A Manual of
Neo-Scholastic Philosophy

BY

CHARLES R. BASCHAB, Ph.D.

SECOND EDITION

B. HERDER BOOK CO.

17 SOUTH BROADWAY, ST. LOUIS, MO.
AND
33 QUEEN SQUARE, LONDON, W. C. 1.
1924

NIHIL OBSTAT

Sti. Ludovici, die 17. Juli, 1923

F. G. Holweck,
Censor Librorum

IMPRIMATUR

Sti. Ludovici, die 18. Juli, 1923

✠ Joannes J. Glennon,
Archiepiscopus
Sti. Ludovici

Copyright, 1923
by
B. Herder Book Co.

Printed in U. S. A.

VAIL-BALLOU COMPANY
BINGHAMTON AND NEW YORK

FOREWORD

The present generation, while extremely self-satisfied on account of its scientific and technical achievements, is profoundly pessimistic in respect to philosophical knowledge, *i. e.,* an adequate, comprehensive, and unified interpretation and explanation of the universality of things. In other words, what modern knowledge has gained in quantity and extension, has been achieved at the sacrifice of depth and harmony. As a consequence, in the midst of its possession of detailed wealth and apparent splendor, the modern mind lives on a food which neither nourishes its substance nor invigorates its energies. Its achievements are manifold and widespread, and its activities multifarious in scope and feverish in intensity; but since its aims and methods are more variable than the proverbial moon, the final result is nil, and its ways are strewn with intellectual corpses, *viz.,* dead theories and stillborn hypotheses.

In view of these facts, thoughtful men are everywhere beginning to turn their eyes back upon scholastic philosophy, hoping to find there an island of rest and a haven of peace in the surging sea of conflicting philosophies. Thus, the *Philosophia Perennis,* unshaken and venerable in the garb of ancient Greece, enriched in depth and breadth by its contact with Christianity in the glorious XIIIth century, looms big and strong again to-day as the one philosophy which, in the opinion of the deepest and best-equipped minds of our time, is able to absorb and assimilate whatever new facts have been discovered and whatever new methods have been invented.

To satisfy this new and rising interest in the philosophy of Aristotle and St. Thomas Aquinas, there are books aplenty, large and small, and yet the author ventures to add a new volume, with the thought and hope of filling a void and thus serving a useful purpose. It seems to him that few of the existing books, if any, appeal to the average mind of the present generation or respond to the needs of the general educated public. Many of them were inspired by scholarly aims and intended for specialists and intellectual gastronomers to gratify their laudable curiosity in regard to the historical or speculative aspects of Scholasticism. Others were written exclusively to serve as textbooks for students in ecclesiastical seminaries and in colleges and universities conducted by religious orders. The rest are monographs or treatises on special parts or particular subjects and problems of scholastic philosophy. However, there has never been published in the English language, as far as the author knows, a complete and systematic exposition of the whole subject-matter, based upon the sound principles of Aristotle and Thomas Aquinas and brought into contact with the facts of modern science, at once responding to the needs of the college and university student, and presented in such a form as to render it accessible to the educated public in general.

Such are the reasons for compiling this volume. The considerations which have guided the author in its composition are chiefly two: he wished both to *modernize* and *popularize* the *Philosophia Perennis*.

His first intention was to modernize it. In order to realize this intention he renounced, as far as it seemed necessary or useful, the technical terminology and the philosophical language of the School, and where he thought that the old principles demanded the retention of the old formulæ, he correlated the venerable expressions of the ancient and ever new wisdom with the terms of the present age.

The author's second intention was to popularize, as far as possible, the study of Neoscholasticism. The simplification of the vast subject-matter appeared to him the only feasible way for the achievement of his purpose. Upon reflection he judged two measures appropriate for the simplification of the subject-matter,—(1) the unification of its systematic structure, and (2) the concentration of the attention upon the fundamental problems, thus bringing out more clearly the vital organization of the system.

The first measure—the unification of the systematic structure—was carried out in a twofold manner: (a) by the division of the whole subject-matter into three parts, of which the first two—cosmology and psychology—are co-ordinate with one another and both subordinate to the third—metaphysics; (b) by the organic incorporation of the highly important problems of logic, epistemology, and ethics with human psychology, where they naturally belong, under the caption of synthetic and teleological psychology.

The second measure which the author adopted for the simplification of the subject-matter, was the placing of emphasis on the main questions and their organic interrelation. While neglecting no problem the solution of which seemed necessary for the comprehension of the system, he paid special attention to, and dwelled with particular care upon, such fundamental problems as the *contingency* of the universe, and the human functions of *abstraction* and *self-determination,* because upon the solution of these problems depends the possibility of a satisfactory solution of issues which are paramount in philosophy—the demonstrability of an ultramundane God and of the spirituality and immortality of the human soul.

Of the quality of his intentions the author is quite sure. He is not so sure whether he has chosen the best means to realize them. Therefore, he must leave it to the judgment of others if, and how far, he has succeeded in attaining his aim. Specific and constructive criticisms shall be welcome and will be considered personal favors.

CHARLES R. BASCHAB

Sausalito, California,
   June 23rd, 1922.

GENERAL TABLE OF CONTENTS

PART ONE

PART TWO

SECTION ONE

SECTION TWO

PART THREE

SECTION ONE

SECTION TWO

SPECIFIED TABLE OF CONTENTS

PART TWO

Psychology, the Philosophy of the Organic World

SECTION ONE

Analytical and Causative Psychology

Contents xiii

Contents

SECTION TWO

SYNTHETIC AND TELEOLOGICAL PSYCHOLOGY

Contents

PART THREE

METAPHYSICS, THE PHILOSOPHY OF THE TRANSCENDENTAL WORLD

SECTION ONE

ONTOLOGY, THE PHILOSOPHY OF THE TRANSCENDENT ASPECT OF THE WORLD

SECTION TWO

THEODICY, THE PHILOSOPHY OF THE TRANS-CENDENT AUTHOR OF THE WORLD

CHAPTER ONE

INTRODUCTION

PRELIMINARY DEFINITION OF PHILOSOPHY

We define a real being by assigning the elements which compose its essence. We can do this because every being that comes within our sense experience is a compound. Consequently, every definition starts with an analysis. But in analyzing the being we do not enumerate all the elements singly, one by one, but rather we express by one term all the general elements of a being, *i. e.*, those elements which are common to the class of beings which we define, and to other classes also; and by a second term, we express the specific element which distinguishes our class of beings from all other classes. Thus, we define man by saying that he is a *rational animal,—animal* expressing all the general elements, and *rational,* the distinctive characteristics of man, or the specific element. By way of analogy we define science, which is a logical compound, in a similar manner by simply changing the term element into that of object. Thus, calling philosophy a science in the Aristotelian sense of science, as a complete and well-reasoned knowledge of a subject, we would give a preliminary definition of philosophy by saying that it is the *MOST GENERAL SCIENCE OF THE UNIVERSE.* By calling it the *SCIENCE OF THE UNIVERSE,* we express in a comprehensive way its subject-matter, which is the general or material object of a science; and by calling it the *MOST GENERAL SCIENCE,* we indicate, though not adequately, yet clearly enough, the special view-point from which we study the universe in philosophy, and this is the specific or formal object of a science.

I. *Adequate Definition*

A. THE MATERIAL OBJECT

The universe, then, is the material object of philosophy. It is plain that the universe is the material object, not only of philosophy, but of all other sciences. However, there is a difference between philosophy and the other sciences also in this respect.

1. No science, except philosophy, studies the whole universe. There are many parts and many aspects of the universe, and this is one reason for the multiplication of sciences. The least particular of all sciences is astronomy, and even astronomy is restricted in its material object; it studies only the inorganic world in its general aspect. Some sciences are extremely limited in their extension, for instance, general biology, which studies the phenomena of a cell. Not so philosophy. All that exists or can exist is part of its material object.

2. Besides the universality of its material object, not to be found in any other science, we have its unity. In the other sciences the universe is studied, as it were, piece by piece; in philosophy it is studied as a whole, as an inter-related and inter-dependent system of beings. Therefore, a scientist who has mastered particular sciences, is not thereby a philosopher,—not only because there are many gaps in his knowledge, since there are many parts and aspects of the universe yet unexplored by science, but also because he would have no conception of the universe as a whole, as a harmonious system, in spite of his wealth of knowledge in matters of detail.

3. There is a third consideration of importance in re-

gard to the material object of philosophy. For positivists, who assume that only the material things accessible to our senses can be the object of certain and positive knowledge, there is no real room for philosophical study in its formal object. However, even they admit that on account of the universality and the unity of its material object, there is a useful work to be done by the philosopher. He must collect and sum up the data furnished by the particular sciences, and whatsoever facts he has found, with the immediate conclusions derived therefrom, he must correlate and systematize, thus creating a kind of universal science or science of sciences.

B. THE FORMAL OBJECT

While this work of collecting, correlating, and systematizing the conclusions of scientific research is done by the philosopher, yet it is the least valuable part of his task; it is done to give him the basis upon which he establishes his distinctive and characteristic science which depends upon its formal object. The particular sciences study the phenomena of the universe, and their formal object is, broadly speaking, to ascertain the fact and the manner of relationship which exists between antecedent and consequent phenomena. Philosophy goes deeper than that. Indeed, it starts where the others stop. It penetrates into the very nature of the phenomena, in order to find out three things:

a. What is the subject in which the phenomena take place?
b. What is the adequate explanation of the existence of both subject and phenomena?
c. What is the final end and goal of all the subjects and phenomena that we call the universe?

In other words, the philosopher attempts to explain the universe adequately by assigning its three causes, *viz.*, the *CONSTITUTIVE,* the *EFFICIENT,* and the *FINAL* causes.

1. The necessity of a constitutive causality to explain the nature of beings is based upon the fact that all beings in the universe are *COMPOUNDS,* and not only accidental, quantitative, but also essential, ontological compounds. Consequently, every being studied by philosophy is composed essentially of a *GENERAL ELEMENT,* general because it belongs to many, if not all, classes of beings, and of a *SPECIFIC ELEMENT,* specific because it belongs to one class of beings only. We call these elements *CAUSES,* because they have a direct, positive, and necessary influence upon the production of a being; we call them *INTRINSIC* or *CONSTITUTIVE* causes, because they form a being and constitute its very nature. Again, we call the general element the *MATERIAL* cause, because we conceive it as the passive, indeterminate principle, the subject in which the other is received, and we call the specific element the *FORMAL* cause, because we take it to be the active and determining principle that gives the being its well-defined specific character.

   The evidence for the statement that all beings of the universe are compounds results from the fact clearly established by observation and research that all beings are subject to change and transformation. But a change, whenever it is essential, *i. e.,* when the very nature of a being is changed, can be interpreted only as a process in which a fundamental element retains its being, and the formal, specific element is lost and replaced by another.

2. The necessity of an efficient causality to explain the existence of beings is based upon the fact that all beings composing the universe are *CONTINGENT i. e.,* they have not the reason of their existence in their own nature,

but must be explained by the influence of other beings that brought them into existence. Such an outside influence we call an *EFFI-CIENT CAUSE*. Now the existence of any contingent being may well be explained by the action of another contingent being, but as long as we remain within the series of contingent causes, we have not given an adequate explanation. Supposing the possibility of an infinite series of causes, and assuming that the universe is such an infinite series of contingent causes, the problem has only been indefinitely multiplied. To solve it we must arrive at a cause that is not a contingent being and, therefore, needs no other cause to explain it, *i. e.,* a necessary being that has the reason for its existence in its own nature.

All beings composing the universe are contingent because all are subject to change, and a being which is transformed into another, ceases to be and, therefore, cannot be necessary, *i. e.,* it cannot have it in its nature to be.

The efficient causality is of two kinds: When it is sufficient to explain an effect by its own proper action, we speak of a *principal* cause; when, on the contrary, its own proper action is insufficient to explain it, we speak of an *instrumental cause,* as, for instance, the action of a pen in writing a letter.

3. The necessity for a final causality to explain the activity of beings is based upon the fact that there is *ORDER* in the world. This fact is as plain as daylight. Order is conditioned by the reduction of multiform elements to a unity of existence, or of manifold actions to a unity of purpose. Now, in every being, especially in every living being, we find numberless and heterogeneous elements reduced to a perfect unity, and in the universe as a whole,

we find, again, numberless and multifarious
actions reduced to a most wonderful harmony.
But such a reduction of what is so manifold
and heterogeneous to unity and harmony demands a cause, *i. e.*, an influence that directs
and controls the coming into existence of the
individual beings and their interdependence
and interaction. It is this influence which we
call *FINAL* causality. And this causality we
consider as *PHYSICAL* in irrational beings,
in which we must conceive it as an intrinsic
tendency towards their natural object. In
man, being rational, we call it a *MORAL*
causality, as it is based upon the abstract
knowledge of his immediate and final object,
which he may desire and strive to attain freely
in virtue of his power of self-determination.

We may now enlarge our definition of philosophy
by saying that *it is the general science of the universe, giving an adequate explanation of its constitutive elements, of its efficient causes, and of its
ends and purposes.*

II. Division of the Subject-Matter

To say that philosophy is the most general science
of the universe is a first and preliminary definition; to
add that its object is to give an adequate explanation of
the constitutive, efficient, and final causes of the universe
is an explicit and proper definition. Again, we reproduce
the very same definition when, using an expression more
in harmony with ordinary speech, we say that philosophy
studies the nature, origin, and purpose of all things.
Generally speaking, the most effective means of clarifying
a definition is the division of its object. This applies
also to our subject-matter. Analyzing the universe, the
philosopher finds a threefold object for his study. First,
he finds the *inorganic world,* the vast number of non-
living beings which are the natural basis and necessary

condition oг the living. In the second place, there is the uncountable multitude of living beings, the *organic world,* with an infinite variety of divisions and subdivisions, but all alike in this that they have life. Finally, there is a third object of study expressed by the *common attributes of beings, i. e.,* whatsoever is neither proper to the inorganic nor to the organic world, but belongs to both indiscriminately. Consequently, there are three parts of philosophy: *cosmology, psychology,* and *metaphysics.*

I. COSMOLOGY

In COSMOLOGY, the philosophical study of the inorganic world, three fundamental questions present themselves to the mind: What is the inorganic world? What is its origin? What is its destiny?

a. The solution of the first cosmological problem, which is the most important because it is fundamental, demands an accurate knowledge of the phenomena of the inorganic world. We have no intuition of the nature of anything, but must gain such knowledge by abstraction. Abstraction has its objective factor exclusively in the facts brought into our mental life by observation and scientific research. Consequently, the cosmologist must have some knowledge of astronomy and geology and a very clear comprehension of the general principles of physics and chemistry.

b. The origin of the inorganic world is the second problem of cosmology. The importance of the right solution of this problem cannot be exaggerated, especially on account of its paramount practical consequences in respect to the religious and moral life of man. However, this solution is not so very difficult, provided the first problem, the nature of the universe, has been correctly solved.

c. Also the third problem, the destiny of the inorganic world, is of great importance from a practical as well as a theoretical viewpoint. However, its solution is easily inferred from the other two

2. PSYCHOLOGY

LIVING AND ORGANIC BEINGS constitute the other great class of beings in the universe. They form the object of PSYCHOLOGY. We call this philosophical study *psychology,* following Aristotle, because life is the common characteristic of all, and the principle of life was called by him *"psyche,"* the soul. Life itself, as we find it in the universe, is of a threefold, clearly distinct order,—plant, animal, and human. As a consequence, we have also a threefold psychology, that of the plant, of the animal, and of man.

a. *PLANT PSYCHOLOGY* studies the nature, origin, and purpose of plant life. The knowledge of the origin and purpose of plant life is inferred from the right conception of its nature, which, therefore, is the fundamental problem of plant psychology. Here again, the synthesis of the philosopher must be based upon an accurate knowledge of facts, and consequently, the general laws of life and of vital functions, as modern biology has brought them to light, must be well known to him.

b. *ANIMAL PSYCHOLOGY,* or the philosophical study of sense life, is the second object of the psychologist; the second, because it cannot be studied without the knowledge of the first, since sense life finds its basis and source in plant life. However, sense life, as compared with plant life, has its distinctive features, which give it not only a superiority of degree, but also of kind. This will become apparent in the study of its nature, origin, and purpose. Also here, as the knowledge of origin and purpose depends upon the knowledge of its nature, this is the one great and fundamental problem of animal psychology. And, again, the right solution of this problem is impossible without the proper knowledge of facts. Hence, personal observation and experience, while necessary, are not sufficient preparation for the psychologist: the well-established general results of physiology and psychophysiology must be known to him.

c. *HUMAN OR RATIONAL PSYCHOLOGY*, or the philosophical study of man's rational life, is the highest and most important object of the psychologist. As animal life has for its basis and source plant life, so human life has for its basis and source, animal life. Hence also, as we never find sense life except in conjunction with vegetative life, so we never find rational life except in conjunction with sense life. However, conjunction signifies not necessarily identity of nature. The same as sense life, compared with plant life, possesses a superiority not of degree only, but of order, so also rational life, compared with sense life, expresses not only a higher degree, but a higher kind of life. Also as regards rational life the knowledge of its origin and destiny is derived from the knowledge of its nature, and consequently, the main work of the psychologist in this matter is to determine the nature of the human soul. Here again, the knowledge of facts is indispensable as a basis for his analysis and subsequent synthesis. And while from the nature of the case his own introspection is the main source of his knowledge of facts, yet the knowledge of the general results of experimental psychology is an indispensable aid and corrective.

Human psychology is studied from a double viewpoint:

1. *ANALYTICAL PSYCHOLOGY* studies the facts of rational life to determine their nature and causality.
2. *SYNTHETIC PSYCHOLOGY* takes the knowledge of rational facts and their nature

for its basis in order to determine the teleological relations of man's rational life. In regard to his intellectual operations we call this part of psychology *LOGIC,* and in regard to his moral acts, we call it *ETHICS.*

Finally, there is one other psychological study, *CRITERIOLOGY,* which is a special study on certitude and its objective basis and source. In consequence of Descartes' methodical doubt and Kant's criticist psychology, this study has become of vital importance.

3. METAPHYSICS

METAPHYSICS is the third part of philosophy; the third, because the study of metaphysics supposes the knowledge of cosmology and psychology. It represents the supreme philosophical abstraction and, as a consequence, is the foundation of the highest synthesis of which the human mind is capable. Its object is *being as such, i. e.,* those attributes of being which belong neither to the inorganic world as such, nor to the organic world as such, but to both in the same manner. Hence, the object of metaphysics transcends not only every species and genus, but every class or possible division of beings, and excludes every relation to any other being of any kind. Hence, we say that it is being, transcendent and absolute. Now a being may be transcendent and absolute in two ways:

a. *ONTOLOGY* studies being as such, as we gain its knowledge by the supreme abstractive efforts of our mind. In its objective existence in the universe, every being is a concrete being, belonging to a certain species and genus, with a hundred concrete relations to other beings. But the metaphysician simply does not consider these points, concentrating his whole attention on the being, inasmuch as it is a being considered in itself.

b. *THEODICY* also studies transcendent and absolute being, but this transcendence and absoluteness is of quite another kind. The being of ontology is transcendent and absolute by abstraction. While it is based upon objective reality, it does not exist as such, except in the mind. The object of theodicy on the contrary is objectively and concretely the absolute and transcendent being, God. His existence is a necessary conclusion from the contingent nature of the universe and His attributes are knowable inasmuch as they are expressed and reflected in the universe.

PART ONE

COSMOLOGY, THE PHILOSOPHY OF THE IN-ORGANIC WORLD

CHAPTER TWO

THE MAIN COSMOLOGICAL PROBLEMS AND THEORIES

ARISTOTLE, THE FOUNDER OF COSMOLOGY

In cosmology the philosopher studies the inorganic world. His object is to obtain, if possible, an adequate explanation of the existence, nature, and destiny of non-living beings, individually and collectively. Such being his object, it would appear that a satisfactory cosmology would have been, if not directly impossible, at least extremely difficult in ancient, and even medieval times, when the mechanical, physical, and chemical properties of bodies were hardly known, at least not scientifically, and when geology and astronomy, as real sciences, were not thought of. However, we find that, as a matter of fact, Aristotle, the greatest philosopher the human race can boast of, laid the foundations of cosmology almost two thousand years before any of our modern sciences came into existence, and while in many details his views are erroneous, because he lacked the scientific knowledge of inorganic matter which we have, yet his foundation was so firm and so deep that no scientific discovery has been able to shake it.

I. Theories on the Nature of the Universe

Of the three main problems of cosmology, the nature, origin, and destiny of the inorganic world, the first is the most important because it is fundamental. We shall state in a brief and summary manner the various solutions offered by philosophers at the present time.

Apart from eclectic systems, *i. e.*, such as take some principles from one and others from another system, there are three clearly distinct, nay essentially different solutions proposed.

I. MECHANICISM OR PURE ATOMISM

The *ATOMISTIC* or *MECHANICIST* solution is sponsored by many representatives of modern science. However, the solution itself is anything but modern; it is simply a revival and clever adaptation to some striking features of modern science of a more than two thousand year old *MATERIALISM*. It is a very simple theory, since it supposes but two cosmic elements: *matter and motion;* and *it considers the present universe but the chance result of eternal matter in eternal motion.*

a. Its first element is matter. While the bodies which make up the world are apparently heterogeneous, they are really homogeneous, *i. e.,* they are all structures of atoms of matter, conceived somewhat like atoms in chemistry. They are considered devoid of any inherent force, having but one property: extension. They are supposed to be identical in nature and to retain their identity in the structure which we call body. Consequently, all bodies are proclaimed to be homogeneous and all physical and chemical changes in bodies are said to be apparent, not real.

b. The second element of this theory is motion. The atoms are perpetually in motion, and the quantity of matter, *i. e.,* the number of atoms in a body and the difference in the velocity and direction of their movement, are the sole factors that determine all the phenomena in the universe. How these factors produce such marvelous effects, the theory does not and cannot explain.

2. DYNAMISM, THE THEORY OF SIMPLE FORCES

Another solution offered is the *DYNAMIC* theory. Some really great minds have espoused it. It is diametrically opposed to the atomistic theory and surpasses it in simplicity. Its fundamental proposition is that the bodies are not constituted by extended matter, as they appear to be, but are *groups or systems of forces.* These forces are indivisible, inextended entities. On the nature and number of these forces there is no agreement. Resistance, inertia, attraction, repulsion are mostly mentioned.

In this theory the simple forces, conceived as mathematical points, *i. e.,* having no quantity, act upon one another and thus produce the illusion of extended bodies. Consequently, a body is nothing but a special grouping of a certain number of forces. Thus, bodies are but systems of inextended forces and the world itself is the great primary system of those secondary systems.

3. HYLEMORPHISM OR THE SCHOLASTIC THEORY

While atomism says there is nothing in the world but extended matter and dynamism postulates that there is nothing in the world but inextended forces, there is a third theory, which accepts the presence of both matter and forces as an established fact, and builds upon it its own solution. It is called *hylemorphism,* from "hyle"— matter, and "morphe"—form; two terms which express one of the distinctive features of the theory. It was proposed by Aristotle and revived and developed in the Middle Ages by Albertus Magnus, St. Thomas Aquinas and other great schoolmen or scholastics. Being taught generally in the schools, it has been named the Scholastic Theory.

THE CHIEF PRINCIPLES OF ARISTOTELIAN COSMOLOGY

The whole scholastic theory on the nature of inorganic bodies may be reduced to the following five propositions:

1. *The world is composed of heterogeneous bodies, more or less as we find them by observation and scientific experiment, especially in chemistry.*

   Consequently, there are in the world, not only individual distinctions between bodies, but also specific distinctions, *i. e.,* there are bodies which are of the same kind or homogeneous, such as the many specimens of hydrogen, and there are bodies of different kinds or heterogeneous, such as hydrogen and iron.

2. *Each specifically distinct body has a specifically distinct group of properties inherent in it.*

   Heat, color, electricity are such properties. They are not to be taken as specifically distinct in the sense that each body has other kinds of properties, but in the sense that each body is affected by these properties in a very special and exclusive manner. It is by this group of properties that the various kinds of bodies are known to us, because it is by means of these properties that bodies act upon one another. Thus, we recognize water by the exact degree of temperature necessary for its congelation, liquefaction, and evaporation.

3. *There is in every body an intrinsic tendency which unifies and directs all its actions.*

   This proposition expresses the soul of the entire theory. Evidently, the various forces of a body act harmoniously and by means of such action attain their object with absolute regularity. This harmony in the complex activity of a body, whether mechanical, physical, or chemical, and this regularity in the attainment of its object are incomprehensible, unless we consider them as the expression of an intrinsic tendency of the body. The proper term applied to this tendency is *FINAL CAUSE; CAUSE,* because it is conceived as an active principle of control; *FINAL,* because it directs the body towards the *finis, i. e.,* the natural object or end of its activity.

4. *There is in the world a possibility, nay, a necessity of substantial transformations.*

If there are various kinds of bodies, simple and compound, and if each specifically distinct body has its own distinct group of properties or forces, and again, if these forces are controlled in their activity by an intrinsic tendency, it is an inevitable consequence that bodies are subject to changes and transformations. When these changes are realized only on the surface of the body, as it were, we call them accidental. Such are all the modifications of the mechanical and physical properties of a body. But when the body is changed in its very depth so that, by every test we may apply, it is no longer the same body, we call such changes substantial transformations. This is realized only when the chemical properties of a body are changed. Hence, every chemical change in a body implies a substantial change, *i. e.,* a change in the very nature of the body.

5. *Every body, whether compound or simple, is constituted by a double substantial element, the passive element which does not change and in which the change is realized (MATERIA PRIMA), and the active element which disappears in the change and is replaced by another (FORMA SUBSTANTIALIS).*

This proposition is a necessary inference from the preceding one. Indeed, whenever there is a change, there are at least two elements,—one that remains the same in the change and, consequently, is common to the being unchanged and the being changed, and the other, which is lost in the change and replaced by another.

This is easily perceived in the case of an accidental change, for instance, when an artist transforms a mass of clay representing a lion into the shape of a man. The mass of clay remains the same, but the figure of the lion is lost and replaced by that of the man. It is quite apparent here that the clay is the passive element, the subject in which the change is accomplished—*MATERIA*. However, as in this case the *materia* is in itself a specific substance, a complete body and not only a substantial element of a body, we call it the *MATERIA SECUNDA,* the same as the figure which has been transformed, not being a substantial element of clay, but only an accident, is termed in this case, not a *forma substantialis,* but a *FORMA ACCIDENTALIS.*

While the process of transformation and its elements are more easily known in an accidental and superficial change, yet there can be no difference in the interpretation of a profound and substantial change. When chlorine and sodium combine to produce salt, the chemical elements do not cease to exist altogether, *i. e.,* they are not annihilated, nor is salt an entirely new creation, but an element has remained over from chlorine and sodium and entered into the new body. Now, as this element is not in itself a body, but only the passive, indeterminate, common element of a body, we call it the *MATERIA PRIMA.* In a similar manner we call *FORMA SUBSTANTIALIS* the other element, *i. e.,* the active, determinative, specific element, which distinguished chlorine and sodium from every other simple body, and which has been lost in the change and has been replaced by the active, determinating and specific element which distinguishes salt from every other compound, because this element is not an accidental, but an essential part of the substance of the body itself, which it determines and specifies.

II. Theories on the Origin of the Universe

While the problem of the nature of the universe is fundamental in the sense that every other cosmological problem depends upon its solution, yet the problem of the origin of the universe is at least equally important from a practical as well as a theoretical viewpoint. The solutions proposed by the philosophers show this very clearly.

I. EVOLUTIONISM

By evolutionism is not meant here the scientific theory of evolution as it is generally accepted today in biology, but the application to the inorganic world of a philosophical theory which pretends to explain the whole universe, from the atom of hydrogen to man, and its rich and complex history and activity, by the process of gradual, steady and necessary material evolution without any impulse or aim, and without any direction from within or without. Eternal matter in eternal motion is supposed to be an all-comprehensive and all-sufficient explanation. Of course, such a hypothesis is rather a philosophical atmosphere than a clearly circumscribed and well-founded theory, because at the very bottom of its interpretation of the origin of the world is the incredible assumption that a superior effect can be explained by an inferior cause.

We might well be tempted to wonder how such a shallow philosophy has succeeded in gaining such widespread influence and such a strong hold upon the modern mind! Apparently, only antireligious prejudice can explain this phenomenon. Many are afraid to admit God, as that would do away with their own individual sovereignty, and therefore, having but a superficial education or no philosophical training, they are inclined to admit almost any absurdity which promises to explain the universe without God.

2. PANTHEISM

Besides materialistic evolutionism there is another theory of explaining the origin of the universe without God; we may call it idealistic monism or pantheism.

Like the former, it is a modern revival of an old pagan error. It claims that the world—and not only the inorganic world which alone we consider here—is a gradual, steady and necessary emanation from, or rather expansion of, the eternal divine substance. Apparently, pantheism avoids the absurd assumption of materialism to explain by an inferior cause a superior effect, but it is based upon two other assumptions which are equally contradictory: the substantial identity of matter and spirit, as well as that of the world and God.

The antireligious prejudice which alone affords an explanation of evolutionism in its materialistic aspect, has driven many intelligent and educated thinkers into the camp of pantheism, though it is but a case of falling into Scylla while trying to escape Charybdis.

3. THE ONLY SOLUTION: CREATION

There is only one possible solution to this problem of the origin of the universe,—creation by an infinite and absolute God. Indeed, if, as cosmology shows, the world is a system of contingent beings, *i. e.,* beings which have the reason for their existence not in themselves, but in others, the world, as such, must be of the same nature, *i. e.,* contingent and dependent upon another being for its existence; and if we wish to arrive at a sufficient and adequate explanation for its existence, we must postulate a being which, while the cause of contingent beings, is itself not caused by another, because it is not contingent, but necessary, having the reason for its existence in itself. This being we call God, and the action by which He produced the contingent world, we call creation.

However, we do not claim that the world at the moment of its creation was anything like the universe which we know today. It is not only possible, but exceedingly probable, if not practically certain, that in its primitive stage the world was a more or less homogeneous mass of matter with a minimum of density and differentiation, and spread over an immense area of space out of which the present inorganic universe naturally and necessarily evolved, following the laws of the inherent dispositions of the mass, and in conformity with the design of the Creator.

We base this assertion upon two propositions, which we shall prove in the course of our work, and which we believe no one will question who will give them serious attention. The first is the general principle that the philosopher, like the man of science, in attempting to explain anything whatsoever, must never assume a higher factor than is necessary and sufficient to explain it, and the second is the fact that the factors known to be present and active in bodies are sufficient and necessary to explain cosmic evolution from a primitive and unformed stage of existence.

III. The Object of the Inorganic World

While the third philosophical problem regarding the inorganic world is, theoretically and practically, of the greatest importance, its solution offers no serious difficulty. Indeed, if the world is created by an infinite and absolute God, and if it has evolved into the beautiful and harmonious universe that astronomy sets before our admiring contemplation, it is evident that the object attained by the normal activity of bodies, whether considered individually or collectively, expresses the plan of the creation and, consequently, the purpose of the Creator. Now in this respect the design of the universe and, therefore, the intention of the Creator, are clearly discernible: The simple bodies subserve the complex, and both simple and complex bodies subserve the general order. From this statement of fact we infer the principle that the lower elements must subserve the higher elements, and the higher must subserve the highest. We may even go a step farther and add that this is an absolutely universal principle, applying not only to the inorganic world, but also to living beings of all possible orders, and therefore, we may assert positively that, besides the absolute purpose of the inorganic bodies which is the general order of the universe expressing the power and wisdom of God, there is also a relative purpose in all the different orders of beings. Hence, the world of inorganic beings exists for the service of the living beings, plants exist for the service of animals, animals for the service of man, and man for the service of God.

There is hardly any need to state that there can be no discussion on the object and purpose of the world from the evolutionist viewpoint. Neither for the pantheist nor for the materialist is there such a problem. Neither of them can admit the doctrine of final causes. For the one the world is an endless, necessary, and blind expansion; for the other it is an endless, necessary, and blind evolution; for both, consequently, it is an eternal process, an ever-flowing stream, uncontrolled and aimless. Having had no beginning, it will have no end. And it does not make any difference at all whether it is supposed to be conditioned by matter to which are ascribed the attributes of God, or by God to whom are attributed the properties of matter.

CHAPTER THREE

ON THE NATURE OF THE INORGANIC WORLD

OBJECT OF THIS STUDY

The world is a system of bodies. But before we can interpret it as a system, we must study its elements, *i. e.,* the bodies which compose it. The reason is obvious: what comes to our knowledge first, is not the world as a whole, in a system of bodies, but the bodies themselves, each having its own nature and existence. Indeed, these bodies are not only logically, but also ontologically, anterior to the world of which they are the real and independent elements and parts. They are individual concrete substances, self-sufficient in their existence and action, and as such we study them here. Consequently, the first and fundamental problem of cosmology, *viz.,* the nature of the inorganic world, is, objectively and concretely speaking, equivalent to the question: *What is the nature of inorganic bodies, i. e., these real, concrete bodies that our eyes see and our ears hear and our hands touch?* There is only one way of solving this great question correctly, and that is to base it upon such knowledge as we can gain of the phenomena, either by observation or by scientific experiment. We will consider some of the most important of the well-established facts.

I. The Nature of Bodies as Disclosed by Science

A. CHEMICAL FACTS

For the cosmologist the most important scientific discoveries are those of modern chemistry. We will mention a few.

1. Each body is composed of *atoms,* which are of the same kind in a simple, of different kinds in a compound body. Ninety different kinds of atoms are known to the chemist. Each kind has its own distinctive weight. As the lightest body known in chemistry is hydrogen, it is taken as the unit by which the weight of all others is measured. Hence, its atomic weight is one and the atomic weight of every other body is a multiple of one. Thus, the atomic weight of oxygen is 16, that of silver, 108, of gold, 196, and of uranium, 240. This weight is distinctive for each species and never varies.

2. A second fact is *chemical affinity.* It is a tendency of one element to select another element for chemical combination. Each body has its own preferences. In some cases these are so marked that physical proximity and contact are sufficient to effect the reaction. In other cases, a stimulant is necessary, such as a shock, or heat, or electricity. In still other cases, there seems to be no affinity at all. Only in a roundabout way can the chemist get them to combine. The vital significance of affinity consists in this that it is specific: chemically each body has its own friends and is ever loyal to them.

3. *Atomicity* or *valence* is another significant fact. When bodies combine chemically, the quantity which enters the reaction is always controlled by law. For instance, when oxygen and hydrogen combine to produce water, the proportion is ever the same— 1 to 2. So every body has its own distinctive atomicity regarding its combination with every other body and atomicity, like affinity, is a specific property, absolutely regular and constant.

4. A fourth important fact of great value to the cosmologist is the distinctive character of a chemical reaction as compared with a simple mixture of elements. When chlorine and sodium combine to produce salt, we have a chemical reaction: when we pour water into wine, we have a simple mixture of

bodies. Now, when two or more bodies combine chemically, we find there is in this phenomenon no comparison with a mixture of bodies. In a mixture the elements retain their identity, in a chemical reaction their identity is lost. This profound transformation manifests itself in various ways:

a. A complete physical change is the result of a chemical reaction, characterized by the loss of the physical properties of the elements and their substitution by those of the compound. Thus, physically as well as chemically, salt is an entirely different body from either chlorine or sodium, and water is a different body from either oxygen or hydrogen, and the physical properties of salt and water on the one side could never be suspected as resulting from the combined properties of chlorine and sodium, and from those of hydrogen and oxygen on the other.

Needless to say, such a change of properties is never observed in a mere mixture.

b. There are in every chemical reaction certain physical concomitants such as light, sound, heat, magnetic, electrical and other phenomena, which are ever the same in a reaction of the same kind. This is particularly the case as regards the discharge of heat the amount of which is often very great. And again, the same amount of heat is reabsorbed with absolute regularity when in a chemical decomposition the elements regain their liberty. Nothing like that occurs in a simple mixture of bodies.

c. In all chemical reactions the laws of weight, as regards the proportion of the combining elements, are rigorously complied with. Thus, two ounces of hydrogen would combine with sixteen ounces of oxygen, never with fourteen and never with eighteen nor any other number. In a mixture we may take any amount we please of each element.

5. Bearing in mind all these significant facts we shall understand the obvious though most significant fact of all, *viz.*, that in all the manifold and multiform chemical reactions that take place in the laboratory of nature, there is no confusion and chaos; the same bodies appear and re-appear with absolute regularity, there is a constant recurrence of the same chemical species which serves as the basis of the scientific classification found in mineralogy, crystallography, and other sciences.

B. PHYSICAL FACTS

There are established in physics a few facts of deep significance for the study of the nature of bodies.

1. We find that each body which is specifically distinct in chemistry, has a specifically distinct group of physical properties. We shall mention but the most obvious. The different species have their own figure and form. This is especially apparent in crystals. The crystallographer is able to determine exactly the species of a body by measuring the angle of its crystal. Furthermore, each species always acts and reacts in exactly the same manner as regards sound, heat, light, electricity; each one has its natural state, its regular normal density, etc. It is, indeed, by their specific group of physical properties alone that we are enabled to recognize the different kinds of bodies.

Perhaps it may be useful to add that many of these facts are so obvious that it needs no scientific experience to see and appreciate them. Thus, for instance, in respect to heat, almost any person with common sense can tell with exactness the species of any body by the precise degree of temperature

required to solidify, liquefy, and evaporate it.
2. We wish to call special attention to a mechanical
property found in all gases, *viz.*, the tendency to expand and exert pressure against the container. Also
this property is specific and perfectly measurable.

In this connection the universal phenomenon of
gravitation must not be forgotten. If there is any
regularity and uniformity in the world, we certainly
have it in gravitation. While this property is common to all bodies, inasmuch as it is directly related
to quantity, which is the common property of all matter, yet it is also specific, inasmuch as it always acts
in conformity with the atomic weight of each species.

3. In the last few decades physicists have revealed
another property of matter, the nature of which is
still enveloped in obscurity. Indeed, we are in
doubt whether to group it with the physical or
the chemical properties, *viz.*, *RADIO-ACTIVITY*.
Some physicists have been so impressed by this discovery that they believed that at last the key had
been found to unlock the deepest and most secret
recesses of the nature of matter without the necessity of any philosophy. It was hoped that radio-activity would prove all physical phenomena to be reducible to electrical phenomena, and that the nature of all bodies would be shown, almost experimentally, to be constituted by negative electrons
that circulate with extreme velocity around a positive electron, like the planets move around the sun.
These high hopes have not yet been fulfilled, nor is
it probable that they ever will be.

The facts in regard to radio-activity which are of
importance to the cosmologist are relatively few.
By radiation certain heavy atoms, such as uranium,
thorium, and actinium, lose tiny particles of their
being and as a necessary result disintegrate and
are transformed into new chemical species, each
having its own atomic weight. The tiny corpuscles

discharged are atoms of helium. An example will illustrate this. Radium is the result of the disintegration of uranium. The atomic weight of uranium is 238.5 and that of radium 226.5. Consequently, from uranium to radium we have the loss of twelve units which are equivalent to three atoms of helium, the atomic weight of which is four.

Besides this there are ponderable rays, emitted by radio-active substances called "alpha," which are but two atoms of helium, and there are imponderable rays of two kinds called "beta" and "gamma," which also have a direct influence upon the properties of the substance from which they emanate, but do not modify its atomic weight. These rays travel with great velocity and have an enormous power of penetration. But about their intimate nature nothing is known.

An important inference from the facts of radio-activity from a philosophical viewpoint regards the number of simple bodies and their nature. Evidently, uranium, thorium, actinium, and their derivatives, *i. e.,* all known radio-active bodies, are not simple bodies, but real compounds, though the chemist may not be able to decompose them. Is radio-activity a property belonging to *all* bodies? This is still questionable. If it were, then, indeed, our qualification of bodies as simple would have to be greatly modified. In the light of radio-activity even the simple body reveals itself as a structure of great complexity. However, it is of importance to add, that also here the facts prove that a structure is composed of heterogeneous elements.

II. *The Philosophical Interpretation of the Facts*

The well-established facts—chemical, physical, mechanical—which we find in the inorganic world, point without exception in the same direction: There is not only a vast multitude, but an uncountable variety of bodies in the universe, and they are not isolated units, but there is a manifold and multiform connection between them, a most wonderful order of co-ordination in the individual body between its parts and the whole, and, besides this absolute order, a still more wonderful relative order of subordination between bodies in their inter-action and interdependence. We find, indeed, in the midst of the greatest multiplicity and variety, if not universal uniformity, at least regularity and relative constancy, and thus we have the objective basis and source of the ever-increasing marvelous classifications of bodies, their elements, their forces, and their phenomena, which modern science has established. Now, which cosmological theory can best explain this condition, atomism, dynamism, or the scholastic theory?

A. THE FAILURE OF ATOMISM

Neither atomism nor dynamism can explain the order existing in the universe, *i. e.,* neither the manifold and multiform facts, nor their regularity and constancy.

1. The world is specific and complex wherever we look upon it. But in homogeneous, forceless matter we can discover no principle of differentiation. In an atomist world there might be multiplicity, but no variety. Motion cannot be considered as a principle of differentiation, for even in the most realistic interpretation motion is but a continuous change of position.
2. The real world is not only manifold and multiform, but its variety is harmonized, systematized, unified, because there is order everywhere and there can be no order without a principle of unity. But, in an atomist universe there can be no principle of unity, because in forceless matter there is no principle of any kind, and motion as such, being nothing but a continuous change of position, can have absolutely no influence upon the nature of bodies, and being

a continuous variation, can be no source of unification.

3. Atomism not only does not explain the facts of which it is proposed to be the interpretation, but it directly contradicts them in many instances. The plain facts are heterogeneous, multiform, and specific, whereas in atomism they must be homogeneous, uniform, and general. To say that qualitative differences, such as sound, heat, light, electricity, etc., are the natural result of quantitative differences of matter and motion, is an arbitrary assumption, contradicted by established facts.

4. Far from explaining in a satisfactory manner the qualitative differences found in the phenomena of nature, atomists are not even able to give an acceptable explanation of mere mechanical phenomena, such as the pressure of gas or the action of gravitation.

   a. They have attempted to explain the pressure of gas against the walls of its container in this way: The atoms of gas are equally distributed and fly in every direction, and thus hit the walls of the container uniformly. But this interpretation is impossible. Either the atoms are elastic or not. If they are elastic, the whole theory falls, because it is based upon the assumption of forceless matter. If they are inelastic, the movement must soon come to a full stop, whereas we know that the pressure does not cease or diminish, but is ever the same.

   b. A similar interpretation is proposed to explain gravitation. Infinitely small corpuscles fly with extreme velocity in every direction through space, hitting bodies. Now bodies act as screens one for the other, and consequently give the impression as if they were drawn to one another, since from that direction they

receive fewer shocks, and thus the law of
universal attraction finds its explanation.
This mechanical interpretation is also without basis. The corpuscles must be either
elastic or inelastic. They cannot be elastic in
atomism. But if they are inelastic, the shocks
multiplied *ad infinitum* would have heated all
bodies of the universe long ago to a white
heat.

B. THE FAILURE OF DYNAMISM

Atomism fails to explain the facts: 1. because it rejects
heterogeneous forces which alone can supply a rational
ground for the great qualitative differentiation of the
phenomena of the universe; and 2. because it rejects
final causes, *i. e.*, aim- and direction-giving tendencies in
bodies which alone can explain the wonderful order and
harmony in the infinite multiplicity and variety of cosmic
happenings. Dynamism does not fare much better, because all we have said about atomism is almost equally
applicable to dynamism, and in some respects even more
so. Two considerations will be sufficient to make this
clear.

1. If in conformity with the dynamist theory, we assume mechanical forces, such as inertia, attraction,
   and repulsion, to be the only elements of the universe, we have an explanation of abstract motion,
   but no more. In such a world there would be no
   room for a real objective motion, because in such
   a world there would be no concrete bodies that
   could move. Indeed, in the dynamist's world there
   are only simple, inextended forces, and in such a
   world there can be no quantity. Where there is
   no quantity, there can be no local position, and
   where there is no local position there can be no motion, since motion is but a continuous change of
   position.
2. Furthermore, dynamism, being incapable of ex-

plaining quantity, cannot even attempt to explain the qualitative differences in inorganic phenomena, because quantity is the common basis and condition without which these cannot be realized or perceived by us. Apart from this insurmountable difficulty, there remains the impossibility of explaining how the qualitative differences of physical phenomena can be the product of purely mechanical forces.

C. OTHER INTERPRETATIONS OF ATOMISM AND DYNAMISM

Atomism and dynamism in their traditional form are rejected by practically all scientific men of the day. Some still cling to a dynamic atomism, *i. e.*, an atomism mitigated by the inclusion of mechanical forces, just as others proclaim a mitigated form of dynamism, *i. e.*, a dynamism characterized by the acceptance of various heterogeneous forces which they call energies, and hence the name *energism* given to the theory. Evidently, we have in these attempts a plain acknowledgment of the failure of both atomism and dynamism. However, the modifications introduced do not save them, as some of the principal difficulties are left untouched.

The great majority of present-day scientists recognize this, and have assumed an attitude of skepticism and pessimism regarding the possibility of any certain knowledge of the nature of physical and chemical phenomena, and of the bodies in which they are realized, and in consequence they have proclaimed the principle that the student of nature should abstain from inquiring into the nature of the phenomena he studies. As if such a principle could ever be acceptable and satisfying to the human mind! Indeed, not even in the study of the *phenomena* are scientists agreed. Under the powerful, though perhaps secret, impulse of contrary philosophical prejudices, many continue to look upon all the phenomena of nature as homogeneous—being of a purely mechanical character, not appreciating their obvious qualitative differences, while many others, recognizing various forms of energy as necessary to explain the qualitative differentiation of the phenomena, are led to see nothing but the phenomena themselves with the positive exclusion of real extension and the substantial body.

III. Demonstration of the Scholastic Theory

There is only the scholastic theory or hylemorphism left as a cosmological interpretation of the facts. For various reasons this theory is acceptable as a sufficient and adequate solution.

1. It is a COMMON SENSE VIEW of the inorganic world. We all accept in everyday life water as water, wine as wine, and salt as salt, and we all recognize them by the group of physical properties which are found in each species and not in any other. When we see them act in a regular, uniform manner we are not surprised, but attribute it to an intrinsic principle, and thus we say it is in the nature of salt to season food, of wine to cheer the heart, and of water to quench the thirst.

2. The argument based on common sense is only a strong presumption, but this presumption is greatly confirmed by the fact that all our modern languages have embodied expressions evidently in harmony with the scholastic theory. Such are all the terms that denote the substance or nature, the properties or forces of bodies and also processes such as transformation and many other expressions of a similar order.

3. Another presumptive argument of great strength in favor of this theory consists in the harmony of all known facts with the theory. When the theory was first conceived by Aristotle, few facts were perfectly known. Since then thousands have been ascertained by observation and experiment, but none have ever contradicted the theory. This same argument acquires still greater strength, indeed it becomes almost conclusive, when we bear in mind

that so far there is no other theory by which all the facts receive a reasonable explanation.

4. Our final argument is the conclusive proof of the theory, and therefore, we will present it as simply and as clearly as possible.

The greatest fact in the universe that cosmology must explain, is the cosmic order plainly apparent everywhere. The scholastic theory alone explains it. And how? By its position regarding final causes, for final causes form the very soul of the theory.

For the sake of greater clearness let us propose the argument in syllogistic form:

MAJOR: Order, wherever found, implies direction either from within or from without.

MINOR: The order in the universe excludes direction from without.

CONCLUSION: Consequently, the direction productive of order in cosmic evolution is intrinsic.

Only the minor premise needs an explanation. Evidently, direction implies intelligence, and the direction of the universe in all its elements throughout all the ages could be understood only upon the basis of the infinite mind of God. Bearing this in mind we reason as follows: the cosmic order excludes direction from without, because to claim such a direction is unnecessary, arbitrary and unscientific;—unnecessary, because an intrinsic direction is sufficient;—arbitrary, because such direction would mean direct divine intervention, and for such an assumption there is no reason;—unscientific, because it is always unscientific to assume a higher factor than is necessary to explain an effect.

CHAPTER FOUR

PHILOSOPHICAL ANALYSIS OF INORGANIC BODIES

THE NATURE OF BODIES IN THE LIGHT OF SCHOLASTICISM

We have solved the basic cosmological problem, the nature of inorganic bodies, by adopting the scholastic or hylemorphist theory. We have examined and rejected atomism: (1) because it is not based upon the facts of which it is supposed to be the philosophical interpretation; (2) because it is, in most instances, directly in contradiction with the facts; and (3) above all, because it does not explain, and is absolutely incapable of explaining, the most wonderful as well as most conspicuous fact in the universe—the marvelous cosmic order. For similar reasons we have rejected dynamism. On the other hand, we have accepted the scholastic theory, not on the authority of Aristotle or St. Thomas Aquinas, much as we appreciate their philosophical genius, but for these very good reasons: (1) It is based upon the real concrete phenomena as ordinary observation and scientific experiment reveal them to us; (2) It is in conformity with all the facts, and contradicted by none; and (3) It does what no other theory succeeds in doing, *i. e.*, it explains the cosmic order that savage and scientist alike recognize and admire.

The world, therefore, is a system of heterogeneous bodies. The chemical differences are substantial differences, and each body, substantially different from others, has its own specific group of physical elements which, because they are proper to the chemical species, we call properties, and it is by means of these properties that bodies act upon one another and are accessible to our sense experience. Most important of all, in the very substance of the body there is a specific tendency, unifying and directing the body's complete activity.

THE ELEMENTS OF A BODY

So far we have studied the inorganic bodies as units, and as members of the great universal system of bodies which we call the world. But, while the bodies are elements in relation to the world, they are not simple indivisible elements, as is clearly evident, and as we have already seen repeatedly, but they are in themselves systems of elements, and consequently, a careful philosophical analysis will both widen and deepen our knowledge of their intimate nature.

I. The Substantial Elements

Our first consideration will be devoted to the *SUBSTANCE* of the body, *i. e.*, those elements of the body without which it would cease to be the same specific body. Here it is well to remember that, when speaking of substantial elements, we do not mean chemical elements, for chemical elements are themselves specific bodies, whereas substantial elements are only elements of a specific body, they are not themselves specific bodies. They have no existence of their own, individually, *i. e.*, each by itself, but they exist only in and through the body which by their union they constitute, and to which alone existence can be attributed. Of course, they are real objective elements, *i. e.*, they are not the product of the mind, they exist really and objectively apart from the mind that analyzes them, because they are the constitutive elements of the body. However, the existence of the one is not really distinct from that of the other, as, what exists, is not the elements as such, but the body which results from their combination. Consequently, when we speak of substantial elements we refer not only to compound, but also to simple bodies. How do we know there are such elements, and how do we know their nature? By the analysis of a chemical transformation which, in the scholastic theory, is equivalent to a substantial transformation.

I. ANALYSIS OF A SUBSTANTIAL TRANSFORMATION

Everything in the world is subject to change, but not every change is of the same type. Some changes are superficial and physical; others are profound and chemical. When there is a change in the physical properties only, such as sound, heat, light, electricity, and magnetism, the body is thereby modified, but remains the same specific body. When there is a change in the chemical properties also, such as its atomic weight, its chemical affinity and its atomicity, the body itself is thereby not only modified,—it does not remain the same specific body at all, it is radically transformed, *i. e.*, it has become another specific body. While we call the physical changes *accidental,* because they leave the intimate nature of the body intact, we call the chemical changes *substantial,* because they transform the very nature or substance of the body.

Such changes occur every day, nay every minute of the day, everywhere, because all beings of the universe are active and every action implies change. While the great majority of the changes going on constantly in the world are purely accidental, the substantial changes are nevertheless uncountable. To mention but a few kinds: every oxidation of a metal, every combustion of any kind, every part of the process of nutrition in millions and millions of plants and animals, are substantial transformations.

Let us take a concrete example. We place ice, *i. e.*, frozen water, into a container and put it on the fire. Soon the ice will melt. We leave it on the fire and very soon it will evaporate. Many changes have taken place in the water, however its nature has not changed, they were only *accidental* changes. But if we continue to heat the steam, we will effect another change of quite another type: each molecule of water will split and then, instead of water, we have its chemical constituents, oxygen and hydrogen. The nature itself of the water has changed, there is no more water, and in its place we have two bodies, each of a distinct species.

How must we interpret this change? Surely, all are agreed that the water has not lost its whole entity—all that constituted its being; if so, there would have been an annihilation of water, whereas we have had only a change, even though profound. Consequently, there is one element of the entity of water which remained the same, *i. e.,* unchanged in the change. Nevertheless, it is just as indisputable that the water has lost an important element, indeed, the most significant element of its nature, *viz.,* that element which gave it its substantial determination— its specific characteristic, because it was precisely that element which made it water, and thereby made it distinct from every other body that is not water.

So far we looked upon the transformative process from the viewpoint of its "terminus a quo," its point of departure, *i. e.,* we studied it inasmuch as if affected the body-water—which has changed; now let us look upon it from the viewpoint of its "terminus ad quem," its point of arrival, *i. e.,* from the viewpoint of the new bodies— oxygen and hydrogen, which are the result of the change. Evidently, here again everybody is agreed that the new bodies are not wholly and absolutely new, they are not the product of a creation, but only of a transformation, which means that some element of the new bodies already existed before, and it could not exist before but in the body—water—from which they originated. This element is, of course, the very same element which, as we saw already, was not lost in the change but remained unchanged throughout. Something absolutely new, surely an element of the greatest significance has made its appearance in each of the new bodies—oxygen and hydrogen—because it is on account of this new element that they are two new bodies, each of a distinct species. Clearly, this new element in oxygen and hydrogen is equivalent to the element lost by the change, because in the same manner as that element gave to water its substantial determination and its specific characteristic, *i. e.,* made it water—a specific body essentially distinct from every other body that is not water—so also this new element in oxygen and hydrogen gives to each of them its substantial determination and its specific characteristic, *i. e.,* makes the one oxygen and the other hydrogen, two chemical species, essentially distinct from every other chemical species.

2. THE INTERPRETATION OF THE ANALYSIS

Such is the analysis of a substantial transformation of bodies. There can be no room for doubt about the conclusion to be drawn from it: the body is evidently constituted by two substantial elements. One of them is essentially passive, since it undergoes no change; it is essentially indeterminate, since it is indifferent to any change; and it is absolutely common, since it is identical in all bodies before and after they change. Surely, its name was well chosen—*MATERIA PRIMA*. The other element of the body is essentially active, since it is in every change the element which disappears and is substituted by another; it is essentially determinative, since it gives its substantial determination to each body; and it is always specific, since it characterizes each body as an individual of a distinct species. Here again, the name given to the element is highly expressive—*FORMA SUBSTANTIALIS*.

3. CHARACTERISTICS OF THE SUBSTANTIAL ELEMENTS

Of the nature of the two constitutive elements of a body we have no direct perception. What we perceive is the body in which the elements are actualized. The reason for this is simple enough, for the elements have no distinct existence apart from the existence of the body.

Having no distinct existence, they have no distinct action. Only the concrete body as it exists in its objective reality can act upon our senses, and only through our sense experience does the body become an object of our knowledge. However, if we consider carefully the above analysis of a substantial transformation, the characteristics of the elements are partly disclosed.

a. THE FORMA SUBSTANTIALIS

The active element which is the one that is lost and replaced by another, is the less obscure because, being the element which gives the body its distinctive and specific character, it is more apparent in the concrete body than the other element. Its *main rôle* is to actualize and concretize the potential and passive element, and thereby to determine it as an individual of a chemical species. Its *secondary rôle* is to be the source and basis of the immediate principles of action which we call the forces or active qualities of the body. It is in this same active element of the body that we must place the seat and center of that all-important intrinsic tendency of a body which we call its final cause. We express this active and determinative character of the element when we call it *FORMA SUBSTANTIALIS*.

b. THE MATERIA PRIMA

The passive element—the one which remains unchanged in a substantial transformation and which is common to all bodies—is knowable only inasmuch as it is the basic subject in which the substantial form is received, and the potential principle which the formal element actualizes and specifies. Its indetermination is as absolute as its determinability is unlimited, and therefore, it is capable of receiving any kind of determination and specification if we consider it theoretically. However, in practice, its determinability and potentiality are limited, because it exists in reality only in concrete bodies, and in a specific concrete body its capacity to receive new substantial forms is regulated by the chemical affinities of that body. Besides this primary rôle to form the body, it has also a secondary rôle—to be the source and basis of quantity and all the purely mechanical properties of bodies. To express this passive and potential character of the element we call it *MATERIA PRIMA*.

We have a clear indication of the identity and permanency of the materia prima in a substantial transformation, and even more than an indication, for we have, generally speaking, an exact measure for that element in the quantity, which is the philosophical equivalent to the mass or weight of a body. The quantity of the bodies transformed undergoes no change whatsoever. Thus, in a combination of chlorine and sodium the mass of salt is exactly the sum of the combined masses of the two elements, chlorine and sodium.

4. PHILOSOPHICAL IMPORTANCE OF THE HYLEMORPHIST DOCTRINE

We have dwelled upon the discussion of the hylemorphist constitution of a body because it represents the last word regarding our knowledge of the nature of inorganic bodies. Our philosophical investigation on this subject, paramount in cosmology, can go no further. Its importance, moreover, is not only cosmological but psychological also. We will see later that in all our discussions on the nature of living beings, we shall have to come back to the same doctrine, whenever we push our intellectual inquiries to the very end of our power.

There is a second reason for enlarging upon the hylemorphist doctrine. Not being well understood, it is often the object of raillery and even scorn on the part of savants and philosophers, because it is considered as a typical indication of the subtlety, abstruseness, and even futility of scholastic philosophy. Yet, as is clearly apparent from our discussion of a chemical transformation, if we are philosophically in earnest and go to the limit in our intellectual analysis, the hylemorphist interpretation is the only possible one. The clear simple facts of the substantial change of a body present to the mind the premises from which the doctrine of its hylemorphist constitution is the inevitable logical conclusion. Consequently, there is no other alternative in the matter: the cosmologist must accept the doctrine of hylemorphism, or resign himself to the fate of being drowned in a sea of intellectual pessimism.

II. *The Accidental Elements*

After the analysis of the substantial elements, which are the primary elements of a body, we will now pay attention to the secondary elements, to which allusion has already been made repeatedly. They are not substantial, inasmuch as they may change without a change of substance, and especially, inasmuch as they have no existence apart from the substance in which they exist, since it is their nature to exist in another being. To express this insufficiency for a distinct existence of their own, we call them *ACCIDENTS*. However, we must not conceive them as contingent in their relation to the substance in which it is their nature to exist. They belong, as a specified group and system, to the body of which they are the natural properties. It is only by means of these properties that the body is related to other bodies and becomes an object of our perception. In the normal course of nature there can be no accident without its proper substance, and no substance without its proper accidents, because it is only when united in one existence that the substantial and accidental elements constitute the concrete body.

Apart from the primary and fundamental accident of quantity, to the discussion of which we shall devote a special chapter, we may divide, for the sake of greater clearness, all the secondary accidents into three classes, *viz.,* mechanical, physical, and chemical properties.

I. MECHANICAL PROPERTIES

We must discuss the mechanical properties first because they are the most fundamental, *i. e.,* they are, of all secondary accidents, the most closely attached to the very foundation of the body. The foundation of the body is the materia prima, and it is in the materia prima these properties have their seat and source. Thus it is explained, why, strictly speaking, these accidents are really not properties, because they are not proper to any species of bodies like the physical and chemical properties; but they are as common to all bodies as the materia prima itself. Thus a pound of gold has exactly the same mechanical accidents as a pound of hydrogen. The reason for this correlation between the mechanical properties of the body and its fundamental substantial principle— the materia prima—is not far to seek. The mechanical properties are directly and intimately related to the quantity of the body, but, as we have already seen and shall see more fully in the next chapter, the quantity, or its scientific equivalent—mass—is the direct expression and exact measure of the materia prima.

The best known of these accidents are gravitation and inertia. We call them forces, because they are the immediate principles of action, and mechanical forces, because their action is local motion.

2. PHYSICAL PROPERTIES

The physical properties of a body are, strictly speaking, *properties,* because they form a group or system of accidental elements which belongs, as such, exclusively to one chemical species. Consequently, their source and basis in the body is not the materia prima—the common principle, but the forma substantialis—the specific principle. We may call them, therefore, *accidental forms,* because in the same manner as the substantial form determines the body in its specific nature, the physical properties determine the body in its manifold individual characteristics. They have this in common with the substantial form that they both determine the body, but differ in that the forma substantialis determines it substantially and specifically, whereas the physical properties determine it accidentally and individually.

The physical properties are also physical forces, inasmuch as they are direct causes of action by means of which the body expresses its own nature, and, by entering into relation with other bodies, attains its natural object. It is quite evident that these forces are objective and distinct realities in the body, because the body itself is one and undivided in its substance, whereas its actions are of various kinds, specifically distinct from one another. Hence, the immediate principles of these various activities must be specifically distinct from one another. Such specifically distinct forces are sound, heat, light, electricity, and others.

When we say that these physical forces are specifically distinct, we mean that they are numerically distinct ontological elements or objective realities, each having its own specific nature, and not merely various forms or aspects or degrees of one and the same element or reality. When we base their specific distinction upon the objective distinction of their action, we base it upon clearly recognized facts of our sense experience. Indeed, not only do we not perceive the various physical properties of bodies, such as sounds, colors, odors, flavors, etc., by one and the same sense as we should if they were objectively identical, but by our several anatomically and physiologically different senses. Even the phenomena themselves appear altogether as irreducible elements even in the minutest and most careful scientific analysis.

Such are the plain facts. However, many modern scientists deny them. But it is well to add immediately that they deny them not as scientists—the language of the facts is too clear for that—rather they base their denial upon the philosophical assumption of mechanicism, that all phenomena of the universe are purely mechanical in nature, due to peculiar forms of atomic motion. Their reason for applying this mechanicist assumption to the various physical properties is this—all physical properties have a mechanical equivalent as can be shown very easily. With a certain amount of heat, for instance, we perform a definite amount of mechanical labor, just as with a certain amount of mechanical labor we produce a definite amount of heat. Thus, we possess a fairly exact common measure for the physical properties in the quantity of mechanical labor which may be produced by them or may be expended in producing them.

Now we have no difficulty in admitting the premises, but we reject the conclusion, because it passes far beyond anything that is logically contained therein. To claim that the fact of a common mechanical equivalent for the various physical energies demonstrates that the physical phenomena are but more highly developed mechanical phenomena, is deducing an identity of nature from a mere common relationship and interdependence of action. Such a relationship and interdependence, perfectly sufficient to explain the common mechanical equivalent, does really exist, because there is in the constitution of the body an element which appears to be the natural and obvious basis for a common mechanical aspect regarding all the physical and even the chemical phenomena of nature. This element is quantity. Indeed, we know already, and shall see still better, that quantity is the common basis and necessary condition for the existence and action of all physical as well as chemical forces, for we shall explain in our next chapter that all motion and, therefore, all mechanical phenomena, are conditioned by quantity. Consequently, there can be no mystery about the fact that all physical phenomena can be measured by mechanical phenomena, since motion is the common condition, concomitant, and measure of all material action.

3. CHEMICAL PROPERTIES

The chemical properties are those which are in closest connection with the specific nature of the body. Therefore, of all scientists, it is the chemist who comes nearest to the knowledge of the nature of the body, because the chemical properties express this inner nature more directly and more clearly than the others. Indeed, so intimate and direct is the relation between the chemical properties of a body and its very nature, that any change whatsoever in its chemical properties involves a change in its nature. However, even the chemical properties must not be identified with the substance itself, for they are several and various, whereas the substance is one.

The best known chemical properties are chemical affinity, atomicity, and atomic weight. Chemical affinity is evidently a force because it is a cause of action. It is the deepest and noblest force of the body, because its action has a most direct and an absolutely decisive influence upon its very nature, as it is selective in its object. Consequently, it is in the affinity of the body that we possess the most obvious expression of its finality, and the clearest indication of the orientation of its activity. This consideration is sufficient to show that it must have its source and seat in the forma substantialis, the active and specific principle of the body.

Atomicity and atomic weight are not forces, they are but the condition and measure of the chemical affinity and of the quantity of the body, respectively. Hence, the atomicity must be considered as having its root and basis in the forma substantialis, whereas the atomic weight is based on the materia prima.

CHAPTER FIVE

NATURE OF QUANTITY. ITS SPECIES: SPACE AND TIME

COSMOLOGICAL IMPORTANCE OF QUANTITY

Analyzing the nature of inorganic bodies, we have found and defined two kinds of elements: (1) the substantial elements, two in number, *viz.*, materia prima and forma substantialis, and (2) those accidental elements which, divided into three classes, we call the mechanical, physical, and chemical properties of the body. This classification does not exhaust the wealth of ontological elements that make up the real concrete body which we study in cosmology; there is quantity, another element of the highest cosmological importance. Indeed, without quantity no body would ever be accessible to our knowledge. Our first and deepest impression of a body is as an entity occupying a certain portion of space, *i. e.*, as having quantity, because it is on account of its quantity that a body occupies space. In the same way the other properties of the body are inconceivable unless we consider them as existing and acting in a certain portion of space, consequently, they also seem to demand quantity as the basis and condition of their existence and action. It is for this reason that we call quantity the primary, and the other properties the secondary accidents of the body.

There is another reason which shows the cosmological importance of quantity, *viz.*, its relation to position, space, motion, and time. Without motion we should have no time; without position, no motion; without space, no position, and without quantity and extension, no space.

I. Nature of Quantity

Our first question in this respect is: What is quantity? We shall find that it is not a simple question at all. In order to gain a clear idea of it we will first compare it with the elements of the body which we already know, and then study it in itself.

A. QUANTITY IN ITS RELATION TO OTHER ELEMENTS

In comparing quantity with the other elements of the body, we notice that it differs from both kinds, *i. e.*, the substantial and the accidental elements already studied. While it is an accidental element, as we shall prove, yet it is so closely related to the substance, that Descartes mistook it for the very essence of the body, and it is also in such intimate relationship with the mechanical, physical, and chemical properties, that we can only describe its place in the systematic composition of the body, as an intermediate position between the substance and the other accidents of the body.

1. QUANTITY, AN ACCIDENT

With reference to substance, quantity is evidently an accident, because it has no existence of its own, but exists exclusively in and through the substance. To prove this assertion it will suffice to mention three points:

a. The substance of a thing expresses the answer to the question: What is it? The quantity is an answer to the question: How much is there of it? These two questions are adequately distinct. The answer to the second supposes the answer to the first. But if the questions are adequately distinct, the objects to which they refer must be distinct realities.

b. The substance of a body is ever the same. It cannot vary because any variation, however slight,

would make it another species of body. It is not
the same with quantity. In all living beings there
is a great variability of quantity compatible with
the same substance; take the grain of mustard-seed,
for instance.

c. In the Holy Eucharist we are taught on divine authority that there is a change of the substance of
bread and wine without any change of their quantity. Here, substance and quantity appear not only
distinct, but separable through divine intervention.

2. QUANTITY, A QUASI-SUBSTANCE

Compared with substance, quantity is undoubtedly
an accident, but compared with the other accidents it
rather appears to be a quasi-substance, because all the
other accidents find in quantity their common condition
and basis, and without quantity we could neither perceive
them nor could they exist. Two important considerations will help us to understand this peculiar position of
quantity in respect to the other properties which, to express their distinction from quantity, we call qualities.

a. The qualities, *i. e.*, the mechanical, physical, and
chemical properties which we determined as forces
or causes of action, are conditioned in their exercise by space and time, because it is clearly established, both in physics and chemistry, that there are
neither physical nor chemical phenomena without
the mechanical concomitant of motion, and motion,
of course, implies both space and time, and space
and time are nothing else but quantity specified and
applied.
    Our perception of the qualities of bodies shows
the same relation to quantity. Sense perception is
spread out over our sense organs, *i. e.*, conditioned
by space, it is never instantaneous but successive,
i. e., conditioned by time.

b. Though its qualities are manifold and multiform,
being the different means and ways by which the

body enters into relation with other bodies and thus attains its proper object, yet they form a harmonious and unified specific group, manifesting and expressing its inner nature and tendency. It is on this account that these properties of the body are called qualities. Only by means of these qualities can we learn something about its substance. It is very different with quantity. In its specified application of time and space, it is a common condition of all material phenomena in exactly the same manner, betraying in no sense whatsoever the distinctive specific character of the phenomena. From this we infer that quantity has its seat and source in the passive and indeterminate substantial element—the materia prima—and shares in its passivity and indetermination. Consequently, to know the quantity of a being does not increase our knowledge of its specific characteristics, nor does it tell us anything about the distinctive type or class of the being, but simply how much there is of it—how large or small it is.

However, there is one significant exception. The substantial forms of inorganic bodies are the lowest in kind, and are so restricted in their specific determinative power that they can appropriate, actualize, and concretize only a well-defined portion of matter, not more and not less; and consequently, the chemist, not by direct perception, but indirectly by analysis, can determine the species of the body by the knowledge he has of its exact quantity, *i. e.,* of the atomic and molecular weight which expresses the quantity.

B. QUANTITY AND ITS ESSENTIAL CHARACTERISTICS

I. DEFINITION OF QUANTITY

We are now prepared to come to the main question: What is quantity in itself? Our first impression of quantity is its divisibility. However, a being to be divisible, must be composed, *i. e.,* it must have parts. Thus, we speak of quantity whenever we can add or subtract, multiply or divide something, *i. e.,* whenever we can add or take away parts of a being. We cannot do that unless the being we add to or take from be of the same order. Strictly speaking we add water to water, but we mix water with wine. When we add water to water, we have a larger quantity of water; when we mix wine with water, we have two quantities, one of water and the other of wine. Hence, this kind of divisibility does not refer to the division of the body into its substantial and accidental elements, but to the body as a whole, divisible into parts of the same order, *i. e.,* every part being really integral, representing not one element of the body, but the whole body.

For the sake of greater clearness we will present here the various compositions which we have already studied:

a. *CHEMICAL composition* refers to the chemical elements which unite to produce the chemical compound; thus chlorine and sodium constitute salt.

b. *PHYSICAL composition* belongs to the concrete body inasmuch as it is made up of substance and accidents.

c. *SUBSTANTIAL composition* expresses the union of the two ontological elements—materia prima and forma substantialis—that enter into the constitution of the substance.

d. *QUANTITATIVE composition,* or simply quantity, is an attribute of the concrete body inasmuch as that body is made up of parts of the same kind.

2. CHARACTERISTICS OF QUANTITY

From the above definition of quantity various characteristics follow spontaneously:

a. There is first its *INFINITE DIVISIBILITY.* To be composed of parts is the very essence of quantity; but what is composed of parts can be divided into its parts. Hence, any quantity, no matter how small, is essentially divisible. Practically, there may be a limit in the possible division of a definite quantity because of physical difficulties in realizing the division, but theoretically there can be no limit put upon it.

We can show this plainly by an illustration. If we try to convert the common fraction one-third into a decimal fraction, we will never be able to express this quantity exactly. Let us put it in five figures— 0.33333. Surely, we are near a third, but only near it. If we continue to add threes we come nearer and nearer but we will never come to express a full third exactly, even if we continue to add threes forever. However, the whole process is but a process of division.

b. The second characteristic of quantity refers to the *HOMOGENEITY* of its parts—they are essentially homogeneous. All other compositions which we have discussed, are unions of *heterogeneous* parts. As a consequence such compositions are not at all divisible in the same sense as quantity. Since the compound, in its distinctive characteristics, is the result of a combination of heterogeneous parts, if we take away any one of them, it is intrinsically changed, *i. e.,* a qualitative change has been realized. Not so in respect to quantitative composition. We may take away any amount of its parts without in any way affecting the quality of the body, because only the quantity itself has been affected. The reason is precisely in the homogeneity of all the parts: each part representing the whole body in its qualitative aspect—thus, each part of an apple is apple.

c. Another essential characteristic of quantity is the *CONTINUITY* of the parts that compose it. The reason is very simple. Quantity is divisible, but it is not divided; its parts are not actual, but potential. Though they do not co-exist like the heterogeneous parts of the other three compositions discussed, which compenetrate one another in constituting a united whole, yet they also constitute a united whole —quantity—they are united by juxta-position. However, their juxta-position or contiguity is such that there is no line of demarcation between them, consequently their mode of composition or union is by continuity.

If you take an apple and cut it in two, you still have juxta-position of the parts or contiguity if you do not take them actually apart; but you have no more continuity as a line of demarcation is established. To be continuous, which is essential to quantity, the body must be whole. Of course, each portion of a division is again a quantity inasmuch as that portion is itself continuous.

d. From the contiguity and continuity of quantity a few other characteristics follow logically. There is first *EXTENSION,* the most important of all the immediate effects of quantity. In respect to quantity the body is composed not of heterogeneous parts that compenetrate one another, but of homogeneous parts that are joined together by juxta-position. It occupies and fills a definite portion of space. It is this portion of space, circumscribed by the limits of the body, *i. e.,* its periphery, which we call its extension.

Again, because the quantitative parts of a body are continuous and occupy a certain portion of space, every other body is thereby excluded from that same portion of space. We express this when we say that a body is *IMPENETRABLE.*

Finally, because of its continuity and therefore, because of its quantity, every body is *MEASUR-ABLE;* we may take any one part of the body as a unit and thereby measure the whole body.

II. *The Chief Species of Quantity: Space and Time*

The species of quantity called space and time are of vital concern to the cosmologist. The reason is obvious. To explain the universe is the comprehensive problem of cosmology. The bodies that compose the universe are not in a state of absolute repose or stability, but rather in a condition of continuous fluctuation and transformation. The modern, rather happy expression for it is *evolution*. Thus, we say, and say well, that all bodies in the world are subject to constant evolution, either progressive or regressive. However, this aspect of the universe cannot be explained except upon the basis of *MOTION*, and motion again is, on the one hand, conditioned by the *POSITION* of bodies and, on the other, necessarily involves the ideas of both *SPACE* and *TIME*.

1. THE POSITION OF THE BODY

As we explained above, that portion of space occupied by the body on account of its quantity, is called extension. In scholastic philosophy this is also called the *external POSITION* of a body to distinguish it from the *internal POSITION* or the *"ubi."* It is in this sense that we generally speak of the position of a body. The "ubi" is a much discussed subject and not easy to conceive clearly. However, it seems evident that we must look upon it as an intrinsic accident of the body in virtue of which the body takes its own position in space, *i. e.,* an accidental property which localizes the body. There are two good reasons for our statement:

a. Motion is not a logical but a real objective entity— great energy is often expended to produce it. But motion is merely a continuous change of position; therefore, if the position were nothing real, motion could not be real either.

b. Again, distances are real, objective; there is a positive science that measures them. However, what is a distance but a relation between positions? Hence, if the position of a body were not real, distances would be without any objective foundation.

2. MOTION

We have just stated that MOTION is a continuous change of position. We cannot conceive it otherwise. That a body moves, means that it has left its position and has not yet reached another definite position; it is on the way to it. Its march to the new position is uninterrupted, continuous. The moment it stops, there is no more motion. Consequently, the *CONTINUITY* of change is essential in motion, and the only reality of the body changed by it, is its position. No matter how carefully we study and analyze motion, we find that the substance of the moving body and all its accidents remain absolutely unchanged with one exception—its position in space.

From this analysis it is clear that motion is a quantity, as it is a continuous whole composed of homogeneous parts. However, there is this determinative characteristic which makes it a distinctive species of quantity: its parts are successive, not simultaneous; they do not co-exist at the same time, but follow one another in such a way that some have always gone and others are to come, but with no break between.

3. SPACE

It is imposible to explain motion without space as its indispensable condition. What is space? What is its objective foundation? We generally conceive space as if it were a great vacant receptacle or vast container in which all the bodies of the universe exist and move about. Even at the confines of the real universe we imagine there are more infinite stretches of space in which bodies could exist and move about. Evidently, such conceptions are rather the product of the soaring imagination than that of the abstractive mind.

The objective and concrete foundation for our idea of space is very simple, since it is based upon the analysis of motion. That a body moves, means it is continuously changing its position. Now, between the "terminus a quo," *i. e.,* the position of the body before it begins its movement, and the "terminus ad quem," *i. e.,* the position the body holds at the end of its movement, there is a relation of distance. This *distance is the real foundation of our idea of SPACE.* As a body may move in different directions, taking positions accordingly, there is a relation of distance in *length,* another in *width,* and another in *depth,* and, thus, we have the idea of the *three dimensions* and of the complete portion of space occupied by a body, *i. e.,* its extension. Consequently, we might define *space* by saying that it *is the abstract idea of a distance.*

Of course, we have as many real distances as we have positions to compare and relate to one another, and evidently we have as many real spaces. However, we have not only the various positions which one and the same body may successively occupy whenever it moves, but besides, as all bodies occupy their own position, we have all kinds of distances and spaces in the universe. Where there is no body and therefore no position occupied by a body, there can be no question of real space. Hence, when we speak of space outside the real universe, we indulge in a play of the imagination.

4. TIME

The idea of time is closely related to that of space. It appears to us as a kind of beginningless and endless stream upon which all the beings and the happenings in the universe make their appearance, linger for a while, and then disappear to make room for others; in other words, we look upon it in the same way as upon space, as an infinite receptacle, with this difference, that space is a simultaneous, and time a successive receptacle. In this regard we conceive periods of time which might have preceded the creation of the universe, or might follow its annihilation. Evidently, here again, we have rather the work of the imagination than of the intellect.

The true or intellectual idea of time is like that of space —a result of the analysis of motion. Motion is continuous, and therefore, measurable like all quantity. But the continuity of motion is of a peculiar order. It is not like the quantity in space—simultaneous, but *successive, i. e.,* one part of it follows another in uninterrupted succession; one part cannot make its appearance till the other has disappeared, however, without any line of demarcation between the parts. Now, if we look upon motion in this special aspect, as one part following another, we have the idea of time. It is, indeed, nothing else but *a measure of motion inasmuch as part of it is gone and the other part is to come.* Thus, we have in the very idea of time its division into past and future; the dividing line is the present. Looking upon the present closely we find we can never seize it, it is ever flowing and has no extension, because the division thus introduced in time is not real but logical. Consequently, the only objective reality there is in time, is motion, and speaking concretely, the motion of some being. From the analysis of motion the true idea of time is logically inferred: *Time is the abstract idea of motion inasmuch as motion is a quantity in which the composing parts succeed one another.*

Bearing in mind this definition of time, we shall understand that each being has its own time; there is no other objective time but individual concrete beings changing and, therefore, moving. However, our mind divides the motion of beings into two portions, one that is gone and one that is to come, and thereby motion becomes time. Again, our mind measures the motion of one being by comparing it with that of another. The concrete motion chosen by all races as the unit of time, is the movement of the heavenly bodies on account of their regularity, uniformity, and general and easy perceptibility. This explains how our idea of time has become so closely associated with the classification of hours, days, years, and centuries, applied to our own life in particular, and to life in general, because in living beings the idea of time as continuous motion is clearly apparent.

CHAPTER SIX

COSMOGONY, THE SCIENCE OF THE WORLD'S HISTORY

The Importance of this Study

We have solved the basic problem of cosmology—the nature of the universe. However, the second problem —that of its origin—is not less important. From a theoretical viewpoint its value is apparent. There can be no satisfactory explanation of the universe till its coming into being is accounted for. From a practical viewpoint the solution of this problem is even more valuable, indeed, it is of the most far-reaching consequences. The solution of this problem must determine whether man is capable of attaining to a certain knowledge of God. However, the knowledge of the existence and nature of God is the only possible foundation for such individual and social phenomena as religion and ethics, which have been the cornerstone and the only genuine criterion for the value and signification of human civilization and of man's private life. Consequently, it is the plain duty of the philosopher to study this question with utmost care and attention, since its solution is of the most profound and most vital concern to every man in his individual as well as in his social life.

The Method of this Study

In the study of the origin of the universe we shall use the same method as we used in the study of its nature: we shall first examine the facts, as observation and science reveal them to us, and upon the facts we shall build our theory. In ancient and even in medieval times it was much more difficult to offer a philosophical theory on the origin of the world, because of the world's history nothing whatsoever was known except by Revelation. This has changed profoundly since the advent of modern astronomy. Since men like Kepler, Copernicus, Galileo, and Newton blessed the world with their discoveries, we have a true conception of what the universe is, and since Kant with a stroke of genius presented his history of the world, and some decades later Laplace placed it upon a scientific basis, we have a real cosmogonic science, *i. e.,* a serious scientific attempt to explain by natural factors the existence and form of the universe as astronomy presents it to our view.

I. The Cosmogonic Theory

The scientific theory of cosmogony is based mainly upon the results of modern astronomy and geology, and in a smaller degree upon the data of mechanics, thermodynamics, and spectral analysis. In this study the scientist proceeds in fundamentally the same way as the astronomer when he foretells the eclipses of the sun or the moon, or as the farmer when he sows in the spring and expects to harvest in the fall, with this exception that they look forward and he looks backward. The same forces that are active at present and, therefore, prepare the future, have been active ever since the world first came into being, and, consequently, calculating as approximately as possible their action and results in the past, the scientist is enabled to trace, at least in outline, the history of the universe. It may be presented more or less in four or five periods.

I. THE PRIMITIVE PERIOD OF THE UNIVERSE: NEBULA AND THE ORIGIN OF MOTION

The primitive stage of the universe is, with good reason, supposed to date back millions of centuries. It is assumed that the universe existed then in the form of a tenuous, more or less uniformly spread mass of homogeneous appearance, somewhat like a fog or cloud, and therefore, called *NEBULA,* which covered at least all the space traversed at present by the moons and planets as well as by the suns and stars. Of the immensity of this area it is impossible to form even a proximate conception, when we bear in mind, on the one hand, the velocity with which light travels, and on the other, the fact that the light of some stars needs many years to reach us.

The nebula was in a state of perfect equilibrium. However, this universal equilibrium did not last long, because in the peripheric portions of the nebula the force of gravitation would tend to produce motion towards the center of the mass, and perhaps also the distribution of the mass itself was not perfectly uniform in all parts of the nebula, and thus, a tendency to move in a special sense was inevitable. In such a way, though perhaps only after millions or even billions of years, definite movements came about which necessarily resulted in breaking up the primitive nebula into many separate masses.

2. SECOND PERIOD: STELLAR EVOLUTION

The second period of cosmogony is that of stellar evolution. In each one of the vast nebular masses which resulted from the breaking up of the primitive nebula, we see a future star. Let us outline the history of our own star, the sun. This mass is already moving in a definite sense. But how did *rotation* start in our sun? Undoubtedly, not all masses were equally large, and when smaller masses would come near the larger, the force of attraction would draw them irresistibly, and with great impetus they would fall into them. As such falls would not be perfectly concentric on account of other attracting nebular masses, and again, as they would not always be perfectly neutralized by other falls, in the course of time a definite rotatory movement would set in. Now, two processes would go on simultaneously in the solar mass:

gradual condensation of the mass towards its center, and
in consequence thereof an acceleration of rotation. In
this period of evolution, the mass, though not red-hot,
begins to shine, probably the effect of an electrical phenomenon—a brightness like that observed in the actual
nebulæ and in the comet's tail. On the further development of the process of condensation heat is produced
and the heat would eventually produce incandescence,
which accounts for the fiery aspect we perceive in the
stars.

3. THIRD PERIOD: PLANETARY EVOLUTION

During the latter part of the preceding period a new
and striking evolution has set in—the formation of planets
and probably at the same time that of satellites. In the
first stages of solar condensation, the great mass must
have covered at least—probably much more than—the
space included in the orbit of Neptune. While the great
mass began to concentrate its matter more and more towards the center, new and secondary centers of attraction and condensation formed at various distances from
the common center—the nucleuses of the future planets.
They revolved with the surrounding mass about the common center, and with increasing condensation three things
happened: (1) They began to move faster than the mass
around them; (2) They were gradually drawn closer
and closer to the common center till the centripetal force
of attraction and the centrifugal force produced by the
revolutionary motion, were equalized; and (3) In consequence of these two factors, they began a rotatory movement around their own center in the sense of the solar
rotation, because moving faster than the mass around them
and encountering more resistance on their inner side, the
production of such a rotation was inevitable. Exactly
the same principles apply to the formation of the satellites.

There seems to be no doubt that such was, more or less,
the primitive history of our planetary system. However,

one remark is necessary here. Some planets do not rotate in the same direction as the solar rotation. Probably their production is due to the formation of rings around the solar equator. Such an origin would explain their retrograde motion, and the possibility of such an origin is beyond doubt as we see in the rings of Saturn.

4. FOURTH PERIOD: GEOGONY

The last period of cosmogony refers to our own planet, the earth. We may call it, therefore, geogony. Probably our earth began its evolution early and being a small body it developed fast. It was a star for a relatively short time; as very soon more energy was discharged by irradiation than was produced by condensation, it grew old and cold; a gradually thickening crust covered its fiery mass, and within a few million years, when, one after the other, plants and animals and man made their appearance upon it, they depended for light and heat upon the sun.

II. *The Rational Basis of Cosmogony*

Such is in outline the great story of cosmic evolution. It has been written during the last century by the synthetic efforts of various scientists who gathered the material for this history from many different sources. While in its detail the narrative is obscure and meagre, yet in its great comprehensive lines the theory has gradually found favor with all classes of people, till today there is hardly an educated man or woman that does not accept it, not only as highly probable, but as practically certain. There are sufficient reasons in the theory itself to account for this fact, as it is a very serious scientific attempt to explain the existence and phenomena of the universe as we actually find them, by the natural processes of action and reaction of well-known forces of nature. Some people have objected to the theory on philosophical and religious grounds, but, we think, without good reason. We shall examine these objections after presenting the main facts of which the theory is supposed to be the rational interpretation.

A. COSMOGONY AND SCIENCE

1. When Kant proposed the theory, about a century and a half ago, he had in mind the following facts which it was intended the theory should account for:

   a. All the planets then known revolved about the sun in the sense of the solar rotation from West to East.
   b. All the planets had their orbits practically on the same plane, which is that of the sun's equator.
   c. The orbits of all the planets were concentric.

   At the time the theory was proposed by Kant only six planets were known. Now we know more than five hundred. Even all the secondary systems, the satellites, are in perfect harmony with the theory in that they all revolve around their planets in the sense of their rotation and on the same plane with their equator.

   There is but one exception to the general rule and that only in one respect, *viz.*, Uranus, Neptune, and their systems have a retrograde movement of rotation and revolution, *i. e.*, from East to West, probably attributable to the fact of their formation by equatorial rings of the solar mass as mentioned above.

2. However, since Kant and Laplace, not only hundreds of new planets have been discovered, which of course increase the probability of the theory a hundredfold, because they all act as the theory requires them to act, but a vast number of other facts from various sources have been brought to light, which all tend to confirm the theory We will mention a few:

a. From geology we know some very significant facts. Even today the earth is, to a large extent, *i. e.*, with the exception of the thin crust of a few miles, composed of magma, a kind of liquid fire, and in the stratification of the crust itself we have a clear indication that all the earth passed through a stage of liquid fire. However, before it came to a state of magma, *i. e.*, before the radiation of its heat, it must have been in a state of gaseous incandescence. It is true an enormous quantity of heat energy was necessary to produce this state of incandescence. But, then, that is easily explained by mechanical energy produced by condensation. In the early stages of this condensation the volume of the earth must have been of vast proportions.

All these inferences are based upon the action of well-known laws of nature, and of course, they are equally applicable to all the planets.

b. The astronomer confirms the geologist in this respect. What the earth was once, the sun still is, a gaseous ball of fire. He is losing heat by radiation, but probably gaining still more than he loses, by condensation. Gradually it will come to pass that his loss of energy will exceed his gain, and then, the sun will become what the earth is today. Here, again: the sun, though he still occupies a large area of space, in his early stages of condensation must have had a volume of immense proportions.

The astronomer also points out these significant facts: the elements composing the sun and the stars are of the same chemical species which we know from experience on earth; the yellowish, red, and white stars are indicative of the degree of their incandescence;

the new stars that suddenly appear and then disappear are the last flicker of star-life; and above all, the various nebulæ actually present in our skies are manifest confirmation of the nebular theory.

B. COSMOGONY AND PHILOSOPHY

From the viewpoint of the philosopher, cosmogony, as we just presented it, is an acceptable scientific theory, because it is a natural and rational interpretation of the history of the universe, and this interpretation being the only one so far proposed deserves the credit which it has universally received. While none of its arguments is, strictly speaking, conclusive, yet the cumulative evidence gathered from so many and various sources, gives it, to say the least, the highest degree of probability. But is it, as prejudiced and shallow minds have claimed, a full and perfect explanation of the origin of the universe? Surely not, and it is not strange that it should not be, as the scope and methods of experimental science preclude such an explanation. In respect to this problem, as is generally the case, where the scientist stops, the philosopher starts: the former lays the foundation upon which the latter builds.

I. THE NATURE OF THE PRIMITIVE NEBULA

The scientific cosmogonist simply assumes the primitive nebula to act in conformity with certain mechanical and thermo-dynamical laws of matter, as we know them from our present experience. This is a perfectly legitimate assumption, and the scientist could not proceed without it. However, the philosopher will naturally ask a few questions about the intrinsic nature of the nebula, because, unless certain conditions are found in the nature of the nebula, cosmic evolution will remain without a rational explanation. The following conditions are logical conclusions from our former discussion on the nature of inorganic bodies:

a. The primitive nebula, being the first stage in the evolution of the cosmos as we know it today, must be conceived as a mass of heterogeneous corpuscles. The reason is obvious. Cosmic evolution depends to the greatest extent upon chemical reactions, but as far as we know from experience, chemical reactions are not realized except between heterogeneous bodies; evidently, as regards the number and nature of the various species of gaseous corpuscles represented in the primitive nebula, we can say nothing, as we have no scientific data upon which to form a judgment.

b. The second condition necessary to explain cosmic evolution from the primitive nebula refers to the properties of the corpuscles composing the mass. They cannot possibly be supposed to be either simple forces without extension, nor extended masses without forces, as in the first case the presence of quantity, and in the second, the possibility of action, and therefore of evolution, would find no explanation. Even if we were to assume motion in a homogeneous and inert mass, such an assumption, as we saw in the preceding chapters, would lead us nowhere, since through motion the only change produced in a body is its position in space.

c. The most important of all conditions requisite in the primitive nebula is the presence of final causes. Cosmic evolution did not proceed in a chaotic manner, by chance. It followed certain clearly defined lines and laws. Its results were, generally speaking, good for the individual bodies and good for the universal system. System and order were the natural product and concomitant through all the stages of the evolution. Consequently, it would be absurd to speak of a chance system or transitory order, as it is a question of a most marvelous system and order, the constancy and regularity of which have remained unbroken and undisturbed in the midst of the most stupendous, manifold, and multiform upheavals and cataclysms through which the cosmic masses have passed in the long course of their evolution. To imagine that such wonderful effects could be obtained without any adequate cause, would be the height of folly. Hence, within the corpuscles themselves must be sought, as the noblest part of their natural endowment, the principle of direction which alone explains the orderly course and systematic orientation in the age-long processes of evolution.

2. THE ORIGIN OF THE PRIMITIVE NEBULA

The scientist simply assumes the presence of the primitive nebula, and he is perfectly correct in assuming it. His scope and methods once admitted, no one can ask him to go any farther. But the philosopher is not satisfied with assuming the existence of any being, he demands an explanation of it, and a full and adequate explanation. It might not be possible in a certain case to obtain such an explanation, but as a philosopher he cannot rest content unless he finds it. In attempting an explanation based upon the various theories of philosophers, three possible answers might be given to the question regarding the origin of the primitive nebula.

a. MATERIALISTIC EVOLUTION

Materialistic evolutionists would say that there is no need of explaining the origin of the primitive nebula because it has no origin, matter being eternal. This is a very sweeping statement, but without any basis in fact or reason. The eternity of matter is an arbitrary assumption, and, what is worse, an assumption very difficult to conceive. Even if matter were eternal, we should still lack an explanation of its existence.

(1) If matter were eternal, the primitive nebula could not be really the first stage of cosmic evolution. We could either suppose it to be in repose: if so, it would still be in repose, and there would have been no evolution; or, we could suppose it to be in motion: if so, it must have been eternally in motion, and must have already passed through an infinite multitude of phases in its process of evolution. However, the possibility of an infinite multitude is seriously disputed by great thinkers, and it would be intellectually disastrous to build the solution of this paramount problem upon such an obscure foundation.

(2) What is worse for the proponents of evolutionism —eternal matter does not explain its own existence. Even if, for the sake of argument, we were to grant not only the possibility or probability, but also the reality of eternal matter, we should not have thereby explained its existence.

A being which has the reason for its existence in itself and therefore needs no other to explain its existence, we call necessary, whereas a being which has not the reason for its existence in itself and, therefore, needs another to explain its existence, we call contingent.

Matter, even if supposed eternal, still remains contingent. The contingency of its nature is beyond question, especially in the theory of evolution, since it never remains the same, but is subject to eternal change. But evidently, a being that substantially changes and thereby ceases to be, cannot have it in its nature to be—cannot possibly be necessary. If matter is contingent, it does not explain its own existence, and if it exists, it must be explained by another.

b. PANTHEISTIC EVOLUTION

Pantheistic evolutionists assume that the primitive nebula is the divine substance in the first stage of its material externalization and expansion. In the minds of pantheists, of course, the origin of the primitive nebula is accounted for by the divine substance from which it draws its being.

True it is, indeed, that there is no other way of accounting in an adequate manner for the existence of the primitive nebula but by an appeal to the divine substance, but not the divine substance as pantheists conceive it. A divine substance in this sense involves, the same as the eternal matter of the mechanicists, an eternal process of evolution. Consequently, the very same reasons that compelled us to reject an explanation of the primitive nebula by eternal matter in eternal motion, are, "mutatis mutandis," equally conclusive against the theory that accounts for the primitive nebula by the divine substance in an eternal process of expansion. Here, as well as there, we have the difficulty of conceiving an eternity that implies an infinite multitude of phases in the beginningless and endless process of the divine evolution, and here too we have the impossibility of accounting adequately for the existence of the primitive nebula, because the divine substance from which it is supposed to draw its origin is itself not accounted for. The reason for this failure of the divine substance of pantheism is obvious: The divine substance is not conceived as a spiritual, absolute, and all-perfect being, which would explain its existence because it is in the very nature of such a being to have existence, but it is conceived as a substance in the very nature of which it is necessarily and eternally to evolve, grow, and expand. However, a divine substance of such a conception is not essentially different from the eternal matter of the mechanicists, or, to express it briefly: the god of pantheism is as material as the matter of mechanicism is divine.

c. CREATION

There is only one possible adequate solution of the question of the origin of the primitive nebula and that is *CREATION BY GOD*. We have an indirect conclusive

argument for this solution in the fact that both materialistic and pantheistic evolution fails to solve the problem,
because there is, apart from creation, no other hypothesis,
since evolution and creation are contradictory terms, and
therefore, if it is not evolution, it must be creation.

However, we shall not content ourselves with this
negative argument. In view of the paramount speculative and practical importance of the solution, we will devote the next chapter chiefly to the presentation and examination of the positive evidence.

C. COSMOGONY AND THEOLOGY

There are people that have kept all through life the
naïve interpretation of the biblical story of creation as
they understood it in their childhood days. They believe that about six thousand years ago, in six days, or
at least, in six intervals of time, the world was created,
more or less as we see it, *i. e.,* in its present-day size and
proportion, nature and attributes, divisions and subdivisions. Of course, such people find it hard, if not impossible, to accept cosmic evolution from a primitive nebula
as taught by modern cosmogony, and thus, they are often
tormented by a mental discord between the results of
science and what to them is the voice of faith. The great
theologians and doctors of the Church, from St. Augustine down, were not so scrupulous in this matter.
They did not interpret the story of creation so literally.
However, it is hardly necessary to add that it would be
rash to consider the Biblical account simply as an allegory
of fictional character. To understand it correctly it is
well to bear in mind a few considerations:

1. In the Divine Revelation, God was the *teacher* of
   mankind, and as an infinitely *wise* teacher He
   would adapt Himself to the capacity and needs of
   His pupils.
2. The object of Revelation was to teach *religion*
   theoretically and practically, not the history of the
   race, and much less the history of the universe.

Such historical and scientific knowledge as we find in the Bible was not foreign to the mind of the Hebrews and, consequently, was the natural pedagogical means of religious instruction.

3. The outstanding points of religious doctrine contained in the story of creation are two: the fact of the creation of all things by God, and the consequent divine command that the people should devote each seventh day of the week to acknowledge the Divine Sovereignty over them and their own submission to the Divine Will. Surely, these points of religious instruction are brought out most impressively and most effectively.

4. While the Bible is a valuable aid in many instances, and a necessary corrective always, yet the man who wants to write the history of the human race or the history of the universe, must not go to the Bible for his sources.

CHAPTER SEVEN

THE DIVINE INTERVENTION IN COSMIC EVOLUTION

THE SIGNIFICATION OF COSMOGONY

In our last chapter we outlined the history of the universe such as the wonderful discoveries of modern science in various fields have made it possible to construct. To this general account of cosmic evolution we unhesitatingly give our assent. However, we have already proved that it cannot be a complete and adequate solution of the great problem of the origin of the universe, because it does not account for the existence of the primitive nebula, nor for the intrinsic dispositions and tendencies of the corpuscles composing the nebular mass, and this alone can explain the actual process of evolution and its final results. The proper and distinctive task of the cosmologist in respect to this problem begins here. He must show where the primitive nebula came from, and how it was possible that it could produce by natural development the great cosmos that we admire. If he can prove by positive, clear, and conclusive arguments that the primitive nebula is the product of creation by the infinite and absolute God, then the second question will offer no difficulties, for the nature of the nebular mass as constituted by the Creator would easily account for the issue of its activity.

We take, then, modern cosmogony, as outlined, for the basis of our argumentation. In doing so, we have a two-fold reason: First, we believe that the great and important points of the theory represent cosmic events as they really happened, i. e., they are facts upon which we

75

may safely build; second, if we can show that in the explanation of the existence of the universe we cannot do without creation even when we admit the cosmogonic theory, which goes as far as the combined efforts of science are able to go in accounting for the origin of the universe, then, a fortiori, we will have proved the creation of the world for those who do not admit the theory.

I. *The Primitive Nebula, the Product of Creation*

We have already seen that, whether we take evolution in its materialistic form or in its pantheistic coloring—which is but a veiled and disguised materialism,—it is not capable of accounting for the existence of the primitive nebula nor for the direction or the result of its evolution. From the inacceptability of the theory of evolution we have already inferred the necessity of creation. This inference was legitimate because evolution and creation are contradictory terms, for creation is the production of a being of which there was no pre-existing element whatsoever—a totally new production, whereas evolution is the production of a being of which there were elements already in existence in some way or other, and, therefore, not a totally new production, but only a transformation. They are contradictory terms: what the one affirms the other denies and vice versa. Hence, if the existence of the primitive nebula was not due to evolution, it must have been due to creation: there is no other alternative. However, as we promised, in a matter of such paramount importance we will not content ourselves with an indirect and negative demonstration, but will present our argument in a direct and positive form and as clearly and firmly as possible.

A. DEFINITION OF TERMS

Before we propose the argument itself, it is of vital interest to clarify perfectly the terms in which we shall present it.

1. In the first place it is important for us to know very clearly what we mean by *CONTINGENT* and *NECESSARY* in this connection; they are given here as contradictory terms. Any explanation of one implies an explanation of the other; and what is affirmed of the one is denied of the other in the same way as what is denied of the one is affirmed of the other. When we speak of beings here, we refer to beings as they exist in their objective reality, *i. e.,* concrete beings. The existence of such a being can be explained in either of two ways: either it exists because it is its nature to exist, *i. e.,* existence is an essential attribute without which it cannot be conceived: such is a necessary being; or it exists because it came into existence by the influence of another being, *i. e.,* its existence is contingent upon the presence of an external cause: such is a contingent being. It is evident there can be no middle term between necessary and contingent. In the necessary being essence and existence are identical; in the contingent being they are really distinct. The one, therefore, explains itself, the other needs another to explain it.

2. We must apply these terms to our subject matter—the primitive nebula. It must have been either contingent or necessary, there is no middle term possible. In order to solve the question of the contingency or non-contingency of the primitive nebula, we must have an exact idea of what we mean when we speak of it. It is not a question of abstract entities, we refer to the whole universe—this real concrete universe which our eyes see and our mind analyzes in the first stage of its existence such as modern cosmogony presents it to us. In other words, it is the sum of the gaseous corpuscles composing the nebular mass. Evidently, this mass, being the sum of concrete individual corpuscles, must be considered itself in the manner of a concrete body. The question that must be decided is a ques-

tion of fact: Did this primitive nebula exist because it was its nature to exist, *i. e.,* was it a necessary being, or did it exist because some other being brought it into existence *i. e.,* was it a contingent being?

B. THE ARGUMENT FOR CREATION

Having thus clarified our terms, we are able to propose our argument. For the sake of greater clearness we shall present it in syllogistic form, and after the solution of the main question shall consider some difficulties and draw some important inferences.

1. As we have explained above, when we speak in our argument of the primitive nebula, we take it to be the sum of all concrete beings having existence in the first stage of cosmic evolution. Upon this basis we argue as follows:

   MAJOR PREMISE: A contingent being does not explain its own existence, and since its existence cannot be explained adequately by another contingent being, it must be due to the act of a necessary being,—such an act as we call creation.

   MINOR PREMISE: The primitive nebula was totally and essentially contingent.

   CONCLUSION: Hence, the primitive nebula existed because it was created by a necessary being.

   EXPLANATION OF THE MAJOR: The existence of a contingent being can be explained by the act of another contingent being, but such an explanation is not adequate, as the contingent cause, again, needs an explanation, and thus, unless we come to a necessary cause, we shall have no adequate explanation. We call the productive act by the necessary being a creation, meaning that the being produced is a totally new production and not an evolution or transformation of a pre-existing element.

DEMONSTRATION OF THE MINOR: The primitive nebula was contingent if it was not necessary; but surely it was not necessary because it ceased to be, it is no more. For the same reason that a necessary being cannot achieve its existence, it cannot lose it, because *to be* is an absolutely essential characteristic of its nature, in just the same way as a circle can neither begin nor cease to be round. The very fact that the primitive nebula exists no more, is evident proof of the contingency of its nature.

2. Some philosophers reject the solution of the existence of the primitive nebula by creation because to them the idea of creation is *inconceivable*. We admit that we cannot *imagine* creation because we have no experience of it. However, we can *conceive* it perfectly. All that is required to make an idea conceivable is that there be no contradiction between the constituent parts of the idea. But creation implies on the one side an absolute infinite power—God's—and on the other, an existing contingent being; surely there is no contradiction between the two.

There is, besides, nothing incongruous in the idea of creation. To create is an absolute, independent manner of producing something. If contingent beings produce things in a dependent and restricted manner, why not the necessary being, the absolute God, in a way that corresponds to His independent nature?

Evolutionists insist that we need no creation to explain the universe because the universe, being an infinite series of successive phases of evolution, explains itself: each phase is explained by the one that precedes it and explains the one that follows it and thus, all are explained. This is a logical "circulus vitiosus." Indeed, not one is explained. Each phase is explained only inasmuch as the preceding one is explained, which means that all explanations are only provisional, dependent, and inadequate. Even an infinite multitude of provisional, dependent, and inadequate explanations cannot produce one that is definite, independent, and adequate. Instead of solving the problem it only multiplies its difficulty and its obscurity infinitely; it is like multiplying zeros.

3. In consequence of our demonstration that the only possible solution of the problem of the origin of the universe is an act of creation, we have arrived at the idea of God as the *NECESSARY BEING*. There are a few expressions that are perfectly equivalent to, and easily deducible from, that of necessary being. God being the creator is the cause of the universe, and having the reason for His existence in His own nature, He is only a cause, not an effect, therefore, the *UNCAUSED CAUSE*. For the same reason, not being dependent upon another for His existence and action, He is the *ABSOLUTE BEING*. Again, as in Him essence and existence are identical, *i. e.,* it is His nature *to be,* His perfection of being cannot be limited, and thus we call Him the *INFINITE BEING*.

The full significance of this truth will be brought out in a later part of our course—theodicy.

II. *Modes of Divine Intervention in Cosmic Evolution*

Having shown by positive and direct conclusive demonstration that the universe in its primitive stage came into existence by a creative act of the infinite God, the intrinsic dispositions and capacity for cosmic evolution, as cosmogony proposes it to our admiration, are but natural inferences. The infinitely wise Creator had a definite plan in His creation and ordained the very nature of the various corpuscles composing the primitive nebula in such a way that they could and would realize the divine design. However, we may ask ourselves a further question: Was this act of creation the only divine intervention in the universe, and if not, how are we to know when there is such an intervention? Evidently, the cosmologist is interested only inasmuch as the inorganic universe is thereby affected. A few general considerations will help to understand and solve the question.

There are two kinds of divine intervention, which we must clearly keep apart, the natural and the supernatural. The divine intervention is natural when the nature, existence, and natural action of bodies absolutely demand it. It is supernatural when the divine intervention takes place not for the sake of the world itself, but for the sake of a higher cause.

A. THE NATURAL DIVINE INTERVENTION

The assumption of the natural divine intervention must not be arbitrary, it must be based upon the demonstration of strict necessity; *i. e.,* we must assume it only when its object can be explained neither by any particular natural factor nor by any possible combination of such factors. Whenever any phenomenon can possibly be explained by contingent causes, an appeal to the direct action of God is unphilosophical. Based upon this principle, we find a divine intervention in the inorganic world for two objects only:

1. An appeal to God is necessary to explain the existence and nature of the universe as well as its continuation in existence and its ever adequate disposition for action. The contingent nature of the world necessitates this divine intervention.

2. A second appeal to God is necessary to explain the natural result of cosmic evolution, *i. e.,* the marvelous order clearly apparent in all cosmogonic periods. This absolute and relative universal order cannot be explained except by a commensurate design and plan, but such a plan and design cannot come but from the mind of the Creator.

   We do not mean to imply that God must intervene directly in the carrying out of the divine plan and design: It is sufficient if the contingent beings are directed in their action by intrinsic tendencies, the so-called final causes, which are the most precious element in their God-given nature.

It is but a logical inference from these principles of the natural divine intervention in cosmic evolution to look upon the universe as the objective ontological expression of the mind and the will of God.

B. THE SUPERNATURAL DIVINE INTERVENTION

MIRACLES: THEIR NATURE AND SIGNIFICATION

We speak of a supernatural divine intervention when God interferes directly in the universe for the attainment of a higher purpose. This purpose may be a divine manifestation of simple ratification and confirmation by means of which the natural divine plan, which is already expressed in the objective conditions of the universe, becomes more easily understood and more profoundly impressed. However, its proper purpose is a divine manifestation of a new plan, and a design of a higher order than the objective conditions of the universe could express.

This kind of divine intervention we call miraculous. We are able to recognize such a divine intervention not by the general and absolute impossibility to explain the miracle by natural factors, but by the clearly perceived discrepancy between the phenomenon in question and the factors available for its production. In other words: the miracle itself is not necessarily beyond the power of contingent agencies, but the agencies present are evidently unable to produce it.

1. From the very nature of the case it is plain that miracles are rare events. They are, practically, a suspension, or rather interruption, of the laws of nature, *i. e.*, of the uniform and regular manner of material action, and as the laws of nature are our

only normal and natural rule and guide in the knowledge of the divine plan and will in the universe, in order to accept a phenomenon as a miracle two conditions must be realized:

a. The object of the divine intervention must be a worthy one. We cannot assume that anything insignificant or frivolous should call forth such a stupendous thing as an interruption of the normal history of the universe.

b. The second condition for our acceptance of a miracle is the objective and conclusive evidence of the fact reputed to be miraculous, and of the direct and positive intervention of God in the fact. The evidence for the fact must be of the same character which the historian would demand and find sufficient. The evidence for the miraculous nature of the fact consists in the absolute insufficiency of the actually available factors to explain the event.

2. Is there any positive objective criterion of certitude in cases of reputed divine intervention? *i. e.,* have we ever any means of judging with absolute certainty when and where natural factors are insufficient to explain an effect? Undoubtedly, there are cases where the probable or possible factors are not known thoroughly, for instance, in the many strange phenomena recorded by practitioners of the so-called occult sciences. To speak here of miracles would be, to say the least, imprudent. But when the natural factors applicable to the case are well known and the phenomenon is in direct contradiction with them, we are perfectly justified in pronouncing it a miracle. To illustrate: If the wind and the waves obey the voice of a man, or if the dead body of a person exhales not the stench of corruption, but the sweetest fragrance, we no doubt have a divine intervention, because we are quite sure that

a man's voice has no control over wind and waves, and that a dead animal body does not smell sweetly.

3. The proven miracle has a meaning. It is not simply an extraordinary phenomenon, it delivers a divine message. The will of God as known from the normal happenings in creation is superseded by the divine plan manifested in the miraculous event. Hence, miracles are the natural basis for a divine Revelation and prepare the way for, and accompany, man's supernatural relationship with God. This relationship is in itself miraculous, and therefore, the factors that produce and explain it are a continuous series of miracles, but these miracles do not concern the cosmologist.

PART TWO

PSYCHOLOGY, THE PHILOSOPHY OF THE ORGANIC WORLD

CHAPTER EIGHT

THE MAIN PSYCHOLOGICAL PROBLEMS AND THEORIES

DEFINITION AND SCOPE OF PSYCHOLOGY

Psychology is the philosophy of the organic world. In giving this definition we know we are plainly at variance with most modern psychologists, for to them psychology is the science of conscious phenomena. This definition clearly indicates two things: first, that psychology is conceived as an experimental science, differing from the physical sciences in the subject-matter, but hardly at all in its aims and method; and secondly, that the vegetable world is entirely excluded from its study. For us, however, psychology is an essential part of philosophy, for the study of which the experimental science of conscious phenomena is only a necessary source and basis, and by no means the only or even the principal source and basis, and, besides, we consider the explanation of the vegetable world one of the chief objects of psychology. In doing so, we are guided by two reasons: the first one is of a philosophical nature; it was proposed by Aristotle, the real founder of psychology. It consists in this that the fundamental principle of life, the "psyche" of Aristotle, is to be found not only in man and the animals, but in plants as well, *i. e.,* the whole organic world. Consequently, life in its basic characteristics, such as they exist in all orders of organic beings, constitutes logically the object of psychology. Tearing away the conscious phenomena from the general biological phenomena would make the knowledge of their inner nature and meaning almost impossible because a deep and full understanding of the higher orders of life is based upon their analogy with the simple organic life as realized in plants.

We have another reason for not excluding the world of plants from psychology, and this is taken from modern science itself. There is today a perfect agreement amongst biologists, as far as they base their conclusions upon recognized facts, that there is a profound, yea an unbridgeable gulf between the non-living and the living universe whereas there is no such general agreement amongst them when the question arises regarding the boundary line between plants and animals; indeed, many are of opinion that there is no such boundary line. While in no sense granting this contention, we are surely authorized to draw from it the general conclusion that the gap between non-life and life is greater and more clearly recognized than the gap between non-conscious and conscious life, and consequently, we are justified, even in the light of modern biology, to remain faithful to Aristotle's division and look upon psychology as the study, not of one branch of organic beings, but of the whole organic universe.

From this general definition of psychology it follows clearly that a threefold division of our subject-matter imposes itself spontaneously upon us, because the most simple observation and the most common experience plainly show that the organic world contains three general orders of life, *viz.*, vegetable, animal, and human. The more we study these three orders of organic beings, the more we are convinced that we are justified in speaking of the threefold psychology, of the plant, of the animal, and of man.

I. *Analytical and Causative Psychology*

Our initial viewpoint in the study of psychology must evidently be analytical and inductive. We must analyze the phenomena of the various types of living organisms and from such analyses we must form inductions about the nature of the phenomena themselves and of the agents in which they are realized. After determining the *nature* of life in respect to each of the several orders of living beings, we must try to discover the causes, immediate and remote, that account for the existence of the various types of organisms, *i. e.,* our task will be to explain their *origin*.

A. PLANT PSYCHOLOGY OR THE PHILOSOPHY OF ORGANIC LIFE

The first and chief problem of PLANT PSYCHOLOGY is to determine the nature of life. While the problem of its origin attracts greater and more general attention, its solution is impossible unless the problem regarding the nature of life is solved first. Three distinct solutions are offered for this problem:

1. The *mechanicist* theory assumes that life is the natural and necessary product of certain combinations of physical and chemical factors, and therefore, is itself of no higher nature than that of inorganic beings.
2. The *vitalist* interpretation claims that in the organic world there are new forces or properties, not found in the inorganic beings—vital forces— the presence of which explains vital phenomena.
3. The *scholastic* solution shows that a fundamental principle of life, Aristotle's "psyche," *i. e.,* an essentially higher forma substantialis than that of inorganic beings, is both necessary and sufficient to explain the specific characteristics of life.

   The problem of the origin of life is solved by the different schools of philosophy in conformity with their solution of the fundamental problem, *i. e.,* either by evolution or by creation. No other solution is possible as the terms are contradictory.

B. ANIMAL PSYCHOLOGY OR THE PHILOSOPHY OF CONSCIOUS LIFE

The problems of ANIMAL PSYCHOLOGY are much more complex and therefore, of a more difficult character than those of plant psychology, as we would naturally expect from the more complex phenomena of sense life. What complicates the matter still more is the fact that we must rely for the knowledge of these phenomena chiefly upon introspection or the observation of our own inner conscious experience, where the phenomena of sense life are always mingled with, influenced, and therefore, modified, by those of rational life. We can apply this knowledge to the facts we observe in animals only by analogy.

Here, again, the fundamental problem is the nature of sense life. The manner of solving the problem of its origin must depend upon the manner of solving the fundamental problem. In the study of sense life the following threefold solution is proposed:

1. It is not strange that here again, we should find that there are philosophers who propose a purely *mechanical* explanation of the nature of sense life. If life itself is the function of a natural and necessary mechanical combination of elements, why not sense life as well? If life is homogeneous with non-life, why should sense life not be homogeneous with merely organic life? In this hypothesis, the vegetative functions naturally culminate in, and determine adequately, the sense phenomena, just as a certain combination of physical and chemical actions explains the vital phenomena, or, to go still deeper, just the same as merely mechanical factors explain physical and chemical phenomena.

   Do mechanists not see the real difficulty—the question of explaining the specific characteristics of conscious phenomena? Some do, but try to disguise it. We hear Taine call it the inner face of the functions of the nervous system; others call it the epi-phenomenon of nervous functions; others, again, frankly deny the difficulty by asserting that it is but a chemical secretion of the brain, or atomic and molecular vibrations of the brain cells. Du Bois-Reymond, the great physiologist of Berlin

University, more honest than many, openly admitted that sensations are an unsolvable riddle, since it is quite unintelligible to present them as an equivalent of physical and chemical functions.

2. The second solution proposed and accepted today by a majority of professional psychologists, it seems, is the theory of a so-called *PSYCHO-PHYSICAL PARALLELISM*. It is assumed that two really distinct series run side by side, the physical or rather *physiological* phenomena in the nervous system, and the conscious or *psychical* phenomena which accompany them. Between the two series, it is claimed, there is really no causal connection of any kind, though, apparently, organic stimulations produce conscious effects such as sensations, perceptions, feelings, impulses, and, on the other side, conscious phenomena, *e. g.,* volitions and impulses, apparently produce physical effects, such as muscular contractions. This apparent causal connection is denied, not on account of any real scientific facts militating against it, but rather for the sake of a philosophical assumption: the system of physical actions and reactions, causes and effects is assumed to be a closed system, and consequently, a real interaction and causal interdependence of physical and psychical phenomena, inasmuch as they are considered as belonging to two different worlds, is simply assumed to be impossible.

However, the very nature of modern, *i. e.,* experimental, psychology necessitates a correlation between them. There is no way of making experiments in psychology unless it be either by the artificial application of nervous stimuli and comparing with them the consequent conscious phenomena, or by measuring the muscular contractions or relaxations which follow upon conscious phenomena. If the psychologist intends really to analyze and systematize conscious phenomena and establish the laws of their succession and intrinsic connection experimentally, he must base his conclusions on the physical concomitants of the mental phenomena, because only between the phenomena of the physical series can there be any real basis for causal connection. There is no room for the experimental study of causal connections between the phenomena of the psychical series, because this series is a flowing stream, each part of which has disappeared when the new part is present, and in addition, because many interruptions occur which are beyond the psychologist's control. As a consequence, psychologists, who are not absolute mechanicists and yet are bent upon the study of psychology in the manner of an experimental science, must assume the method of psycho-physical parallelism, by which they attribute the causal connection discovered between the phenomena of the physical series to the phenomena of the psychical series.

3. The *scholastic solution* does not assume an unbridgeable gulf between physical and psychical phenomena. On the contrary, it admits the reality of that so clearly apparent interrelation and causal interdependence; and from the distinctive characteristics of consciousness it draws the conclusion that the fundamental principle of the animal, while material because intrinsically dependent upon matter in all its actions, is, nevertheless, of a higher order than that of the plant, and that is of a superphysical and superchemical nature.

Regarding the problem of the origin of animal life, the solutions proposed are the same as those proposed for plant life: either evolution or creation.

C. HUMAN PSYCHOLOGY OR THE PHILOSOPHY OF RATIONAL LIFE

We come now to the distinctive psychology of man, *i. e.,* the PSYCHOLOGY OF RATIONAL LIFE. Here, once more, three solutions are proposed for the great and fundamental problem of the nature of rational life, solutions which are, more or less, parallel to those proposed for the problem of sense life.

1. *Mechanicists* consider man simply as the best developed mammal. What we call rational life is to them nothing else but a higher degree or form of sense life—not a new order of life which would transcend in any sense the powers of the material organism. Consistent in their attempt to explain the universe by one simple element—matter in motion—they attempt to reduce, not only plant and sense life, but also the noblest products of the human mind to purely mechanical functions.

2. *Psycho-physical parallelism* also plays a rôle in the explanation of rational life, because psychologists of this philosophical denomination make no distinction between the multiform phenomena of human consciousness, but present them as one continuous series, speaking in a general way of simple and complex, or, at most, of lower or higher elements of consciousness. In truth, a clear boundary line cannot be drawn, since all the elements are the mixed actions of one and the same agent; only a careful philosophical analysis can introduce discrimination, and such a philosophical analysis is beyond the scope of experimental psychology. Thus, limited both by their method of study and by the assumption of the parallelist theory, a really independent or philosophically valuable theory of the nature of rational life is impossible to the psychologists of this school. Logically, whenever their interpretation is not based upon pure idealism or phenomenalism, it must lead either to materialism or to pantheism.

3. The *scholastic* solution of the problem of rational life is definite, and therefore, quite clear and comprehensible. While man is an animal, and consequently, all that is proper to the animal is found in man, yet it is evident from the analysis of the ele-

ments of his consciousness, that there are functions in man clearly beyond the power of animal and organic nature. Upon the knowledge of these rational functions is based the conclusion that the fundamental principle of life in man is super-material or spiritual.

Regarding the problem of the origin of man there is again the same twofold solution proposed that we found in plant and animal psychology: either evolution or creation.

II. *Synthetic and Teleological Psychology*

A. ITS DEFINITION AND SCOPE

Once we have obtained through analysis and induction a knowledge of the nature and causes of the various orders of living organisms, our study becomes synthetic, *i. e.,* we no longer study life in its elements because they are now known to us, but in its organized activity and in its systematic structure. We do this to determine the immediate objects and aims that reduce to unity and order the manifold individual actions as they follow one another in their frequent recurrence, as well as the final and supreme object and aim which gives its distinctive value and significance to the whole life of man in its totality.

It is this viewpoint and method of work in psychological studies that we call *synthetic* and *teleological.* Here we are well aware of the fact that in this division of the subject-matter of psychology we stand, as far as we know, alone. The reason for this viewpoint shall be discussed in chapter seven, where we enter upon the study of this, the crowning part of psychology.

After the definition we have given of it, it is hardly necessary to add that synthetic and teleological psychology refers to the psychology of man exclusively, because man alone is, through his rational nature, in a position to choose the aims that give direction and order to his activity, whereas the other types of living beings are directed and controlled in their action by innate tendencies over which they have no control.

Another remark is necessary. The problems of teleological psychology are absolutely ignored in mechanicism. In a world ruled by the iron law of mechanical determination there is no room for aims and ends. Hence, the questions will be studied upon the basis of Aristotelian and scholastic philosophy.

B. ITS VARIOUS PROBLEMS

1. The first psychological problems which we must study from the synthetical and teleological viewpoint are *LOGICAL*. The problems of *LOGIC* refer to the intellectual life of man, inasmuch as there is a teleological order between the various acts of the mind. Its principal object is to show, on the one hand, the means and methods of clarifying, verifying, and ascertaining the constitutive elements of the logical order—concepts, judgments and reasonings; and on the other hand, to provide the intellectual architect with the proper methods as well as with the general aim and plan for man's whole scientific work.

2. Having solved the problems of the logical order, it is imperative that we should determine the precise value and meaning of the relationship which exists between the logical and ontological orders. We call these problems *CRITERIOLOGICAL*. The real signification of the logical order depends upon the nature of the solution given to these problems. The most perfect knowledge possible of the laws of logic would be useless, unless knowledge itself be based upon objective facts and be truly representative of their nature and properties.

In the intellectual atmosphere of modern skepticism, agnosticism, subjecticism, and criticism these problems are of great actuality, as well as speculative importance.

3. After the study of the problems of the intellectual

order, those of the moral life of man present themselves to the mind. This science is called *ETHICS*. Its chief concern is to lay the rational foundation of the moral order, *i. e.,* to determine and prove the objective nature of morality, thus providing man with an objective criterion and standard of moral action on the one side, and on the other, to point out the subjective dispositions and conditions requisite for the realization of his ethical ideals, and the application of the theory of ethics to man in his individual and social life.

4. Having studied in logic the aims of the mind of man, and in ethics the aims of his moral life, we are prepared to consider the supreme aim and end of man. Here the paramount problem of the immortality of the human soul, the great questions of heaven and hell, will offer themselves for our discussion and must be settled by solid and conclusive arguments.

Thus, the philosophical study of the organic world will lead us, just as that of the inorganic world has led us already, and even more so to a spiritual interpretation of the universe. The inorganic world simply demonstrates the existence of an absolute and omnipotent spiritual God, because, being contingent in its nature, it supposes the presence of a necessary Cause to explain its origin, and because, manifesting in age-long and far-spread cosmic evolution a most wonderful plan and design, it shows clearly the infinite wisdom of the divine Mind. However, the organic world in its chief representative, man, does much more than that. Man lives and moves in a spiritual atmosphere. His supreme intellectual and moral object and aim is the infinite God Himself.

Consequently, acknowledging the principle already alluded to that the lower elements exist for the higher, it is evident that the purpose of the inorganic world is the service of the organic, the purpose of the organic, the service of man, its natural king, and the purpose of man, and therefore, the supreme purpose of the universe, is the service of God.

SECTION ONE

ANALYTICAL AND CAUSATIVE PSYCHOLOGY

CHAPTER NINE

PLANT PSYCHOLOGY: THE NATURE AND ORIGIN OF LIFE

OBJECT AND METHOD OF THIS STUDY

From the philosophical viewpoint, the basic problems of psychology refer to life such as we find it in all organisms from the monocellular plant through the uncounted species of vegetable and animal life up to, and including, man. It is quite plain that these problems cannot be solved a priori, because our principal object is precisely to determine the nature and essential characteristics of life as such, the knowledge of which does not come to us by intuition, but must be acquired by abstraction and reflection, slowly and step by step as it were. The steps in the gradual acquisition of an insight into the nature of life are the degrees of knowledge that we gain by the study of organic phenomena. When we speak here of organic phenomena, we refer to those phenomena of organic life which are common to all orders of living things, because it is the common characteristics of all organisms that must give us the material for our inductive knowledge of the nature of life. We exclude here the distinctive phenomena of animal and human life.

The knowledge of the nature of life is in itself of great importance, speculative as well as practical. After all, though we possess the higher life, *viz.:* sense life, and even the highest, *viz.,* rational, which is a spiritual life, yet the lowest life in us, that which we have in common with plants and animals, is the ground and soil in which the other orders of life find their natural hold, root, and nourishment, without which they can neither act nor exist.

There is a second reason why the study of life in its common characteristics, *i. e.,* plant life, is supremely valuable to us. Of this life we can acquire a direct, proper, and perfectly clear knowledge, as clear and adequate as we are able to obtain of inorganic bodies. Not so of the nature of sense life. The idea of conscious phenomena, which is essential to sense life, can be gained only by introspection, and it is anything but of simple and easy acquisition; therefore most people's knowledge of the nature of sense life is rather indistinct and obscure. The most natural and most fruitful method for obtaining a clear and distinct concept of sense life is to build it upon the analogy it has with vegetable life,—a method which we will apply in its proper place.

As in cosmology, the only objective and valuable source and basis for a philosophical synthesis is the analytical and inductive knowledge of the facts as we find them by observation and scientific experimentation. Fortunately, these facts are today well known after almost a century of highly successful biological research work. They were known to the ancient and medieval philosophers only by simple observation. Here we have another proof of the clear and profound mind of Aristotle, who is as truly the father of psychology as he is the founder of cosmology.

I. The Nature of Life

We follow, then, the same method which we applied in cosmology. There we first considered the facts as ordinary observation and scientific research make them known; then we examined the various theories which were proposed as interpretations of the facts, adopting that theory which is based upon the facts, is in harmony with all of them, and gives a rational account of them. This we must do in plant psychology. The facts which our own observation and experience, as well as the work of biologists who have studied ex-professo the phenomena of plant life, have brought to light, we must attentively bear in mind, and by comparing and correlating them, we must determine their common and essential characteristics before we attempt to examine any of the various theories advanced on the nature of life.

A. THE COMMON FUNCTIONS AND CHARACTERISTICS OF ORGANISMS

The facts of organic life come to our knowledge from the study of the *vital functions.* There are three such functions: nutrition, quantitative and qualitative growth, and reproduction. The first—nutrition—is the fundamental function: it exists without the others, while the others are absolutely dependent upon it. Hence, the analysis of nutrition will give us all the facts we need.

1. What is *NUTRITION?* It is a process in which three distinct stages are noticeable:

    a. It is an *INTUSSUSCEPTION* of a foreign substance which is called food. We find in non-living beings similar processes, such as crystallization: the crystallizing body receives new particles of matter, adding them to its own, as in the freezing of water. It is by no means the same as nutrition—it is an *addition by juxtaposition,* not by intussusception.

    b. It is in the second stage an *ABSORPTION* of the food, *i. e.,* the foreign substance taken into the organic body is no longer distinct from it, but loses its identity. Nothing like this happens in inorganic bodies: the new crystals, added to the mother-crystal, retain their identity, they are not absorbed.

    c. The third stage of nutrition is the *ASSIMILATION* of food, *i. e.,* the foreign substance taken into the organic body and absorbed by it becomes homogeneous and consubstantial with it; in other words, the final result of a series of chemical reactions is the substantial identification of the subject and object of nutrition—the foreign substance is now fully and substantially identified with the organic body.

2. What are the distinctive *characteristics* of nutrition? They are two:

a. The first is *CONTINUITY:* the process of nutrition never ceases. The moment it does, life itself ends; the body may still have the appearance of an organism, but in reality it has ceased to be an organic body. If we take motion, not in the superficial sense of local movement, but in its deeper metaphysical sense of an intrinsic change, especially as an advance from a potential to an actual stage of being, life is, indeed, perpetual motion. The process of assimilating new matter and dissimilating, *i.e.,* eliminating waste or used matter, suffers no interruption.

There is nothing like this in the phenomena of the inorganic world. The nearest approach to it is a chemical reaction, but a chemical reaction is merely a *transitory* process. The affinity of the re-agents is roused, they act upon one another more or less violently till their atomicity is satisfied, and then the action ceases. No matter how strong or feeble the affinity of the re-agents, the reaction tends by its very nature to an equilibrium and to stability. The greater the affinity, the greater the stability of the result.

How different the process of nutrition! It is true that its most essential element is also chemical reaction, indeed, it is a complex series of chemical reactions. The characteristic feature of this series is its continuity, one reaction follows another without interruption:

as soon as one combination is realized another takes its place. We have here a tendency to disequilibrium, a condition of perpetual instability.

b. The second characteristic of vital actions is their *IMMANENCE*. Physical and chemical actions in the inorganic world are *transitive, i. e.,* there are two bodies affected by the action, one from which it proceeds—the agent, and one in which its effect is received—the patient. On the contrary, in vital actions there are not two bodies affected: the organism is both agent and patient, *i. e.,* the action proceeds from the very same living body in which its effect is received. In other words, the process of nutrition benefits the one that realizes it.

B. PHILOSOPHICAL INTERPRETATION OF THE FACTS

We are now in possession of the main facts and the most important distinctive characteristics of organic life. We shall proceed to determine its nature as revealed by them; and we do so by examining, in the light of the facts, the various solutions proposed by philosophers.

I. MECHANICAL INTERPRETATION OF LIFE

In the first place let us consider the mechanicist theory. Is it possible that life is nothing higher than the natural and necessary result of physical and chemical factors, just as in the mechanicist interpretation the physical and chemical phenomena themselves are nothing higher than the natural and necessary result of purely mechanical factors? Such a theory is inacceptable because, far from explaining the facts of life, it is directly contradicted by them. We know that the basic function of life is nutrition, and that the complex process of nutrition belongs to organic beings exclusively. There is no trace of it found in the inorganic world. Consequently, its essential characteristics of continuity and immanence put a natural barrier between the distinctive activity of inorganic and organic bodies, a barrier which no sound philosophy can ignore.

It is nothing short of ignoring the problem for mechanicists to say that life is simply the function of the organism. To start, build up, continue, and perpetuate the organism is precisely the direct and proper object of life, and therefore, to explain the organism itself is the crux of the question. We have no intuition of the nature of the organism, but come to the knowledge of it only by the careful analysis of its functions. We cannot explain the action by the nature of the agent because we know the nature of the agent only by its actions. Consequently, the mechanicist claim is simply a "petitio principii," a begging of the question.

2. VITALIST INTERPRETATION OF LIFE

The vitalist interpretation represents the other extreme by assuming in the organic body vital forces, in addition to the general physical and chemical properties. We cannot accept this assumption because, while it is sufficient to explain the phenomena of life, it is not necessary, and, furthermore, it is a mere assumption, having no vital facts for its basis. The most careful biologist has never found any trace of a specific action which, in its analysis, was not physical or chemical. It is quite evident that there can be no justification for assuming distinctive forces where there are no distinctive actions to demand them, for such a proceeding is both arbitrary and unscientific.

3. THE ARISTOTELIAN THEORY OF LIFE

We accept the solution proposed by Aristotle, commonly called the scholastic theory of life, because it is both necessary and sufficient to explain the facts. Before we prove this statement, let us determine the theory itself more clearly and completely. We may reduce it to three propositions:

a. *The organic bodies or living beings are not the possessors of any specifically higher properties because all their actions can be explained perfectly by the ordinary physical and chemical forces.*
b. Nevertheless, *they constitute a new order of beings, essentially superior to all inorganic substances, because they are capable of functions performed by all of them, and never by any other, and these functions are of a higher nature than those of the inorganic bodies.*
c. Consequently, *the specific and determinative substantial principle in organic bodies, i. e., their forma substantialis, is of an essentially higher order than the forma substantialis of inorganic bodies,* and therefore, with good reason, the scholastics, following Aristotle, gave it a special name, namely, *"anima vegetativa."*

The first proposition as already stated has been proven clearly in biology. The second proposition offers no difficulties if we bear in mind the plain vital facts of the case. The continuity and immanence of the functions of living beings are plainly features of an activity of a higher order which mark a clear boundary line between the inorganic and the organic world. The third propositon, again, hardly needs any demonstration, as it is a necessary conclusion from the second. A few remarks will clarify this.

From the analysis of vital phenomena it is quite evident that genetically the chemical elements that enter the organism are the same as those that enter into chemical compounds. However, the composition of the two is very different: in a compound it is homogeneous, *i. e.,* each part is the same as every other part; in the organism it is heterogeneous, each part being different from every other even in the most simple organism. Heterogeneousness in composition is essential to the organic body, as all vital functions are dependent upon it. Hence, it is plain that organic bodies are of an incomparably superior complexity: superior, because together with, and in spite of, great multiplicity and variety of parts and functions, there is clearly noticeable a greater ontological unity, absolutely necessary to explain both the cohesion and co-ordination of the multiform parts to one integral whole, and the concentration and subordination of the manifold functions to the permanent welfare of the individual and the species. This superiority of the organism over the compound is not only one of degree, *i. e.*, expressive of greater unity in the midst of greater variety, and therefore, of a higher degree of the same order, but it is, as the analysis of its specific functions has plainly shown, one of an essentially different nature, because this higher order is achieved and maintained by superior laws of action which are directly contradictory to the laws of action that regulate the inorganic world.

Such being the well-established principles from the analysis of organic functions, and bearing in mind the cosmological solution regarding the nature of a body, our demonstration of the third and main proposition of the scholastic solution of the problem of life will be simple enough.

To understand the value and significance of this demonstration we must remember the general principles that we have established in cosmology about the nature and constitutive substantial elements of the body, because the organism also is a body. The same chemical elements which go into the constitution of inorganic bodies, go also into the structure of organic bodies. The chief principles in this connection which apply to our case are those that enunciate the twofold substantial element of the body: the passive element—the materia prima, and the active element—the forma substantialis.

MAJOR PREMISE: The presence of an essentially superior order in the composition and functions of a body demands an essentially superior substantial principle to explain it.

MINOR PREMISE: This superior substantial principle cannot be the passive and indeterminate principle—the materia prima, since it remains unchanged through all substantial transformations.

CONCLUSION: Hence, the principle that explains the essential superiority of the organism must be an essentially superior forma substantialis.

II. *The Origin of Life*

The origin of life is the second main problem of plant psychology. It admits of a threefold application: We may refer to the genesis of the individual plant, or of the species of organic bodies, or again, to the primary origin of life on our globe. We will discuss the first and third questions now, leaving the second for another occasion, namely, when we come to the problem of the origin of animal life.

A. THE GENESIS OF THE ORGANISM

The genesis of the individual organic body is at present perfectly known from biology. "Omnis cellula a cellula," is accepted as an evident principle by all biologists. Every organic body comes from one original cell, which, by division and manifold subdivisions and multiform differentiations, develops into the adult living being.

The original cell itself is produced by the parent organism, either by simple division, as in the lowest forms of life, or, in the higher forms, by the fusion into one of two heterogeneous cells, produced respectively by the male and female parent. The development of this original cell proceeds with absolute regularity in the sense of a complete reproduction, not only of the specific type, but often also of many individual and family features of both parents.

B. THE ORIGIN OF THE FIRST ORGANISM

The genesis of the first living organism on the globe is a question upon which scientists and philosophers do not agree. In spite of biology some still assume the possibility and probability of spontaneous generation, which was commonly accepted in the Middle Ages even by Christian philosophers. Others suppose that the germ of life dropped upon the globe from some heavenly body, a theory rather far-fetched and offering no adequate solution. However, let us formulate the question with precision.

There are two possible explanations of the primary origin of life, and not more than two, because they contradict each other, *viz.*, EVOLUTION AND CREATION.

I. THE THEORY OF EVOLUTION

Can life be explained by EVOLUTION? Let us analyze the term and its meaning. To evolve is the same as to unfold, *i. e.*, to bring out what is within; to make patent what has been latent. From the philosophical viewpoint evolution means what the scholastics would call an "eductio entis e potentia ad actum," *i. e.*, the progressive ontological movement of a being from a state of potentiality to a state of actuality: what exists in an implicit and less perfect form at the starting point, exists in an explicit and more perfect form at the terminal point.

From this analysis it appears evident that the being, in order to evolve, must already exist, *i. e.*, the starting point cannot be a pure negation or a mere possibility, which is, indeed, no more than the conceivability of a being. There must be a real positive intrinsic capacity for the acquisition of the new degrees of perfection which are the effects of the evolution. For instance, take the intelligence of an infant. There is as yet no degree of intellectual perfection in actual existence; however, it is far from a mere negation as it would be in a puppy. There is in the infant a positive intrinsic disposition which is entirely absent in the puppy. There can be therefore, and generally is, intellectual evolution in the infant that grows up; there is none, and can be none, in the puppy. As with intelligence, so with life: in order to evolve, it must already potentially exist, *i. e.,* there must be a positive intrinsic disposition to explain its evolution. To say that life evolves from non-life, or organic beings from inorganic beings, is the same as to say that being comes from non-being, or something from nothing, which, of course, is absurd because contradictory.

Evolution could be accepted as a possible explanation of life on the globe only if it could be shown that life is not a reality of a new order, essentially superior to the properties of the inorganic bodies. The opposite has been clearly and conclusively proven: there is not the least trace of life to be found in the inorganic universe.

2. THE SOLUTION: CREATION

Since evolution does not explain the first apparition of life on the globe, creation alone can explain it. While we admit that we are never justified in the study of science or philosophy to appeal to a divine intervention to explain a phenomenon as long as any possible natural factor can explain it, yet as soon as we have demonstrated that life cannot be the product of evolution, we must perforce conclude that it is the product of creation, because the terms are contradictory, and therefore the negation of the one necessarily implies the affirmation of the other.

We will present the argument for creation in a direct and positive manner. What we have said in cosmology with reference to the creation of inorganic bodies, considering the universe, from the dynamic point of view, as a series of successive phases, each one being explained by the preceding one and explaining the one that follows, we can apply with much better reason to the organic world. Living bodies, as both biology and philosophy show, form an exact series of successive generations, each conditioned by the one that precedes and conditioning the one that follows. It needs no proof to bring out the contingent character of each generation that comes and goes. If each generation, *i. e.*, each link in the chain, is contingent, the chain itself is contingent. Even if we were to suppose that the chain be infinite, granted that such a supposition be possible, it will make no difference: an infinite multitude of contingent causes can produce no necessary cause. As shown in cosmology, only a necessary cause can explain adequately the existence of contingent beings. Consequently, the existence of the organic world can be explained adequately only by an act of a necessary Being, God, and such an act we call creation.

It is hardly necessary to add that, speaking of a creative act as the only possible explanation of life on the globe, we do not refer to the materia prima of the first organism, which, of course, was taken from the inorganic world. Only the superior forma substantialis demanded direct divine intervention. We attribute the existence of the first organic body to creation, because in the superior character of its essence it surpasses the highest possible effect of all possible combinations of inorganic factors. Our appeal, therefore, to divine intervention in this instance is legitimate because of the absolute impossibility of another explanation.

CHAPTER TEN

THE PHENOMENA OF SENSE LIFE

<small>THE ANIMAL WORLD: ITS PLACE IN NATURE'S SCALE
OF BEINGS</small>

Perhaps it will be well here to call attention to the gradually increasing complexity of the bodies that have formed the object of our study. We started with the so-called simple bodies. We found that regarding the real objective universe, simplicity is a relative idea. Even simple bodies, *i. e.*, chemical atoms, are complex systems of elements, substantial and accidental, active and passive, absolute and relative; they are simple only in the sense that they are less complex than compounds. The compounds themselves are relatively simple when their constituent molecules, which represent the individual of the species, are composed of only two or three heterogeneous atoms, but become more and more complex as their constituent molecules enclose more and more atoms. Here can be applied the saying: *"Natura non facit saltus,"* nature evolves gradually, step by step, making no leaps in her progress. To the thoughtful philosopher it would appear that only when she reaches the limit of her resources, the Creator intervenes and lays, as it were, a new and nobler gift in her lap—the seed of life. Again, nature seems to start her work in as simple a manner as possible—a monocellular plant is her first achievement. Simple it is, indeed, when compared with the complex organism of an oak, but when compared with inorganic bodies, even the most complex, or when studied in itself, what a wealth of constituent elements, each one different from every other in structure and function, and at the same time, what a perfect unity of structure and function when we look upon them as a system, as a whole! Here again, it would appear that nature uses God's gift to the very limit of her resources, progressing step by step till the highest development in plant life is attained. Then once more nature stops, for she can go no further unaided by her author.

So far have we advanced in our philosophical interpretation of the universe. But plants are only the smaller and less important portion of the organic world. Even to the casual observer and to the untrained thinker animal life with the vast multiplicity and rich variety of its representatives constitutes a new and nobler order of living beings which in its specific characteristics surpasses essentially that of the vegetable world. This animal world, in its specific superiority to the vegetable world, is the object of animal psychology.

METHOD AND SCOPE OF OUR STUDY

Our method of study must remain the same as heretofore. We must study the specifically animal functions, analyze them carefully, and then, once we have come to a clear knowledge of what they are by means of induction, we can draw logical inferences and conclusions about the nature and origin of the animal.

The distinctive functions of animal life are called sense functions. There is a twofold aspect to sense functions —the one *physical* or *physico-chemical,* and the other, *PSYCHICAL, i. e.,* characterized by *CONSCIOUS-NESS.* As each aspect contains various elements which follow or accompany one another, we may well speak of a double series of phenomena, one physical, the other psychical. The physical phenomena are much better known than the others because they are studied by the physiologist with the exact methods of physical science. Not so the psychical phenomena. Their positive and specific contents are known by introspection alone. Two reasons, however, influence the introspective method unfavorably: 1. The elements of consciousness are by their very nature unsteady and fluctuating, and therefore, consciousness itself is of the utmost instability, incomparably more so than the process of assimilation in cell life. Consequently, it is difficult to fixate and determine sense phenomena exactly. 2. In our consciousness the elements of the animal and the human psychical life are always mingled, and in many cases hard to disentangle.

For the exact interpretation of the contents of our consciousness we possess, happily, at present a fruitful aid, *viz.,* the ingenious methods invented by experimental psychologists, based upon the interrelation of the psychical and physical series of phenomena, which have been a wonderful help and corrective to introspection, the place of which, of course, they cannot take.

I. The Physical Basis of Sense Life

Let us begin by considering the series of physical phenomena. The length and complexity of the series depend greatly upon the species of animal life. In the higher species it is much more complex than in the lower, but the essential elements are ever the same.

I. ANATOMY AND PHYSIOLOGY OF SENSE LIFE IN GENERAL

From the anatomical viewpoint there are three distinct parts of the sense organ which is the nervous system, *viz.,* the central part, the peripheral part, and a double connecting link between the central and peripheral parts, *viz.,* one centripetal and one centrifugal. In the higher animals, for instance in mammals, the three parts are clearly differentiated, and therefore, easily known. The central part is constituted chiefly by the various portions of nervous matter in the *brain* and *spinal cord,* the peripheral part by the *external sense organs* such as eyes, ears, etc., and the double link connecting both by the *sensory nerve* parting from the external and leading to the central organ, and by the *motor nerve* parting from the central organ and leading to some muscle.

From the physiological viewpoint we have a stimulation from without in the peripheral sense organ, a transmission of that stimulation to the central sense organ, a retransmission of it to a peripheral muscle, and in the muscular contraction the final result of the whole animal reaction. This is the most simple *physical or physiological arc* of a sense function. Even in the lowest forms of animal life we find it, at least to a certain extent, represented.

The network of a telephone system is the best illustration of the sense organism. The outside world acts upon the peripheral part and thus delivers, as it were, a message to the animal. The peripheral sense organ receives the message and transmits it by the sensory nerve to the central organ—the switchboard of the system, and there the answer to the message is formulated and transmitted by the motor nerve to a peripheral muscle, and the result is a muscular action whereby the animal reacts upon the outside world.

2. ANATOMY AND PHYSIOLOGY OF SENSE LIFE IN THE HIGHER SPECIES

The physiological arc of sense functions becomes more and more complex as we ascend in the order of animal species. It is most complex in the higher mammals and in man. To show this complexity we will give a brief general description of the arc of a visual reaction in man.

The eyes, the peripheral parts of the organ of sight, are of a very complex structure so as to have the light waves coming from the external object hit the cones and rods on the retina in the proper manner. To the several thousand cones and rods correspond as many nerve fibres which leave the retina in a bundle to carry the excitation to the occipital lobes of the brain. On the way the two bundles of nerves cross each other in a very peculiar manner: half of each bundle, *i. e.,* the nerves coming from the right side of the right eye unite with those of the right side of the left eye and terminate in the left brain lobe; and the other half bundle, *i. e.,* the nerves coming from the left side of the left eye and from the left side of the right eye terminate in the right brain lobe. Undoubtedly, we have in these lobes the central organ of sight.

However, the visual sense stimulations do not come in these lobes to an absolute stop. From the occipital lobes rich nerve bundles leave which carry the nervous stimulation to and fro between the higher nerve centers located in the upper parts of the brain, often called *association centers,* which are clearly differentiated, if not in their structure, at least in their functions, some being sensory, others motor centers, some having for their special object excitations that correspond to sound sensations, and others such as belong to color perception, etc. These higher sense organ centers are receiving stimulations simultaneously and successively from every direction and part of the organism. Between these centers themselves there are manifold and complex connections.

To use again the illuminating simile of the telephone: It is these higher nerve centers that, like the central offices of a great telephone system, receive and exchange the messages from all the peripheral parts of the sense organism, and the motion and pain sensations from the inner parts of the animal, and formulate and transmit the orders for the right kind of muscular reaction in every part of the body.

II. *Analysis of Psychical Phenomena*

With this illustration we approach the series of psychical phenomena which accompany and follow the physical phenomena so far analyzed. We have no direct knowledge of the presence of psychical elements in brute animals, but we find that their sense organs are similar to our own, and when they are stimulated we see that the animal behaves as we behave in consequence of consciousness, and therefore, we feel perfectly justified in assuming that its muscular contractions following regularly upon sense stimulations are not simply physico-chemical irritations, but, as we know from ourselves—spontaneous reactions upon sensations. So when we observe by the microscope and amœba recoiling from an injurious matter, or approaching and apprehending its food, we cannot interpret it as a simple effect of chemical affinity or of gravitational attraction, but as a result of conscious selection. Of course, how high or low is the degree of consciousness in animal life, especially in its lower species, we have no way of ascertaining.

A. SIMPLE PHENOMENA OF CONSCIOUS LIFE

Regarding the psychical phenomena of sense functions we will use the same method that we applied to the physical series, beginning with the most simple arc, as we just insinuated speaking of the amœba. Psychologically, we interpret the action of the amœba as perceiving an object as desirable or undesirable, and as a consequence, moving towards, or away from it. We assume this to be the correct interpretation of the action of the amœba because we have ourselves many similar experiences. Let us analyze one of our own experiences which, of course, are generally much more complex.

I am sitting at my desk writing. A fly alights on my hand. I feel it vaguely as a disturbing object. Attending to it as it begins crawling, I move my hand and feel it no more. But it comes back. Now my eye falls upon it also, and I feel it distinctly as an annoyance, and try to kill it. This is the series of conscious phenomena. What are they psychologically? First, there is the tactual sensation on my hand, little noticed at first as my attention is perhaps on other things. Gradually, through more attention to it caused by the unpleasant crawling of the fly, the sensation becomes more pronounced and I have the vague perception of a disagreeable object on my hand, and move it half consciously to get rid of the fly. When it returns, my attention is fully drawn to it, and I perceive it distinctly as obnoxious and make an attempt to kill it. This, then, is the full *psychical arc:* First the tactual sensation, which leads to a vague perception. Then, when the visual sensation is added, the perception of the fly becomes perfect. Thus, sensation is followed by perception; perception is, indeed, but a circumscribed, clarified and objectivated sensation. Now comes the third element of the series. I feel the object as unpleasant, *i. e.,* the perception is followed by an immediate discrimination—the object is taken to be either good or bad. This spontaneous discrimination leads to an *appetition* or sense volition in the affirmative or negative sense, *i. e.,* the object is either accepted or rejected.

Consequently, the psychical series or arc consists of these four essential elements: SENSATION, PERCEPTION, DISCRIMINATION, AND APPETITION. Besides these there is another psychical element of great importance which accompanies every conscious action, at least in a vague manner—EMOTION, *i. e.,* a feeling of pleasure or displeasure; of pleasure when the action is natural, energetic, and successful; otherwise of displeasure. This concomitant element of pleasure or displeasure is strongest in connection with appetitions and their corresponding muscular reactions.

In the illustration used the series of psychical phenomena originated from an external stimulus—the fly alighting on my hand. In many instances it draws its origin from internal stimulation, as experience amply shows.

B. COMPLEX PSYCHICAL PHENOMENA

After analyzing the simpler psychical phenomena, we must add a few remarks on the more complex.

I. FUSION OF SENSATIONS

We have seen how the tactual and visual sensations of the fly on the hand united and aided in the formation of a more complete and clearer perception. Let us take another example.

I hold an apple in my hand. A number of sensations originate directly from this simple fact. There are first the sensations of smoothness, temperature, weight, and various colors—a number of heterogeneous sensations referring all to the same object. Besides these distinctive sensations, *i. e.,* those produced by one particular sense, we have the sensations of volume and figure, of spatial and temporal relations, which are common sensations, *i. e.,* realized by the concurrence of several senses. Even this is not all. Now I lift the apple to my nose and smell it, I bite it and taste it. What a complexity of sensations all referring to one and the same object—the apple! Undoubtedly, the physiological action which is the basis of this adding and summing and grouping of sensations is done in the higher nerve centers described above. The natural result of it is the clearer, richer, and fuller perception of the object, which, again, is followed by a more pronounced discrimination, a more energetic appetition and a more useful reaction, and all these elements accompanied by an enhanced tone of feeling, consequently, an all-round enrichment of consciousness. We may call this the *FUSION* of sensations.

2. REVIVAL AND ASSOCIATION OF PSYCHICAL PHENOMENA

This is a substantial increase in psychical complexity. However, it is small compared with the process called *ASSOCIATION*. Though we cannot explain how, there remains a trace of all the psychical elements so far analyzed in the nervous system, because, under certain conditions fairly well known, they revive, mingle, and combine in manifold and complex ways with the actual contents of consciousness.

We call these elements of consciousness, inasmuch as they are capable of psychical revival, *images* or *repres-*

entations, and speak of the association of images or representations.

The general laws of association are two: that of *contiguity* and that of *similarity*. The law of contiguity is realized when an element of our actual consciousness awakens an element of a former consciousness because the past element was together simultaneously or successively with the element of our present consciousness. So if I see a certain dog, he revives in me the conscious image of his master, in whose company I have seen him before. The law of similarity is realized when an important element of our present consciousness resembles an important element of a past state of consciousness; for instance, when my mother's portrait revives in me the conscious image of my mother with its train of associations.

In conformity with those two laws of association and in consequence of the multiform combinations of present with past psychical elements, ever-varying chains of rich and complex conscious phenomena follow one another ceaselessly, with hardly any interruption except in sleep, and even in sleep only apparently, as dreams and other occurrences plainly show. Thus, elements of our past experience and consequently, elements accumulated in our consciousness during a lifetime, may become part of our present, and this never-ceasing and ever-changing adding, summing, and grouping of psychical elements evidently enlarges and enriches our whole inner life and has a powerful influence upon our muscular reactions.

The tendency of psychical elements to revive appears to be most pronounced in those that have been present in our consciousness *most vividly, most frequently,* and *most recently.*

C. FACTORS THAT INFLUENCE CONSCIOUS LIFE

There are a few more factors that exercise a most powerful influence upon the contents of consciousness and their inner arrangement. Such are attention and inhibition, physical reaction, and above all, instinct operations.

I. ATTENTION AND INHIBITION

Modern psychologists make much of the phenomena of attention and inhibition. In attention, the psychical life is focused in a certain direction, and thereby the elements that lie in that direction become more distinct and vivid. Inhibition is the negative aspect of attention : as the elements favorable to the focus of attention are clarified and enriched, the antagonistic elements are obscured and impoverished.

There are in animal life two kinds of attention, subjective and objective. Subjective attention follows the natural and spontaneous course of conscious life in conformity with the laws of association, whereas objective attention is drawn away from this subjective course by a striking sense impression, such as a brilliant color, a piercing sound, a peculiar odor, etc.

The significant meaning of this factor is that it is a principle of order and harmony in conscious life. There is in the normal life of the animal, at least, the higher animal, such a constant onrush of stimulations from the surrounding world and from the uncountable number of elements of its past inner experience with a tendency to revive and mingle, that, if a definite selection were not made by attention and the rest more or less eliminated from consciousness by inhibition, the animal simply could not stand it, it would go mad and perish. Consequently, attention and inhibition constitute a fundamental condition of animal consciousness.

Attention and inhibition are not a discovery of modern experimental psychology. Inasmuch as attention is active and self-determinative, having its source in the initiative of the conscious subject, it is not a part of sense life at all, but the most important action of the rational will and consequently, it belongs to human psychology. Inasmuch as it is passive and instinctive, having its source, as explained above, in instinctive direction or new sense impressions, it is a part of sense life, but by no means a new factor in our knowledge of consciousness. Both attention and inhibition were presented by the scholastics as the operations of the "vis æstimativa," *i. e.,* the process of conscious discrimination described above, which follows upon the perception of an object, taking it to be desirable or undesirable.

2. INSTINCT IN ANIMAL LIFE

Instinctive operations are another highly important factor in conscious life; indeed, for the life of the species they are paramount. They are less pronounced in man because in him, mind and will have mostly superseded them. However, in babyhood even man would die without them. Such are, for instance, the complex reactions of sucking and swallowing, and the still more complex series of reactions necessary in breathing. In the life of the mere animal their necessity never ceases nor diminishes. Let us mention a few instances of such instinctive animal operations.

We are familiar with such things as the wonderful nest building of certain birds, the migratory wanderings of others, and, generally speaking, the manifold actions necessary for the perpetuation of the animal species, for the care of the young, etc. Also the amazing behavior of bees, ants, and other insects with a highly developed social life must be mentioned.

Such operations animals never learn. The young, as soon as normally developed, perform them with just as much perfection as the parents. Yet they are not a mere physical process such as the selection of the proper food elements by a plant, for they are really conscious, as we can easily ascertain. Destroy partly the work of a bee while busy on it, and the bee mends it. Transport animals into new surroundings, and they learn to adapt themselves gradually to the new elements of their life, at least to a certain extent. The same holds good for the instinct operations of the infant: remove him from his mother's breast, and he cries and protests; he is plainly conscious of his actions and their direct effects.

3. THE PHYSICAL REACTION OF CONSCIOUS PHENOMENA

Another factor which exercises great influence in the psychical life of the animal is the physical reaction. By this reaction we mean, physiologically, the motor discharge of sense stimulations. The natural purpose of sense actions is to apprise the animal of the conditions of its surroundings, so that it may select its course of behavior, *i. e.,* accept what appears useful and necessary, or reject what seems harmful and dangerous. Consequently, it is but natural that the desirable or undesirable objects, as they are present in consciousness, should directly prepare the motor apparatus of the animal for its proper exercise of approach and seizure, or of aversion and flight. This condition of tension in the motor apparatus, *i. e.,* the motor nerves and their endings in the muscle, we call the motor setting. Thus we say that each sense stimulation produces by means of a certain well-defined state of consciousness its own motor setting. The muscular contraction and relaxation which spontaneously follow this motor setting, we call the motor discharge of sense stimulations or simply the physical reaction of consciousness.

While in itself the last member of the *physical* series of sense life, as we saw above, the muscular reaction is also a factor in *conscious* life for a twofold reason: first it is the organic expression of the contents of consciousness, and as such it is both a physical manifestation of the inner experience and the natural means by which the animal attains its direct and immediate ends. Therefore it is an advancing step in the completion and perfection of its nature, and as a consequence, it reacts strongly on the conscious operations from which it proceeds; *i. e.,* when the good selected or the evil rejected is seized or avoided, the whole field of consciousness is thereby intensified and enriched,—especially and more directly, the tone of feeling. A second reason is that the reaction, be it simply turning the eye or the head, blushing or weeping, perspiring or smiling, or be it shouting or walking, grasping or jumping, becomes a new and complex sense stimulation, because we are not only conscious of the motor discharge itself, but of its conscious reaction in us, and of the perception of its effects in our surroundings. Consequently, the reaction has two very definite results: 1. It affords a favorable setting for new sense impressions: I see and hear better when I look and listen; 2. It affords a favorable setting for new reactions. On account of the association of the pleasure of former reactions the appetition is greatly intensified.

CHAPTER ELEVEN

THE NATURE AND ORIGIN OF SENSE LIFE

The Parallelist Hypothesis in Psychology

In order to proceed methodically, and thus to be better assured of success, the scientist bases his experiments upon certain assumptions, *i. e.,* he postulates certain hypotheses as probable interpretations of the phenomena that form the subject-matter of his study. Such hypotheses are perfectly legitimate and scientifically valuable, they are, as it were, guides that direct him in his work. Thus, the physicist assumes that there is an intimate relationship between physical and mechanical phenomena and this assumption has been highly fruitful because it gave him a common measure for the various kinds of physical phenomena, and thereby the formulation of many laws of the physical properties of bodies was made possible. Thus, the biologist assumes that vital functions are maintained, developed, and perfected in a stable manner, that these perfective dispositions are transmitted by inheritance because they are useful, and again, that with the end of their usefulness they gradually disappear. Also the biologist's hypothesis has been very successful —in virtue of it wonderful progress has been made in the knowledge of the laws of vital phenomena.

Within the last half century even the psychologist has become a scientist in the strict sense, making experiments in the manner of the physicist and the biologist. He also bases his experiments upon an assumption, and there can be no question about the many valuable achievements that have been made thereby in the knowledge of psychical phenomena. The psychologist's hypothesis is this:

There is such an intimate interrelation between the stimulations of the organs of the nervous system and the phenomena of conscious life that the causal links discovered between the sense stimulations can be attributed to the psychical phenomena as well.

Now as long as the scientists are aware of the fact that their assumptions are only hypotheses, and that, no matter how helpful they may be in explaining certain aspects of the reality, they are, at best, only one-sided and, therefore, partial interpretations of the facts, even the philosopher can have no objection to them. However, he cannot rest satisfied with them, no matter how plausible they may be. Why? Because, the philosopher seeks a complete and adequate interpretation, based upon the knowledge of all the facts of the case and of all the aspects of the reality. Thus, in physics, while plainly acknowledging the common mechanical aspect, he does not overlook the specific and qualitative aspect of physical phenomena, and in biology, while thankful to the scientist for the discovery of facts which show that usefulness is a potent factor in the explanation of life and living beings, yet he wants to know more than the mere facts, he wants to know why useful functions persist, are reproduced regularly, and are perpetuated in the species. So also in psychology, he is not satisfied with the knowledge of the fact of the parallel series of physical and psychical phenomena and their interrelation but he tries to ascertain the nature of the relationship between the two parallel series of phenomena, and, above all, the specific nature and origin of the psychical series.

I. The Nature of Sense Life

If we wish to determine the nature of sense life, we must begin with its specific phenomena which we studied and analyzed in our last chapter. After this has been successfully achieved, we shall be able to determine the immediate principles which explain their production. Finally, when the sense phenomena and their immediate

principles have been determined and classified we can draw
from this knowledge definite conclusions about sense life
itself, *i. e.,* we shall be able to define what is the nature of
the animal.

A. THE NATURE OF SENSE PHENOMENA

To determine the nature of psychical phenomena two
things are necessary. First we must consider them as
elements of vital functions, and secondly, study them in
their specific characteristics.

I. VITAL CHARACTERISTICS OF SENSE PHENOMENA

In the first place sense functions, being vital functions, are characterized by continuity and immanence.

a. THE CONTINUITY OF CONSCIOUSNESS

Conscious life is like mere organic life, a series of
successive phenomena, where one follows another without interruption; it is like an ever-flowing stream. The
stream remains constantly, but its water, *i. e.,* the conscious phenomena, is ever moving. This stream is not
equally deep, wide, and clear at all times, it is, on the
contrary, ever changing like the physical stream of life
on which it depends. A little introspection will show this
clearly.

At times we are conscious of many things present
within us simultaneously: various sounds, sights, flavors,
odors, sensations of temperature, of muscular movement,
of pain or pleasure, together with a strange mingling
of manifold past conscious experiences revived in conformity with the laws of association—the stream of consciousness is wide and deep. However, its contents are
rather colorless and vague, not clearly defined and distinct
from one another. The water of the stream is abundant.

A change comes suddenly. A striking color or sound
or a sudden sharp pain rouses our attention and draws
it in a definite direction. The things to which our attention is thus strongly drawn, become clear and vivid,

whereas all others are thereby obscured, and those farthest away from the focus of attention, *i. e.,* those near the periphery of the field of consciousness, seem to fade away entirely. The stream has been narrowed, its water is less abundant, but clearer and brighter.

Again, at times our attention seems in a state of complete dispersion. While there are really very many and complex things present in our consciousness, yet we are hardly aware of their presence, they make no sensible demand upon our attention, they enter the stream and pass by to make room for others equally unnoticed. Here the stream is wide and shallow, its water has no depth or color. We are hardly awake, we are, as we might say, day-dreaming.

There is a still lower degree of consciousness possible. At intervals, *e. g.,* during sleep, it becomes so low and colorless that we speak of unsciousness, but by this we mean, not *"non-consciousness,"* but rather *"subconsciousness."* As a matter of fact, we often wake up when the clock stops ticking, which plainly proves a certain degree of conscious life even in sleep.

b. THE IMMANENCE OF CONSCIOUSNESS

Like plant life, conscious life is based upon immanent action. Since sensation in animal life corresponds to nutrition in plant life, we ought to be able to determine sensation as an intussusception, absorption, and assimilation of foreign elements, *i. e.,* other objects than the animal. Let us try:

By *intussusception* the object seen, heard, touched, tasted, or smelled has acquired another subjective presence within the animal. It is taken in really as food, though in another way.

By *absorption* the inner presence loses its identity with the external presence of the object from which it originated. Hence we have now two presences of the same object: the object itself is the objective, external presence: the inner presence is the subjective reproduction of the object which caused the sense impression from without. Consequently, with good reason we call the subjective conscious presence which originated from the other and of which it is another or second presence, a *RE-PRESENTATION* of the object.

Finally, by *assimilation* this inner presence becomes an integral element of the specific nature of the animal, *i. e.,* its conscious life. Let us bear in mind the vital character of this assimilation, otherwise we cannot understand it correctly. The intussuscepted and absorbed object is not simply added to consciousness as a crystal is added to the mother crystal in the process of crystallization, or as in a river new water appears, passes on, and out of sight to come back no more. On the contrary, it is fully and intimately incorporated with the organic structure of consciousness as food is incorporated with the organic structure of the plant. Though its law is that of perpetual motion, consciousness is not like a physical stream in which one wave follows another in regular succession, ruled by the laws of mechanical motion, but it is a stream of living water in which each new drop and each new wave is, like the cell and the organ in the physical life, an integral element and essential part of the psychical life. Contrary to appearances, the elements of consciousness constitute a stable, organized structure with which the new elements are literally incorporated, because, though in appearance like a stream, they do not flow on the stream of consciousness for a while only and disappear never more to return, but they leave, as it were, psychical sediments capable of conscious revival, which enter into the psychical structure as permanent organic elements. This organization of the new elements assimilated is generally called by modern psychologists *AP-PERCEPTION*.

2. THE SUPERPHYSICAL CHARACTER OF SENSE PHENOMENA

While the sense functions are continuous and immanent because they are vital functions, their continuity and immanence is of another type, of a higher order than those found in plant life. The elements that make them so, constitute the specific nature of sense phenomena.

Mechanicists assume that psychical elements are perfectly homogeneous with physical elements—a secretion of the brain, vibrations of nerve cells, the inner face, or, again, the epi-phenomena of nerve functions. The more honest of them frankly confess their ignorance.

Psycho-physical parallelists wisely attempt no explanation. On the one hand they assume the distinctive perfection of psychical phenomena because they consider them as a special series to be explained by its relation to the series of physical stimulations of the nerves to which it is supposed to run exactly parallel; and on the other, by denying a real causal interdependence, they make all objective explanations groundless. If they were consistent, they would be either mechanicists or pantheists.

Against the mechanicists we assert that the physical and psychical phenomena of sense life are not homogeneous but heterogeneous, and that the difference is not one of degree, but one of kind, and against the parallelists we affirm that there is a real causal interdependence between the two kinds of phenomena.

a. DEMONSTRATION OF THE SUPERPHYSICAL CHARACTER

The failure of the mechanicist explanation is a negative proof of our first proposition. Mechanicists do not succeed in explaining the mechanical character of consciousness: to say that it is but a secretion of the brain or the vibrations of brain cells, is nonsense; to say that it is the inner face or an epi-phenomenon of nerve stimulations is a veiled confession of ignorance, of which Du Bois-Reymond made a public avowal. The positive proof of our thesis is based upon the analysis of the psychical phenomena.

We have seen above that we possess an excellent analogy for sensation, which is the basic function of sense life, in the process of nutrition, which is the basic function of plant life: they both are the intussusception, absorption, and assimilation of a foreign object. But what a world of difference between them! In nutrition the object is literally incorporated and made one with the organism, so that, at the conclusion of the process, there is nothing whatever left of the object assimilated—it is a physical, chemical, and substantial transformation of the object. In sensation, on the contrary, the object intussuscepted, absorbed, and assimilated is not affected at all in its physical, chemical, and substantial constitution, but by its action upon the senses a conscious representation of it is realized. We call this product of sensation a *rē-presentation* of the object because it is *another* presence of it. What existed before in its proper, physical, and chemical nature only, exists now in a new and higher form in the animal. Inasmuch as this new subjective or inner presence of the object mirrors, and corresponds exactly to, it as it is in its objective presence, we call it a picture or *representation* of it. However, it is not a picture of it as a photograph or a painting would be. Such a picture of an object is itself another concrete being, having its own quantity and all the other physical and chemical properties of a body. Not so the subjective sense picture of an object. While it represents the object in all its physical and chemical characteristics inasmuch as they are accessible to the various senses, it has itself neither quantity nor any other physical or chemical property. Therefore, it does not occupy any space nor is it subject to any microscopic experiments. It is an animal function and as such it mirrors, not only the objective qualities of bodies such as sounds, colors, flavors, odors, etc., but just as perfectly the inner subjective qualities of the animal, such as pleasure, pain, lassitude, sadness, etc. Consequently, its distinctive characteristics are not of the same type at all as those of the physical body. Sense representations may be spoken of as vivid, distinct, faithful, and their opposites, but not as small or large, heavy or light, colorless or colored, etc. Their properties are those of consciousness, which is irreducible to a physical or chemical condition of matter. To express these distinctive characteristics of sense phenomena we call them *psychical,* which is the proper manner of saying that they are *superphysical* and *superchemical.*

b. CAUSAL INTERDEPENDENCE OF PHYSICAL AND PSYCHICAL LIFE

The physical and psychical phenomena are not only parallel series of elements, but are really interdependent as causes and effects. The opposite supposition is a mere assumption without any basis of fact. The facts find a very natural and obvious explanation if we assume causal relationship. To proclaim the impossibility of such interrelation between the physical and the psychical world is simply begging the question. The basis for the theoretical interpretation of the phenomena must be the facts and nothing but the facts, and in no way any preconceived mechanicist or idealist philosophy. If ever there is to be found a perfect demonstration by induction, the method so highly extolled by scientists, we have it here. Let us apply the three principal rules of the inductive method:

Applying the law of concordances—I open my eyes and see an apple on the table: "Posita causa, ponitur effectus." Presenting the cause, the effect also is presented.

Applying the law of differences—I close my eyes and see the apple no longer: "Sublata causa, tollitur effectus." Removing the cause, the effect also is removed.

Applying the law of variations—I take the apple and hold it in my hand, grasping it I feel the muscular movement, holding it I feel its pressure, its smoothness, its temperature, lifting it to my nose, I feel again the muscular movement and its fragrance, and finally, I bite it and I feel the movement of my jaws, its touch and temperature on my lips and its taste in my mouth: "Mutata causa, mutatur effectus." Modifying the cause, the effect also is modified.

The conclusion is evident—there is plainly a relation of cause and effect between the physical stimulations of the organs of sense and the concomitant or subsequent conscious phenomena. The very same method proves just as clearly the opposite side—there is a relation of cause and effect between conscious phenomena and muscular contractions and relaxations.

B. THE NATURE OF SENSE FACULTIES

Psychical phenomena, then, are superphysical and superchemical, and yet depend absolutely upon physical sense functions as their direct source. But what is the immediate subjective cause of these functions? Is it only one, or are there various direct causes?

Our solution will be analogous to the one adopted in regard to the various physical and chemical actions of the inorganic body, for we have the same reasons. The animal as a substance cannot be the immediate and direct cause or principle of the sense functions, because the substance is one, whereas the functions are many and of various kinds. Besides, as we saw in cosmology, the substance of a being as such never changes, whereas the functions produce manifold modifications in the agent. Hence, in addition to the substance there must be in the animal accidental dispositions which explain the complexity and variability of the functions. These inherent dispositions, which we called forces in cosmology and in plant-psychology, we call *faculties* in animal psychology to express a distinctive characteristic of their nature: they increase, develop, and are permanently perfected, at least to a certain extent, by their functions, whereas forces are ever the same—*faculties are plastic, forces are rigid*. The proper name of the specific faculties of the animal is sense faculties or simply senses.

Such faculties are psychical or super-physical and super-chemical because they are the immediate principles of sense functions which, as we have seen, are essentially superior to physical and chemical action, and evidently, the effects cannot be superior to their causes.

I. THE EXTERNAL SENSES

We distinguish the senses, the same as the physical forces, by the adequate distinction of their actions, which, again, depends upon the adequate distinction of their proper objects. Thus, we have two kinds of senses, the external and internal, and both kinds are, again, differentiated into various species. The two kinds of senses have their name from the fact that one kind, the external senses, have, generally speaking, parts of their organ on the surface of the organism, whereas the other, the internal senses, have their whole organ within the animal. However, the real distinction is this: the external senses introduce new elements into consciousness because their objective stimulus is foreign to the sense itself, whereas the activity of the internal senses has its objective origin within the conscious life of the animal.

The external senses in the higher animals, particularly in man, which are generally admitted as distinct by experimental psychologists, are nine, namely, sight, hearing, taste, smell, touch, pressure, temperature, pain, and the kinesthetic or muscular sense. For each of these, various organs have been found to exist, and their objects seem to be really distinct from one another. There is no question about the adequate distinction between colors, sounds, flavors, odors and touch qualities, such as smooth, rough, hard, soft. But psychological opinion is not quite unanimous about the adequate distinction and exact number of the others. The sensations of pain, pressure, and temperature can hardly be reduced to those of touch. About the distinctive identity of the kinesthetic sense there is hardly any doubt possible; its object: to inform the animal of the position and movements of the parts of the organism, is surely proper and distinctive.

2. THE INTERNAL SENSES

We come now to the internal senses, *i. e.,* those whose organs have apparently no peripheral part. From the phenomena of the revival and association of psychical elements, as described above, we know clearly there is the faculty of *RETENTION, REPRODUCTION,* and *COMBINATION* of psychical elements, to which we give the name of *IMAGINATION*. If we add the power of *recognition* of psychical elements to the faculty of the imagination, we call it *MEMORY*.

While it seems that there are great individual differences as regards the natural power in clearness, breadth, depth, and length of memory, yet a great deal can be achieved toward its development by rational exercise. To the general conditions for such exercise and its success we have alluded above, where we spoke of the tendency of conscious elements to revive. These conditions are chiefly three: 1. Conscious elements must be as clear and vivid as possible. 2. They must not remain isolated, but must be organized, and consequently, must be retained in the conscious state together with other elements long enough for such organization. 3. They must be frequently reproduced lest they grow stale and vague and at last fade away. The fundamental condition, then, is the clearness and vividness of consciousness, and since they depend mainly upon attention, it is evident that an intense and well directed attention is the keynote of rational memory work. As a second factor may be added careful, frequent, and timely repetition.

There can be no doubt that the power of *discrimination* is another special internal sense, as its function: to discern between what is desirable or undesirable, has a very proper object, which is of supreme importance for the life of both the individual and the species. This sense is the basis for the principle of direction and order in conscious life, and for the so-called instinct operations, by means of the phenomena of attention and inhibition.

These phenomena, as we pointed out above, with the instinctive operations are of paramount importance, the former chiefly for the life of the individual, the latter for the life of both the individual and the species.

There is another significant aspect to this sense. Being a sense of *conscious selection,* it corresponds to the force of non-conscious selection in the lower orders of being which we call chemical affinity and, like affinity in cosmology, it is the clearest expression of teleology in the animal. This sense, already highly developed when received by inheritance, is like the other senses, and even more so, capable of being developed by individual experience.

There seems to be one other internal sense, the faculty of *sense volitions or appetitions,* the "appetitus sensitivus" of the scholastics, from which the action of accepting or rejecting the desirable or undesirable object proceeds and which, therefore, explains the spontaneous movement of approach or escape.

Some psychologists add another sense in order to explain the presence of *emotional elements* in consciousness. If they were due to an active sense power, this would not be an internal but an external sense, since the emotional elements are elements of a new type in conscious life. However, emotions are not active sensations equivalent to conscious functions, but passive states of the organism, which accompany and follow all conscious functions and vary in kind and degree according to the kind and condition of the function. When the functions are natural and successful, the concomitant emotions are pleasurable; when the functions are extremely feeble or exceedingly strong, or do not succeed, their emotional echo is on the contrary, unsatisfactory and displeasing.

About the value of these passive dispositions called passions, which explain the variety and intensity of the emotional elements, there can be no question. Being the thermometer of the well-being of the organism, they both increase and insure that well-being. They are useful and necessary as a protection and safeguard for the preservation of both individual and species.

C. THE NATURE OF THE ANIMAL

Having determined analytically and inductively the nature of psychical functions and their immediate principles—the sense faculties, we are prepared to draw general conclusions about the nature of the animal as a whole, *i. e.,* as a self-sufficient substance, as an independent agent. After all, just as the phenomena explain the faculties, the faculties explain the subject in which they exist and the agent whose means of action they are.

I. THE SUPERPHYSICAL CHARACTER OF THE ANIMAL SOUL

To facilitate comprehension of our argument we must again recall the Aristotelian doctrine of the substantial constitution of the body as discussed and dwelt upon with sufficient largeness in its proper place in cosmology. We presented it again, briefly, in its application to the nature of the organism, where we established the conclusion that the fundamental explanation of the nature of vegetative life consisted in the essential superiority of the forma substantialis of the organic body as compared with that of the inorganic body. This is the foundation of our present demonstration.

There can be no question about the lower element of the substance of the animal, since organic life is the natural basis and source of conscious life—the materia prima is common to both, not only because it is identical in all bodies, but chiefly because the organs of sense are maintained and developed by the same food elements and vital functions as the vegetative organs. The difference, then, must be in the other substantial element. Consequently, the active and determinative element of the animal—its forma substantialis—must be of a new and essentially superior order as is plainly evident from the essential superiority of the sense faculties over the physical and chemical forces of nature, because these faculties are, strictly speaking, the specific properties and qualities of the animal which manifest and express its nature. Following Aristotle we express this specific perfection of its forma substantialis calling it "anima sensitiva," the animal soul.

2. THE MATERIAL NATURE OF THE ANIMAL SOUL

Though the nature of the "anima sensitiva" is plainly superphysical and superchemical, it is by no means supermaterial or spiritual, because there is no function in animal life which is not perfectly explicable by sense experience in conjunction with the innate powers of instinct, and surely if there were any spirituality in the nature of the animal, it would manifest itself somehow in its functions. The conclusion to be drawn from this proposition is evident: psychical is by no means equivalent to spiritual or supermaterial.

The reason for this materialistic interpretation of the "anima sensitiva" is not far to seek: The animal soul is completely immersed in its atmosphere of matter with its deepest roots and its finest blossoms and fruits. This fact is quite evident from the absolute and intrinsic dependence of the sense phenomena upon matter. All animal functions without exception are subjectively and objectively dependent upon material conditions: subjectively, inasmuch as their relative perfection is in exact proportion to the dispositions and conditions of the sense organ, and objectively, inasmuch as there is an exact correlation between the degree of perceptibility of the object and the degree of its perception by the functioning sense organ. Therefore, speaking of a concrete case: the vision of an object by the animal depends for its relative perfection proportionately upon the relative visibility of the object and the relative quality of the eye.

II. The Origin of Sense Life

Having a definite knowledge of the nature of animal life, we are prepared to propose the question of its origin.

We may omit the question of the origin of the individual animal, because what we said about the origin of individual plant life is perfectly applicable here: "Omnis cellula a cellula." Our problem, then, has two sections: where did the first animal come from? And what is the origin of the various species of animal life?

I. ORIGIN OF THE FIRST ANIMAL

Can we consider the first animal on the globe as the fully and perfectly developed fruit of plant life? And if so, was it the natural product of intrinsic forces and dispositions, the "terminus ad quem" of the gradually progressive evolution of a thousand previous generations of vegetable organisms, or was it the chance result of a happy combination of external circumstances? Both these questions have been affirmed with more or less assurance, though there is not a shadow of reason nor the least basis of fact for either.

As regards the latter, it is absurd to assume that by a chance combination of fortunate circumstances a plant might have developed into an animal. The principles established above in regard to the origin of plant life are apposite here. Wherever there is order, there must be direction, and where the order is so complicated as in an animal organism, it is absolute folly to account for its first production by chance, and sevenfold folly to account for its continuance and perpetuation by a regular and steady recurrence of chance.

While the other assumption, which takes animal life to be the natural and necessary fruit of the full display of the intrinsic forces and natural tendencies of a thousand previous generations of plants, is not quite so absurd, because it does not attempt to explain order without direction, yet it is plainly insufficient, and therefore inacceptable as an explanation of the first animal organism. The reason for the insufficiency of such an explanation is the absolute and essential superiority of the animal over the plant, which we demonstrated above. It is here not a question of a new degree or a higher proportion of the same perfection, but altogether another kind and order of perfection that must be accounted for. As we have seen, psychic life is not only a higher degree of plant life, but an entirely new element of a superior nature, of which no trace whatever can be found in plant life, and evidently, from nothing, nothing can evolve. Hence, to bridge over the gap between the physical and psychical world, nature being absolutely powerless, a divine intervention, or creation is necessary.

2. ORIGIN OF SPECIES

What about the manifold and complex divisions and subdivisions of animal and, also, of plant life, the different orders, families, genera, and species? Did God intervene directly in the formation of the different species? If so, are the species so created absolutely permanent in their specific characteristics, or do they admit of definite and stable modifications? Again, what would explain these modifications? Such is the problem of the origin of species.

It is plain this problem cannot be solved a priori, as the nature of the living being in its positive and negative powers for selective adaptations of a hereditary character cannot be known to us except by the facts of such adaptations. Taking all the evidence in the matter that has been gathered by paleontology, botany, zoology, and biology with its branch sciences, the general conclusion seems unavoidable that, at least to a considerable extent, evolution is highly probable if not practically certain. While none of the arguments for it are directly conclusive,—from the nature of the case this can hardly be expected,—yet the facts pointing in the same direction are so numerous and coming from so many different sources that their cumulative value is great if not overwhelming. The force of these arguments is doubled by the consideration that, while the facts which speak in favor of the permanency of species can be explained very well in the transformist theory, there are many facts which cannot be accounted for rationally except by evolution.

Thus, to give but one illustration: If we find two species of a certain genus of insects which are perfectly alike except for one characteristic, and if upon investigation we perceive clearly that the change or modification of the characteristic in question responds to the natural requirements of their respective environment, we cannot help but conclude that these two species were originally one and became differentiated because of their adaptation to different conditions of life. Of such species there are many, and as what is practically certain in their case, is applicable to others in a similar manner, the fundamental question of the problem appears to be solved: species change and thereby new species are formed.

There is no need of calling attention to the difference in our interpretation of evolution and that proposed by Charles Darwin. The theory that means to account sufficiently for the transformation of species by natural selection and the survival of the fittest in the struggle for existence, has long been exploded. It represents at most a mere negative factor, which might explain the disappearance of deficient individuals and species, but can by no means explain the production of new organic characteristics, and therefore, of new species. The origin of new species by evolution can only be accepted upon the condition of positive, adaptive, and selective dispositions existing in the animal organism.

While it seems fairly certain that numerous species and genera, and probably different families, draw their origin from a common stock by evolution, we are not justified by the facts to assume a blood relationship between widely divergent orders of animals. There is no ground for even a probable opinion that lions and bees descend from common ancestors.

Considering the facts as we know them at present it would seem probable that God created a certain number of different orders of plants and animals with an immanent tendency and power to adapt themselves to changing conditions and to transmit the acquired adaptations to their offspring. Whether these original species were created simultaneously or successively is not apparent from the facts so far known.

CHAPTER TWELVE

PHENOMENA OF INTELLECTUAL LIFE

Man's Superiority over the Animal

In its natural tendency to progressive evolution nature is intrinsically limited. When a being reaches that limit it can go no farther because its natural powers are exhausted. If progressive evolution is to continue, God must directly intervene and add a new substantial element with new powers to its nature, so that another series of phases of progressive evolution may start and work till this new element also attains the limit of its powers. We have noticed several such gaps, where only direct divine intervention could realize the passage from one side to the other. Such a gap bridged over by creation was the first production of life on the globe, such was also the first appearance of sense life on earth. Now we have reached another boundary line with another big gap. Human life is obviously not a mere progressive degree of evolution from animal life. We need not be scientists or philosophers to see the yawning gap between the two. What a profound difference there is between the highest animal and the lowest man! Then, taking the animal and the human world as a whole, what a vast discrepancy!

As regards his social activity, man has produced science, art, literature, philosophy, religion, in a word, the complex of achievements which we call culture and civilization. There is nothing in animal life parallel to this. It is true that some species, such as bees and ants, have a certain analogy with social organization, and other species, such as the beaver and certain birds, are wonderful architects, but neither their life nor their work is ever the free expression of social aspirations, but simply a racial and instinctive characteristic, which is practically stationary throughout thousands of years, and absolutely subordinate to the primary physical necessities of the individual or of the species.

In respect to the individual, the obvious line of demarcation between animal and man appears to be this: *Man is perfectible,* indeed, indefinitely perfectible, whereas the animal is not. While this distinction is clear enough, the philosopher is not satisfied with it. He wants to know why man is perfectible and why the animal is not, or only to a very limited degree. In his desire to find this explanation he examines and analyzes the facts and functions of man's life to determine his nature and thus to find a rational solution for the problem of man's indefinite perfectibility, and incidentally, of the animal's lack of it.

I. Intellectual Phenomena

As we have no intuition or direct perception of intellectual functions, but gain our knowledge of them only indirectly by an analysis of the phenomena, our first task must be to examine and classify the phenomena of intellectual life. Evidently, the phenomena which we must examine here are those of knowledge, inasmuch as human knowledge is different from animal knowledge, this difference referring to the quality rather than to the quantity. We will present the main facts of the distinctive human knowledge under five heads:

1. Man's knowledge is naturally *SCIENTIFIC*. Once in possession of sense representations in his consciousness, he considers, reflects, and reasons upon the grounds of his sense knowledge. Thus, he succeeds in finding out in many instances the connection between cause and effect, means and end, and other manifold relations between the beings which he per-

ceives by his senses. A few applications will show this clearly.

The normal man has sufficient knowledge of the ways and means to provide safety and protection from all kinds of enemies; food, clothes, and shelter for himself and his family. This knowledge he has not like the animal by instinct and inheritance, but from personal experience and reflection.

Man speaks and writes. This fact implies the knowledge of a complex relationship between the sounds of the spoken and the letters of the written word; between the words of a proposition; between the different propositions; and above all, between the terms and their meaning; all things clearly not perceptible by animal sense.

Even the savage knows the elements of arithmetic. He has a clear idea of unit and number, of the elementary principles based upon them, such as addition and subtraction, division and multiplication.

2. Man is naturally a *RELIGIOUS being*. Even the most degraded savage has some conception of a higher power that rules him and the whole universe; in whose presence he feels awe and reverence and a sense of his absolute dependence; and some idea also of immortality and of punishment and reward. Otherwise we could not explain the practical universality of religious worship amongst all races of man. Of these facts of religious signification there is not even a trace or faint analogy in animal life.

3. Man is naturally an *ETHICAL being*. Just as he knows the causal connection between things, he finds out the teleological relation between actions. Being conscious of the freedom of his decisions, he feels a sense of obligation, and therefore, a responsibility for his deeds, worthy of praise for some, worthy of blame for others. Here again, we have a number of ideas, such as freedom, obligation, responsibility, virtue, sin, crime, etc., *i. e.*, knowl-

edge plainly never present in the animal, but always present in man, even under the most primitive conditions.

4. Man is naturally a *SOCIAL being.* As soon as he awakens to the use of reason, he learns to know his rights and duties in the family, the social position of his family in the group of families associated in a tribe or a state, and what it is to be loyal or disloyal to his country. Many other relations of social life, such as friendship or business dealings, are perfectly understood and acted upon even by uncivilized man. Nothing of the same character exists in animal life. The apparent social organization in the life of ants and bees is but a faint analogy; a real knowledge of social relations is nowhere manifest.

5. Finally, man is a *METAPHYSICAL being.* He is naturally a philosopher because he is self-conscious. He knows himself as distinct from everything else. He knows his position with regard to his fellowman, to the inorganic and organic world upon which he depends in many ways, and to Almighty God, upon whom he depends absolutely. In other words, man knows the system of which he is an element and also the part he ought to play in that system. Is there anything like that in animal life?

II. Philosophical Analysis of the Intellectual Phenomena

Such are some of the facts, plain and unmistakable, of human life, inasmuch as it is distinct from animal life. How can we explain them? *Mechanicists,* who, in this respect, are also called *sensualists, associationists,* and *positivists,* do not really attempt an explanation, they simply deny the facts. But with strange inconsistency, while in theory they deny them and thereby proclaim themselves the highest species of mammals, pure and simple, in practice they live as if they were human, *i. e.,* they live and act the facts which, with their lips, they deny.

Psycho-physical parallelists cannot do much better. By denying the causal interdependence between physical and psychical phenomena, they undermine the foundation upon which their own theory rests, *viz.,* the objective reality of their parallelism. Furthermore, by presenting human consciousness in its concrete complexity and mixture of the general animal and the specific human elements without any attempt at discrimination, their method precludes any possible definite solution in the matter. No wonder that a great many desirous of some explanation seem to accept plain idealism with an ingredient of pantheism.

Rationalist philosophers assume these facts to be rooted directly in the very nature of man and not due to specific powers or faculties which would explain them by their natural and proper action. Thus, Descartes claims that thought constitutes the very essence of the human soul, and rationalists generally postulate the presence of ideas in the soul as part of its very nature, which would account for the facts of man's intellectual life. Evidently, such attempts at an explanation are not based upon the facts, but are aprioristic interpretations, and consequently, being plainly arbitrary and unscientific, do not deserve our attention here.

Much less do *ontologistic* interpretations deserve our attention because we are perfectly sure from the most simple introspection that we do not see things in God, since we are not even conscious of the existence of God. As far as we can judge, only two really serious solutions have been proposed, the one by Aristotle, the other by Kant. We will examine Kant's theory first.

A. KANT'S THEORY

To understand Kant's psychology we must know his viewpoint. He was confronted with two opposite schools of philosophy: sensualism and rationalism. In the sensualism of Hume and Locke, human knowledge was the natural product of sense experience, nothing essentially beyond that. Kant rejected this interpretation because in his mind the necessity and universality, or as he would say, the "objectivity" of scientific knowledge was incontestible, whereas it was evident to him that concrete sense experience could produce only contingent and particular knowledge. He also rejected the rationalism of Descartes and Leibniz because scientific knowledge was being added to constantly, whereas real objective additions to knowledge would be impossible to explain if all knowledge were fundamentally derived from the reading of the innate ideas in the mind. This rejection of both theories was the starting point of his own criticist theory.

I. KANT'S ANALYSIS OF THE HUMAN MIND

In Kant's mind, there are chiefly two things to explain: the objective additions to human knowledge on the one side, and on the other, its universality and necessity, which he calls its "objectivity." To explain the first, *i. e.,* the clearly apparent objective additions to our knowledge from experience, he justly supposes that our senses are passive faculties, and therefore, in order to account for their action it is necessary to assume an outside factor acting upon them. As a consequence of this action, we have sense impressions. Being merely impressions, they are indefinite and have no meaning as yet. How do they acquire their meaning? By a first reaction upon them when we place them in space and time. How is the reaction accomplished? Time and space are innate mental conditions, psychical moulds or *pure intuitions,* a priori forms belonging to man's mental equipment. They are empty forms, but as our sense impressions pass through them they acquire a content. Now they are representations—phenomena with a definite meaning.

Such is Kant's explanation of the objective additions to our knowledge. How does this mass of new impressions objectivated by their temporal and spatial determinations become necessary and universal knowledge from particular and contingent representations? By a second reaction of the mind. This time it reacts upon the representations by passing them through a twelvefold mould—the so-called *categories,* by means of which the representations become universal and necessary knowledge. The categories must be conceived somewhat like the pure intuitions of time and space, as *pure ideas, i. e.,* intellectual moulds or innate conditions of the mind, having no content or objective value till they are applied to representations, because, like time and space, they are a priori forms, independent of, and prior to, all experience.

2. CRITICISM OF KANT'S ANALYSIS

We refuse to accept Kant's theory of human knowledge for various reasons.

In the first place we reject it because it is arbitrary and artificial. It is arbitrary because not based upon the facts. Like rationalism it is an aprioristic conception. The facts show that the ideas of time and space as well as the categories, such as substance and accident, absolute and relative, do depend upon experience, because they are very imperfect in early years of life and grow in perfection with mental development and with the growth in thought and reflection. Furthermore, the theory is artificial because there is no natural basis for just twelve general a priori conceptions. Why not ten or fourteen? However, our main reasons for rejecting the theory are two: First, it does not explain what it is supposed to explain, and secondly it is the natural source of disastrous errors.

Against sensualism it is supposed to explain the universality and necessity of human knowledge; against rationalism, its objective growth. In reality, by making all knowledge dependent upon subjective, a priori conditions in the individual mind, it explains neither the one nor the other.

In the first place, it does not explain the objective

growth of knowledge from experience. The only objective factor in the whole psychology of Kant is the external influence which accounts for the action of the passive senses. About the properties or nature of this objective factor we can learn nothing, as the impressions caused by it have no meaning whatever by themselves, but must acquire it by passing through the pure intuitions of time and space. However, this meaning, such as it is, is necessarily subjective as time and space are subjective mental conditions. Even if we were to consider, contrary to the theory, this meaning given to the sense impressions as objective, our objective knowledge would simply denote a factor endowed with time and space relations, no more; surely a very meagre dose of objective additions to our knowledge from experience.

Furthermore, Kant's psychology does not and cannot explain the necessity and universality of our knowledge. His basis for the assumption that it does, is his hypothesis of the perfect identity of the categories in all human minds. Evidently, this is a mere hypothesis: it has no facts and no experience for its foundation. In reality, things are very different. The general ideas which Kant calls categories are not the same, not only not the same in the minds of various individuals, but not the same in the same mind at various periods of life. Do we not know how by study and reflection our ideas, even the most simple and general, grow more distinct and more adequate, and consequently, change? But if they change at all, we can surely not consider them as the root and source of the necessity and universality of our knowledge.

As the second main reason for rejecting Kant's psychology, we referred to the disastrous errors which are its logical consequences. Indeed, subjectivism and phenomenalism follow from the theory spontaneously and almost necessarily, because, as pointed out, there is just one tiny thread left by which the mind hangs on the objective world,—the external influence that explains the sense impressions. But as we can know nothing whatever about this objective factor, since all real signification

which sense impressions may obtain, comes from subjective conditions of the mind, such objectivity is not
worth the name. If subjectivism and phenomenalism
have a fruitful source in Kant's theory of knowledge,
idealistic pantheism is just as legitimate an offspring of
its doctrine. Indeed, if, taking Kant's psychology for
granted, we want a real objective basis to account for the
necessity and universality of human knowledge, there is no
other alternative but to accept the universal mind of pantheism, manifesting its divine modes of knowledge in
the categories of the human mind.

B. THE SCHOLASTIC THEORY

Having examined and refuted the theory of knowledge
proposed by Kant, which bears the name of *criticist,* we
are going to discuss our own solution, which in its main
principles is based upon Aristotle, and which is generally
known as the *scholastic theory.* However, before we enter upon the subject, let us define and determine the problem itself. The study of Kant's psychology has been of
great profit to us in this connection. Kant understood
the problem well, far better than any of his predecessors.
In our opinion, this is the great merit of Kant's philosophy: by him, the whole significance of the problem was
proposed and expressed in exact and precise terms.
There are, in truth, two essential characteristics in human
knowledge, the one, its *objectivity* and the other, its *necessity and universality,* or as we prefer to express it in one
term, its *absoluteness.* To account in a plausible and
adequate manner for these two characteristics is the
problem which we must try to solve.

What we mean by the objectivity and absoluteness of
knowledge needs hardly any explanation. *To be objective, knowledge must be an interpretation of facts, and
to be absolute, it must be applicable not only to some
cases but to all possible cases.* Examining the actual
knowledge of man as given in the first part of this chapter, we find that it bears out just what we were saying:
All scientific, ethical, social, religious, and metaphysical

which we may call psychical images or *percepts* of things.

a. THE OBJECT OF ABSTRACTION

The proper object of abstraction will appear sufficiently clear to us if we point out briefly the most obvious difference between percepts and concepts, *i. e.*, between sense knowledge and mind knowledge. *Sense knowledge applies to the individual things as individual mind knowledge applies to classes of things as classes.* Why? Because a percept represents the totality of the body which is its object, and therefore, can refer to one only; it is like a portrait, expressive of singleness. This is quite evident, as a being in its totality cannot be multiple, it can belong only to itself. It is very different with mind knowledge. A concept represents one essential element of the being to which it refers, or several elements conceived as one, but never to all its elements at once, and of course, this one or several essential elements are naturally applicable to many individuals, since in reality they are often found in many. The being considered in its totality, *i. e.*, with all its elements as it actually exists, we call *the concrete being,* the being considered without the contingent conditions of its actual existence, we call *the abstract being,* and thus, we say that *the proper object of a percept is the concrete being, the proper object of a concept is the abstract being.* Consequently, *the specific function of the intellect is the production of the abstract being which, as such, exists in the mind only.* And this function we call abstraction.

b. THE NATURE OF ABSTRACTION

What does abstraction consist in? While it is the specific function of the intellect, yet we must bear in mind that the intellect is not independent in this function, but depends upon sense knowledge, and that in a double way: first, as the material object of sense and mind is identical—this world in which we live and of which we are a part—the mind depends upon the senses for the pres-

entation of its objects: nothing can come into the mind
except through the senses. Secondly, the mind depends
upon the senses inasmuch as the intellect does not act
without the concurrent action of the imagination. This
is made evident by experimental psychology and especially, by psychiatry. Any lesion in the association centers of the brain has its proportionately harmful influence
upon the work of the mind. When the lesion is substantial, all mind work ceases. Even a functional dis-
turbance in those centers reacts proportionately on the
mind. We all know from personal experience how the
mind work is influenced for good or evil by certain
stimulants, such as coffee, tea, alcohol, and drugs of various kinds. Evidently, they cannot affect the mind directly, but help or hinder the action of the concurrent
cause, the imagination. Consequently, abstraction is a
function of the intellect in which the imagination co-
operates. Acknowledging the evidence of these principles, we can present the whole theory, which is the
cornerstone of human psychology, in two propositions:

FIRST PROPOSITION: *Abstraction is the act by
which the intellect abstracts ("abstrahit," i. e., pulls from
the percept) all the elements which represent the contingent conditions of the being in actual existence,* retaining
some or all of the essential elements which represent the
being independent of the conditions of its actual existence.

We have here a case of primary abstraction, by which
we acquire the knowledge of what the being presented
to the mind in sense knowledge is. It is the concept or
idea of the being and represents what we call its essence
or nature. But there are other cases of what we may call
secondary abstraction. For instance, of a being presented
to the mind in sense knowledge, we may take any one
element and consider it by itself apart from the being
in which it exists, and apart from the other elements which
are together with it in the percept.

SECOND PROPOSITION: *We express the nature
of the concurrence of mind and sense in abstraction when
we say that the intellect and the imagination co-operate*

as principal and instrumental causes. Such a concurrence explains, on the one side, the essential unity of the abstractive action itself, and on the other, it explains both the objectivity of human knowledge and its absoluteness. Furthermore, this interpretation is in perfect harmony with the psychological, psycho-physical, logical, and criteriological facts apparent in human knowledge.

III. Analytic Study of Abstraction

The subject being of such paramount importance on account of its speculative and practical inferences and consequences, we shall try to elucidate both propositions of the theory by a careful analysis of abstraction, as it is the keynote of the theory.

I. THE PROCESS OF ABSTRACTION

Abstraction in the primary sense as defined in the first proposition is generally called an *intellectual apprehension,* because the intellect apprehends, *i. e.,* takes hold of an object. Thus, we may speak of abstraction as an intellectual or mind perception of an object, just as we speak of a sense perception of an object. No wonder, then, that sense perception is the best analogy for this fundamental act of the mind. Like sense perception, abstraction is a vital function and as such it is an intussusception, absorption, and assimilation of the being which is its object. Consequently, it will be illuminating to examine this process of intellectual perception closely in order to see in what it resembles the process of sense perception and in what it differs from it.

In our last chapter we pointed out that the process of sense perception bears a close analogy to the process of nutrition, because like it, it is a process of intussusception, absorption, and assimilation of an object. We also showed the essential differences between the two vital processes of the animal: The process of nutrition converts its object physically and chemically, *i. e.,* by a series of chemical reactions, into its own material substance, so that the object has no longer any existence of its own, whereas in the process of sense perception the object is intussuscepted, absorbed, and assimilated in conformity with the essentially superior nature of the animal in an absolutely different manner: the object is not physically and chemically transformed, but by its action upon the sense powers an inner conscious and, therefore, superphysical representation of it is produced in the animal. Though fully aware of this enormous difference between the assimilation of an object by nutrition and that by sense perception we must not exaggerate it: they are both essentially material processes. The psychical image produced by sense assimilation is purely material, because it is the product of two concurrent causes—the concrete object and the sense organ, both purely material, and therefore, it represents, and responds to, its material object in all its concrete details as it exists in the objective order of the universe.

In the same manner as we have thus for sense perception a valuable analogy in nutrition, so for abstraction, the fundamental act of mind perception, we have an illuminating analogy in sense perception. Like this, abstraction is essentially the psychic intussusception, absorption, and assimilation of an object. We conceive the process to be as follows: *an object present in the imagination,* which is the sense representation of an external object, is *intussuscepted by the intellect* without losing its presence in the imagination; *it is absorbed by the intellect and thereby an intellectual presence of it is produced,* entirely distinct and separate from the mere psychical presence in the imagination; and finally, *it is assimilated, i. e., it enters as it were, into the very nature of the mind, increasing, deepening, and widening its native powers.* From the mere indication of these vital phases of the process of intellectual perception, it is apparent what a world of difference there is between the two functions compared and analyzed. The object itself is different, different its intussusception, different its absorption, different its assimilation, and therefore, radically different also the result.

a. The first difference refers to *the object*. The object of the sense perception is the individual concrete being which acts physically upon the sense powers of the animal and thus contributes to the production of the sense representation as an objective independent cause. On the contrary, the object of abstraction is not the individual concrete being having its objective existence outside our consciousness, but the psychical image of that object, *i. e.,* the object as it exists in the imagination. While its influence upon the production of the concept, *i. e.,* the being as it exists in the intellect, is a true and positive causality, it is not a causality of the same, but of a very different type, as we shall see clearly before we come to the end of this chapter.

b. In the second place, there is a profound difference in the *intussusception of the object* in both cases. In the intussusception of the concrete individual by means of sensation the object is apprehended with all the conditions and determinations which belong to the concrete individual, in so far as they directly or indirectly act upon the sense powers. It is a material apprehension. Far different is the intellectual intussusception of an object. The psychical image or the object as it exists in the imagination, is intussuscepted by the intellect not as a concrete, material picture of the objective individual, but as an abstract immaterial image of the object, so that it corresponds to the object present in the imagination minus the material conditions and determinations that individualize and concretize it.

c. In the third place, the intellectual *absorption of its object* widely differs from the sense absorption of its object. Through sense perception the object present in man's consciousness becomes distinct and separate from its external presence; however, the inner, subjective reproduction of the object still corresponds exactly to the external object itself; though psychical in its nature, it is still a concrete image of a concrete reality. The very opposite happens in the absorption of its object by the intellect. Here the object intussuscepted and absorbed no longer represents the individual being in its objective existence, but the species or class of beings, which as such has only a subjective existence in man's mind.

What we said with reference to the abstraction of a substance having its own existence, refers also, "mutatis mutandis," to the abstraction of any essential or accidental element of a substance.

d. The final phase in the abstractive function—*assimilation of its object,* manifests the same profound difference in character when compared with the assimilation of its object by sense perception. The image of the object produced by sensation does not remain isolated, but is incorporated as an organic element into the structure of man's imagination, to be revived whenever the occasion calls for it according to the laws of association. Evidently, this organic structure of the imagination, though psychical in nature, is a material structure representing the objective material environment as it appears to the senses, *i. e.*, with the conditions of its material existence. There is nothing like that in the assimilation of its object by the intellect. The object intellectually intussuscepted and absorbed cannot become a part or element in an organic structure; because an immaterial object cannot enter as an element or a part into the constitution of any spiritual being, since such a being is necessarily simple. Consequently, we cannot conceive the assimilation of its object by the intellect except as an increase in abstractive power, *i. e.*, as a perfective disposition for other abstractions—it is a development in intensity, not a growth in quantity.

e. In view of these great differences between the object as well as between each vital phase of the two processes, it is no wonder that there should appear a profound discrepancy between the *two processes considered in their totality.* The material object, *i. e.,* the "terminus a quo" of sense perception, is the concrete reality, its formal object or distinctive product, *i. e.,* its "terminus ad quem," is the psychical image representing the concrete reality. Hence its nature, while superphysical and superchemical, is not immaterial or spiritual. From this sense process the mind perception differs in every detail: its material object, *i. e.,* its "terminus a quo," is the concrete object as present in consciousness, its formal object or characteristic product, *i. e.,* the "terminus ad quem," is the concept or intellectual image which represents not the concrete reality, but the abstract species or class to which the concrete object belongs. Hence, *its nature is not only superphysical and superchemical, but also immaterial, or rather supermaterial or spiritual.*

2. THE CAUSALITY OF ABSTRACTION

In the second proposition of our interpretation of intellectual phenomena it is stated that there are two efficient causes in abstraction, the intellect and the imagination, but that they do not contribute to the common production in the same manner because the one, the intellect, acts as a principal, the other, the imagination, as an instrumental cause. Let us first clarify the meaning of these expressions.

By a principal cause we refer to a being that exercises its causative influence as an independent agent, independent, of course, in the sense of its relation to the causative action; whereas by instrumental cause we express a being which, not exercising its causative influence as an independent agent, is in its causative action absolutely controlled by the principal cause. It is clear that the instrumental cause, while it is a real cause because it shares positively and directly in the causative action, yet is only a cause of secondary significance. All its specific determination and value as a cause depend upon the principal cause to which its action is subordinate. A simple illustration is the pianist playing on the piano. The piano is only the instrumental cause of the play, but on account of its positive and direct contribution to it, it shares in the dignity and beauty which the pianist as the principal cause may give to his play.

This is precisely what the theory claims. The intellect needs for its production sense representations of its object, *i. e.,* it uses the imagination which reproduces the sense representations as the pianist uses the piano which produces sounds. The pianist uses the sounds of the piano and manipulates them according to the laws of harmony so as to express a definite object, a certain state of mind, for instance,—a thing absolutely unthinkable if the piano were left to its own action. So also the intellect uses the representations of the imagination and in conformity with the laws of intellectual vision perceives in the variety of the objects represented in the imagination a common aspect, and thus, seeing unity where only multiplicity is represented by the senses, the concept or the abstract image is realized, which represents not the individual, but the class to which the individual belongs.

Such we assume to be the co-operation of mind and sense in the product of abstraction because we have no other way of conceiving it in a rational manner.

a. THE FACT OF THE TWO CONCURRENT CAUSES

On account of the importance of the matter, we will present the reasons for our interpretation at some length.

(1) First of all, there can be no doubt about the necessity of a double causality to explain the production

of intellectual knowledge, and consequently, the fact itself of the co-operation is quite evident. Abstraction, as we saw above, is a process of which the sense representations of objects are the "terminus a quo," the starting point, and the mind representations or the concepts of things, the "terminus ad quem," the point of arrival. But to account for such a process adequately, we must assume a causality that explains both the seizure of the "terminus a quo" and the attainment of the "terminus ad quem." However, it is absolutely impossible that one and the same causality should explain both actions because, the "terminus a quo" being concrete and therefore material, and the "terminus ad quem" being abstract and therefore immaterial, it is plain that the causality which explains the seizure of the "terminus a quo" must be material, whereas the causality which accounts for the attainment of the "terminus ad quem" must be supermaterial. The latter is evidently the intellect, the former the imagination, in and by which the sense representations of objects are reproduced.

(2) This argument is confirmed decisively by a consideration of the product of abstraction, *i. e.,* the intellectual images in consciousness or the concepts which represent the classes of beings and not the individuals. It is evident that only individual things have an objective existence, the classes of things as such have existence in the mind only. Consequently, sense powers or organic faculties cannot explain such a product, because they are intrinsically passive and become active only upon the condition of stimulations which cannot proceed but from individual concrete objects. Therefore, there can be no doubt that only an inorganic faculty, essentially superior to sense, *i. e.,* a supermaterial faculty, can explain the product of abstraction. We call this faculty the intellect.

Though necessary, the intellect is not sufficient

to explain the product, because, while the concept does not represent the individual things that have an objective existence, it does represent a real object, not a simple negation or an imaginary being. This objective reality which the concept represents has clearly its foundation in the individual beings of the universe, since it represents these very same beings, but exclusive of the determinations and conditions that concretize and individualize them. Therefore the object of abstraction cannot possibly come into the mind but through the senses, and it cannot remain in the mind except in and through the imagination. Hence, the imagination also is indispensable as a factor of abstraction.

(3) The necessity of the double causality of intellect and imagination in abstraction has been proven conclusively by experiments of various kinds which show that there is an exact correlation and interdependence between intellectual activity and the structural and functional integrity of the upper brain centers which are the organ of the imagination.

(4) Finally, there is an argument pointing in the same direction which can be verified by anybody at any time. The most obvious introspection of our consciousness manifests the double causality fairly well: whenever we are engaged, and as long as we are engaged, in the work of abstraction,—and every intellectual act shares in the character of abstraction—our imagination is always busy offering images suitable in some way to the abstraction which we are producing.

b. CORRELATION BETWEEN THE TWO CONCURRENT CAUSES

The fact of the co-operation of mind and sense is incontestable. However, there are only two ways of conceiving such a co-operation: either they work together in team work as two independent causes;—such is the co-operation of sound and ear in audition, of light and eye in vision—or they work together as principal and instrumental causes. The first alternative not being acceptable, we must assume the other. The first alternative is not acceptable because it is impossible for us to conceive how a sense representation and, therefore, a material reality can act upon and move the intellect, a spiritual factor. While it is also difficult for us to conceive clearly how the intellect, a spiritual factor, can use the imagination, an organic and therefore material factor as the instrument of its action, yet we know from a thousand facts of personal experience that this sort of co-operation is the most common and familiar thing in human life; indeed, our whole intellectual and moral life is accomplished and expressed by the instrumentality of the body and its organs.

3. MODES AND DEGREES OF ABSTRACTION

From the principles enlarged upon so far, various inferences of importance follow logically; some refer to the modes, others to the degrees of abstraction.

a. How does the mind proceed in abstraction? In either of two ways: either it uses various objects presented by the senses, or it uses the same object presented by the senses at various times. In the first case, comparing various objects, the mind discovers what is common to several or to all of them, and what is distinctive of each one. Thus, it distinguishes not only between individual and class, but also between a more general and a less general class. In the second case, where the intellect uses the same object presented by the senses on various occasions, it compares the various representations of the object and discovers two classes of elements: such as always reappear the same, and such as always appear more or less modified. From this analysis it forms the induction that the elements which always remain identical, belong to the essence of the object and that the others are only contingent accidents.

b. From the modes we pass naturally to the degrees of abstraction already alluded to in the first mode. Our mind goes on naturally from one degree to another. This procedure is based upon the manifold elements which constitute the concrete being represented in our consciousness. We may start by abstracting only the individual elements, and thus we obtain the concept of a species. If we continue by abstracting the specific elements, we come to the idea of a genus. Again, we may abstract the least generic elements, and thus obtain the knowledge of a higher genus, and so we may continue till we reach the very last element, and thereby approach the transcendental concept of being. Let us take a certain live-oak. If we abstract the individual elements, we have the species: live-oak. Taking away the specific elements, we have the genus: oak. Now, we separate mentally the least generic elements and we have the higher genus: tree. Once more, we take away the least generic elements and we have the still higher genus: plant. Once again, we pursue our abstraction and we have the genus next to the highest: body. If we still continue, we will have next the highest or supreme genus: substance, and lastly, the transcendental concept: being.

CHAPTER THIRTEEN

PHENOMENA OF VOLITIONAL LIFE

DISTINCTION BETWEEN INTELLECTUAL AND VOLITIONAL PHENOMENA

We have examined the most important phenomena of the intellectual life of man and have come to the certain conclusion that there is a knowledge in man which is not found in any other organic being, and is, therefore, specific and proper to human nature. Upon critical analysis, we determined abstraction as the basic function of this knowledge. By this we mean that, while the human mind may apply its specific powers of knowledge to many objects, there is in every intellectual exercise this specific feature: the perception of unity in multiplicity, of simplicity in complexity. While there is an objective foundation for such a perception in nature, yet in themselves all bodies, organic and inorganic, are manifold and complex, and therefore, the ideas or concepts which represent them as one and simple, exist as such exclusively in the mind of which they are the natural product.

However, human activity is not exhausted in purely intellectual productions. With the presence of ideas in man, a new source of activity opens up, and this new activity is so characteristic of his individuality and so expressive of a distinctive human energy that, when we speak generally of human actions, we refer to this energy with the exclusion of his purely intellectual activity. The principle of these actions, the *will*, as we call it, appears to be really distinct from the intellectual principle, because the two sorts of acts are different from one another in many ways. Knowledge, even mind knowledge, is objective and in a sense, passive. It originates from an object acting upon the senses, and as we have seen, even the intellect in its specific act of abstraction depends objectively and instrumentally upon the imagination which reacts upon it, and therefore, its product is just as truly an expression of the object as of the subject. How different the acts of the will and their product! 1. They appear absolutely subjective inasmuch as they proceed altogether from within the subject. 2. They are felt as essentially active because they have no other efficient causality but the will. 3. They are themselves the direct efficient causes of all other human activity. It is hardly necessary to add that, when we speak here of human actions, we include all specifically human acts with the exception of the intellectual, though even they are not exempt from volitional influence.

I. *Characteristic Human Actions*

As distinctive human actions we take all such as are performed with a purpose or an aim in view. Such actions are everywhere in human life; indeed, human life is above all else, human action.

A. A FEW TYPES OF PURPOSIVE ACTIONS

Man knows not only the reason for things and their manifold and complex relationship, but he acts upon the knowledge thus acquired for the purposes of his life.

1. Above all else, man speaks, writes, reads. But speaking, writing, reading are not simply outward signs of a certain state of consciousness. They are in themselves complex combinations of actions with their own intrinsic aims, expressive of the relation between letters, sounds, and phrases. Furthermore, to the extrinsic aim—to manifest human thoughts and feelings, they often add the literary ideal—to express the inner experience more adequately and more beautifully.
2. Domestic work, hunting, fishing, farming, all the

common arts and professions, industry and commerce, are, one and all, human actions, *i. e.,* actions performed for certain well-defined purposes.

3. Man acts morally throughout. His ethical knowledge and his standards may not be perfect. But whenever he acts as man, he has ends in view and his actions are the means for his ends. Whether his ends and means be holy or wicked, he is conscious of responsibility of his acts, and the thought of this responsibility directs and controls his activity in a thousand ways, in such a manner, that his whole life becomes the performance or neglect of duty.

4. Man lives in society. He knows not only his social relations with others, his rights and duties in the family, in the state, in the church, but he practices or neglects them. And with what spirit of generosity, patience, and endurance at times! He even risks his life in a social crisis, as in times of war or other public calamity.

5. Who can enumerate the efforts and sacrifices made, and the time and money and energy spent in the pursuit of scientific aims and ideals! And science is not an aim in itself, as a rule, but is studied for a hundred practical applications.

6. Man practices religion. Who can count the deeds performed from the fear of God or from love of God! There is hardly any man whose life is not filled with them on a smaller scale, not to mention the heroic life of a million saints. Was there ever any man, a real normal man, whose actions were never influenced by religion? But religious actions are, above all others, actions with spiritual aims and ideals.

B. INTERPRETATION OF PURPOSIVE ACTIONS: FREEDOM OF THE WILL

These are a few selections of human actions. We could multiply them indefinitely. They are exclusively human. We find them, at least in an elementary form, in all men and not at all in animals. What makes them human actions, what is the specific characteristic of them all? They are *teleological,* they are performed in the pursuance of definite aims, and these aims are *self-chosen, self-proposed,* and therefore, the actions performed under the inspiration and direction of these aims are *self-determined.*

1. Such is the obvious interpretation of human actions as it becomes clearly manifest to any one from the most simple *introspection.* The voice of consciousness in this regard is unmistakable. I feel most clearly that the actions which I perform are my actions; I control them, I am their master and therefore, I feel responsible for them. Whatever praise or blame they deserve, I feel, is due to me. While I am conscious that many influences, from without and within, may bear on my decisions, the final voice in each decision is of my own free choice. In the last instance, it is I who declare pro or contra, it is I who say internally yes or no to each proposition that comes before me. Even more than this; in addition to the concrete cases of a free decision I am conscious of an outright impossibility of being unfree in any possible decision, *i. e.,* I feel there is no power within or without me that can force my will, so that the freedom of my decisions from which all my human activity flows, I perceive to be the formal basis and source of my individuality.

2. The voice of the *collective consciousness* of the race speaks in the same terms. As long as a man has not been declared by competent authority to be insane, society holds him responsible for his actions. All nations have pantheons for their heroes, prisons and gallows for their criminals. The pantheon is meant to be a reward for merits, prisons and gallows are meant to be a punishment for crime. But

the ideas of reward and punishment necessarily imply freedom of action. To reward or punish an action which is not born of freedom, but of necessity, would be the height of foolishness. We prepare delicacies for a pet dog or bird, and put a lion or a cobra in a steel cage, but no one ever thinks of reward or punishment in this connection.

3. A third argument for the freedom of human actions, an argument by no means negligible, is derived from a *comparison between human and animal actions.*

The obvious distinction which imposes itself on the mind between human and animal actions is this: animal actions are spontaneous, *i. e.,* produced dependent upon knowledge, and besides, they are conscious in themselves. However, they are not free, they are determined from within by instinct and impulse, over which the animal has no control. They are, as psychologists would say, spontaneous muscular discharges of certain motor settings in the nervous system, but these motor settings depend directly and absolutely upon definite contents of animal consciousness. Not so human actions. While, materially, they are also muscular discharges of certain motor settings, formally, they are the deliberate expression of the ideas that are in the human mind. These ideas in this connection receive another name: we call them aims and ideals. Not being concrete representations, they do not exist as material elements in the organism, and therefore, cannot act in the manner of motors or efficient causes that set the body in motion. However, they do influence the production of human actions since without them there is never any normal human action. The question is what is the nature of this influence exercised by aims and ideals upon human activity? They act as *final causes* that draw the will in a certain direction offering it its proper object; and the will, being a principle of rational action, moves when it knows whither and why.

We have met in our study with a threefold manner of selection in the beings composing the universe. The first is the selection which we found in mineral and vegetable bodies. Their actions attain their object by a necessary and blind selection which is based upon chemical affinity. The second kind of selection is proper to animals. Their actions attain their object by a selection which is as necessary as that characterized by chemical affinity, but it is not blind, but based upon the knowledge of the object and accompanied by the knowledge of the actions themselves by which the object is reached. This is spontaneous selection. The third type of selection is the most noble because it is neither necessary or blind, nor is it simply spontaneous, but is born of a deliberate and free choice, free in the selection of the object itself and free in the selection of the actions necessary to obtain it. This selection is proper to man.

There is no question here of a simple difference in degree in regard to the threefold selection analyzed; it is plainly a difference of kind and order.

II. *Analysis of Free Actions*

It is evident then from the voice of the individual and collective consciousness of mankind that the most distinctive characteristic of human actions is their freedom. They are not forced upon man from without, because the will is not subject to compulsion, nor are they the result of innate and intrinsic necessity such as we find in all other beings. How must we conceive this freedom of action, how can we explain it? Here we are again discussing a subject about which philosophers apparently will never agree. There are many who go so far as to deny, in spite of the manifest evidence of consciousness, the fact of human freedom for no other reason than because they cannot explain it on the basis of their philosophical assumptions. In truth, the subject-matter is difficult and some points in it will probably always remain rather obscure, but it is plainly poor philosophy to deny facts because they do not fit personal theories, or because we find no satisfactory interpretation for them. The only wise policy in philosophy as in science, is to ascertain the facts and then, if possible, to build a theory upon these facts.

A. POSSIBILITY OF FREEDOM

We will first study the matter from a negative viewpoint. Is it impossible to conceive the idea of free actions, *i. e.,* is there a contradiction implied in the very concept of free actions? If so, we would have to speak of a metaphysical impossibility of freedom. Many ancient and modern authors assert such an impossibility. Or, if the concept of freedom is not contradictory, are there any reasons for the assumption of a physical impossibility of freedom, *i. e.,* are there any laws of nature which make free actions impossible? Many scientists believe so. We will examine both objections to freedom.

I. METAPHYSICAL POSSIBILITY OF FREEDOM

We admit that the concept of freedom is not simple and easy, because a free action implies the assumption that it is in a sense a *"PRIMUS MOTOR"* or an *uncaused cause.* So far we have known only one really "primus motor," *viz.,* the creative will of God. Divine creation is a "primus motor" because it is the adequate efficient cause of a series of beings that evolve from one another, *i. e.,* where one being is the efficient cause or motor of another. These beings by their causative action are "secundi motores," the divine creation, however, is the "primus motor," because it does not depend upon another action as its cause. While it moves the whole series, it is not itself moved by another, *i. e.,* it has itself no efficient cause. In a restricted though true sense, the free act of the human will runs parallel to the creative act of the divine will: it starts a series of actions and their consequences as their first efficient cause, or as their "primus motor."

Of course, there are many and essential differences between the creative act of God and the free act of man: 1. In God will and nature are essentially identical, in man the will is but one of the many properties of human nature. 2. The divine nature is absolute for existence and action, human nature is plainly contingent for both existence and action. 3. There are a thousand limitations imposed upon the human will by the complex internal and external conditions upon which human actions depend, from which the creative will of God is altogether free.

While thus acknowledging, we must not exaggerate, the difficulty of conceiving self-determination or freedom of action. After all, the whole difficulty arises from the fact that our idea of causality is taken from sense experience, and, as a consequence, we are quite certain that in respect to the material universe, the interrelation of causes is ruled by the law of *determinism, i. e.,* each cause in the series is determined and conditioned in its action by the cause that precedes it. Therefore, the first link in the chain of causes is hard for us to conceive as appearing to be undetermined and unexplained by a preceding one. Yet it is quite evident from the fact of free will itself, and still more so from the nature of its causality, being a principle of direction and orientation, that the causative influence of the will is spiritual or supermaterial. But if so, it surely cannot be strange that the law of determinism, which rules material interdependence, should not apply to the activity of the will. On the contrary, we would naturally expect the laws of causality of spiritual actions to be different from those of material actions. If that is the case, there can be nothing inconceivable or incongruous in the analogy of the action of the free will of man with the creative act of God; it would seem rather reasonable to assume that a greater likeness exists between two kinds of spiritual activity than between spiritual actions on the one side and material on the other.

2. PHYSICAL POSSIBILITY OF FREEDOM

While the concept of free acts is admittedly difficult, because the only good analogy we have of it is that of creation by God, yet some philosophers make more of physical difficulties in explaining it. The greatest, in their mind, is to harmonize it with the law of the conservation of energy *i. e.,* the principle that energy is never lost or created in the world, but merely changed.

This whole difficulty is based upon a pure assumption: it is assumed that there is only one kind of energy in the world, *viz.,* physical energy, and consequently, that all energy, even will energy, is ruled by the same physical laws. But this is a mere assumption that involves the begging of the question: it fits the facts to the theory instead of fitting the theory to the facts.

In our previous studies we have found repeatedly that there are various kinds of energy, and that each kind is ruled by its own laws. Thus, mechanical energies are ruled by mechanical laws, physical, chemical, and psychical energies are ruled by physical, chemical, and psychical laws. We found that all these energies co-exist and work harmoniously together in the animal. The principle which explains their co-existence and co-operation in the same substance, being the same which we expounded in the preceding chapter, is that the highest energy directs and controls the lower as the principal cause directs and controls the instrumental. Consequently, while the animal's life is ruled by consciousness, yet the interplay of mechanical, physical, and chemical actions is not disturbed, but they are the very instruments of psychical life.

In man we find a still higher energy—the will energy, and while it is the directive and controlling principle in man, the laws of the lower energies are thereby not in the least affected, they are instrumental causes wielded by the principal cause.

If we bear in mind the proper interpretation of such a double causality concurring in one and the same action, as we explained in the preceding chapter, the whole difficulty vanishes. It is not a question of two actions succeeding each other, the one being the cause and the other the effect, as it would be between the hand and the pen in writing, nor is it a question of a joint effect of two distinct actions, as we would have in the case of a carriage being pulled by two horses. The will does not move the hand in the same way as the hand moves the pen. All the material energy necessary to account for the motion of the pen in writing is perfectly explained by the animal motor apparatus without any influence of the will. The whole object of the causality of the will is to use that material energy in a definite sense by giving the action its proper direction. There are not two actions, one spiritual by the will and another material by the animal motor apparatus, there is only one action, that of writing, which is both spiritual and material on account of proceeding from a double causality.

The illustration of the two horses pulling the carriage is still more to the point. The will and the animal motor apparatus are not two horses pulling the same carriage, but the will is the driver and the various organs of the body that are involved in writing are the horses pulling together. Just the same as the causality of the driver does not interfere in any way whatsoever with the causality of the horses in accounting for the motion of the carriage, the driver neither adding to, nor substracting from, the horses an ounce of their physical strength, so is the influence of the will as regards the action of writing. Both, however, are active in the best sense of the word, giving direction to the action, or as we express it more precisely and properly, being the principal causes of the same action in which the horses and the motor organs of the human body are the instrumental causes. There is only one difference between the two and that is in favor of the will in its influence over the body: while the horses are mere instruments in the action of the driver, and therefore, the double causality is more loosely connected and even separable, the double causality of the will and the human motor apparatus is much more intimate, the bodily organs being the organic and consubstantial instruments of the spiritual power in man.

B. EXPLANATION OF FREEDOM

Neither the metaphysical nor the physical difficulties in the explanation of evident facts must ever prevent us from accepting the facts. If our preconceived theories do not square with the facts, the only rational method is to abandon these theories and look for others that explain the facts.

We will offer a few suggestions that, we believe, will facilitate the comprehension of the freedom of the will.

I. CORRELATION BETWEEN MIND AND WILL

The best explanation of the freedom of the will is found, in our judgment, in the correlation between mind and will. While both faculties are plainly interdependent, the relation between them is not reciprocal in the same sense. Between the mind and the will the dependence is in the nature of *finality,* whereas the relation between the will and the mind is rather in the nature of an *efficient causality.* Though the mind exercises a great and positive influence over the will, this influence has not the character of a driving and compelling force against which there is no resistance, but rather a power of attraction and invitation against which resistance is possible. In the same way, the will exercises a great and positive influence over the mind, and even more so, because this influence, being in the nature of the power that a principal cause wields in respect to its instrumental cause, is an almost absolute controlling power against which the mind cannot prevail. As a logical consequence of this correlation it is clear that, while the mind is not free because the will has almost perfect control over it, the will is free because the only power of control to which it could be subject, is the mind, and as we have just explained, that power consists exclusively in an attraction and invitation. The reason is simple enough: *the mind in regard to the will exercises not an efficient but a final causality.*

If such be truly the nature of the correlation between mind and will, the freedom of the will finds a natural and logical explanation. The question that remains to be answered is a question of fact: Is our interpretation of the interdependence between mind and will correct, *i. e.,* is it based upon fact? We do not think there is any possible doubt about it. All we have to do in the matter is to examine our own consciousness. There we perceive very clearly that we possess control over our mind, we direct it in one sense or another as we please, or, as we generally say, we turn our attention to one subject or another. With almost as much facility and rapidity as we turn our eyes or our head to the right or to the left, we change our attention at will. Thus, we might say that the will controls the mind almost as perfectly as the violinist controls his violin.

However, the opposite is not true. Observing the happenings in our consciousness, we see very plainly that the mind does not control the will, though it does influence its action. What is the precise manner in which this influence is exercised? We shall arrive at a clear knowledge of that by an analysis of the act of the will as it manifests itself in our consciousness. The act of the will is plainly an act of *selection,* of a free selection at that. We decide upon a definite course—upon one out of several, or at least, we choose one of two alternatives, rejecting a proposition that comes before us or accepting it, affirming or denying it. Being a free decision or choice of one course rather than another, such a selection cannot be blind or instinctive but must be enlightened and deliberate, *i. e.,* it must be based upon the presence of an aim that gives the direction, and upon reflection that shows the relative value of the aim. But evidently, both the presentation of an aim and the judgment of the value of the aim are acts of the mind, and, being the means by which the mind enters into relation with the will, they express the influence of the mind over the will. To understand the nature of this influence is not difficult. The aim is nothing else than the idea of an object inasmuch as it appears desirable to the will, and the value of the aim nothing else than an intellectual viewpoint of the same object inasmuch as it possesses a measurable attraction for the will or is a motive, *i. e.,* is able to move the will. This power to move depends upon the degree of its desirability. An aim, however, no matter how desirable and attractive, does not and cannot determine the action of the will, because there are always in the mind a great variety of aims and a still greater complexity of motives, and it is precisely the act of the will to determine the choice of the aims and motives.

From the foregoing analysis certain conclusions showing the correlation between mind and will are inevitable. Some explain the influence of the will over the mind; the others, the influence of the mind over the will. In the first place, the controlling influence of the will admits of no doubt. It is *a direct ontological influence.* It is even more than that of an efficient causality over its effect. It is, indeed, paramount as it is in the nature of the influence which the principal cause possesses over its instrumental cause. The will is the horseman on his horse or the pilot on his ship.

Very different in character is the influence of the mind over the will. It is not direct and ontological, but *indirect and moral,* because it acts on the will by presenting to it its object and offering it various viewpoints of that object. It is to the will, what the road-sign is to the traveler, and what the marine maps and the compass are to the sailor. It is like a friend that inspires the traveler with the narrative of the beauties of his destination, and warns him of the hardships and dangers of his journey, while encouraging him with the hope of the oases on the roadside. Thus, we see clearly that the influence of the mind over the will, though only indirect and moral, is very powerful, and in a sense necessary, because, being a faculty of selection, the will could not act properly. *i. e.,* rationally, without the mind, having no object to select, no aim to strive for. But however great and necessary this influence of the mind be over the will, it does not compel or determine its action, and therefore, its action is essentially self-determined. The will is so free that it may reject the light presented to it by the mind, thus acting as foolishly as the horseman who would turn his eyes away from the road-sign, or as the navigator who would throw into the ocean his compass and his marine maps. Hence, the human will may imitate the proverbial despot at any time, acting without any objective reason: "Stat pro ratione voluntas."

2. RELATION OF THE WILL TO ITS OBJECT

Another consideration of decisive value for the comprehension of free actions refers to their object, and not to the object alone, but also to the manner in which the object is seized by the will. The force of this argument will be best appreciated when the object of the will and the manner in which the will seizes it, are compared with the object of sense appetitions and the manner in which their object is seized.

In sense appetition the *material* object is the objective concrete reality, inasmuch as it is assimilated by sense experience, and the *formal* object is that very same concrete reality present in consciousness, inasmuch as it appears desirable to some one of the various senses. Consequently, it is a *sense object, a material good.* The manner in which the senses appropriate that good enhances the fact of its material nature. As soon as the object is perceived by the senses, its desirability or undesirability is felt immediately and instinctively by means of another concrete organic function—the sense discrimination, and again, this organic function leads directly without any possible break to its acceptance or rejection and the consequent muscular reaction which simply expresses that acceptance or rejection. Here we have *one continuous series of organic and, therefore, material actions,* each one determined absolutely by the one preceding it, from the sense impression caused by the object to its seizure by the muscular reaction. This uninterrupted chain of causal connections is accounted for by the fact that the object is a concrete sense good.

In respect to rational volitions both the object and the manner of seizing it are radically different. Their *material object,* being the *abstract idea* in the mind, is not and cannot be the product of a sense function, but must be the product of an intellectual and spiritual function, and its *formal object* is the same abstract idea, inasmuch as it represents a *desirable aim, i. e.,* an object which is considered a means of completing and perfecting human nature in some way, or, as we express it properly, it is an *abstract good.*

The manner of its appropriation is equally different. Of course, the original starting point is necessarily the same, since all food for the mind and will must come through the senses. But the series of sense functions suffers an absolute break, or at least an interruption incompatible with a chain of purely material actions. The moment the object of the sense perception is apprehended by the mind, the series of sense functions comes to a complete stop. *The function of sense discrimination* which would necessarily follow in the mere animal, *is superseded in man by the function of mind discrimination, i. e.,* the desirability or undesirability of the object becomes a matter of intellectual reflection till the will determines its decision and by this determination sets the animal motor apparatus again in motion. Evidently, it would be absurd to claim that the reason or motive which is the only possible causative factor in question, determined the will in the manner of an efficient cause, because, being but a desirable aim or motive in the mind, *i. e.,* an abstract good, it cannot exercise any function or produce any action. In other words, *the influence of the abstract good* which is the object of the will, is not direct and ontological, but indirect and moral, and consequently, its causality is not and cannot be in any sense that which is proper to an efficient cause which alone determines an action, but is *that of a final cause which draws and guides the action in a definite direction.*

If we bear these considerations in mind we shall be able to answer the objection of some philosophers who have thought that man in acting must always act upon the stronger motive and therefore, cannot be free. This is a mistake, the facts speak differently. While it is true, of course, that the will, if it acts according to its nature, *i. e.*, rationally, cannot act without a motive, *i. e.*, the will has for its proper object the abstract good, and therefore, must pursue some good when it acts, yet in this life there is never offered to the will any object which is good from every viewpoint, and consequently, the will by turning the mind to a reflection of the unsatisfactory viewpoint, may reject any object. Thus, the will is free to decide affirmatively or negatively in any question whatever. Even when there is no apparent objective reason for a decision, the will can, as we said above, take its own act as a motive to act, and thus decide simply to come to a decision, to break a suspense.

CHAPTER FOURTEEN

THE NATURE AND ORIGIN OF MAN

The Various Human Functions and Their Interrelation

In the two preceding chapters we have described and analyzed the phenomena of human life in so far as they are distinct from those of the mere animal. From this study we concluded that there are two kinds of elements clearly distinct from each other, the intellectual and the volitional. To account for these elements we were compelled to assume in man two specifically distinct characteristic functions, that of the intellect or mind, and that of the will—the "appetitus rationalis" of the scholastics. They appear to be specifically distinct because their specific and proper object is, while materially the same, formally the very opposite: *the mind function is the abstract apprehension of the concrete reality, the will function is the concrete realization of abstract aims.* However, they are closely related to each other because they are interdependent in their action, both being subordinate to human nature as a whole. As the result of the intellectual function we have an aim present in the mind, *i. e.*, an object that is judged to be desirable as a factor that would complete and perfect human nature in some respect. Such is the distinctive work of the intellectual function in its relation to the will. The distinctive work of the volitional function is to start a series of actions the general object of which is the actual attainment of that aim in the mind. In other words, the intellectual function produces the aim in the abstract, the volitional function initiates the realization of the aim in the concrete.

The Emotional Phenomena in Man

In modern books on philosophy much is said of a third distinct function in man—the emotional, as it is assumed that the distinctive human elements are based upon a threefold faculty: that of knowledge, appetition, and feeling. With Aristotle and the scholastics we believe that this is a mistake. What we said in a former chapter is as applicable to man as it is to the animal. Every conscious function is accompanied by a certain tone of feeling—a passive affection of the conscious agent, expressive of pleasure or displeasure, of comfort or discomfort, and so forth. The differentiation in kind and degree is dependent upon the kind and relative perfection of the conscious action on one hand, and on the other, upon the innate emotional dispositions.

The emotions of joy born of the acquisition of knowledge are distinctively human inasmuch as they are related to the perception of beauty, which implies an object which is at the same time rich and complex and yet of a relatively facile and quick perception on account of a striking unity harmonizing the manifold elements. These we call the esthetic emotions or sentiments. They are distinctively human because they are based upon the power of abstraction, the knowledge of order, or unity in multiplicity. They presuppose a certain degree of education in abstractive perception in order to arrive at the knowledge of an important matter quickly and with a certain facility. Also the emotions which accompany volitional functions and which, generally speaking, are much more intense and are found in all men, are distinctively human and not animal, when the aim striven for and achieved is of an abstract nature. Thus, while emotions are not the function of a specific third power in man, they are an essential concomitant of the other human functions. They are an integral part of human nature and of paramount practical importance: to man's knowledge they give light and color, to his actions power and success, and to his character sweetness and fullness. They are to man what the aroma is to the flower.

I. The Nature of Man

Having described and analyzed human functions, it is now our task to determine their nature as far as it is manifested by the functions themselves. Once we have determined the nature of the functions, it should be easy to arrive at a knowledge of the nature of the agent that performs them.

A. THE SUPERMATERIAL CHARACTER OF HUMAN FUNCTIONS

The distinctive human functions, as we have seen, are of two kinds, the intellectual and the volitional. We shall study each kind separately, analyzing them carefully, or rather determining the result of the analysis we made of them in the preceding chapters. We shall find that the supermaterial or spiritual character will appear quite evident in the intellectual and the volitional functions, and it will be confirmed by a comparison of these human functions with the purely animal.

I. THE SPIRITUALITY OF MIND FUNCTIONS

We will first consider the nature of the intellectual functions. One of them we have studied with some care —abstraction. There are others which we did not analyze: the acts of reflecting, judging, reasoning. For our purpose that is not necessary, because the general object of all intellectual functions is the same: to find out and explain what a thing is, to know its constitutive, efficient, and final causes. All this implies abstraction. There may be a difference in degree, but the kind never varies: it is the perception of the abstract. But what is the abstract? As its very name indicates, it is a material object shorn of the conditions and determinations of its material existence, which is as much as saying, it is the object inasmuch as it is *IMMATERIALIZED*. *Abstraction is the process which accomplishes this immaterialization of a material object.* Evidently, such a function and the power in man which makes such a function possible are of a supermaterial character.

Looking upon the abstract from another viewpoint we come to the same conclusion. Surely, to perceive the abstract is to perceive an object which is not concrete, since abstract and concrete are contradictory terms. It is evident that only the concrete, and not the abstract, is accessible to the material senses and, therefore, not the abstract, but *the concrete alone can be seized by sense organs.* Hence, abstractive knowledge cannot be the function of a sense organ, it cannot be a material function at all, but must be in its very nature supermaterial or spiritual.

This conclusion is confirmed by an analysis of the act of *reflection*. When we speak of reflection we refer to two distinct acts of the mind:

We reflect—from "reflectere": to turn back—when we turn our mind back upon an object already known in order to know it better. Reflection in this sense is the ordinary means to increase our knowledge of things. Again, we reflect when we turn our mind back upon ourselves, as when we think our own thoughts and reflect upon our own reflections. This is reflection in the strict sense in which we take it here. Such a turning back upon one's self, where the subject becomes also the object of the same act, is absolutely impossible in a material action, which is by its very nature transitive, *i. e.,* is either one body acting upon another body, or one part of a body upon another part.

Here we must bear in mind what we said about immanence in respect to the nature of vital functions. Those functions are plainly material and yet we called them immanent, and so they are in a very proper and legitimate sense. Cause and effect of the functions are in one and the same being: the same being assimilates and is benefited by the assimilation. Such is immanence in a broad sense. But here we take it in a strict sense. While the function of nutrition in its totality is immanent, each part action of it is plainly transitive, because each part of it is accomplished successively in another part and organ of the body. Not so the action of reflection. Here it is the thought thinking itself and reflection reflecting itself. You cannot divide a thought or a reflection into parts and then assert that one part of it thinks of the other. Such a division is clearly impossible, and consequently, such an assertion would be absurd. Besides, such a reflection would no longer be a reflection. Hence, reflection being strictly immanent, and strict immanence being impossible in a material substance, *i. e.,* a substance constituted by quantitative parts, *the fact of reflection in man proves beyond question the supermateriality of the mind.*

By the power of reflection, by which man is able to take himself for the object of his knowledge, the fact *of self-consciousness* is explained. Animals, too, are conscious; indeed, all specifically animal acts are conscious acts. But they are not self-conscious, which implies an act of strict immanence, and thus *the ability of self-consciousness in man is another evidence of a spiritual function of knowledge in man.*

2. THE SPIRITUALITY OF WILL FUNCTIONS

We proceed to examine the nature of the volitional functions. According to our analysis of volitional functions their proper and specific element is a free decision, of which is born a series of actions which are the means selected for the attainment of a definite aim, *i. e.,* it is a free teleological decision. Teleological determinations and selections we have met with before we came to study man. We met them first in inorganic bodies, where they are expressed especially by chemical affinity. In plants we notice them much more clearly because the great complexity of the constitutive and functional elements demands an enormous selective and determinative power in order to insure the life and well-being of the organism. A new and striking element is observed in the teleological determinations and selections of animals: they are based upon consciousness, and consequently, they are spontaneous and therefore, superphysical and superchemical. However, they are still material, ruled by the iron law of causal interdependence, *i. e.,* by *determinism*, in consequence of which an action is conditioned by the one that precedes it and conditions the one that follows. Only in man this law of determinism that rules the interaction of all things material, ceases to act in the same absolute sense. *In him the teleological determinations and selections are free decisions which have no efficient antecedent but only an aim in the mind* which shows their way and illumines their goal, as we have amply shown in the preceding chapter. If such is the case, *i. e., if human volitions are not subject to the laws of matter, evidently they must be of a supermaterial or spiritual nature*.

Here again, we have a plain confirmation of the supermaterial nature of the will functions in the fact that also *the will is capable of reflection*: we can take and often do take our own volitions as the aim of our volitions, *i. e.,* we can decide on a matter, and often do, for no other reason than to come to a decision. But as explained, such an identification of subject and object in the same act is unthinkable in a mere material agent because it is strictly immanent. Thus, it happens that in the same way as the mind is able to reflect upon itself, taking itself as an object distinct from any other, and thereby becomes self-conscious, so also the will is able, not only to direct the mind and determine the whole animal organism, but to determine and direct itself and thereby it becomes *self-determinative* and *self-directive*. *This evident capacity for self-determination and self-direction is another plain evidence of the spirituality of the will.*

3. COMPARISON BETWEEN SENSE AND MIND FUNCTIONS

There is another argument, already mentioned by Aristotle, which shows clearly the fundamental distinction between the nature of sense functions and that of rational functions.

Sense functions, being material, are of a measurable quantity and therefore, their capacity has a definite limit. Experimental psychology has proved this scientifically. The greater the actualization of a sense power, the smaller is its susceptibility for further actualization; in other words, the more intensely a sense is stimulated, the less sensitive is it to more stimulation, till it reaches a point where its sensitiveness to stimulation ceases entirely.

If you put three lighted candles in a dark room and then add a fourth, the addition is noticed. But if you have ten candles and add another, the increase of light will make no impression upon your eye, you would have to add more than one, possibly three or four. If you have the light of a thousand candles, even fifty more would not be noticed by the eye. If the full sunlight falls upon your eyes, no addition of light, no matter how great, can impress it, for its capacity for stimulation has reached its limit.

The very reverse happens in rational functions. Their capacity for development is not a measurable quantity and consequently, it has no definite limit. Apace with its actualization and growth in development grows also proportionately its capacity for further actualization in general, and its potentiality for more diversified and more delicate objects. For instance, the deeper our intellectual knowledge of things, the better we are able to understand and discern even the more delicate points and obscure relations between them.

The same principle applies to will functions. The more we exercise our will the better prepared it is for further action. There is no definite limit in its power of development. *The only rational explanation for this plainly contradictory manner of procedure between sense and rational functions is the contradictory character of their nature*—the one is material, the other spiritual.

B. THE HUMAN COMPOUND

If, as we believe we have proved, mind and will functions are specifically distinct supermaterial functions, it is evident that the mind and the will themselves, *i. e.*, the intrinsic stable dispositions which explain the permanency and regularity of the functions, must be specifically distinct supermaterial faculties because the effects cannot be superior to their causes. Nor must these functions and faculties be identified with the substance of man because the substance is one and unchangeable, while the faculties and functions of man are manifold, various, and subject to continuous change.

Such are the main conclusions arrived at by the method of induction applied to the distinctive functions of man. We must not stop here; our purpose is to acquire a more profound and a more comprehensive knowledge, we want to know what man is as a whole, *i. e.*, we want to know human nature.

I. THE SPIRITUALITY OF THE HUMAN SOUL

The most superficial knowledge of man is sufficient to convince us of his animal nature. There is no mistake possible about this: he is a mammal. Consequently, about the lower substantial element of his nature there can be no doubt: it is the same materia prima that we found in all the inorganic and organic bodies. The same material elements enter his body as enter the body of mere animals. But what about the specific, determinative principle in human nature, *i. e.*, the forma substantialis? Evidently, it is here that the difference lies, and the difference is enormous. In cosmology, as well as in plant and animal psychology, we have found that the nature of a body is manifested in its properties because they are the natural means by which it realizes its proper object. Therefore, it is in the knowledge we have of the nature of the distinctive human properties that we must seek an explanation for the specific substantial determination which distinguishes man from every other being, *i. e.*, the forma substantialis, the essential, determinative principle in human nature. We found that these properties are the mind and the will. But if mind and will are essentially supermaterial or spiritual, it is evident that the forma substantialis in which they have their source and root, and which they naturally manifest in their functions, is supermaterial or spiritual. To affirm the contradictory statement would be absurd: spiritual properties cannot possibly have their seat and root in a mere material substance. Consequently, the forma substantialis in man, or the human soul, as we call it, is, speaking strictly and properly, of an essentially spiritual or supermaterial nature. Thus we have arrived at *the general conclusion which constitutes a clear verification of the scholastic definition of man as a rational animal; rational and, therefore, spiritual expressing the specific, and animal expressing the generic part of human nature.*

2. THE NATURE OF THE UNION OF SOUL AND BODY

We have proceeded so far building our arguments upon a perfectly logical basis, and yet we have arrived at an astounding conclusion, a proposition apparently contradictory, *viz.*, that *man is a body that is spiritual, and a spirit that is material*. How is such a union possible? What is the precise nature of this union?

We confess that we have nowhere found a perfectly satisfactory answer to these questions and we do not think it will ever be found. But the lack of an adequate explanation must not prejudice us against the facts. No matter how obscure or inadequate our interpretation, *the plain evidence of a real substantial union is not thereby affected.*

a. *Plato* thought the soul was in the body as a prisoner is in a prison or a bird in a cage. *Descartes* considered the soul as a sailor in his boat or a horseman on his horse. Such an external and accidental union is in plain contradiction with the facts as we find them in our consciousness. The only union that is *in harmony with these facts is an intrinsic substantial union,* such as we express when we say that the soul is the forma substantialis of the body, and that man is a rational animal. It is on account of such a substantial union that we may say that man is an animal, but an animal that lives and acts as a rational spiritual agent, or that man is a spirit, but a spirit that lives and acts in and through an animal body. There is no division between the animal and spiritual elements in man except by mental analysis, and as the spirit depends for all its functions upon the animal and the animal upon the spirit —their vital substantial interrelation is obvious. All the functions of man, the vegetative, sensitive, and rational, are interdependent because they are all plainly the functions of one and the same substance. The most obvious introspection shows clearly that it is the same agent who eats and drinks, who sees and hears, who reflects and decides.

b. Such is the evidence of our consciousness, and *such is also the evidence of objective facts.* I hear the voice of a friend, of a teacher : they awaken the noblest sentiments and the most spiritual ideals in me. However, materially, they are but air waves hitting my ear. Again, I open my mouth and speak, or I take my pen and write : what is deepest in my mind is communicated once more to material air waves or to a white surface of paper by means of material organs and instrumentalities. Surely, these facts of spiritual and material co-operation and interdependence are so evident that to deny them would be equivalent to denying one's own existence. Yet they are the natural expression of the substantial union of soul and body. Consequently, no matter what may be one's difficulties of understanding and explaining it, the fact of its real existence and effective action is incontestible.

c. How can we conceive the action of the soul, which is spiritual, in a body which is not simply a body but an organic, sensitive body, *i. e.,* an animal body? Is there first a forma substantialis that gives the materia prima the character of a body, and then a higher forma, the "anima vegetativa," that gives the body the character of a plant, and then, again, a still higher forma, the "anima sensitiva" that gives the plant the character of an animal, and last, above all others, the "anima humana," the spiritual soul, that gives the animal its human character? There were philosophers in the Middle Ages that proposed such a complicated interpretation. Not so St. Thomas Aquinas. According to the prince of scholastic philosophy, this would introduce a threefold substantial division in man, since the forma substantialis gives its specific nature to a body, and thus, man would possess four specific natures, one on top of the other, *viz.,* inorganic, vegetative, sensitive, and rational. Therefore, the only acceptable solution is that the spiritual soul is the exclusive forma substantialis in man, and that the power of the lower functions is included in, and exercised by, the spiritual soul in a similar sense as a higher force includes a lower and a larger number includes a smaller.

3. THE INTERACTION OF SOUL AND BODY

a. The first and fundamental interdependence between soul and body results from the part they play respectively in the constitution of the human substance. The body is the passive, determinable element, the potential part of human nature which is substantially actualized and specifically determined by the soul. Evidently, we take body here not in the sense of the materia prima, the common underlying element of all bodies, but as the "materia disposita," *i. e.,* the organism so prepared as to be capable of receiving the soul as its determinative and specific principle. The part the soul plays in the constitution of man is the very opposite. Its object is to inform and animate the body, *i. e.,* to actualize and vitalize it, to communicate to it the powers of sense as well as of mind, in other words, to determine it as a living and animate organism and to specify it as man.

Bearing in mind this mutual rôle of body and soul, there can be no doubt about their reciprocal substantial interdependence. The body is substantially deficient without the soul because it lacks the essential principle which alone can constitute it a human body. But also the soul is substantially deficient, because without the organism which it is its main object to vitalize, animate, and rationalize, it lacks the natural subject in which to exist and act as a human soul. However, there is this difference: the body's dependence as regards the soul is absolute, as without the soul it is not substantially and specifically determined, and no being can have existence without substantial and specific determination because only the concrete being can exist, and a being to be concrete must clearly be a substance of a certain species. The dependence of the soul as regards the body is not of the same absolute nature: *while the soul can constitute the human substance only in and with the body, yet, being supermaterial or spiritual by nature, it cannot be intrinsically dependent upon matter for its existence on account of its essential superiority to matter, and being specifically determined in its being, there is no reason why it should not be capable of enjoying an independent existence.*

b. Besides this fundamental interdependence between

body and soul, based upon the part they mutually play in the constitution of the human substance, there is another interrelation between them which is just as important though less profound. It refers to the complex character of human activity and the part which corresponds to the soul and body respectively in this activity.

Little observation and reflection are sufficient to show that human activity is never that of a spiritual being or that of a mere body. While it shares in the dignity and power of a spiritual agent, it is likewise affected by the natural limitations and imperfections of a material agent. The highest and noblest productions of the human mind demonstrate upon close examination their material origin, and on the contrary, the most trivial exercise performed by some part of the bodily organism may be consecrated by sublime ideals which they express or serve. It is not difficult to comprehend the reason for such a mutual interchange and reciprocal communication of properties and attributes between body and soul. Let us bear in mind in this connection the interdependence of the intellect and the imagination which we discussed in chapter twelve, and the interdependence of the will and the animal motor apparatus which we expounded in the last chapter. It cannot be strange that the same principles should apply also to the interaction of the spiritual and the material parts of the human compound when we consider it as such, and not the elements which compose it. Just as the product of abstraction and the realization of a purpose are the result of one undivided action by two concurrent causes, one principal and the other instrumental, so *human activity in its entirety and in all its parts is the one undivided issue of a double concurrent causality, the rôle of the soul being that of the principal, the rôle of the body being that of the instrumental cause.* Hence, in the same way as the ar-

tistic productions of the violinist are both helped and
hindered by the quality of his instrument, the violin,
so the spiritual soul meets with many aids as well as
with many obstacles from the body which is its organic and consubstantial instrument in its intellectual
and moral activity. As a compensation; in the
same way as the violin participates in the glory of its
player's achievements, so also, and even more so,
the body enjoys a participation in the value and
dignity of the spirit that animates, directs, and
uses it.

II. The Origin of Man

We have solved the chief problem of psychology—the
nature of man. In doing so we have paid no attention
to the attempts at a solution made by mechanicism or pantheism, because, in our opinion, they do not deserve it, as
they are not serious efforts to explain the facts. How
should a mechanical interpretation of the specific human
life be possible when, as we have found, not even mere
mechanical phenomena, such as the pressure of gas or
the universal attraction of matter, can be explained by
homogeneous matter in motion?

In the same manner, every pantheistic attempt at an
explanation must prove fruitless, because the most elementary testimony of our consciousness is plainly expressive of absolute individualism with not a tinge of
universalism: each mind thinks its own thoughts and each
will decides its own course, the universal mind and will
are nowhere apparent. Pantheism is a philosophical
dream, not a scientific theory.

The scholastic theory, then, is the only solution acceptable because it is based upon the facts, is never contradicted by them, and is both sufficient and necessary to
explain them. Man is a compound of body and spirit, in
which the spirit is the forma substantialis, *i. e.,* the specific determinative principle, and the body is the passive

and determinable principle. While it is the main rôle of the soul as the forma substantialis essentially to determine and specify the body, and thus to produce the compound—man—yet, being spiritual in its nature, it cannot be intrinsically dependent upon the body for its existence, and consequently, in its coming into existence or in its acquisition of existence it cannot be intrinsically dependent upon the physical act of generation, *i. e.,* it cannot be the simple product of the parent organism. Hence, the problem of the origin of man takes on quite a different aspect and importance from that of animal life.

I. THE ORIGIN OF THE HUMAN SOUL

Man is an animal, and the questions referring to the origin of his animal life must be solved by the same principles which apply to animal psychology. But in addition to, and above, his animal life, is his spiritual life, and the principles upon which a solution of the origin of his spiritual life must be based, cannot be the same as those which explain his animal life. The animal soul—the "anima sensitiva"—being intrinsically dependent upon the organism, is begotten and born with and in the organism itself and dies when the organism is dissolved. They are as inseparable and dependent upon one another as the forma substantialis and the materia prima in a plant or inorganic body, for the simple reason that the "anima sensitiva" is, though psychical, material in its nature. Not so the human soul.

Having demonstrated the spirituality of the soul, it is evident that its origin cannot be due to generation because generation is a mere material process which cannot produce a supermaterial effect. But there can be no doubt that, *if the human soul is not the product of generation, it must come into existence by creation.* There is no other solution possible. Generation is but a special form of evolution, and since evolution and creation are contradictory terms, as we proved in cosmology, if the soul cannot be accounted for by evolution, it must be explained by creation.

Furthermore, if we were to assume that the soul is begotten in generation, we would attribute to matter the power to produce a spiritual being, but *an evolution of spirit from matter or non-spirit is equivalent to an evolution of something from nothing,* which is a plain contradiction.

There is another reason why the human soul must be considered the product of creation. The soul, as shown above, is capable of an existence of its own because it is intrinsically independent of the body—it is a spiritual being. A body because it has quantity can begin to be or cease to be by evolution, because, being essentially composed of parts, when its essential parts are acquired by the influence of external agents, it begins to be, and when one of the essential parts is lost, it ceases to be. Not so a spiritual being, because a spiritual being is devoid of quantity, has no integral parts, is essentially simple. Such a being can never begin to exist or cease to exist except it begins to be or ceases to be at once, instantly, in its totality. It either is or it is not, it cannot grow and develop its being gradually, one part after another, and lose it by an inverse process of regressive evolution. Such a manner of coming into existence at once in its totality is what we term the creation of a being. Since an act of creation is plainly not in the power of a contingent cause, but of the absolute cause alone—God,—it is clear that each soul is directly the product of divine creation.

2. THE ORIGIN OF THE HUMAN COMPOUND

From the principles evolved so far in our study of the nature of the human soul, we have drawn the logical conclusion that its origin is due to creation by God. There is no other possible interpretation of the origin of the spiritual part of the human compound. However, there are in this connection two other questions of great interest to the philosopher. What is the relation between the act of God creating the soul, and the process of human generation in which the organism takes its origin? Again, what is the relation between the creation by God of the first human soul, and the organism which it was to animate and humanize?

a. We know from animal psychology that the new organism is the product of the parent organisms. The question arising is this: is this new organism in its first stages of evolution of a vegetative or animal nature? Or, is it from the very beginning, while it is still a monocellular organism, a human being with a rational soul? Some of the great scholastics, St. Thomas included, thought that the organism in its initial stages was neither human nor animal but vegetative, and that only when the vegetative organism was sufficiently developed, an animal soul would replace the vegetative forma substantialis, and that finally when the organism had reached the limit of animal capacity, the spiritual soul created by God would replace the animal soul. Their arguments were based upon the general principle of Aristotelian philosophy that in every substantial transformation the new forma substantialis replaces the preceding one when the condition of an evolving body demands it and not before. The body thus disposed and prepared for the reception of the new forma was called *"materia disposita."* Today this opinion is not shared generally. However, to us its ground appears solid and we have nothing better to put into its place.

To claim that the divine intervention is effected at the moment of conception, when the new organism in its monocellular form starts its distinctive individual life, is a mere assumption for which no philosophical reason is given. The phenomena of the new organism as discovered by embryology seem to confirm absolutely the opinion of the old scholastics.

b. The second question of concern to the philosopher in this respect is that of the origin of the first human organism. Did God, when He created the first human soul, take an animal organism already prepared by the natural evolution of a thousand or a million generations, or did He create the human organism from nothing? Evidently, this question cannot be solved a priori, its solution must be founded upon the facts of the case. So far, our knowledge of the facts is not sufficient to justify any definite assertion either one way or the other. There is, however, no intrinsic impossibility, not even improbability that God should not have used an existing animal organism as the body into which He infused the spiritual soul at the production of the first man. It would appear to us rather that there are reasons which create a probable opinion for the other side. We will mention two: 1. It is evident that God is not jealous of the work of His creatures. He does not interfere except when necessary, *i. e.,* where the powers of contingent causes are insufficient to produce the necessary effect. From the reasons adduced in our discussion of the origin of the animal, it would seem that natural evolution would account to a great extent for many perfections of the animal organism. 2. The reasons which are the logical basis of the opinion of the great scholastics that the spiritual soul is not infused into the new organism at the time of generation but at a later period when the organism is sufficiently prepared, would lead to the same conclusion in respect to the creation of the first human soul.

Against these reasons for an intrinsic probability for animal progenitors of the organism of the first man it is alleged that the traditional view is contrary, and that the dignity of man as a rational creature, destined from the beginning to the still higher dignity of the divine sonship, demanded the direct creation also of the animal organism. We frankly confess, we can see no essential difference between an organism created by God directly or indirectly. In the book of Genesis we are told that God did not create the body, but formed it of the slime of the earth. The argument from tradition, of course, has some weight, but is not conclusive. It is but an argument from human authority, and it is of this argument that the great prince of Christian philosophers said: "Locus ab auctoritate humana est infirmissimus."

SECTION TWO

SYNTHETIC AND TELEOLOGICAL
PSYCHOLOGY

CHAPTER FIFTEEN

THE CONSTITUTIVE ELEMENTS OF THE LOGICAL ORDER

Place of Logic and Ethics in Philosophy

So far we have made chiefly an analytical and causative study of human psychology. We analyzed the distinctive phenomena of human activity with a double aim: first to determine their specific nature as distinct from the nature of mere sense phenomena, and secondly, to trace their history so to speak, *i. e.,* to discover their causal relations, defining both the immediate principles from which they directly proceed, and the fundamental principle—human nature as an hypostasis or the self-sufficient individual in whom they exist. From the knowledge thus acquired we drew some general conclusions about the origin of man.

In all this we traveled more or less on the highway of traditional Aristotelianism. While on some questions of detail we went our own way, formulating and solving them according to our own conception, in a general way we followed the order of problems as is customary amongst scholastics. Though we injected here and there new matter and more modern viewpoints into the traditional forms, we adhered faithfully to the old principles and methods. But now we come to the parting of the ways. Logic and ethics—the study of the order of intellectual and volitional operations respectively—are, as far as we are aware, commonly presented, not only as outside the scope of psychology, but as outside the scope of philosophy altogether. They are treated like distant relatives whose connection with the family cannot be def-

initely established, and for whom, therefore, no place is
reserved at the family board. Not wishing to be rude,
throwing them out of the house entirely, philosophers
group them loosely together and introduce them as the
practical branches of philosophy, *i. e.,* they are only step-
children—real Cinderellas in the household of their royal
mother.

No, logic and ethics are twin sisters and their true
mother is psychology. Why? Because, if human psychology is the philosophical study of human life, logic, the
science of the teleological relations of intellectual operations; and ethics, the science of the teleological relations
of volitional operations, are surely psychology. They
are not only vitally correlated to, and interrelated with,
one another, but also in a direct relation of co-ordination
and super-ordination with the analytical and causative
psychology, because, being synthetic in their method and
purposive in their object, they are the controlling and
aim-giving psychological studies. Like all true philosophy they are essentially speculative sciences because their
direct and proper aim is knowledge, and knowledge of
the highest speculative value. The simple fact that it may
be applied, and indeed, should be applied like all knowledge to action, does not destroy its fundamental scientific
character. To call logic and ethics *arts, i e.,* mere systems of rules of logical and moral activity, is to look upon
them with the eyes of the mechanic, not with those of the
philosopher.

Logic, the Synthetic and Teleological study of Intellectual Operations

Logic, then, is the synthetic and teleological study of
intellectual operations. It is synthetic because our point
of departure is the simple, and our aim is the compound:
we start with the intellectual elements, *i. e.,* the acts of
the intellect which we already know, and with these elements we hope to build up the complex structure of the
logical order. In the second place our study is teleological,

because, knowing the causal connections between the mental elements, we want to know their relations of finality. Consequently, while our former study was rather *subjective* psychology, because we studied mental life in its relation to itself and the subject in which it is realized, logic, and also ethics, is an *objective* study of mental life, for only by the determination of its natural and proper *object* can we determine its final cause.

There are *three elements of the logical order*: *concepts, judgments, reasonings; the first two are essential,* as without them no logical order is conceivable, *the third is integral,* as without it the logical order would be of the most simple kind and restricted within very narrow limits. The three elements are not co-ordinated but subordinated to one another. *Concepts are the material, judgments are the formal elements of the logical order, reasonings are the means, and judgments are the end.* The technical expression for a concept is *term,* for a judgment, *proposition,* and for the reasoning process, *syllogism.*

I. Concepts: *The Material Element of the Logical Order*

We already have a clear knowledge of concepts. They are the natural product of the first intellective act—apprehension. They represent objects, not as they are in their own objective individuality but as they are intellectually, *i. e.,* in the mind by abstraction. In logic, concepts are studied not in themselves, but in their relation to judgments, and therefore, they are considered not in their subjective reality as acts of the mind, nor in the subjective conditions of their production, but in their *object. i. e.,* in respect to their contents, or still better, in respect to their *representative value.* We call concepts terms because they are the *"TERMINI,"* the end points, to be joined by the judgment in a mental synthesis. Regarding their object, they are divided into various classes:

1. We speak of *concrete* and *abstract* concepts. Of course, there is really no concrete concept. We call it concrete when we consider it in relation to an hypostasis. Such is the term *man* against the term *manhood*. In this connection the concrete term is important as the *subject of a proposition, i. e., the term of which something is predicated.* Also abstract terms may be subjects; but on analyzing complex judgments and reducing them to the absolutely simple judgments upon which they are based, their *subject is always concrete.* Why? For two good reasons: 1. Logically, the object of the abstraction is taken from sense experience, which is always concrete; 2. Ontologically, the hypostasis alone is self-sufficient for existence and is therefore able to be the subject in which all other realities exist. Hence, it is but natural that also in the logical order, which represents the ontological, the subject to which the terms expressing all other realities are attributed, should be concrete.

   On the contrary, *the predicate of a proposition, i. e., the term predicated of the subject, is always abstract,* and it could not be otherwise because it represents but one element of the subject, and only the subject itself—the hypostasis—can be considered as having objective existence.

2. According to their contents, concepts are *simple* or *complex.* They are simple when their object is one element, *v. g.,* the concept of action against that of life or organic action. The term action expresses a logical element; that of life or organic action adds the elements of continuousness and immanence.

   In this respect terms vary greatly; we call them *specific, generic,* and *transcendental, v. g.,* man, animal, being. The specific term is the most complex because it expresses all the elements of a being except the individual determinations; the generic is less because it expresses the elements of a being minus the individual and minus the specific;

the transcendental term is simple because it refers to the being as a being without expressing its elements. The generic term, again, subdivides into the most generic, the least generic, and the intermediate terms, according to the smaller or greater number of the elements of the being which they express. The most generic expresses the highest or *supreme genus,* enclosing the smallest number of essential elements belonging to any category of beings; the least generic, the lowest genus, enclosing the greatest number of essential elements except the specific; and the others, the number of whose elements vary between the highest and the lowest, are the intermediate genera, *v. g.,* the highest: substance; the lowest: animal; the intermediate: living being, and body.

This supreme genus—substance—expresses the order of hypostases; but there are nine other supreme genera or orders of accidents called by the scholastics *CATEGORIES* or *PREDICAMENTS.* The ten categories are: 1. substance, 2. quantity, 3. quality, 4. relation, 5. time, 6. location, 7. action, 8. passion, 9. intransitive action, and 10. a passive state. As stated, transcendental terms are of supreme simplicity. They are called transcendental because they transcend all genera, and are attributable to all beings of all genera indiscriminately, as they are the predicates of being as such.

3. The division of concepts into simple and complex leads to what is called the *COMPREHENSION, and EXTENSION of concepts. Comprehension refers to the object, or the representative value of a concept, extension to the subjects to which a term is attributable.* The relation between the two is of an inverse order: the less comprehensive a term, the more extensive it is and vice versa. Thus, the strictly concrete term, referring to the individual, being the most comprehensive, *v. g.,* Peter, is the least extensive, it extends to one individual only;

whereas the transcendental term, being the least comprehensive, as it is absolutely simple, is the most extensive, it extends to all individuals of all classes.

4. Again, concepts are *adequate or inadequate:* adequate when they comprehend all the essential elements of their object; inadequate, when they do not. Inadequate concepts may be *distinct, clear,* and *definite,* or *confused, obscure, and vague.*

5. Concepts or terms are *positive* or *negative, proper* or *analogical.* A concept is proper when its object is known by its own properties directly or indirectly; analogical when its object is known only in so far as it possesses a likeness to an object which is known properly. Thus, life applied to the plant is a proper term, to the spirit, it is an analogical term. A proper term is either *univocal,* having one sense, or *equivocal,* having several senses.

6. Finally, terms are *opposed* to one another or not. In this respect they may be only different but *compatible, v. g.,* animal and rational; or *incompatible, i. e.,* exclusive of each other, *v. g.,* a square circle.

   a. Terms are *contradictory* when one denies what the other affirms: something and nothing. There can be no middle term. Privation adds an element: a denial of what could and should he, *v. g.,* sight and blindness.

   b. Terms are *contrary* when they are opposed as extremes admitting middle terms, *v. g.,* to laugh and to weep.

   c. Terms are *relative* when one implies the other: Father and son.

II. Judgment: *The Formal Element of the Logical Order*

The judgment is the formal element of the logical order. The logical order is based upon the relation between objects in the mind. In the concepts the objects are presented to the mind, they are the material element of the relation. *The mind perceives the relation and, aided by the will, enunciates it,* and this is the judgment. This relation we call true or false; true when the relation between concepts perceived and enunciated by the mind corresponds to the relation between the objects themselves represented by the concepts. Otherwise the judgment is false. Consequently, the judgment is as much the formal element of truth as of the logical order, for the logical order is the order of truth.

Expressed in language we call the judgment a *PROPOSITION.* A simple proposition is made up of two terms, the subject and the predicate, and of the auxiliary verb "to be," which links them together. A complex proposition is made up of various subjects or predicates, or also of various simple propositions. According to the adverb that binds such propositions together, we have different kinds: conjunctive, disjunctive, causal, conditional, and relative. From the logical viewpoint it is important to know that they can all be reduced to simple propositions, and therefore, the fundamental laws of a judgment apply to all propositions.

I. We have various ways and distinct terms to distinguish propositions from one another.

    a. Propositions are *positive* when the connection between subject and predicate is affirmed; *negative,* when it is denied. They are *apodictic, assertory,* or *problematic,* according as the attribution is declared necessary, certain, or possible. This is called *the form of the proposition.* As an example let us take the proposition: Man is free. Positive: Man is free. Negative: Man is not free. Apodictic: Man must be free. Assertory: Man *IS* free. Problematic: Man may be free.

    b. Propositions are *universal, particular,* or *singular* according to the subject of the proposition. This is termed the *quantity of a proposition, v. g.,* Universal: All men are wise, or no man is wise. Particular: Some men are wise. Singular: Peter is wise.

c. The truth or falseness of the relation between subject and predicate is spoken of as the *quality of a proposition.*

2. These distinctions are logically important in reference to the relation and *opposition* of propositions to one another.

a. Propositions are *equivalent* when they express the same meaning in different terms, *v. g.,* All men are mortal—No man is immortal.

b. They are *convertible* when subject and predicate are exchangeable without change of quality, *i. e.,* truth. This is possible in two cases in which both terms have the same extension, *viz.,* the universal negative and the particular affirmative, *v. g.,* No man is sinless—No one sinless is man. Some men are artists—Some artists are men.

c. They are *contradictory* when opposed in form and quantity, *v. g.,* All men are saints—Some men are not saints.

d. They are *contrary* when, both being universal, they are opposed in form, *v. g.,* All men are saints—No man is a saint.

e. They are *subcontrary,* when both being particular, they are opposed in form, *v. g.,* Some men are saints—Some men are not saints.

f. They are *subaltern* when opposed in quantity only, *v. g.,* All men are saints—Some men are saints.

The laws governing the opposition of propositions are these: If propositions are contradictory, one is necessarily true, the other false. If contrary, both may be false, but they cannot both be true. On the other hand, if subcontrary, both may be true, but both cannot be false. If subaltern, the truth of the universal implies that of the particular. The knowledge acquired by the application of these rules is called an *inference* as distinct from a *conclusion* which is part of a syllogism.

3. The most important consideration about judgments refers to *the nature of the connection between subject and predicate.* Is it necessary or is it contingent? In modern philosophy, especially since Kant, there is a great deal of confusion about this question. Based upon Aristotle's doctrine of the so-called PREDICABLES, the solution is simple and definite.

There are five predicables, or manners in which the predicate is attributable to the subject. It is attributable either because it expresses: (1) The whole essence of the subject, or (2) The generic part of the essence, or (3) The specific part of the essence, or (4) An element in necessary connection with the essence—the essential *property,* or (5) A contingent accident. All propositions in which the connection between subject and predicate is based upon the first four predicables are of cogent value in logic, because, when well apprehended, their simple simultaneous presence in the mind is sufficient to force assent. These judgments are called *a priori.* The value of the judgment based upon the fifth predicable must be shown each time by experience; therefore, these judgments are always *a posteriori.*

An example will show plainly what is meant by the five predicables. First: Peter is a man. Second: Peter is an animal. Third: Peter is rational. Fourth: Peter is free. Fifth: Peter is sick.

III. *Reasoning Acts: The Integral Element of the Logical Order*

When concepts are of utmost simplicity we have, as it were, an *intuition* of their nature, we know directly what their objects are, and when two such concepts are together in the mind we have a similar intuition of their connection, *i. e.,* we perceive the relation between them quickly and surely, and thus, we have *judgments of immediate evidence.* However, such concepts are few, and therefore, such judgments are also few, and thus our field of certain knowledge would be restricted within narrow limits if our mind had not an additional power—*the power to reason,* by means of which a proposition which is not evident in itself is shown to be evident indirectly. Such an act of reasoning is expressed formally in a SYLLOGISM.

A. THE NATURE, STRUCTURE, AND VALUE OF SYLLOGISMS

1. The *NATURE of the reasoning act* is not hard to understand. We have a proposition in which the connection between subject and predicate is not evident. We want to make sure of it, *i. e.,* discover its evidence. What must we do? We must analyze and simplify the subject of the proposition, because the reason why we do not perceive the connection clearly is, generally speaking, the complexity of the subject, since the predicate, being more abstract, is also more simple. We simplify the subject by analysis, retaining the more generic elements of its contents. Thus, we have a third term. Of course, the subject and this new term are related to one another since it is taken from the subject. Now we compare it with the predicate, and if the connection between it and the third term is apparent, we have achieved our aim, *i. e.,* the relation between the subject and the predicate of our proposition has also become evident, because, if two terms are like a third, they are themselves alike.

Let us illustrate this. The proposition: Man is mortal, is supposed to be inevident. We analyze the subject, man, retaining the generic element, animal; or, if the connection is not yet clearly apparent, a still more generic element, organism. This is our third term to which we compare both subject and predicate. There is no doubt about the connection of the subject and the third term: Man is an organism. Now we take the predicate: an organism is mortal. About this also there can be no doubt: as soon as we put the two ideas, organism and mortal, together, we perceive the necessary connection, because life, the function of an organism, depends on manifold internal and external conditions which are not absolutely constant nor are they found everywhere. But if organisms are mortal and if man is an organism, our first proposition: man is mortal, has become evident, because this last proposition is implicitly and potentially contained in the first two, just the same as an effect is contained in its cause.

The important points to bear in mind regarding the nature of a syllogism are three: 1. A third term as a term of comparison must be found. 2. It is found, generally speaking, by analysis of the subject, and 3. The necessary connection between the third term and both the subject and the predicate must be evident.

2. Such being the nature of the reasoning act, we can understand the *STRUCTURE of a syllogism* and the technical terms applied to its elements.

A syllogism contains THREE propositions with THREE terms, no more and no less. The proposition to be proven is the *CONCLUSION.* Its subject is the *MINOR TERM,* its predicate, *THE MAJOR.* Minor and major refer here to the extension of terms. The third term is the *MIDDLE TERM.* The middle term must never be found in the conclusion, but must appear either as subject or as predicate in each of the other two propositions, which are called *the PREMISES*. The other subject or predicate in each premise is either the minor or the major term, which gives its own name to this premise. Consequently, the premise in which the minor term figures is called *the minor premise,* that in which the major appears is called the *major premise*. Again, the two premises together are called the *ANTECEDENT,* and the conclusion, the *CONSEQUENT* of the syllogism.

Such is the form of the regular syllogism. In practice we often abbreviate it, omitting either the minor or the major premise or adding either the one or the other to the conclusion as incidental propositions. At other times we complicate our syllogisms by combining two or three and even more into one structure.

To illustrate our meaning we present the above syllogism in an abbreviated form: Man is mortal because man is an organism.

Let us add as an illustration the same argument in more complex form involving various syllogisms: Man is mortal because man is an animal; animals are mortal because they are organisms; organisms are mortal because life is the function of the organism, and organs depend for their functioning on various subjective and objective conditions, and the objective conditions for life are not found everywhere available to the organism nor are the subjective conditions of the organism absolutely constant.

However, it is important to notice that the same fundamental laws apply to all syllogisms, whether abbreviated or complicated. Whenever in doubt about their demonstrative value, all we have to do is to transform them into regular syllogisms.

3. There is a tendency amongst modern scientists to minimize the *VALUE of the syllogism*. However,

such a tendency can only be accounted for by a grave misunderstanding of the nature of the syllogism as the formal expression of the act of reasoning. It is a plain matter of fact that the great mass of our knowledge is not immediately evident, but comes to us by reasoning, and consequently, syllogisms in some form or other are of the highest practical importance. Of course, it is perfectly true that the simple knowledge of the seven rules generally given by logicians for the construction of syllogisms does not produce thinkers. Their value is more negative than positive, more critical than constructive, *i. e.,* they facilitate the detection and refutation of errors.

B. THE GENERAL LAW OF SYLLOGISMS AND ITS INFRACTIONS

The general law governing syllogisms which includes all other rules is this: *THE PREMISES MUST BE TRUE AND THE CONCLUSION MUST BE A REAL CONCLUSION, i. e.,* must follow logically from the premises; and it cannot follow logically from the premises unless it is potentially contained therein. Infractions of this rule are *PARALOGISMS* or *FALLACIES*. When they are perpetrated intentionally we call them *SOPHISMS*.

To understand how it is possible that even scientists and philosophers are the victims of logical fallacies, it is well to bear in mind that it is in the very nature of a judgment that the will has a share in it. The mind perceives the relation between two concepts, but the will is the decisive factor: it shifts attention as it pleases and decides, *i. e.,* affirms or denies when it pleases. It is unfortunately true that even the scientist's will is not exclusively influenced by purely intellectual motives.

1. We have repeatedly met with fallacies in our course. We will first mention the most common *FALLACIES OF DEDUCTION.*

a. *"Petitio principii,"* or *the begging of the question,* when what is to be proven is surreptitiously assumed, *v. g.,* when it is assumed that an eternal universe explains its existence.

b. *"Circulus vitiosus,"* or the *fallacy of the circle,* such as that of Descartes when he proves the certainty of clear knowledge by the divine goodness and wisdom, and the existence of God by the clear knowledge we have of the divine existence.

c. *The fallacy of non-causa,* when from simple concomitance or succession, causality is inferred: "Cum hoc vel post hoc, ergo propter hoc."

d. *"Ignoratio elenchi,"* or the *fallacy based upon the ignorance of the matter in discussion,* which is also realized when an argument proves too much or not enough, or is irrelevant, *i. e.,* beside the point.

2. To the fallacies of deduction we will add a few *FALLACIES OF INDUCTION*.

a. *The fallacies of observation.* Scientists often see things they like to see and do not see things they do not like to see. *E. g.,* the famous Bathybius of Haeckel, or biologists who do not see the difference between plant and animal life.

b. *The fallacies of interpretation.* From the mechanical phenomena which accompany all material action, scientists conclude that there is only one kind of energy in the world, *viz.,* mechanical energy.

c. *The fallacies of inductive inference.* Such are all generalizations without any abstract basis, *i. e.,* from particular cases. Its false source is the proverb: "Ab uno disce omnes."

CHAPTER SIXTEEN

THE STRUCTURE OF THE LOGICAL ORDER

OBJECT AND AIM OF THE LOGICAL ORDER

In the last chapter we determined the viewpoint of our present study of psychology as objective and teleological. After enlarging upon the elements of our intellectual life from this viewpoint, we are prepared to ask ourselves: what is this object, this aim of our intellectual life? To this question the answer cannot be doubtful. The object of our mental life is to build up the logical order, and the aim is to have this order built as perfectly as possible. But what is the nature of the logical order, and what is the criterion of its perfection? The logical order is the intellectual reproduction of the ontological, and the more faithfully the subjective represents the objective order, the more perfect it is. A few considerations will show the profound significance of this definition.

The objective or ontological world in which we live and of which we form the noblest element, is composed of concrete individual beings which have their distinct existence and action. These beings we seize with their total individuality in our sense experience. Thereby we acquire the knowledge or psychical reproduction of beings, but not of the world as a system of beings with interrelations and interdependence. Hence, this sense knowledge is not, and cannot lead to, logical order. From this sense reproduction of concrete beings our mind abstracts and produces concepts. Even these concepts do not constitute a logical order, they are only the material elements of it, because they only represent beings in the abstract as beings of a class. This is, indeed, a step in advance of concrete sense reproduction. However, concepts do not reproduce the manifold and complex interaction and interrelation of beings. This decisive step is made by the mind, when in judgment it approaches and synthetizes two concepts, and when in reasoning it extends and universalizes this synthetizing construction. Thus, a subjective reproduction of the objective world as a system is realized in our mind, and this we call the logical order.

A SUBLIME VIEWPOINT OF THE LOGICAL ORDER

The perfection of the logical order consists in reproducing faithfully, and as completely as possible, the real or ontological order. This is the highest natural aim of the mind of man. Why? Because the ontological order, as it exists objectively in the universe, is the created expression of the mind and the will of God, and in proportion as we succeed in building up the logical order in conformity with the ontological, we acquire the knowledge of the mind and the will of the Creator. The universe, then, becomes a gigantic work of art, produced by the hand of the Almighty, spread over the immensity of space and passing through the immensity of time, in which the infinite power and wisdom of God are revealed to us by the uncountable billions of elements composing it, reduced to a striking unity in the midst of the greatest variety, thus manifesting a harmony and beauty so perfect and marvelous that the great master-pieces of human art are but faint imitations and feeble shadows. Or, to use a simple and more proper expression: *The ontological order is the embodiment of the divine plan in the universe, the logical order is the human perception of that divine plan.*

I. Methods of Clarification

Aware of the object and aim of the logical order and, therefore, of its depth of meaning, and knowing also the logical elements that enter into the structure, our next problem is to find methods of intellectual architecture, *i. e.,* some practical way of procedure by means of which we may be better assured of a faithful and complete subjective reproduction of the objective conditions of the universe. There are two distinct kinds of such methods: One refers to the elements of the logical order, the other, to its construction. When we build a house, we first examine and select the material and then study the general plan and the detailed designs. In building up the structure of the logical order, we must proceed in the same way. First, we want to make sure of the material elements, *i. e.,* the representative value of the concepts which, as subjects and predicates, constitute the logical order. There are two methods at hand for such a purpose: The *definition* and the *division* of a concept or term. We may well call them *methods* of *clarification,* as their obvious object is to determine and thereby to clarify the exact signification of a term. Consequently, to obtain a clear knowledge of the representative value of our concepts, we first define them, and to clarify our definitions, we divide them.

I. DEFINITION

The definition of an idea explains its comprehension, *i. e.,* it tells us what elements are represented in the idea. There may be many elements or there may be few. The aim of a definition is not to enumerate them all; if necessary, that work is done by the division. The definition presents all the generic elements under one term, expressed in the lowest genus, and under another term, the specific elements. In this connection the lowest genus is called the *PROXIMATE GENUS, i. e.,* proximate to the species, and the specific elements as distinct from the others are called the *SPECIFIC DIFFERENCE,* because they establish the difference between genus and species. Hence, to give a definition of a being is to GIVE ITS *PROXIMATE GENUS AND ITS SPECIFIC DIFFERENCE, v. g.,* Nutrition is a vital action by which food is assimilated. Vital action is the proximate genus. Action would be the higher, and in this case, the supreme genus. The assimilation of food gives the specific characteristic of nutrition. Both together define it. It is not sufficient to give a higher genus because, while the lower genus includes the characteristics of the higher, the higher does not include the lower, and thus, the characteristic expressed in the lower genus would not be found in the definition, and consequently, the definition would be inadequate, it would not respond to *the basic law of a perfect definition: to be equivalent to the defined.*

Such a definition, while the logical desideratum, is in most cases not possible, because in the complex reality placed before our mind, our abstraction, *i. e.,* the production of concepts, is slow, laborious, and more or less imperfect. It is only when analyzed and decomposed into their elements that we see clearly and adequately what things are. Whenever this is not done, or cannot be done, we must give inadequate, accidental, descriptive definitions, *i. e.,* instead of defining what objects are, we describe and circumscribe them, pointing out sufficiently certain combinations of accidents which in their totality belong exclusively to the distinct objects which we have in mind.

2. DIVISION

When proper and adequate definitions are possible, and such is the case whenever our concepts are adequate, the definition itself is already a division: it divides the object into its generic and specific elements. But the generic elements may yet be very complex and obscure. To clarify them, we divide them into their natural constituents, giving the generic elements in their order, the supreme, the intermediate, and the lowest. Thus, applying this rule of division to our illustration, we would divide the concept of vital action into its genus, action, and its specific difference, life or immanent action. From this we see that the division is but the natural continuation of the definition. The two are inseparable elements of the same process, the object of which is to clarify and to classify our concepts. The greatest possible degree of clearness is reached when the division is pushed to the really simple elements of our concepts, *i. e.,* concepts that represent the transcendental attributes of being, or at least, the supreme genera or categories of beings.

3. SIMPLE AND SELF-EVIDENT KNOWLEDGE

The application of these methods of clarification leads to the possession of a perfectly clear knowledge, because, if persisted in, they make us ascend to the very elements of our mental life, *viz.,* truly simple concepts. Such are the concepts of the categories, and especially the transcendental ideas, which, on account of their supreme simplicity, are of supreme intelligibility, so that all that is necessary to assure their clear perception is to present them clearly to the mind. When such simple concepts are placed before the mind, also their objective relations are perceived directly and with perfect clearness, and the consequent judgments, *i. e.,* the affirmations or negations of such relations, are of immediate evidence. They are called *first principles.* We call them so because they are, indeed, the first and fundamental judgments of the mind and have a controlling influence upon all other judgments. Such are above all the *PRINCIPLE OF IDENTITY* : A is A, and the *PRINCIPLE OF CONTRADICTION* : A is not non-A. To this class of first principles belongs the proposition that serves as the logical basis of the syllogism: Two things which are like a third, are themselves alike; and the famous *PRINCIPLE OF CAUSALITY:* A contingent being needs another to explain its existence.

II. *Methods of Construction*

When judgments are of utmost simplicity, *i. e.,* when the concepts between which the connection is affirmed or denied, are themselves simple, we have propositions of immediate evidence. Such mental syntheses we form with the greatest facility and with no fear whatever of a mistake. The objects are so clear in our mind that we cannot but give our assent. But logical constructions are not always so simple. To make sure of our construction when the concepts are not quite clear to us, we need methods of construction. We might also term them methods of demonstration, as their object is to make a relation appear evident which is in itself inevident. *Propositions of immediate evidence need no demonstration and do not admit of any,* just as simple terms do not need a definition and do not admit of any. Why? Because both definition and demonstration must be based upon the fact of terms and propositions better known than those that are to be defined and demonstrated, but there is not and cannot be any clearer knowledge than that of simple terms and of propositions composed of simple terms. The great mass of our knowledge comes to us in propositions which are not only complex themselves, but are based upon terms of great complexity, *i. e.,* of rich comprehension. The reason for this fact is quite obvious: as we have shown above, the logical order must faithfully reproduce the ontological order of the universe, and the great manifoldness and variety in the universe is everywhere clearly apparent in the individuals themselves and their multiple relations. Therefore, such complex propositions not being of immediate evidence, the necessity of demonstration to show forth their evidence imposes itself. There are two distinct methods of procedure in demonstration: Either we analyze and simplify the complex reality as it comes to us in our sense experience in order to determine the nature of the constitutive elements—the *ANALYTICAL AND INDUCTIVE method,* which proceeds from the particular to the general; or we take simple concepts and their relations to one another, *i. e.,* simple and self-evident propositions as our principles, and by logical deduction we synthetize, *i. e.,* build up a system of propositions which we call science in the most proper sense; and this is the *DE-DUCTIVE AND SYNTHETICAL method,* by which we proceed from the general to the particular.

I. ANALYTICAL AND INDUCTIVE METHOD

We will first discuss the analytical and inductive method, as it has the right of priority logically and chronologically. The human mind is first analytical and inductive because its basic work is abstraction, and *abstraction is essentially an analysis and an induction.* The intellect finds in sense experience the complex reality of a concrete being and immediately analyzes and separates the elements. It puts the elements that vary on one side, and those that are permanent on the other. If on different occasions, by repeated abstractive actions on the same being present through sense experience, the same result is achieved, it forms an induction, *i. e.,* it attributes the constant variation of the one sort of elements and the constant permanency of the other sort to the very nature of the being, and decides that the one sort are contingent, and the other necessary elements of the being. Thus, the mind gains the knowledge of what things are, or, as we say more technically, it produces concepts of beings.

Such being the fundamental act of the mind as interpreted in Aristotelian philosophy, it is evidently absurd to claim, as modern writers often do, that the inductive method is an achievement of modern times, due, above all, to the work of Lord Bacon. While Lord Bacon and others have done much to improve the practical procedure of the method, the method itself was used by the first man in his first intellectual act.

a. *THE RATIONAL FOUNDATION of induction, i. e.,* the reason that justifies induction is expressed in this syllogism:

MAJOR PREMISE: When in the changes realized in a being some elements constantly reappear the same and others just as regularly vary, the reason for this difference must be either intrinsic or extrinsic.

MINOR PREMISE: It cannot be extrinsic because the external circumstances are not always the same.

CONCLUSION: It must be an intrinsic reason, *i. e.,* a principle which belongs to the nature of the being.

b. The *LAWS* that regulate the application of the inductive method are chiefly three: 1. That of concordances; 2. That of differences; and 3. That of variations. In a former chapter in which we showed the real causal interdependence of the physical and psychical phenomena in sense life, we applied these three laws.

However, let us use another illustration. We have observed at various times that whenever A, B, and C are together, we have as a concomitant or consequent R. We suppose therefore that R is the effect of A, B, and C. To make sure we experiment, applying first the law of concordances: We bring together A, B, and C to ascertain whether R also appears. "Posita causa, ponitur effectus." Presenting the cause, we present the effect. If successful, we apply the law of differences: We remove A, B, and C to ascertain whether R also disappears. "Sublata causa, tollitur effectus." Removing the cause, we remove the effect. We are certain now that the cause of R is contained in A, B, and C. However, to make sure that each of the three factors is causally related to R, we apply the law of variations: We remove any one or any two of the three to find out if and how much R is thereby affected, and thus we have a complete inductive knowledge about the causal connection of A, B, and C conjointly and separately with R. "Mutata causa, mutatur effectus." Changing the cause, we change the effect. The application of the law of variations is necessary in all cases where the law of differences cannot be applied. For instance, in the study of gravitation where we cannot remove the factor of attraction.

c. *The VALUE of induction* is often misunderstood and greatly exaggerated. Scientists sometimes speak of it as the only scientific method. O course, it is fundamental in all intellectual work because it is necessary to lay the foundation of the logical order, but to lay the foundation, or to provide the material and the necessary conditions, not to raise the structure itself. By means of a primary kind of induction, such as is implied in every abstractive act of the intellect, we learn to know what things are, form our first and fundamental ideas, distinguish between beings, and between the elements of the same being. When simple observation is not sufficient, as often occurs in complex realities, experimentation with the application of scientific inductive procedure becomes necessary to find out whether certain phenomena are linked necessarily or only contingently with certain conditions produced artificially by the scientist. The result of such experimentation is the formulation of what is termed *the laws of nature, i e.,* regular and uniform connections between two sets of phenomena. The philosopher does not rest satisfied with the knowledge of the laws of nature, but seeks an explanation of the regularity and constancy of the phenomena and finds it in the very nature of the being in which the phenomena are realized. To express the value of the inductive method in one proposition we would say that *it is the scientific and philosophical profundization and extension of simple observation and of ordinary mental analysis and induction.*

From these considerations the signification of the analytical method for science and philosophy becomes apparent. The elementary material and conditions for the construction of the logical order are thereby prepared. Beings are revealed to the scientist in their concrete actions, in the concrete relationship between their actions, and between their own actions and those of other beings; to the philosopher they are revealed in the abstract, *i. e.,* the necessary connection between the inherent properties which explain the constant regularity of their actions, and the beings themselves in which they exist as accidents in their substance. Now, both the scientist and the philosopher have all that is needed to build the logical order; for its complete and perfect construction the inductive method is of little or no value because construction means synthesis, but the inductive method is essentially analytical.

2. DEDUCTIVE AND SYNTHETICAL METHOD

The deductive and synthetical method begins where the other ceases. They are not antagonistic but equally necessary for the construction of the logical order, the one supplementing the work of the other. The inductive method goes from the complex to the simple, from the particular to the general, from the effect to the cause, from the action to the agent. On the contrary, the synthetic method goes from the simple to the complex, from the general to the particular, from the cause to the effect, from the nature to the accident. Consequently, *the analytic method proceeds A POSTERIORI, the synthetic method, A PRIORI.* It is deductive because it proceeds by deduction, it is synthetic because it puts together the logical elements and builds up the logical order. It takes the logical elements, the simple concepts and the self-evident propositions which express the relation between these simple concepts, and by deduction arrives at propositions, from step to step more complex, or, what is equivalent, the general propositions are used as principles from which their particular consequences are logically deduced. The most perfect application of this method we have in mathematics. The principles of Euclid—simple, self-evident definitions, are placed at the head, and upon these principles the whole complicated science of geometry is built up by logical deduction. Again, the definitions of unit, number, addition, subtraction, and such similar ideas lead by logical deduction to the vast science of arithmetic. From this it appears evident that *the synthetic method is simply an extension and universalization of the syllogism.* What is done in the syllogism for one proposition, is done in the synthetic method for a system of propositions. Consequently, what the inductive method does for the accumulation of evident propositions, the deductive method does for the putting together or the synthesis of these propositions into the systematic structures of the logical order.

a. The logical *FOUNDATION* and the general *LAW* of the synthetic method are identical with those of the syllogism. Both are legitimate mental modes of procedure because, on account of the necessary correspondence between the logical and the ontological order, as ontologically the causes contain the effects and the nature of a being explains its phenomena, so logically the simple propositions contain potentially the complex, and the general principles explain the particular propositions that follow from them.

b. About its *VALUE* there can be no question. The construction of any science is impossible without it. The purely rational sciences need no other; all other sciences, philosophy included, depend necessarily upon it. While simple general judgments must be formed first and made sure of by analysis and induction, it is only by a methodical synthesis that these propositions can be joined together in logical sequence to constitute a well arranged structure or system of propositions, and all the sciences are such structures or systems of propositions.

While in theory we distinguish these two methods of logical construction very well, assigning to each one its own field of application, yet in practice they are so mingled and interdependent that there is hardly any mental operation of any consequence in which both are not applied with equal necessity. They compenetrate and supplement one another in logical construction as bricklayer and hod-carrier in the construction of a house. *Just the same as observation and reasoning are indispensable elements in any work of the mind, so are the analytical method which deepens and widens observation, and the synthetical method which extends and applies reasoning to a whole complex series of relations.*

III. *The Logical Order: Systematized Knowledge*

In definition and division we have studied the methods of making sure of the logical elements that are already in our mind; in the analytical method we have seen the scientific procedure of acquiring, and making sure of, new logical elements, in the synthetic method we have dwelt upon the manner in which the intellectual architect—the scientist and philosopher—puts his material together and builds up the logical order. But, what is this logical order, which is the aim of all thought and all intellectual activity? It is evidently, as already stated in the introduction to this chapter, a system or systems of coherent and interrelated knowledge which mirrors and represents subjectively the objective system or systems of interrelated phenomena and interdependent beings.

I. ELEMENTARY SYSTEMS OF KNOWLEDGE: THE PARTICULAR SCIENCES

The elementary structures of the logical order are the particular sciences. They have their origin in the methodical application of the mind to a certain subject-matter. The result of such an application is called a science when the being or beings and their manifold attributes and complex relations are studied from a special viewpoint which unifies and harmonizes the various propositions which enunciate and determine the attributes and relations of the being or beings studied. Consequently, *a science is a system of propositions referring to the same subject-matter studied from a special viewpoint.* The subject-matter is the *MATERIAL OBJECT*, the special viewpoint is the *FORMAL OBJECT* of the science. Thus, man may be the material object of a number of sciences if he is studied from different viewpoints, *v. g.,* human biology, human psychology, sociology, politics, etc.

The particular sciences are generally divided into rational, experimental, and mixed, with many subdivisions according to the manifoldness of their material, and the variety of their formal object.

Rational sciences are those which depend for their construction mainly on the deductive and synthetical method. Such is, above all, mathematics. On the contrary, we call experimental sciences those which are built up chiefly by the analytical and inductive method. Such are chemistry, biology, and most of the physical sciences. Mixed sciences, as their name implies, are tributary in their structure equally to the application of both methods. To this class belong astronomy and some other physical sciences, and chiefly all the historical, political, and moral sciences.

2. HIGHER SYSTEMS OF KNOWLEDGE: COSMOLOGY AND PSYCHOLOGY

The normally developed man does not rest content with the possession of the particular sciences. He studies the world from a higher viewpoint, anxious to obtain an adequate explanation of all the phenomena of the universe and their underlying causes. Thereby he produces a general or *SUPER-SCIENCE of the universe—PHILOSOPHY*. This super-science evidently includes in a sense all the particular sciences, as it takes from them the data necessary for its construction.

The philosopher studies the whole inorganic world in

cosmology, and the whole organic world in *psychology* from the philosophical point of view, and thereby constructs the two general sciences of which one gives the key for the synthetic interpretation of the particular sciences the subject-matter of which is the inorganic, and the other for that of the particular sciences the subject-matter of which is the organic universe.

3. THE SUPREME SYSTEM OF KNOWLEDGE: METAPHYSICS

Even the possession of cosmology and psychology does not satisfy perfectly the philosophical mind of man. When he finishes this double study, he ascends to a still higher plane—the transcendental viewpoint—and thereby creates a supreme logical system or science—*metaphysics,* which is not only a general or super-science but also a general or *super-philosophy.* Is the philosopher justified in thus crowning the logical order with metaphysics? Undoubtedly.

Let us bear in mind that the logical order is the intellectual reproduction of the ontological. It is true that the objective universe is composed of concrete individual beings and not of systems of individual beings superposed upon one another. However, we know very well that the individual beings which are, each and all, self-sufficient for existence and action, are systems of ontological elements, and that there is a manifold complexity and multiform variety in the combination of those elements. This complexity and variety in the constitution and activity of concrete beings is the ontological foundation for the logical distinction of specific, generic, categorical, and, at the top, transcendental being, which is the formal object of metaphysics. Consequently, the study of transcendental being has its proper place in human knowledge and it is precisely the highest as well as the most profound, because it is the most simple, and therefore, the most general—truly all-comprehensive.

CHAPTER SEVENTEEN

CRITERIOLOGY

Object of Criteriology and its Place in Psychology

Intimately attached to the study of the logical order are the consideration and solution of the criteriological problems. Like the logical problems, they refer to knowledge. Their object is the examination of the objective foundation and conditions of knowledge in order to determine its precise representative value. Here again, as in the study of the logical order, we must base our investigation upon the knowledge acquired by the analytical and subjective study of psychology, particularly upon the analysis of abstraction. Hence, the same as logic, criteriology is synthetical and objective psychology.

There are two problems in this connection which deserve our careful attention. The first is fundamental: it questions the very capacity of the human mind for objective knowledge. The second refers to the objective value of knowledge. The first problem arises from the fact that throughout human history there have been skeptics who denied the very possibility of any certain knowledge. The second problem has assumed great importance in modern philosophy, because, owing to the sensualist school of Locke and Hume, and the criticist theory of Kant, the tendencies of the modern mind are largely either positivist, or idealist and subjectivist.

I. The Problem of Skepticism

Evidently, it cannot be our purpose here to enter into any detailed discussion of skepticism. We will present the problem as briefly as possible and point out the principles that must guide us in solving it.

About the fact of our spontaneous knowledge and certitude of many things, there is not and cannot be any question. A doubt may arise when, upon reflection, we ask ourselves whether we have any objectively solid ground on which to base our spontaneous knowledge. Skeptics reply that we have not. The arguments for their position are of two kinds, one based upon so-called facts and the other deduced from assumptions.

Our parents, our teachers, our friends have led us astray, innocently or wilfully, in many instances. We have been induced to accept erroneous views many a time by our own faculties. Therefore, the wise man is the skeptic who will trust neither himself nor others.

To be certain about anything we must first prove it; to prove it we must have a criterion of knowledge, *i. e.*, a test proposition which we can apply like a touch-stone of truth; but this criterion of knowledge we will have to prove again by another criterion, and this again by another and so forth, which means we can never be certain about anything because we can never come to an end in proving it.

The nature of the arguments used by the skeptic manifests plainly the shallowness of his mind. Because we have been deceived either by others or by ourselves nine times is surely no proof that we shall be deceived every other time; and if in analyzing our knowledge we come to propositions which are so simple that their evidence imposes itself upon our mind, we need no other proposition to prove them.

Skepticism seems to be a disease of the human mind. Its natural causes would appear to be intellectual pride and impatience. Some people, especially the young, are super-inquisitive like Mother Eve and the wife of Lot. They would like to know everything knowable and a little more, and to know it quickly, easily, and perfectly. Hence, when it dawns upon them that human knowledge is at best imperfect and must be acquired slowly and laboriously, they begin to fret and are liable to fall a prey to skepticism.

I. DESCARTES' SOLUTION

Descartes, in his desire to defeat skepticism once for all, used the very weapons of the skeptic, advocating a method of doubt. He says, it is wise to doubt always as far as we possibly can, in order to be quite sure of our foundation of knowledge. To show the wisdom of doubt, he adds to the arguments for skepticism two more:

In my dreams I am certain of many things. But who knows whether I am not always dreaming?

When I am certain, it may be only the trick of an evil spirit in my mind.

Thus, Descartes doubts everything till he comes to his own existence. There he stops: Why, he says, I could not doubt if I did not exist. Hence, his famous phrase: "Je pense, donc je suis." Upon this fact of his existence he pretends to build his whole philosophy.

Descartes was wrong. If he had been consistent, he had no right to be certain of his own existence. How did he know that he was not dreaming? Or that no evil spirit was tricking him? What is his criterion? Oh, he says, I see very clearly that I could not doubt if I did not exist, and so I conclude that whenever I see anything very clearly, I cannot be mistaken. Why? Because God's goodness and wisdom could not permit that. But how was Descartes certain of God's goodness and wisdom, nay of God's existence? Because he saw it very clearly that there must be a God. But, again, how could he be sure he was not deluded by a dream or a malign spirit? Besides, that *he* saw it very clearly, is of little consequence to anybody else, and of no consequence to the skeptic. Not all, not even many see very clearly in respect to the existence and nature of God. Hence, Descartes' criterion is without value, as all its logical force is derived from a subjective knowledge of the goodness and wisdom of God.

Furthermore, his arguments in favor of methodical skepticism, if true, would be disastrous. If we had no objective reasons for discriminating between the consciousness of our dreams and that of our waking hours, or between our own mentality and the mental influence of a malign spirit, we would be necessarily doomed to intellectual shipwreck; there could be no means of finding a port of certain knowledge anywhere. Consequently, if Descartes was not a skeptic, it is exclusively owing to his inconsistency.

2. A DOGMATIC INTERPRETATION

A second solution to the problem of skepticism has been proposed by a large number of philosophers, especially Catholics, who oppose to the assertion of the skeptics about the hopeless incapacity of man to attain to certain knowledge, their own dogmatic assertion of the positive capacity of the human mind to attain to certitude. They proclaim that the admission without proof of a positive power for certain knowledge is an indispensable condition for fruitful philosophical work.

They are mistaken. They will not convert one skeptic. Their affirmation without proof is a surrender of their position. Their ground leads to intellectual despair. If they were consistent, while fierce dogmatists in practice, in theory they would be absolute skeptics.

The source of skepticism is precisely this—that in the opinion of skeptics the power of the mind to attain to any certain knowledge cannot be positively demonstrated. Consequently, as regards their fundamental principles, dogmatists and skeptics are perfectly agreed. If, nevertheless, they occupy extremely opposed positions, the fault lies with the former, who do not dare accept the logical conclusions which follow necessarily from their principles. The skeptics, at least, deserve respect for their consistency.

3. THE TRUE SOLUTION

In regard to the question of the capacity of the human mind to attain to certain knowledge, there is only one attitude justified, and this is one of neutrality. Positive dogmatism is not better founded than the negative dogmatism of the skeptics. Whether we are able or unable to know anything with certitude, we cannot and must not decide beforehand: let us first try and find out. What would we say if on the birth of a baby the doctor and the nurse started to discuss whether the baby had the power of digestion and assimilation of food? Surely, we would laugh at such an absurd procedure. They let the baby have its nourishment and very soon they know if it has the power of assimilation or not. So it is with our capacity for certain knowledge. The question is plainly one of fact and not of theory. We have used our faculties of knowledge since our childhood, and therefore, the question can easily be answered by each one for himself.

II. *The Objectivity of Human Knowledge*

We have disposed of the preliminary problem—the position of skepticism. The second and main problem refers to the objective value of knowledge. To understand the nature and importance of the problem, we must bear in mind the result of our discussion of the logical order. We saw that knowledge is constituted by two elements—the material element, concepts, and the formal element, judgments. Consequently, the problem of the objective value of knowledge is twofold: when we speak of the objectivity of concepts, we refer to the objective existence of the objects represented by our concepts, and when we speak of the objectivity of judgments, we refer to an objective reason or motive in the mind which induces us to predicate one concept of another. Evidently, the two problems are closely interrelated: the solution of the second depends absolutely upon the solution of the first.

A. THE OBJECTIVE VALUE OF CONCEPTS

It is in the very nature of a concept to be representative. What a concept represents we call its object. The question that arises in this connection is: Is this object of a purely subjective character, *i. e.,* is it an absolute and exclusive production of the mind, representing nothing except subjective conditions and dispositions of the mind itself; or is it of an objective character, representing also conditions and dispositions of beings which exist outside and apart from the mind? If so, how great is this objective value of our concepts, *i. e.,* how far are the objective beings represented in our knowledge?

Such is the fundamental signification of the problem. For the solution we must go back to chapter four, where we discussed the analytical and subjective psychology of human knowledge. There we pointed out that only two really serious efforts had been made to explain adequately the specifically human knowledge, one by Kant, the other by Aristotle, and their respective schools. Hence, it will not surprise us to find that here again, only two attempts at a solution deserve our serious attention, that of Kant and that based upon Aristotle's psychology.

I. KANT'S SOLUTION

To understand Kant's criteriology, we must bear in mind his psychology, because his psychology of human knowledge was excogitated precisely to explain the representative value of human knowledge. In Kant's mind all moral, religious, and metaphysical knowledge is of no speculative value because it is purely conceptual knowledge, and it has no objective value because it cannot be submitted to a personal test by sense experience. While Scientific knowledge is of speculative value because it is not purely conceptual knowledge, and it has objective value because it can be tested by personal sense experience. However, Kant knows that sense experience is individual and contingent, whereas scientific knowledge is universal and necessary. How can these two things be explained? Let us recall how Kant accounts for them.

Our senses are passive faculties, and when affected by an outside influence we have sense impressions. Impressions, however, are not yet knowledge, they represent nothing as yet. But then our mind reacts upon them applying to them the pure intuitions of time and space. These, being intrinsic, a priori forms, are anterior to all experience. They are like moulds through which the sense impressions pass and which are thereby placed in time and space, and become representations. They are representations of phenomena, *i. e.,* of the appearances of things, not of the things themselves. However, even these phenomena are still individual and contingent. Now the second reaction of the mind sets in, for, besides the two pure sense intuitions of time and space, there are in the mind twelve pure concepts or categories, like so many moulds through which, in this second mental reaction, the representations pass and thereby become scientific knowledge, *i. e.,* the representations are now universal and necessary. Why? Because these categories are a priori forms of the mind, are anterior to any experience, are the same in all minds, and this explains the universality and necessity of human knowledge. Thus, while Kant repudiates the innate ideas of the rationalists, yet in another form he introduces them in his psychology because the pure intuitions of time and space and the twelve categories or pure concepts—such as unity, reality, substantiality, possibility, and etc.,—are nothing else in reality.

It is evident that human knowledge would possess but a minimum of objective value if Kant's psychology were based upon fact. Sense impressions are due to external influence. What is the source and the nature of that influence? Is there any outside being having an existence of its own, and are we able to know anything about its objective properties? In Kant's theory of knowledge there is no possibility of solving these questions in the affirmative. Substance, accident, time and space, and consequently, extension, figure, motion, etc., are all subjective forms of the mind. Not based upon experience, they can have subjective and phenomenal value only. It is hardly necessary again to call attention to Kant's inconsistency. Had he been consistent, he would have been both an idealist and a pantheist; an idealist because all that is essential and significant in his theory of knowledge is purely subjective, and a pantheist because the only real foundation possible for the universality and necessity of his knowledge can be the assumption that the human mind is but a spark of the universal mind, or the pantheist god.

Consequently, the objectivity of our concepts admits of no satisfactory interpretation in Kant's psychology. The only objective feature in the elaborate intellectual process is the factor causing the sense impressions. But of the conditions and dispositions of this factor we are not able to know anything. Hence, the whole objectivity of our conceptual knowledge would be limited exclusively to the bare existence of an objective factor.

2. THE SCHOLASTIC SOLUTION

Kant recognized and proposed the criteriological problem better than any of his predecessors. It became the source and centre of his whole philosophy, which therefore, has been called *criticist philosophy*. While he grappled seriously with the difficulties of the problem, he was not able to conquer them. It is doubtful whether Kant was aware of the fact that a true and solid foundation for a correct solution had already been laid more than two thousand years before by Aristotle. Upon the basis of the Aristotelian psychology, a solution may be built which is in harmony with the facts and satisfies the requirements of the most critical mind. Here we must call to mind once more the interpretation of intellectual life which we gave in chapter four, since, evidently, any valuable explanation of the matter must have for its source and basis the facts of intellectual knowledge. In proposing our interpretation of intellectual life then, we had already in mind the special requirements of the criteriological problem. Even then we presented the two main points of the problem and the basis for an explanation—the objectivity of our knowledge and its absolute value. The explanation of the objectivity of our knowledge is based upon the scholastic interpretation of sense knowledge, and the absolute value of our knowledge is inferred from the scholastic conception of abstract knowledge. Let us recapitulate and determine the points at issue.

a. THE OBJECTIVITY OF SENSE KNOWLEDGE

Sense knowledge is the psychic intussusception and assimilation of sense objects. This vital function is realized by two causative factors—the subjective factor, the sense, and the objective factor, the external being or reality. The sense alone is powerless to act because it is essentially passive, an object from without must supplement its intrinsic deficiency by acting upon it. The result of the two concurrent causes manifests the nature of both, *i. e.,* that of the subject which knows and that of the object which is known. The nature of both is manifested in this way: while the function itself manifests the nature of the subject because it is its function, the nature of the object is manifested inasmuch as it is represented by the function.

Let us recall in this connection a former illustration. The eye is like a photographic camera, the ear like a dictaphone. We know that the light picture of the camera and the sound reproduction of the dictaphone are truly representative of the objects which they reproduce in a special manner. So are the senses with this difference based upon the nature of sense which is much more perfect than a mechanical apparatus could be : while sense knowledge reproduces the object just as really as a camera or a dictaphone, it represents it much more perfectly than a photograph or a phonograph could do, be-

cause a photograph or a phonograph, being physical light
and sound pictures, can represent only one aspect of the
object, while knowledge, being a psychical image, represents the total object with every aspect accessible to the
senses. Consequently, sense knowledge is really representative of an object, which is a concrete element of the
material world : it is objective in the strictest sense.

b. THE OBJECTIVITY OF MIND KNOWLEDGE

Such is human sense knowledge. It represents the objective world in which we live and of which we are members. With this objective world the mind enters into direct and intimate relation. It immediately seizes upon,
and assimilates, it in the process of abstraction. The objects as represented by the senses being complex, the
mind abstracts, *i. e.*, it takes one element of an object to
consider it by itself and apart from the others with which
it is united in sense knowledge, and thereby the mind
knowledge become representative, not of the individual
being but of a class. However, the simple object
which the idea represents, is not an element created or
produced from nothing, but taken from the complex object of the sense image, and consequently, it is just as
really representative of an objective reality as the sense
image itself.

This argument for the objective value of our conceptual knowledge is confirmed by the manner in which
the abstractive process is realized. Like the sense process, it demands a twofold cause : the intellect, the principal cause, and the imagination, the instrumental cause.
While the specific work of the intellect is subjective, *i. e.*,
assimilative, the specific work of the imagination is objective, *viz.*, the imagination presents to the intellect the
sense object which is the mental food. Here again, the
result of the combined action of a subjective and an objective factor must manifest the nature of both, and
even more perfectly than the concurrence of sense and
concrete object because of the more intimate co-operation of the mind and sense as principal and intrumental

causes. Just the same as the voice contributes directly, objectively, and powerfully to the expression of a speaker, so the imagination to the mind.

Hence, there can be no doubt that the ideas of the human mind are representative of objective realities. Have they also absolute value? The absolute value of our concepts will appear quite evident when we reflect upon the nature of abstraction. Objects become intelligible only inasmuch as they are abstracted, *i. e.,* pulled away from the conditions of their concrete existence and considered in and by themselves. Thus, evidently, their concrete relations disappear and they become necessarily and indiscriminately applicable to all possible individual cases, which is another way of saying that they obtain absolute value.

B. THE OBJECTIVE VALUE OF JUDGMENTS

The objective and absolute value of our conceptual knowledge has been shown to be evident upon the basis of Aristotelian psychology. Abstraction expresses the keynote of the solution. Our task is thereby not completed, indeed, only the foundation has been laid. While ideas constitute the indispensable elements of our intellectual life, they are elements only. If we wish to come into the possession of true knowledge, they must be put together in a mental synthesis, because truth is not in a concept but in a judgment. A concept as such is neither true nor false, it becomes formally true or false only when we compare one with another and affirm or deny a relation between them. Hence, truth does not belong to the concept, but to the relation between concepts. Here the second part of the main problem of criteriology presents itself to our mind : When we consider two concepts simultaneously and affirm or deny a relationship between them, do we do so in consequence of purely subjective factors, such as the will, the emotions or intrinsic necessity, or do we act under the influence of objective reasons which do not depend upon ourselves? In other words, formally speaking, is our knowledge of truth subjective or objective? If objective, what is the nature of the objective reason which justifies our judgments?

I. VARIOUS INTERPRETATIONS

This problem like all criteriological problems, is a product of modern philosophical thought, and consequently, many attempts have been made by modern thinkers to solve it. We will first examine the attempts made on a wrong basis or in a false direction, and thereby prepare the ground for our own solution.

a. In the first place we have to consider the opinion of a number of Catholic philosophers who, preoccupied by the intellectual chaos produced by modern philosophy on all the great and vital questions of human life, intended to apply a remedy by an appeal to *FAITH* in a primitive divine Revelation, which would be, in their mind, the only unshakable foundation for the certain knowledge of truth. This theory is called *TRADITIONALISM*, as most of its proponents take tradition to be the means by which the substance of the primitive Revelation was preserved. There is a number of objections to this view. Truth is evidently a question of the mind and must be decided by the mind. But this view proposes the will as the primary judge of truth, since an act of faith is an act of the will. Besides, this criterion is not definite and final: Man will naturally ask for a reason to accept the divine Revelation other than the Revelation itself. Still more serious: being an act of the will, it is not objective and of universal value, but subjective and personal. It will appeal to some and not to others.

b. Somewhat related to traditionalism is the view of the Scotch school of Reid and Hamilton, who consider *COMMON SENSE* the final criterion of truth. Here, again, not the individual mind is to decide the matter, it must submit to the verdict of common sense. This could be at best only a mediate and provisional solution because we shall want to know on what ground common sense rests. Again, the decision of what is matter of common sense or not, is left to the individual disposition rather than to objective considerations.

c. *DESCARTES'* interpretation, as we saw in a former chapter, is of a similar type. He holds to be certain what he sees quite clearly, because the divine wisdom and goodness could not permit it otherwise. Also this criterion is unintellectual and subjective, being dependent, not on the mind which reasons, but on the will which assumes, and furthermore, it is altogether of a provisional character, as it rests upon faith in God and the divine attributes, which must be proven first.

2. KANT'S INTERPRETATION

We have left the most important attempt, that of Kant, to the last. From what we said before about Kant's psychology and the subjectivity of conceptual knowledge, it is plain enough that there can be, in his theory, no judgment whatsoever of objective and absolute value, because, as the judgment is the expression of a relation between concepts, this relation must be purely subjective if the concepts themselves are purely subjective products of the mind; and such they are in Kant's psychology.

However, it is well here to pay attention to another aspect of Kant's philosophy, since no other philosophical system has taken such a hold of the modern mind. We have already seen how Kant drew a sharp boundary line between what he called scientific knowledge and the knowledge embodied in ethics, religion, and metaphysics. The one, in his view, has been successful, the educated world agrees about it; on the contrary, the other is a failure as the cultured people have never agreed about it. Why? Because scientific knowledge, based upon sense experience, admits of a personal test, whereas the other, being beyond sense experience, does not. This is not the place to refute Kant's argumentation; and, indeed, it hardly needs a refutation. Clearly there is no absolute agreement about scientific knowledge, nor is there either an absolute disagreement about ethical, religious, and metaphysical knowledge. There is a fairly general agreement about any kind of knowledge when it is expressed in proposititions which are simple and of easy perception, and also a fairly general disagreement about subjects of any class which are profound and of difficult comprehension.

The important point, however, is this. Kant was by no means a man who would be satisfied to live on the mere surface of things, nor would he be inclined to accept a philosophy that would open the gates to irreligion and immorality. He realized that man, in all the endeavors of his higher life, cannot succeed without ethics, religion, and metaphysics. Yet because, according to his psychology, they could not be based upon speculative grounds, he claimed a moral foundation for them. Though excluded from theoretical reason, they are *POSTULATES OF PRACTICAL REASON,* without which human life would be impossible.

It is plain that this is substituting for the speculative certitude which belongs to the mind, a practical certitude which belongs to the will. Consequently, what we said about traditionalism, the common sense theory, and Descartes' view, is applicable here: The postulates of Kant's practical reason are inacceptable as a criterion of truth because it would be extrinsic, subjective, and provisional: extrinsic because the decision is not in the mind itself; subjective because the decision is in the power of the free will, and provisional because the human mind does not rest satisfied till it finds an objective and sufficient reason for its knowledge.

3. PRAGMATISM

The great importance of this discussion will come home to us when we consider the latest issue of Kant's practical philosophy which generally goes by the name of *Pragmatism,* and the inroads of which into Christianity were condemned by Pius X under the name of *MODERNISM.*

Pragmatism and its theological twin brother, Modernism, are rather an intellectual atmosphere than a definite body of doctrine. They are born of the frank acknowledgment of the sterility of the mind and its incapacity for the attainment of objective, definite, and absolute truth. Truth itself is but relative, and therefore, its conquest is unimportant. The important thing is action, and any view or theory is true in so far as it leads to right action. What people think and believe is of little value, it is action, it is their conduct that counts. The scholastics, like the rationalists, are called contemptuously *INTELLECTUALISTS.*

We all know how this false philosophy has poisoned the modern mind. Its fallacy is so obvious that its prevalence proves the general superficiality of modern intellectual life. Can there be any serious doubt that the value of actions and the standard of conduct depend absolutely upon the intellectual principles from which they proceed?

And, indeed, the present political and social conditions in the world prove better than the strongest logical arguments what the standard of conduct comes to be when the religious and ethical principles which underlie conduct are cast to the winds. Upon intellectual despair no practical and fruitful system of action can be built either in private or in public life.

4. THE CORRECT INTERPRETATION : OBJECTIVE EVIDENCE

The foregoing discussion taught us some of the conditions of a genuine criterion of truth which may serve as a touchstone in regard to the objective and absolute value of our judgments: 1. It must be intrinsic and not extrinsic, *i. e.*, it must have its basis in the judging mind, not in the will or the emotions; it must be open to reflection by the mind. 2. It must be definite and absolute in its character and not provisional, requiring an indefinite continuation of intellectual search. 3. It must be objective and not subjective, *i. e.*, there must be objective conditions directly influencing the mind's judgment, and over which the mind itself has no control. Such a criterion of truth we have in *objective evidence*.

a. DEFINITION OF OBJECTIVE EVIDENCE

To understand the nature of objective evidence, a few considerations will be necessary. Our concepts, while the fruit of abstraction, which is a subjective function of the mind, represent objects, and consequently, when by another subjective function of the mind, judgment, two concepts are compared, they are compared not as subjective functions as such, but with reference to their contents, *i. e.*, the objects which they represent. But, as we have seen, these objects do not depend upon the mind, and when the mind by a complex abstraction perceives clearly that there is a relation between them, this relation itself does not depend upon the function of the mind but upon the objective contents of the concepts, *i. e.*, the objects represented by them, and this relation, when clearly perceptible as existing or not existing, is called objective evidence.

From this analysis of a judgment we see with perfect clearness that our mind is just as dependent upon objective conditions for its judgments as it is dependent upon objective conditions in simple apprehension. The very same thing we must affirm about reasoning, because just as judging is a complex way of apprehending an object—here the objective relation between concepts— so is reasoning but a complex way of judging, *viz.*, the perception of an objective relation between judgments. The reason for this lies again in the very nature of abstraction which is the basic work of the intellect: abstraction is not a creation or a production from nothing, but the perception of a common element, a real objective element, existing in several objects.

b. DEMONSTRATION

The proof of our theory is in our own inner experience. When two concepts are simultaneously present in our consciousness, if they are sufficiently simple, we perceive immediately with all clearness whether there is a relation between them or not. But when the concepts are rather complex, we hesitate to decide because the relation does not appear to us clear. However, if we reflect upon and analyze the concepts, and thus simplify them, the relation becomes clearer and we judge it in conformity with the degree of clearness more and more probable, and when, at last, the relation becomes quite clear to us, we assent firmly, *i. e.,* we judge unhesitatingly without any more fear of error, we are sure to possess the truth. Throughout this process our consciousness tells us plainly that we do not go on as we please in the matter, but that we act all along under the direct and decisive influence of the objective factors present in the mind.

As a confirmatory proof we may add that objective evidence contains all the conditions which, as we have seen, are necessary in a genuine criterion of truth. 1. It is intrinsic: its source and basis is in the individual mind itself. Each man is able to perceive and apply it himself. No need to appeal to another faculty or tribunal. And so it should be, because the proper object of all intellectual operations is the knowledge of truth. 2. It is definite and final: there can be no appeal from it. When a person forming a judgment is clearly conscious of its evidence, there can be no mistake about the possession of certain knowledge. Thus it is as it must be: each man is and must be the ultimate judge in his own intellectual life, and as a consequence, also in his moral life. 3. It is objective: man does not form his intellectual synthesis from an innate unavoidable impulse nor by a purely subjective cnoice, but under the influence of objective factors present in the mind which bear upon the decision.

Such being the conditions of objective evidence as they affect the individual mind, we have in it a criterion of truth which is of absolute and universal application. It explains perfectly why, regarding immediate facts of our own experience, or very simple propositions, such as the principle of identity or contradiction, the evidence is judged to be overwhelming, and the consequent conviction of being sure in the matter is unshakable. To assure the same result in more complex propositions where we feel doubtful, all that is needed to attain to certainty, is to reduce them to greater simplicity, till, with the increasing clarity of the object of our concepts, the evidence of the positive or negative relations between them will dawn upon us.

CHAPTER EIGHTEEN

THE CONSTITUTIVE ELEMENTS OF THE MORAL ORDER

DEFINITION AND OBJECT OF THE MORAL ORDER

In the same manner as the logical order is based upon the relationship between the intellectual actions of man and their natural object, so the ethical or moral order is based upon the relationship between the normal actions of man and their natural object. We say *moral* and not simply *volitional* actions, because the aim, determined upon and chosen by the will, is the determinative and decisive influence in all human activity which proceeds from the will, and thus shares in the character of morality of the volitions themselves. Hence, it is evident that while the logical and ethical orders are correlative in man's life, yet, from a practical viewpoint, the ethical order is by far the superior on account of its universal application to all human activity, even the specific acts of the intellect not entirely excluded. The reason is that the will controls all other powers in man, not absolutely or despotically as the scholastics said, but politically. It is true that the mind also has influence upon all other powers, but this is not a controlling influence, and it is generally exercised only indirectly through the will. There is another difference between the two orders, which refers to their object. The objectivity of the logical order depends upon the senses in general and the imagination in particular, as the senses seize the object and the imagination presents it to the intellect. While this same object seized by the senses is the primary source and basis of the objectivity of the moral order as well, yet the ethical objectivity as such consists in the object present in the mind, and presented by the mind to the will as an aim. To be exact: the distinction between the object of the logical and that of the ethical order is not real but metaphysical; what to the mind is true, to the will is good. The ethical order, therefore, being the order between the moral actions of man and their aim, or objects conceived as good, has for its objective or material element the law that regulates this relation and for its subjective and formal element the will approving or disapproving, accepting or rejecting that law. As the knowledge of this law is gained exclusively by the study of the objective conditions and relations between the concrete beings of the universe, we may add that just as the ontological order is the objective basis of the logical, so the logical order is the objective basis of the ethical.

I. *The Moral Law: The Material or Objective Element of the Moral Order*

It is evident from the foregoing definition and explanation of the moral order that, when we speak of the moral law or the law of nature, we use the term law in fundamentally the same sense in which scientists speak of *the laws of nature*. The difference is in its application to different relations. Scientists in their observations and experiments strive to discover the laws of nature, this is their chief aim. Bodies, inorganic and organic, have an intrinsic tendency—their final cause, which unifies and controls all their actions in a definite sense towards what we call the natural end, and the uniformity, or at least regularity, in the actions of bodies explained by this intrinsic tendency, are called their natural laws. Thus it is the natural law of oxygen to combine with hydrogen in the proportion of one to two. So it is with all the laws of nature, mechanical, physical, and chemical. In the study of psychology we have found still other kinds of natural laws. Organic life has its own laws; and also sense life, based upon the same intrinsic tendencies, has its own distinct laws of consciousness. We have found that even mind life has laws of its own. We studied in the three preceding chapters the most important laws of mind knowledge, calling them the laws of logic. Our present aim is to study the laws, or rather in a general way, the law of the will. Of course, there is a profound difference between the laws of sense action, and those of mind and will action on account of the difference in both the object and the manner of reaching the object. However, they are all expressive of the natural and normal connection between an action and its object. In sense life the object is a conscious good, *i. e.,* a known good; but, being a sense good, it is a concrete good and as such has a direct efficient influence upon its appetition and seizure by the animal. In mind life the object is also a good known, but, being a mind good, it is an abstract aim or end which has no efficient physical influence upon its acceptance and seizure by man, but only a moral influence, drawing the will in a definite direction. This drawing of the will, *i. e.,* the moral influence exercised by an aim in the mind upon the will, is nevertheless a positive, and generally most powerful influence, giving to will actions, if not the rigid uniformity of chemical and physical laws, at least a normal regularity, and it is from this regularity of will actions produced by aims in the mind that we abstract what we call the law of the will and, for the reason given above, the moral law of man or, briefly, the law of nature.

A. THE OBJECTIVE BASIS OF THE MORAL LAW

The moral law is, then, the law of nature in its application to man. Being a species as it were of the general natural law, it has its specific characteristic in this that in man the intrinsic tendency which in other bodies unifies, directs, and controls all their actions, is not of a compelling but only of an inviting nature and that, as a consequence, he is able to produce and choose his own aims and to determine his actions in the manner he pleases. This condition of human activity is not exceptional but normal, nay essential, and constitutes the formal element of the moral order, because it is in this power of self-direction and self-determination that we have the explanation for both the moral imputability of an action and the moral responsibility of the agent. It would seem, then, that here is a danger to look upon the moral law as all subjective, having its source and basis in the subjective will, whereas the law of nature in its application to all other beings is all objective, having its source and basis in the objective elements of those bodies. However, this difference is not so profound as it might appear. *The subjective element in the moral law consists exclusively in this that man is not like the other beings driven by an intrinsic force against which there is no resistance possible, but only drawn by an extrinsic attraction against which there may be resistance.* In other respects, and especially in its objective source and basis, the moral law, *i. e.,* the natural law in its application to man, does not differ from the general natural law.

I. THE ONTOLOGICAL BASIS OF THE MORAL LAW AND ITS SIGNIFICATION

The moral order is nothing else than the systematic application of the logical order to human action. Consequently, the objectivity and stability of the moral order depend directly upon the objectivity and stability of the logical order. But, as we saw in the study of the logical order, there can be no doubt whatever about its objective and absolute character, because it is really nothing else than the subjective reproduction of the ontological order, *i. e.,* of the real objective universe. Hence, whatever regularity and stability there is in the objective conditions of the concrete beings of the universe and their interaction, must also be found in the law which regulates and stabilizes the moral order, because they are identical laws. It is true, that the ontological order of the universe is itself not intrinsically absolute, because the universe, as we know, is contingent. However we must bear in mind that, its nature and existence being from God, the Absolute Being, the ontological order, as it exists objectively in the universe, is the created expression of the mind and the will of God, and therefore, in a certain sense, shares in the absoluteness and stability of the divine nature. Thus, in its last analysis, *the fundamental source and basis of the law of nature, whether it refers to man or any other creature, is the divine nature itself in so far as it is expressed in the ontological order of the universe. This very same law becomes the moral law inasmuch as man being capable of perceiving it in the logical order is also capable of approving or disapproving, of accepting or rejecting it.*

2. THE APPLICATION OF THE ONTOLOGICAL ORDER TO MAN

Man is not superior to the ontological order of the universe because he is not its absolute master standing above it, but only its contingent master, for, though the highest being in it, he remains a member of it and consequently, subject to it as a whole. Hence, man does not control the order of the universe, but is himself controlled by it. Though he is rational and, therefore, capable of perceiving the ontological order, and though he is free and, therefore, capable of approving or disapproving, accepting or rejecting it, yet he is not less a contingent part and member of the universe than any other being, and, therefore, he is not and cannot be a law unto himself, but is subject to the universal law of all creation.

Consequently, though *free, man is not autonomous.* He is not the absolute master of his actions because he is a contingent and dependent, not a necessary and absolute being. He finds himself in a universe of which he knows he is but an infinitesimal element. He is quite aware that the universe is subject to the Absolute Being to whom it owes its existence, and that creation, being a free act of the Creator, can have no other extrinsic end but to glorify its Author by a contingent expression of the divine power, wisdom, and goodness. Consequently, even if he is free to choose his own aims, he is morally bound in the choice of his aims by the objective conditions he finds in the universe in general and in his own nature in particular, because these objective conditions reveal to him the plan of the Creator to whom, as creature, he owes absolute submission.

3. OBJECTIVE MORAL GOODNESS

From the principles so far discussed, two essential conclusions regarding the objective goodness of human life are logically deduced: 1. Man's aims are good only in so far as they are based upon, and abstracted from, the objective conditions of the universe, or, which is the same, as they are in conformity with his own rational nature. 2. Just as the goodness of his aims depends upon their objective connection with the divine plan, so also his concrete actions are good only inasmuch as they are objectively related to his aims. While there is, indeed, nothing in human nature more subjective than the actions proceeding from the free will, yet, since the decisions are made under the influence of objective aims present in the mind, this influence of the objective motive in the production of the actions gives them the character of objective morality.

Consequently, the main difference between the law of nature as it applies to the life of man and to the actions of the rest of the universe is not a difference in the nature or degree of goodness, but simply a difference in the manner of subjection to the same law: both are bound by the same law, but in man its fulfillment must proceed from self-determination and its course must be self-directed, *i. e., it is the moral law of his nature;* whereas, in the rest of the universe, its fulfillment is by intrinsic necessity, *i. e., it is the physical law of its nature.* One of the consequences of this difference is that man may fail to attain his natural end, whereas the rest of the universe cannot fail. However, there is no objective difference between the goodness of man's actions and that of the actions of other beings.

B. ATTRIBUTES OF THE MORAL LAW

After studying the fundamental objective source and basis of the moral law, it will be useful to consider some of its important attributes. In doing so, the moral law, and particularly its objectivity and absolute value, will be better understood and appreciated. There are, above all, three attributes that deserve a serious examination: the *obligation, promulgation,* and *sanction* of the moral law.

I. THE OBLIGATION OF THE MORAL LAW

The attribute of paramount importance in this connection is the obligation of the moral law: a law is not a perfect law unless it obliges, *i. e.,* unless it binds the person subject to it normally to its fulfillment. It is clear that by obligation we do not mean any physical force that the legislator may possess the power to apply to the subjects of the law in order to compel its fulfillment. Whatever force there is in obligation is of a purely moral nature, *i. e.,* its entire influence is exercised upon the will through the mind. Its basis is, on the one side, the right to legislate and the will to exercise that right, and on the other, the recognition of that legislative right and its exercise, and the consequent sense of submission to it. With reference to the moral law, it is evident that its basis is the authority of the divine Creator and His will expressed in the objective order of the universe, recognized by man as the law of his nature.

It is well here to pay attention to a distinction the neglect of which has often given rise to serious errors in ethical discussions. While the obligatory character is an essential attribute in moral law and indispensable in human life, yet it is not an essential element in the objective law or the objective relation as we find it between the normal actions of man and their natural end. The moral law in this purely objective and material sense is knowable by simple analysis and induction from the regularity of the normal human activity as we have pointed it out already. Not so the character of obligation. Analysis and induction are not sufficient to account for it. Only upon the assumption of a personal God and His sovereignty over the universe can the obligatory character of the natural law be accounted for. The knowledge of it is not analytical but synthetical. Of course, we have a perfect right to predicate moral obligation as an essential characteristic of the law of human nature, because for us the existence of God and His absolute sovereignty is not an assumption but has been demonstrated conclusively in former chapters.

Consequently, while the moral law depends objectively and materially upon the ontological order of the universe, in so far as it is the created expression of the divine goodness and holiness, its character of obligation depends directly and formally upon the will of the divine Legislator imposing upon us respect for the order which He has established in the universe.

Obligation, then, is a moral force consisting in the authority and the will of the legislator, which, acknowledged by the subject, determines the voluntary acceptance and performance of the law. It is evident that the obligation of the law of nature or the natural moral order is absolute and universal. It is absolute because it is the expression of the holy and unchangeable will of the Creator, and it is universal in the double sense that it applies to all human beings without any possible exception, and that it applies also to all actions of a person in so far as they proceed from his free will.

2. THE SANCTION OF THE MORAL LAW

Next to the moral obligation of the law of nature comes its sanction. It is based upon the principle that no legislator can be indifferent in the matter of the laws he has made—he wants to see them carried out. His indifference in respect to the enforcement of his laws would necessarily imply one of two reasons: either the laws are foolish so that the failure of their enforcement would be a benefit, or the will of the legislator lacks the necessary firmness and stability, and therefore, is easily affected and influenced by change. Of course, it would be blasphemy to attribute to the divine Legislator either of those qualities; He is infinitely wise and absolutely good.

Consequently, the fulfillment of the moral law will be beneficial in its results, not only for the general order which the law serves, but also for the person that fulfills it, and on the contrary, the violation of the law will bring about conditions that are detrimental not only to the general order, but also to its violator. From the infinite holiness and justice of God it is evident that the good or evil consequences for the performer or violator of the law must be in exact proportion both to the importance of the law for the general order and to the degree of merit or guilt of the person performing the act. It is quite clear that the knowledge of the proportionate good or evil consequences for the person is a powerful motive for the fulfillment of the law.

From the foregoing explanation the definition of the sanction of the moral law is easily inferred: it is precisely *this disposition of the divine Legislator in virtue of which submission to the law brings about happiness, and rebellion against the law, unhappiness* in some form or measure to him who submits to, or rebels against, the law as a natural reward or as a natural punishment. Such a sanction must be both proportionate and adequate: it must be proportionate because divine justice demands that the reward or punishment be measured by the objective importance and the subjective perfection of the action commanded or forbidden by the moral law; and it must be adequate because divine holiness demands that the reward promised or the punishment threatened be normally sufficient to induce everybody everywhere and in all circumstances to conform to the moral order.

What we said above with reference to the obligation, is equally true of the sanction of the moral law: as there can be no perfect obligation, so there can be no perfect sanction of the moral law without the acknowledgment of a personal God. Nevertheless, from the simple knowledge of the perfect obligation and sanction of the moral law, we could not deduce the existence of God as a legitimate conclusion, because our knowledge of both the obligation and sanction of the moral law is not analytical, but synthetical, *i. e.,* it is inferred from the existence of the divine Legislator, the knowledge of which has come to us, and necessarily must come to us, from other sources.

3. THE PROMULGATION OF THE MORAL LAW

Both the obligation and the sanction of the moral law presuppose in man a knowledge of the law. A law which is not known evidently cannot oblige, nor can anybody be justly liable to reward or punishment for the fulfillment or the violation of a law of which he knows nothing. Hence, the promulgation of the law is indispensable in all cases. In respect to the law of human nature, *by promulgation we mean the disposition of the divine will in virtue of which the mind of man is capable of knowing and understanding the order and plan of God as expressed in the universe, himself included.*

About the possibility and even, at least generally speaking, about the reality of such knowledge in man there can be no doubt. While it is true that in consequence of a poor, or directly bad, education or through perversion wrought by evil habits, the knowledge of the moral order may be very imperfect and obscure, yet any normal man, normally developed, is well able to distinguish between what is plainly morally wrong and morally right. As regards the great general principles from which all moral duties and rights are deducible, there can be no discrepancy of opinion. Let us mention some of those principles.

In this connection we have found some strange specimens in certain books on moral philosophy or even on moral theology. For instance, we have seen this quotation: "Bona facienda, mala vitanda sunt," we must do good and avoid evil. Surely this is a truism, but it is absolutely useless as a moral principle, because the very object of such principles is to teach us how to distinguish between good and evil. Just as inadequate a principle is, in this connection the so-called golden rule: Act towards others as you want them to act towards you. Even if this axiom were objectively correct, *i. e.,* morally perfect, it would apply to only one aspect of moral life, conduct towards one's fellowman, but it is intrinsically wrong. In consequence of this principle we would be justified in acting at times immorally, because not seldom do we want others to act towards us in a manner which is plainly incorrect from a moral viewpoint. Instead of such useless and inadequate general principles, so often foolishly quoted, we venture to propose a few which are sufficient as a general source and basis for a whole code of morality, and about the existence and nature of which there can hardly be discussion:

1. Each being in the world has its natural object and end.
2. There is an interrelation between beings based upon the general fact, plainly noticeable, that the lower exist for the service of the higher.
3. Man, being the king of the material universe, is authorized to use the universe for his benefit.
4. In the use of the universe he is limited by the co-equal dignity and rights of his fellowmen.
5. Man depends naturally upon his fellowmen in many respects, and as this dependence is mutual, a number of mutual rights and duties are the logical consequence.
6. Being a creature, man is bound to accept, approve, and carry out reverently and thankfully this order as the expressed divine will.

Of course, when it comes to a knowledge in detail, there may be doubts, and consequently, discrepant opinions about the moral character of certain actions, but we believe that no norma. adult can ignore the general moral principles just enunciated, unless it be in consequence of moral perversion.

II. *The Acceptance or Rejection of the Moral Law:*
The Subjective and Formal Element of the Moral Order

So far we studied the moral order from the objective viewpoint. In this respect the moral order is fundamentally identical with the ontological order of the universe expressing the objective relations between concrete beings. This is the *material element of the moral order*. We will now proceed to consider *the formal element* which consists in the approval or disapproval, the acceptance or rejection of the moral law by man. Knowing himself to be subject to the divine sovereignty and recognizing in the objective order of the universe the plan and will of God, man applies to himself and to his actions the divine plan as the law of his own nature.

While such an action on the part of man is plainly an act of the will, yet the will, as we know, is a blind faculty and needs the mind to enlighten and guide it as regards both the ends and the means that lead to the ends. If such is the case generally, it is especially so in respect to moral life. Hence, we shall study first the part which the mind plays in moral activity and then examine the work of the will as such.

A. THE MIND IN MORAL LIFE: CONSCIENCE

Speaking in a general manner we call conscience the human mind when it reflects upon and judges of subjects referring to the moral order. However, in the strict and proper sense, *conscience is the mind judging about the morality of a concrete action that we are about to perform*. Consequently, it is not an inspiration from on high, nor an emotional element, nor, much less, a sense function, but an intellectual judgment, based upon rational grounds. These grounds are the knowledge we have of objective ontological conditions about which the judgment is to be pronounced. If the action to be performed corresponds to the natural end of a being, it is morally good; if not, it is morally bad. This is the aspect of moral life which we have called objective morality and upon which conscience must shed the necessary light.

Furthermore, inasmuch as the will depends for guidance and direction exclusively on the mind, it is evident that whatsoever influences the exercise of conscience in a favorable or unfavorable sense, has also a favorable or unfavorable influence upon the will. Thus, *ignorance, prejudices, passions, and evil habits* interfere with, and preclude, at least to a certain extent, the freedom of decision so necessary in moral action.

However, it is hardly necessary to add that conscience, being an intellectual power, does not determine the moral character of its possessor. A saint may possess a rather poor conscience, whereas the conscience of a criminal may be of excellent quality. Moral character does not depend upon conscience but upon obedience to conscience.

I. VARIOUS KINDS OF CONSCIENCE

When conscience is in conformity with the objective morality of our actions, we say we have a *RIGHT conscience;* if not, we speak of a *WRONG conscience.* Both the right and the wrong conscience may be either *CERTAIN or UNCERTAIN.* We call conscience certain when our judgment excludes every doubt or fear of error. The uncertain conscience may be simply doubtful, based upon a suspension of judgment for lack of objective grounds, or it may be probable, having an unconclusive argument in its favor.

From another viewpoint we speak of a *DELICATE, SCRUPULOUS, LAX,* and *PERPLEXED* conscience. A delicate conscience is a desirable possession. It judges correctly and quickly, not only in matters of importance, but in respect to minor points as well. On the contrary, a scrupulous conscience is a mental disease. Its eyes are distorted: it magnifies and multiplies the evil and minimizes the good side of things. A lax conscience is the opposite mental disease: it minimizes the evil and maximizes the good side of things. A perplexed conscience puts a person before an apparently unescapable dilemma: it judges that to perform the action is sinful, and to omit it, is also sinful.

2. THE LAWS OF CONSCIENCE

The first law of conscience is negative: *Never act while your conscience is doubtful.* The reason for this rule is obvious: acting upon a doubtful conscience would be exposing ourselves knowingly and willingly to do wrong, and of course, exposing ourselves deliberately to the danger of wrong-doing is acting immorally.

The second law is the reverse of the first: *When your conscience is certain, you may always act upon it, i. e.,* when you are sure that an action is commanded, you must perform it; when you are sure that it is forbidden, you must omit it; and when you are sure that it is neither forbidden nor commanded, you may either perform or omit it.

Also the reason for the second law in the use of conscience is of easy comprehension: while in theory a right conscience is the great desideratum in moral life, in practice there can be no other guide but a certain conscience, because we have no other possible criterion to pronounce judgment on the objective morality of an action but certainty of judgment. Consequently, if we were not allowed to act always on a certain conscience, we should never be authorized to act at all, which, of course, would be absurd. While thus acting upon a certain conscience, it may happen that our action is wrong from the objective and material viewpoint; yet it would be always subjectively and formally right.

The third law in the application of conscience is much

more difficult to understand. It refers to the mode of procedure in a doubtful state of conscience. While we are not allowed to act upon a doubtful conscience, yet action may be imperative, a decision urgent.

The solution is relatively easy when the question is not of an urgent nature. It is then a simple matter of obtaining light on the subject either by careful study and reflection or, where we are not able to come to a definite conclusion ourselves, by an appeal to the proper authority.

When a decision is urgent, there are two distinct cases practical. Where it is a question whether there be a law commanding or forbidding an action, if after reflection the doubt perseveres, we may act upon the principle that a *doubtful law is no law.* The reason for such a solution is in the doubtful promulgation of the law.

In the second case, the law forbidding or commanding an action is supposed certain, but it is the question whether "hic et nunc," *i.e.,* in the concrete circumstances in which we find ourselves, we are subject to, or exempt from, the law. If upon conscientious reflection the doubt persists we may consider ourselves exempt from the law, if a good and solid reason speaks for such an exemption, though the reason may not be conclusive. The reason for this solution of the question is of a similar nature as the preceding one: we cannot assume that the divine Legislator would oblige us to bear a burden when, even after reflection, we are in doubt about such an obligation.

In the case of a perplexed conscience, *i. e.,* when both the performance and the omission of an action are taken to be morally evil, we must proceed to choose the evil which appears to us the smaller. But if they appear to us equally bad, we may choose either. The reason is clear: there can be no obligation to choose what is evil. Therefore, if we are forced to choose between two apparent evils, evidently neither, or at least one of them, is not a moral evil.

Scrupulosity and laxity are, as already explained, mental diseases and they must be treated as such. Both the scrupulous and lax persons are unable for the time being to direct their own moral life and must depend upon the guidance of others. The first condition for their cure is the recognition of their disease, the second, implicit trust in, and submission to, their moral physician.

B. THE VOLITIONAL ELEMENT IN MORAL LIFE: INTENTION

What conscience is in moral life in respect to the mind, intention is in respect to the will. In conscience the mind presents to the will its proper object, a moral good, "bonum honestum," and by its intention the will directs its action towards the attainment of that good. Consequently, *by intention we mean the deliberate direction of the will towards its object.*

Intention receives various names according to the difference in viewpoint, such as the object, end, aim, motive, and purpose of an action.

Inasmuch as it is an abstract idea of the being's natural good, it is the *OBJECT* of an action, and inasmuch as this object is the "terminus ad quem" of the action, it is its natural *END*. This is the ontological viewpoint which is fundamental.

It is the *AIM* inasmuch as it exercises a directive influence upon the action. The aim is in a moral sense what a goal is in a sense of physical motion. In a similar sense we call it a *MOTIVE* inasmuch as it moves the will to perform the action in the manner of a final cause, *i. e.,* by attraction.

Finally, we term it a *PURPOSE* inasmuch as it is an achievement which the will is bent upon realizing.

I. THE RÔLE OF INTENTION

As has been explained sufficiently, the relation between the action of a being and its natural end is the objective basis for morality. It is an objectively good or bad action according to the character of conformity or non-conformity of the said relation. When the will coincides in its intention with this objective goodness or badness, we have the subjective character of morality or immorality added to it, and thus, we have a morally good or a morally bad action. For the moral goodness of an action both elements are necessary, the material or objective and the formal or subjective goodness. An objectively good action with a bad intention is no more acceptable than an objectively bad action with a good intention; in other words, the end does not justify the means, nor does the means justify the end.

The reverse is, evidently, not true. To spoil completely the moral character of an action, either element is sufficient, whether it be the material or formal element. An objectively excellent action is corrupted by an evil intention, and even the noblest intention cannot justify a morally wrong action. The reason is not far to seek: Neither the objective nor the subjective action must depart from the plan of God as expressed in the universe.

2. SEVERAL INTENTIONS

So far we spoke of one intention only, *viz.*, that by which the will directs the action towards its natural object. However, man is capable of having more than one intention for the same action, for the simple reason that the same action may have various objects, direct and indirect, and thus man may have in mind some or all of these objects. Of the many objects of an action some are better than others, and again, some may be evil and others good.

Thus, the pupil studies his lesson either because he wants to know it, or because he wants to please the teacher or the parents, or because he hopes to earn a prize or praise of some kind, or, again, because he fears some kind of a penalty. The first of these intentions we would call the objective intention because it coincides with the direct and natural object of the act. The others are more or less subjective intentions, though they are or may be all in harmony with the natural object of the act. Evidently, these intentions do not conflict, and therefore, the pupil may be influenced by one only, or by more or all of them at the same time. There might be also and often is, a subjective intention which would conflict with the objective goodness of the act. For instance, if the pupil learned his lesson in order to make a fellow-pupil feel jealous. How is the morality of an action influenced by the presence of various, and even conflicting intentions in the mind?

3. THE MORALITY OF SEVERAL INTENTIONS

In Kant's ethical system there is room for one good intention only, the one that is identical with the direct objective end of the action. *His categorical imperative*: Thou shalt obey the law because it is the law, excludes as morally wrong the intention of any advantage or pleasure that the fulfillment of the law may produce. This would impose upon human nature a yoke man cannot bear, and there is, besides, no justification for such severity.

After all, it is the natural order, which, again, expresses the goodness and wisdom of God, that a good action should produce good fruit and an evil action evil fruit, and that the agent should enjoy or suffer the natural consequences of his action. If such is the natural order, why should a person be precluded from thinking of, and aiming at, the things to which his action gives him a natural right?

Again, when we study the moral conduct of normal people in our own surroundings as well as in history, we find that they are all influenced by this double sort of motives, the objective and impersonal motives, and the personal and interested motives. Hence, we would be obliged to say the absurd thing that the ethical order is superior to the capacity of the normal man, and is appropriate only to people of heroic moral conception and power.

Consequently, man's actions are morally good as long as their objective goodness is not actually or vitually excluded from his intention, even if his direct intention be the personal advantage or reward that his actions will bring him. Thus, a physician curing the sick does not sin if his explicit intention is to earn a livelihood for himself and his family, as long as he does not exclude the implicit intention of taking proper care of his patients. Of course, the moral value of such actions is in direct correlation with the value of the personal intentions. If they are of lower moral quality than the objective goodness of the action, the moral value of the action is lowered, but also vice versa, if they are of higher moral quality, its moral value is enhanced. Evidently, any direct evil intention to which the objective goodness is subordinated, would spoil the moral value of the action completely.

If the principal intention is good and a minor intention evil, the moral character of the action is thereby lowered, but not completely spoiled.

III. *Other Theories of Ethics*

Such is the theory of the moral order based upon the philosophy of Aristotle and St. Thomas Aquinas. It is the only purely philosophical theory in harmony with the ethical teachings of Christianity. This fact explains why the other theories of ethics, whenever in essential points they depart from the scholastic theory, lose themselves in a labyrinth of errors, and when applied to action, lead to disastrous consequences. We will just add a few remarks on the theories mostly in vogue amongst modern philosophers. These theories are, when compared with the one we just discussed, extremely shallow and frivolous, another evidence of the superficiality of the modern mind.

1. The first theory is the *PLEASURE THEORY* or *HEDONISM*: Good is what produces pleasure, evil what produces pain. Such a theory is plainly contradictory: The most shameful deeds of immorality are often done because they produce pleasure, and on the other side, sometimes the most cowardly conduct is explained by a desire to avoid pain.

No better is the *UTILITARIAN THEORY*:
Good is what is useful, bad what does harm. And
it makes no difference whether the utilitarianism is
individual or social; the social is the same selfish
utilitarianism in a slightly disguised form. In this
theory morality would be equivalent to utter selfishness. The greatest crimes and immoral practices
would thereby be sanctified, because such is human
nature that no deed is ever done, no matter how
heinous its moral aspect, which is not done with the
desire and hope of some advantage to be derived
from it.

2. There is another moral theory taught, and unfortunately spread with astonishing success amongst the
people of our time: the *THEORY OF EVOLU-
TIONISM*. It is an application to moral life of
the general principles of materialistic evolutionism. Moral ideas and practices are the natural and
necessary product of heredity and environment.
They have no absolute value and meaning. What
was very moral in the life of our ancestors a million
years ago is perhaps very immoral at present, and
what is morally good now will probably be very bad
amongst our posterity of a thousand generations
hence. Of course, in such a theory of ethics there
is no room for moral obligation nor for moral freedom and responsibility. Human morality is held to
be fundamentally equivalent to the morality of the
tiger and the hog.

There is hardly any need to add that such a theory
is inacceptable, not only because it falls with its
foundation—the general philosophy of materialism'
—but also because it is absolutely incapable of explaining any one of the momentous problems involved in the theory of moral life.

3. The *CRITICIST THEORY* of ethics has been
alluded to above, speaking on the morality of
several intentions. Kant's interpretation of the
moral character of human action as formulated in

the *categorical imperative* is without doubt exaggerated, because it is impossible as a rule of conduct for the average man. On the one hand, Kant decries as morally wrong any motive of action except the objective intention, *i. e.,* the intention implied in the law itself, and on the other, he demands that each individual action be such that it may serve as the law of action for the whole race. We saw above that the demand of the exclusive objective intention for human action cannot be established nor has the second demand any better foundation. While general ethical principles are necessary to determine the morality of concrete actions, yet the conditions and circumstances surrounding them have such a direct bearing and influence upon their moral character that no individual action can ever be considered a rule of conduct of absolute value and universal application.

Apart from these intrinsic objections to Kant's categorical imperative, we reject his theory also on extrinsic grounds. Tearing away ethics from its native root and soil—religion, Kant did not and could not explain sufficiently the character of moral obligation and sanction which are indispensable attributes of any valuable theory of ethics. Furthermore, excluding from his theory the divine Legislator and proclaiming in His stead the autonomy of man, the way was prepared for the practical substitution of the sovereign God by divinized man.

CHAPTER NINETEEN

THE APPLICATION OF THE MORAL ORDER

Rights and Duties: Their Correlation

Discussing the application of the moral order, the ideas of right and duty come to our mind spontaneously. They present themselves together because there is a natural correlation between them. However, this correlation is not absolute. In the presence of God man has duties only, no rights, and towards man God has rights only, no duties. The reason is obvious: man has duties only in the presence of God because all he is and has is due to Him, and God has no duties towards man because He owes man nothing whatever. It would be folly, then, to speak of God as respecting the rights of His creatures: He does respect the created order which He established, but this respect is not due to any right in the creature, but to His own free disposition.

Apart from this one-sided relation, rights and duties are always correlated: To each duty corresponds a right and to each right a duty. This is natural and logical because the order established by God in the universe is such that we all depend upon one another and, therefore, ought to serve one another. The precise nature and importance of the respective rights and duties must be determined by the nature and degree of interdependence. Generally speaking, people know their rights far better than their duties, and even when they know them both fairly well, there is, from a practical viewpoint, always great danger lest they forget their duties, whereas there is not much danger that they will forget their rights. There is, indeed, a general tendency to overestimate rights and to under-value duties. Hence, it is much more necessary to insist upon duties than upon rights.

There are two kinds of rights and duties which, while interrelated, are clearly distinct; those that refer to the individual as an individual, and those that refer to the individual inasmuch as he is a member of society. To each kind we will devote careful attention.

There is one other remark to be made in this connection that may not be useless. Rights and duties being correlated, depending mutally upon one another, any being fundamentally incapable of performing duties is also incapable of possessing rights. Consequently, rational beings only possess rights. A man can have no duty towards his horse or his dog because a horse or a dog is fundamentally incapable of exercising rights.

1. *The Moral Order Applied to the Individual*

There is, as already pointed out, little necessity for enlarging upon the individual rights. However, it is not out of place to state them briefly in a general way. Man has been endowed by God with a spiritual soul and consequently, as we shall see more perfectly in the next chapter, has been called to a never-ending, ultra-terrestrial life for which the present life on earth is meant to be the preparation. For this work of preparation in conformity with the divine plan as visible in creation, man possesses a large number of forces and faculties, physical, psychical, spiritual. Man has a right to exercise all these forces and faculties in a proper manner for the realization of his destiny as long as he does not interfere thereby with the co-equal rights of his fellowman. Particularly, he has a strict right to do or to omit any action that is necessary for such a purpose. This constitutes the source of the so-called *inalienable rights of the individual* which no authority on earth has the power to violate or disturb.

In respect to individual duties, while trying to limit ourselves to the most general principles, it will be necessary to dwell rather extensively on the application to their various objects.

1. DUTIES TOWARDS SELF

The very first object of our duties is our own person. The reason is in our nature. In this connection man is not different from any other being. Any being by its normal action develops and perfects its nature, and consequently, every agent is the first to benefit by its action. This principle applies also to man. He is the first beneficiary of his moral activity which implies an increase in the natural and normal development and perfection of his nature. Inasmuch as his actions are necessary either as ends or as means in this natural and normal development and perfection of his nature, they become moral duties. The source and basis for this broad principle is the fact of man's absolute subjection to God, who has given him existence and nature and all his talents and forces, not to waste or pervert, but to preserve and improve.

To speak concretely, man's duties towards self refer, in the first place, to the care he must take of his life and his health, both from the physical and the moral viewpoint, because life and health are the fundamental conditions for everything else. In the second place, they refer to the proper and systematic utilization of all his powers and possessions, both internal and external, both spiritual and material, in conformity with their proper and natural object and end, being mindful of the necessity of harmony in such activity and being mindful also of the law of such harmony, which demands the subordination of the lower elements to the higher and of the higher to the highest.

2. DUTIES TOWARDS THE FELLOWMAN

We exclude from our consideration here the duties of a social character, limiting our attention to those that affect man as an individual. The source and basis of these duties is the fact that there are fellowmen in the world, *i. e.*, beings endowed with the same nature, dignity, and rights. This co-equality of dignity and rights demands a co-equal respect for such dignity and rights, which is equivalent to saying that every man has the duty not to infringe upon the rights of his fellowman. Evidently, if people live together, especially if they live together in close proximity, conflicts between the rights of the one and the rights of another will necessarily arise. For the just discrimination between the rights of various individuals and the equitable solution of such conflicts this principle, which explains itself, may serve as a criterion: *Rights which are essentially inferior, naturally yield to those which are superior, rights of more practical importance predominate over those which are of less, and rights of an urgent character prevail over those which are less urgent*.

Rights and duties being correlative, whenever it is a question of proper and strict rights, it is also a question of proper and strict duties. Such duties towards one another we call *duties of justice*. The neglect of such duties, involving the violation of strict rights, has for the person responsible a very grave consequence—the duty of restitution. In virtue of this duty the injury or harm caused must be repaired as far as possible regarding both quantity and quality.

There is another class of duties, which, while less strict and circumscribed in their nature and less onerous in their consequences, are just as important for the regulation of the proper intercourse of man with man. Such duties are generally termed *duties of charity*. However, this term, beautiful as it is, is rather misleading as it would insinuate that this kind of duties have their exclusive source and basis in Christian Revelation, in which we are taught that man has been raised by God to a supernatural state in virtue of which all men form one family of which God himself is the head, and that from the love all men owe to their common Father, the duty of brotherhood or charity for one another is a natural conclusion. While, of course, it is true that the duties of brotherly love and charity have been immensely elevated and consecrated through the grace of Christianity, yet they have a natural foundation apart and outside the sphere of Revelation.

For the proper and full realization of his life it is not sufficient for man to find a bare recognition of, and simple non-interference with, his strict rights, he needs the sincere interest and encouragement of his fellowman. To make mutual intercourse of a satisfactory nature it is not enough to respect one another's rights but it must be based upon a mutual desire of fair play and carried on in a spirit of conciliation and benevolence. If such are the natural and necessary conditions of human life for its normal development and activity, it is evidently the will and plan of Him who created and determined man's nature, and consequently, there can be no doubt that the divine Legislator exercises His providential care and sanction just as truly and effectively in respect to these duties of charity as in respect to those of justice.

3. DUTIES TOWARDS GOD

There can be no room for doubt about the supreme object of our duties: it is God, the Creator and absolute Master of the universe. Being the sovereign Author of the moral order, He is just as clearly the crown and seal of all duties as He is the source and basis of all rights. Bearing this in mind it will not be difficult for us to understand that we have a threefold class of duties towards Almighty God:

1. In the fulfillment of all our duties of every description and order, the primary motive and the supreme intention must be simple, humble submission to God, from Whom alone all rights and duties derive their obligatory power and signification. From this

the most profound and most comprehensive moral viewpoint the inference is evident that *every moral duty is necessarily a religious duty.*

2 Apart from this religious conception of the whole moral order, which is an inevitable conclusion of philosophical thought in matters ethical, there are others, specifically religious duties. They are the duties which have for their direct and exclusive object the payment of our debt to Almighty God. Being our creator, He is our absolute Master to Whom we owe supreme reverence, obedience, and gratitude. Such is our debt to God. The sincere and actual acknowledgment of this debt we call *worship.* *We pay our debt to God by worship* since we have no other way of paying what we owe Him. Considering that human nature is both material and spiritual, evidently *our worship must be both internal and external,* and bearing in mind that man is not only characterized by essential individuality but also lives in virtue of natural necessity as a member of social organizations, there can be no doubt this *worship must be public as well as private.*

3. There is a third class of duties towards Almighty God for the knowledge and acceptance of which the study of ethics must and will prepare our mind. They refer to the supernatural order which is disclosed to man by divine Revelation.

The premises of these duties are of two classes. Those of one class are founded upon the nature of God, and those of the other upon the nature of man. We have as philosophers a sufficiently clear and certain knowledge of God's existence, of the absoluteness and sovereignty of His power and dominion, and of His infinite wisdom and incomparable goodness. On the other side, our knowledge of human nature and human life from personal experience as well as from the study of history is just as certain and even more clear and firm, and from this knowledge we derive the intimate conviction of the practical impossibility that the great masses of people should ever come naturally into the firm possession of the doctrines which explain the nature of God and the consequent moral and religious principles which control human life. Such being the case, *it is not only our strict duty to accept and submit in all details to divine Revelation when it presents itself with the clear evidence of its divine source and authority, but it would be a duty as well to pray and hope for a divine Revelation* which would make it possible also for the great masses of people to come to the knowledge and the exercise of the true religion. This attitude of the philosopher, having a natural and genuine concern for the religious interests of both God and the masses of the people that without Revelation would remain in utter religious darkness, would be perfectly justified, even were we to exclude from the hoped-for Revelation the supernatural order which we find in Christianity. Thus, there can be no doubt that the profound and thorough study of moral philosophy prepares and disposes the ground for the intellectual and moral assimilation of the sublime supernatural philosophy which we call Christian Theology.

II. *The Moral Order Applied to Society*

We must begin this study by explaining the nature and object of social organization. Man's natural condition compels him to live in society: that is why we call him a social being. He makes his appearance in the world as a member of society, and he lives and develops physically, mentally, and morally as a member of society. So great is his dependence upon others that if he were left to himself, he would die the day he is born, and if at any period of his life, even after having attained in every respect to natural maturity, he were to be deprived of human intercourse and of all the things derived from other men, he would soon sink into the condition of savagery.

Consequently, it is in virtue of natural conditions both intrinsic and extrinsic, over which the human will has no control, that men live together in groups. The proper term for such groups is *society.* *Societies are* not mere aggregations, like a pile of rocks or a number of trees, related to one another by simple local juxtaposition or superposition, but they are *organized groups, i. e.,* the members of the group are related to one another by a double order of co-ordination and subordination like the parts of an organism. Just as in an organism the various parts and organs have their own specific function, yet all functions are subordinate and subservient to the welfare of the organism as a whole, so in an organized group the various persons have their own offices and functions, but inasmuch as they are the members of the social body, their offices and functions must be subordinate and subservient to the welfare of the group as a group. However, there is a great difference between the natural and social organism. While in the natural organism the object of the secret powers of nature which account for the variety of organs in its structure and functions is the very production of the organism and its individual and specific life, in the social organism or group of organized individuals the common purpose which explains the structure and function of the organization is not the production and welfare of the group as an organization, but the life and welfare of the individuals that form it. The reason lies in the fundamental difference between the proper organism which is a physical being, and a social organism which is a moral being. In the physical organism the constitutive parts have no existence and action of their own, they exist and act exclusively in and through the organism which they constitute, whereas in the social organism the component members have their own individual existence and action anterior to, and therefore, independent of, the existence and action of the social body. The natural object of social organization is not the production of another being of a superior order, but the protection of the individual beings for the full display and perfect development of their own proper nature.

Hence, while *the rights and duties of the whole social body as a body naturally prevail over the rights and duties of any one member or any particular group of members, in so far as they are members, the essential rights and duties of the members, in so far as they are individual beings,* having an existence and purpose prior and superior to the existence and purpose of society, *necessarily prevail at all times and unconditionally over the rights and duties of society.* Such are briefly the principles which must serve both as a source and basis and as a criterion for the determination of social rights and duties.

A. ESSENTIAL SOCIAL RIGHTS AND DUTIES

We cannot possibly discuss the social rights and duties in their manifold applications, but will call attention to those that are paramount, or the discussion of which appears to us most important in our own times. The rights and duties which are paramount in this connection are those which refer to authority or the right of social direction, and the most important from a practical viewpoint are those which control the property and the life of the members of the social body.

I. AUTHORITY: THE RIGHT OF SOCIAL DIRECTION

The right of social direction, *i. e.,* the right to direct a social body and control its action, we call *authority.* The importance of the subject-matter from the theoretical as well as practical viewpoint is evident. It seems, at no time in human history was there less public respect for authority and at the same time more need for it. The whole social fabric of the race is in danger of collapse and the only possible salvation can come from a general return to the recognition of, and submission to, authority. But such a return demands a clear and profound knowledge of the fundamental principles upon which authority is based.

a. NECESSITY AND SOURCE OF AUTHORITY

The necessity of social direction is evident. Whenever two or more people join to form a group for the attainment of any object whatever, common or social action, *i. e.,* action of the group as a group becomes necessary. But as soon as there is common action there is the necessity of social direction, *i. e.,* a power which directs the actions of the members towards the common object. Hence, the rational source of human authority is obvious —social organization is based upon a common purpose, a common purpose demands common action, and common action is impossible without social direction. Consequently, if social organizations are natural, *i. e.,* if there are objects which are necessary for the natural perfection of man and, therefore, ought to be achieved, but for the achievement of which the individual capacity of man is insufficient, the right of social direction or authority is evidently based upon the order of nature and is, therefore, a part of the divine plan in the universe. As a matter of fact, there are many such objects. We will just mention a few. Such is, first of all, the procreation and education of human beings. Such are, wherever people live together, the maintenance of order, the protection of life and property, the harmonization of the conflicting rights, etc. None of these objects can be achieved by an individual but require the action of an organized group. Hence, the Apostle merely confirms a truth of natural philosophy when he tells us that *all powers of social authority are from God.*

b. NATURE AND LIMITATIONS OF AUTHORITY

No doubt, the right of social direction includes the *executive* and *judicial* functions as well as the *legislative* power, because laws without sanction or the sanction of which is not regularly applied, will not be carried out, they will be laws in name only. Laws which are not enforced, are not only futile, but are worse than no laws at all—they are a mockery of authority. However, *the power to legislate is fundamental*, since the others, having no object without it, are intrinsically dependent upon it. Therefore, it becomes necessary to define and explain the nature and limitations of the power to legislate as it exists in man. All members of the race having essentially the same dignity and rights, there can be no question of any man possessing an intrinsic and absolute power over any other man. Wherever authority over others is claimed, it must be proven to be derived from a delegation by God Himself, the Author of human nature. The only basis for such a demonstration is social necessity. *Hence, all, human authority, to be legitimate, must be representative and executive of the divine authority, i. e.,* it must be based upon the will and plan of God as it is expressed clearly in the order of the universe. As a consequence, human authority goes as far as can be clearly demonstrated by social necessity, but no farther.

Human authority is necessarily limited in a double sense: 1. It can only legislate for the social group and its members for whose direction it exists. Therefore, it can bind individuals only in so far as they are members of the group, because, the purpose of its existence being social direction, it has no power to interfere in the use of their individual rights as long as they do not conflict with the rights of other members of the group. This is a limitation in extension. 2. Human authority is also limited in the sense of its comprehension, *i. e.,* as regards the subject-matter of the legislation or the actions which it may command or forbid. Its basis being the plan of God as expressed in creation, it can never and under no circumstances or pretext go against the law of nature, which it has the power to extend, specify, and apply, but never to change or abrogate; and besides, its exclusive *raison d'être* being the direction of the social group, all its laws must have for their object the welfare of the group as a group or, as the scholastics so aptly expressed it, the *bonum commune,* the common good. Hence, any legislation the plain object of which is to benefit individual members or particular sets or classes of members instead of the group as a whole, is intrinsically immoral and consequently without any ethical value or obligatory signification.

2. PROPERTY: THE RIGHT OF OWNERSHIP

Though our present purpose is the study of the social function of property chiefly, we must bear in mind that anterior and superior to the social, is the individual function of property. In virtue of this function every man has a strict personal right to own the things necessary for his life and its full development. God created man and placed him upon the earth to live on it. Consequently, there is no legitimate power under heaven which could deprive him of the right to take and possess as his own the things which he needs. However, since man does not live alone on the globe, and all men have the same natural right of ownership, social authority must step in and determine the application of that right. Hence, property has, besides its undoubted individual significance, a very broad social importance.

The importance of the social function of property will appear to us still more manifest when we consider its relation to the family and to the larger social groups—such as municipalities, counties, states, nations. They all depend upon the right of ownership for the realization of their common life, and consequently, in all these cases ownership is an intrinsic social right. Hence, the social function of property is double: the social groups as such have the natural right of ownership just as much as an individual person, and as such, the right of the group prevails over that of its members; and furthermore,—and this is the chief rôle of society in matters of property —the social groups must exercise the function of equitable adjustment and conciliation between the rights of individuals whenever they are in conflict.

It is hardly necessary to add that when we speak of

social groups we exclude the financial and industrial cor-
porations. Inasmuch as they originate from individual
initiative and function as private institutions, their right is
not social but individual ownership. In this connection
two serious questions present themselves—the question
of *capitalism* and its extreme opponent, that of *socialism*.

a. CAPITALISM

The solution of the capitalistic question is at present
a crying necessity. The facts are evident and they are
pregnant with the danger of a social catastrophe such as
the world has not yet seen. The wealth of the nations
has been accumulating with astonishing rapidity during
the last few centuries, but its fruits were not, generally
speaking, for the enjoyment of the large numbers which
helped to produce them, but for the benefit of a relatively small number of individuals who succeeded in gar-
nering them by fair means or foul, into their barn. At
the side of millionaires and multi-millionaires, of whom
many scandalize the world by the ostentation and extravagance of their life, and others by their insatiable greed
for more wealth and often by the unscrupulous methods
they employ in its acquisition, there are the great masses
of the people, millions of them, either in dire want of the
necessaries, or in abject economic dependence upon the
magnates of finance and industry. Thus, our age which
has been glorified as the era of political liberty, might
more aptly be called the era of economic slavery. And
it is not necessary to prove that economic liberty would be
far preferable to political liberty—in fact, the latter is futile without the former.

To parallel the social misery produced by the criminal
pressure from above, certain combinations of working men
are inclined to reduce the whole fabric of social organization to ruin by interminable strikes. Such is the economic
situation everywhere amongst the so-called civilized
nations today. Is there no remedy possible? No solution to be found for a question fraught with such tragic
eventualities?

No doubt there is a remedy for this modern economic and social disease of the world because God has made the nations "sanabiles," curable. However, the preaching of platitudes about justice and charity will not cure the nations, nor will the boards of conciliation and arbitration solve the social question. These things are well and good as far as they go, but they do not go very far. Nor does it help more to proclaim as a new doctrine the community of interests between capital and labor, because, while it is fundamentally true that all the interests of the members of the social body are interdependent, yet in the present economic organization of society, it is an exasperating falsehood. To the most superficial observer who is not prejudiced by personal interests, it is quite obvious that the ascendency of capital means the slavery of labor, and that the ascendancy of labor promises class-rule or perhaps the complete ruin of society. Therefore, *there can be no efficient remedy, no true solution till the causes of the present economic organization*—we should perhaps say better, disorganization—*are removed*.

The *GENERAL CAUSES* are the result of irreligion and immorality: irreligion because it tends to exaggerate and overestimate the goods of fortune as the means of satisfying the human thirst for happiness, since no ultra-terrestrial happiness is hoped for;—immorality because it tends to make people look upon life as a struggle for existence in which the fittest survive, and consequently, produces an attitude of utter selfishness with an absolute disregard for the rights of others.

A *SPECIAL CAUSE* is the pernicious doctrine that the state must not interfere in the economic life of the people, but leave the economically weak to the tender mercy of the economically strong. It is assumed that the classical formula of the economic regulation of the world by the *law of demand and supply* offers an adequate explanation for all economic problems. There never was a more disastrous fallacy.

We have already pointed out that it is within the essential scope of society to protect the natural rights of its members; the economic rights particularly need constant supervision as otherwise the rights of the little ones would be swallowed up by the rights of the big ones, a process which must produce in the long run social chaos. Hence, the common good, the essential object of social action, absolutely demands interference.

There is another consideration which plainly confirms the right of social interference in the distribution of wealth. What profit would a man derive from the possession of wealth if he lived in complete isolation? None whatever. Hence, the advantages of wealth being due to society, society has the evident right as well as duty to see to it that the essential economic advantages are shared by all its members.

The *MOST SPECIFIC CAUSE* of the economic chaos in the world, we believe, is found in the function which money exercises at present in the world's social and economic life. Its proper function is to serve as a convenient means of exchange; but this function has long since been falsified to such an extent that from a mere means of exchange it has become almost the exclusive representative and expression of wealth. Hence, this thirst for money and more money, which is the principal source of modern capitalism.

While, of course, money, being made of precious metal, has a certain intrinsic value which may make it a desirable possession, yet it is not this true value of money which gives it the all-important and central signification which it occupies in modern economic life. This signification is based upon the economic fiction that money as such bears fruit. Evidently, this is a fiction because it is absurd to say that money bears fruit in the sense in which a flock or a field bears fruit. Fruit-bearing is not an intrinsic attribute of money as it is of the field or flock. It is true, unfortunately, that at present it does bear fruit. However, this fact is due not to the money itself, but to the social sanction and guarantee of money, *i. e.,* because money is a social institution. This obnoxious function of money has become possible because society has feloniously renounced its birth-right, the care of the common-wealth for the benefit of all, leaving it to the manipulation of men who had no other thought but the service of their own individual interests. Hence, it is imperative for society to reclaim its essential right and perform this all-important duty to restore money to its legitimate function. What a quick and fundamental change for the better would be produced if money were divested of its fictitious value and its false glory, returning to be the humble servant of the many instead of being as it is, the arrogant idol of the few.

Perhaps, it is not feasible, it certainly would not be wise for a nation to take such a drastic measure at once on account of the great economic and social disturbances it would create, but in all its economic legislation this end should be kept in view.

b. SOCIALISM

Capitalism is the doctrine and system of non-interference by the state in economic matters, leaving the economically weak mercilessly to the exploitation of the economically strong; socialism, on the contrary, is the doctrine and system of over-interference by the state in economic matters, turning over to the state the entire problem of the production and distribution of wealth. While we condemn both doctrines and systems as economically, socially, and morally wrong, if we were compelled to choose between the two, we would unhesitatingly choose socialism as the lesser evil. Inasmuch as socialism is an economic theory—and this is the only viewpoint from which we consider it here—it is plainly a reaction against the exaggerated individualism in respect to the right of private property which has produced capitalism. And such is the pendulum of human errors: from the extreme position of one side it swings to the extreme position of the other.

There can be no defense or excuse for the extreme form of socialism or *communism,* in which the right of individual property is absolutely abolished. Being a natural necessity for the individual it is an essential individual right, and there is no power under heaven which can lawfully take it away. We cannot condemn so absolutely the economic theory of moderate socialism which proclaims the ownership of productive property or the tools of production to be the exclusive right of society, because here we have not a question of principles, but of expediency in the manner and degree of their application. While in principle the goods of the world belong to the human race and every individual has a fundamental right to a proportionate share in their possession, the distribution cannot possibly be left entirely in the control of individuals who, in virtue of favorable circumstances and not having any scruples of conscience, would be inclined to serve exclusively their own private interests to the detriment of the social group. Can it be left absolutely in the control of the State? We have been having the experience of the first system, more or less, for several centuries and we are tasting its bitter fruits to satiety. Would we fare better if we were to leave the distribution of economic goods to the State? Perhaps there would be less selfishness, unfairness, and down-right injustice than there is in the capitalistic system, but probably after a while there would not be much wealth to distribute. Again, there would surely be less hunger and misery at the side of horrible excesses of extravagance and dissipation, but there might possibly be more hunger and misery for everybody. It is true, such is not and cannot be the intention of socialism, but human nature is so constituted that it needs a *stimulus* to rouse its energies, and from the economic viewpoint the only stimulus which seems sufficient for all sorts of people to induce them to work is *self-interest,* the hope of economic and social betterment. With the universal removal of this stimulus it seems practically certain that the necessary production could be maintained only by the application of methods used by slaveholders. Consequently, in practical socialism the alternative would appear to be either the danger of general misery and starvation for all, or the separation of society into two classes—the slave-drivers and the slaves.

3. THE RIGHT TO LIFE

The right to life is the most fundamental of all individual rights. If human life is threatened in consequence of man living together with others, society must by all means protect and safeguard it. This is, indeed, the first and foremost object of social organization. There can be no doubt that of all things in the universe human life is the most sacred: God alone can give it and God alone can take it. Nevertheless, there are cases in which men believe themselves justified in taking other men's life. We will examine them in the light of the principle of the sacredness of human life just enunciated.

a. THE RIGHT TO LIFE OF THE UNBORN

There can be no question about the criminal character of *abortion*: *it is either actual and explicit, or potential and implicit murder,* it is, indeed, the horrible slaughter of the innocent. The frequency of its occurrence does not diminish its gravity but makes it a social and racial curse. It fills the world with infanticides, and an infanticide is in the sight of God and of truth and, therefore, ought to be in the sight of man, even worse than a parricide. Those whom the order of nature predestined to produce, protect, and cherish the nascent life, turn into fiendish monsters to spoil and destroy it. There is no animal so depraved and so cowardly in its attacks on the defenceless.

Another assault upon the sacredness of human life is *its prevention* by the deliberate frustration of its conception. If the prevention of the conception of human life —"birth-control"—is less heinous as an individual sin or crime because it is not murder, yet, being a violation of the order of nature in so grave and vital a matter, and on account of its social and racial consequences, it is not less a crime against society and a curse of the race. The awful aspect of this crime is its common perpetration, and its disgraceful causes are its saddest feature. So frequent has become this shameful violation of the natural law regarding the production of human life amongst all classes of people, single and married, high and low, that the very sense of its shame is fast disappearing, and in plain day-light the methods of its practice are taught and recommended. Unless an effective means be found to counteract this moral and social danger, it will not need the curse of the Almighty to bring ruin upon the race because the race will extinguish its own stream of life.

And the real or alleged *causes* for such criminal practices? Sad to relate, they aggravate rather than attenuate the gravity of the crime. The first and most general is the *absolute rejection of sex restriction*. People want to gratify their sex appetite without any restraint. Evidently, conception and its consequences impose a manifold restraint upon lawless sex license. What an excuse! The beasts of field and forest obey the law of nature, guided by their instinct, and man, to whom the heavenly light of reason has been confided, uses it to find ways and means to frustrate the law of God and thereby degrades himself below the level of the beast.

The second cause is the complete disappearance of *continency in marriage*. To most married people the very idea of continency appears ludicrous. There are many husbands to whom marriage is *legalized prostitution* and, what is worse, there are modern wives who are perfectly satisfied with such a condition. In such families the natural sanctity of marriage has become an object of mockery and its moral level has reached the lowest possible depth.

The third and most general cause is *the dread of sacrifice* and self-denial, which is another way of saying, utter selfishness on the part of married couples. Because the birth and care of children interfere with the comfort of parents and with their desire for selfish enjoyment, they are not wanted, even if a fundamental law of nature must be violated in order to prevent their coming into existence.

b. INDIVIDUAL AND PRIVATE SELF-DEFENSE

We speak here of self-defense as *the individual and private enforcement of the right to life*. In this connection, it has been an axiom amongst all nations and peoples that in a case of unjust attack the right to life may be defended even by endangering or taking the life of the attacker. This axiom is a moral principle of the law of nature and is based upon the very sacredness of life which, when wantonly or perversely violated, may justify even the destruction of life. To understand its moral foundation it is well to bear in mind that it is a question of choosing between two lives, the life of the person unjustly attacked and that of the unjust attacker, and in the presence of such a dilemma, no sane man can doubt that the life of the innocent is preferable to the life of the guilty. From this explanation it is clear that two conditions are necessary to authorize slaying in self-defense: *it must be a real case of unjust aggression, and there must be no other honorable way available to repel the aggressor*. The right of self-defense applies also to cases in which an unjust attack is made, not upon life itself but upon such goods as are, in the eyes of the person attacked, more precious than, or at least equivalent to, life itself.

Sometimes this plea of self-defense is invoked in the case of a *child in the mother's womb, endangering the life of the parent*. However, the plea is irrelevant—this is not a case of unjust aggression. To insist upon the plea because of the two lives in danger only one can be saved and of the two lives in question that of the mother is preferable since it is more valuable, is begging the question. *In the sight of God the right to life of the child is just as sacred as that of the mother, and, consequently, to slay the child directly and intentionally is an act of murder,* and murder cannot be justified even if it were to save the whole human race. In conclusion we add that the very fact that there is such a question is a sad reflection upon motherhood. It would be, indeed, a complete reversal of nature, were the mother, whose natural office it is to nurse and cherish life, to demand and co-operate with, or even consent to, its destruction.

C. SOCIAL AND PUBLIC SELF-DEFENSE

There are two cases of legitimate social and public self-defense—the one is *war,* the other, *capital punishment.*

A war is a just war only in so far as it is a real case of social self-defense, i. e., it is morally right to make war only on the same conditions which are required to make individual self-defense lawful. Consequently, on the one side the social body must be unjustly attacked either in its existence or in such rights as are in social life equivalent to, or more precious than, that of existence, and on the other, there must be no other honorable means of safeguarding these rights. In every other case war is simply the legalization of the crime of murder in its most aggravated form, *viz.,* murder by wholesale.

The second case of legitimate social self-defense is *capital punishment.* In order to understand the moral nature of this case, it is well to bear in mind why public authority inflicts punishment. There are various subsidiary reasons for the application of punishments, such as the correction of the evil-doer and satisfaction for the scandal caused by the crime. But the *main reason is derived from the necessity of enforcing the law, i. e.,* the sanction of the law. Experience has shown amongst all nations and peoples that for a certain kind of persons the only effective manner of enforcing certain actions, or of compelling submission to certain conditions upon which the every existence of society depends, is the threat of capital punishment. But, if the threat of capital punishment is legitimate, its fulfillment, being a necessary consequence, is also legitimate. And the threat is legitimate whenever it is proven that it represents the only sufficient and perfect sanction for laws upon the enforcement of which the life of the social body depends.

It is simply a case of justified social self-defense—there is the unjust aggression and there is no other effective way of dealing with the aggressor.

St. Thomas Aquinas uses as an illustration the operation performed upon the organism. As we cut off an organ or a part of the body in order to save the organism, so we cut off a member of the social body in order to save society.

B. THE NATURAL SOCIAL ORGANIZATIONS

There are quite a number of social organizations which derive their being from the natural conditions of human society. Such are in ascending order the family, the municipal and district organizations, the county, the state, the nation. While they are all natural organizations, the degree of their social importance and necessity is not the same. Only two are indispensable, the one at the bottom —*the family,* and the one at the top—*the nation* or to use a term more generally applicable, the *sovereign state,* by which we mean the social organization which recognizes no other political power above its own.

I. THE FAMILY

What in the organism proper we call the cell, *i. e.,* the primary element of its constitution, the family is in the constitution of the social organism. It is the social cell because it is the first and fundamental social organization. While it has no other social organization as its source and basis because it is constituted directly by individuals in their individual character, it is itself the source and basis of every other natural organization. Furthermore, being prior to every other natural social organization and having a distinctive natural and necessary social object which is exclusively its own, the family is essentially superior to any other social body on account of the specific superiority of its object. Hence, *in the same way and for the same reason that individuals have their essential rights, over which no social organization has any control, so the*

*family has .s own essential rights which, while yielding
to the essential rights of the individual, precede in dignity
and value the rights of every other social organization.*
Just as individuals do not exist for the family, but
the family for the sake of the individual, so the family
does not exist for the more general natural organizations,
but these organizations exist for the sake of the family.
And evidently, the ends are higher and nobler than the
means because all their dignity and value depend upon the
ends which they serve. From these self-evident principles this important conclusion is inevitable: *no human
authority, not that of the state or nation, not even that of
the Church, can lawfully interfere with the laws of family
life in so far as they are clearly determined by the nature
and the essential object of the family.* However, if human authority does interfere by laws plainly contrary to
the natural laws of the family life, as unfortunately often
is the case, such laws are laws in name only. They are
essentially immoral in character, and therefore, have no
value whatever in conscience.

a. THE NATURE OF THE FAMILY

It is evident from the foregoing discussion how important, and from the social viewpoint, how vital it is to
determine clearly the natural laws of the family, *i. e.,* its
essential rights and duties. However, it is quite impossible to do so unless we have a clear knowledge of its
nature and essential object because the nature and object of a being determine the laws of its action. Fortunately, though of an extremely delicate nature and of the
highest possible significance both individually and socially,
both theoretically and practically, the subject-matter is not
very obscure or subtle in its character and, therefore,
quite obvious in its essential bearings to any ordinary
earnest inquirer.

*The family has for its natural source and basis mar-
riage and for its natural object the proper perpetuation of
the race.* This basic principle enunciating the nature and
object of the family is so simple that it will hardly be dis-

puted by anyone and yet it is so comprehensive that all the essential attributes of the family and the laws regulating its life are easily deduced from it.

Marriage is based upon the natural differentiation of human nature into two sexes, male and female. The reason for this differentiation is obvious,—man is an animal. However, to understand the true nature of marriage, we must not forget the spiritual part of man's nature, because his natural dignity and characteristic position of superiority in the universe are derived from his spiritual, not from his animal nature. Hence, *even in his sex life man is essentially superior to the other animals.* They are guided by natural instinct, man must be guided by reason. For men and women to enter the state of marriage with no other idea but the gratification of sexual desires, is a course of action involving a practical abdication of their rational dignity and would plainly be a perversion of human nature. For the very same reason that man must not eat and drink like a beast, he must not behave like a beast in his sexual life.

We stated that the natural object of the family was the proper perpetuation of the race. There are two things in this definition which we must consider apart. First, the object of the family is the perpetuation of the race. Consequently, *it is not the particular good of the men and women that marry, but the common good of the race which is intended by the order of nature,* and therefore, by God. Evidently, the good of the race, speaking concretely, is the good of the children, *i. e.,* the necessary conditions for their coming into existence and the attainment of their maturity. Hence, if people marry with no other thought in their mind but their own personal and selfish advantage and happiness, we have, again, a plain perversion of the nature of the family, because such a mode of procedure ignores the essential object of married life.

In the second place, it is necessary to insist that the perpetuation of the race must be *proper, i. e.,* it must be realized in a manner befitting the dignity and position of man as a rational and morally responsible agent. The perpetuation of the race is accomplished by two distinct processes, that of *procreation* and that of *education*. Both processes are equally necessary; from the social viewpoint, however, the more important of the two is that of education. *If a normal result is to be obtained under normal conditions the concurrent action of both parents is just as indispensable for the education of the children as for their procreation.* We will understand this if we bear in mind what education is. By education we mean here every necessary and appropriate aid and influence conducive to the attainment of the child's normal, complete, and harmonious development, physical, intellectual, and moral. If, generally speaking, even for the physical part of the educative process the co-operation of the father can hardly be dispensed with, it would be a social and racial crime to leave the intellectual and moral formation of the child normally and permanently in the exclusive control of the mother, not to mention the injustice done thereby to both father and mother.

The criterion by which we must judge the manner and value of the realization of the processes of procreation and education is also of facile comprehension. It is based upon the purpose of the perpetuation of the race. To attain that purpose the race should be kept at least upon the same level of perfection physically, morally, and socially. Consequently, it is the natural and essential duty of both parents to use every appropriate means in their power to promote and advance the amelioration of the race from every viewpoint. If they are not capable of perfecting it, they must at least not contribute to its deterioration.

It is hardly necessary to add that if the duty of education is primarily incumbent upon the family, as is evident from the foregoing explanation, *the right to educate the children is primarily and essentially a family right*. For the state to legislate in matters of education over the heads and against the will of the parents, unless compelled to do so by the open failure of parents to fulfill their duty, would be in violation of the order of nature, and therefore such laws would be without moral value.

b. THE NATURE OF MARRIAGE

To still better understand the nature of marriage, which is the source and basis of the family, we will consider its essential conditions and characteristics. The first and most essential condition of marriage is *its monogamous character*. Even amongst the higher animals where man has not interfered, the sex relations bear the character of a monogamous union. Could it be possible that the Author of nature had assigned to the mere animals a nobler form of sex life than to man? Monogamy is demanded also by a primary emotional instinct, sex jealousy, the object of which is to safeguard the exclusiveness of sex relations. That this strong passion is not the issue of a perversion but the legitimate voice of nature, is apparent from the fact that it is found in the upper species of animals as well as in man.

Consequently, marriage is not the union of one man with several women—polygamy—nor much less the union of one woman with several men—polyandry. Polyandry has been repudiated by all civilized nations as contrary to nature. *Polygamy,* though tolerated by a few, is just as *contrary to the natural law.* Chiefly for two reasons: 1. It lowers the dignity of a woman to share the possession of nuptial rights with other women. There is no reason whatsoever why in sex relations the dignity of the wife should be of lower value than that of the husband. 2. Polygamy precludes the proper home atmosphere, which is equally necessary for both mother and child, but especially for the child during the years of its gradual development.

In the second place the marriage union is not of a transitory but of *a permanent character*. Here again, the higher species of animal life point the way. Where man's influence has not disturbed the natural order, the male and female of the species, after mating, remain together and maintain a kind of community life as long as the care of the young requires the concurrence of both. Shall it be said that animals dependent upon instinct are better equipped by nature to attain the natural object of sex union than man endowed with reason? What a degradation that would mean for man and what an insult to God!

Consequently, *the stability of marriage is a natural and necessary conclusion from the very nature of marriage.* As explained above, both the procreation and the education of the child demand the concurrence of both parents. Who, for instance, would doubt that the mother, before the birth of the child, and both mother and child for a long time after the birth need the quiet, sheltered atmosphere of home life, which would be impossible without the stability of the marriage union? In view of the many years necessary to carry to its completion the process of education in which, for the attainment of proper results, the manly influence of the father is not less essential than the womanly influence of the mother, we cannot but conclude that nature is not fully satisfied with a relative stability, but demands an absolute stability, *i. e., indissolubility.*

Thus, led by the simple analysis of the nature and object of marriage, we have come to the knowledge of its highest attribute, *viz.,* its absolute stability, which excludes the possibility of divorce and remarriage. It is the natural crown and seal of the human sex union and marks its distinction from, and superiority to, purely animal sex life. It is the glory of the race because it is the symbol of its dignity showing forth the victory of the spirit over the flesh and the triumph of the common good of the race over the interests of the individual members by the perfect subordination of the instincts of the flesh and of the ambitions of selfishness to the dictates of the moral order.

The *reasons for the indissolubility of the marriage bond* are of two kinds, one positive, the other, negative. The positive reasons are based upon the necessity of providing the proper moral and social atmosphere for the children's development. If a generation were to grow up without the knowledge and appreciation of home life and its sweet charms and peaceful happiness, the deterioration and even degeneration of the race would be unavoidable. But children whose parents are divorced and remarried, are compelled to grow up and develop in an environment which will necessarily tend to estrange them from the attractions of home life. *Only the family which rests secure upon the unshakable rock of the indissolubility of marriage, can preserve and transmit the hallowed cultural treasures of the past and inspire healthful and noble aspirations for future achievement.* Hence, the disruption of the family is in every normal case the greatest possible disaster for the growing child. As a consequence, if divorce becomes frequent and remarriages common, the proper perpetuation of the race which is the natural object of the family, is in imminent danger of frustration.

The last proposition will lead us logically to consider the negative reasons for the indissolubility of marriage. Granting the irreligion of the present generation on the one side, and on the other, the moral weakness of human nature—and no thoughtful man will deny either—it is an inevitable consequence that *the very possibility of divorce will naturally end in the frequency of its occurrence.* The testimony of the history of the race confirms palpably the teaching of theoretical logic. Periods of immorality and irreligion in any nation were characterized by the facility of divorce and the consequent instability of marriage, and these, again, were the grave-diggers for the greatness and culture of their times.

There is another strong reason against divorce in this that *its very possibility exercises a baneful influence upon the marriage relations* in a double sense : 1. There is the danger that people will enter the state of wedded life on the tacit or even express condition of the hypothetic and provisional character of marriage, and of course, such a union is in its very nature immoral as contrary to the essential conditions and objects of the family. 2. The possibility of a divorce and, consequently, the anticipation of a remarriage, adds another and powerful incentive for the crime of racial suicide by the prevention of conception, because the presence of children might destroy or at least decrease the chances of another favorable marriage.

Such being the chief principles of the natural law in its relation to the sex life of man, we cannot but perceive that *we are living in an age of unparalleled corruption,* both private and public. The first evidence of it is in the voluntary barrenness of marriage and the consequent childless homes. It is a social cancer which eats away the very vitals of society. This condition is even worse by far if, as it commonly happens, it is barrenness without continency. This is, indeed, a moral degradation of the very nature of marriage. But the climax of social immorality, the veritable abomination of abominations, has been attained through the facility and frequency of divorce and the increasing number of successive remarriages. Marriage, the sacred institution of nature and god-ordained fountain of human life, has become legalized concubinage, and the home, the sanctuary of the family and nursery of the race, has become a respectable brothel.

c. FAMILY GOVERNMENT

The family is a society. Hence, there must be a family government, because wherever there is a society, there is social action, *i. e.,* action the object of which is the good of the society, and consequently, a power to direct that social action becomes necessary.

As regards the relation between parents and children, there can be no doubt that the *parental authority is vested equally in both parents* because both parents have co-equal rights and duties towards their children. As this authority has for its object the welfare of the children, it is necessary that parents should consult with one another and always act harmoniously, zealously safeguarding and protecting one another's authority in the eyes of their children. Otherwise, the beneficent influence of their authority would disappear, or at least be greatly impaired. However, should it be impossible for both to reach a common conclusion in a concrete case, *the decision must be left in the power of the father, because the father is the head of the family,* and *he is the head of the family because the husband is the head of the wife*.

Such is the doctrine not only of St. Paul, but of the natural moral order. This conclusion is inevitable: Marriage is a society of two, of which one alone can be the head, and appointed by God is the one who is normally better fitted by nature to perform the functions of government. But about the better natural adaptation for the functions of government there can be no reasonable question. It is a matter of daily experience that the motives influencing and shaping the life and character of the normal man are very different from the motives influencing and shaping the life and character of the normal woman. The sort of motives affecting most deeply the normal woman are of an emotional type, the sort of motives controlling the normal man are more of a rational type. For the object and purposes of the family both types of life and character are equally important, nay equally necessary. However, there can be no doubt that for the exercise of authority, *i. e.,* the directive function in the common life of the family, the rational type is better qualified than the emotional. It has often been said, and the saying is expressive of the order of nature, *that the wife is the heart, and the husband is the head of the home*. Just as the heart in an organism drives the blood through all the parts, thereby not only giving the necessary nourishment, but by the distribution of warmth and moisture providing the proper environment for the well-being of the cells and tissues of the body, so the wife not only bears and nurses the children, but by her love and tender solicitude creates the necessary emotional atmosphere and social environment which constitute the essence of the home. However, it is clear that the heart is not and must not be the directive organ in the body, but the head, and thus also, notwithstanding the paramount practical importance of the wife in the home, the husband is the head of the family.

2. THE STATE

Whenever various families live together in the same territory, certain interrelations based upon mutual dependence will follow. Now it is a common evil or danger that threatens, now it is a common good or advantage that is to be achieved. In each case it is a common necessity which calls for social action. Such is the origin of the wider social organization which we call state. By this term we wish to express its character of social completeness: the perfect state recognizes no higher political authority, it is sovereign or supreme in its own sphere.

Historically, *the ORIGIN of statehood* is not quite clear. The first form of state-life was probably *patriarchal:* the stock family from which the others are descended would naturally exercise a predominating influence over them, and the traditional authority would pass on from the head of that family to the eldest son. However, even in very primitive conditions of social life we find that the chieftains of tribes and clans are elected. This fact is easily accounted for by the necessity of extraordinary circumstances. If a crisis arises and the actual head of the principal family is not capable of dealing with it, a man will be chosen who is better qualified either by the wisdom of his counsel or by his prowess in warfare.

These few remarks are sufficient to show that the *FORM OF GOVERNMENT* is not of decisive importance in a state. It is entirely a matter of expediency. A form of government that would be very good for one people, might be very bad for another on account of their racial and cultural differences. For the same reason, even for the same people the form of government which would be excellent at one stage of its national life might be disastrous at another. Generally speaking, that form of government is best which responds best to the character and needs of a people, whether it be republican or monarchical, democratic or aristocratic, socialist or despotic. *The purpose of government is to govern, and if it governs economically and efficiently, promoting the common good without infringing more than necessary on the rights of the individuals, such a government is ideal, no matter what its form.* Against such a government people will never revolt.

Much has been said of late about the necessity of the CONSENT OF THE GOVERNED *for the legitimacy of a government.* This claim is perfectly justifiable in theory. All men are equal in dignity and rights by nature, and, therefore, in the presence of God no human authority can lawfully exercise its power of social direction whose right to govern is not known to, and recognized by, the people. However, in practice this principle is not of easy application. Who will determine in a particular case how many and what kind of members of the social body are necessary to represent "the consent of the people"? Evidently, purely numerical majority would be an insufficient criterion. Perhaps, we might suggest, the majority of the people who are politically educated and mean to exercise their political rights and duties. Hence, a sudden and radical change in government is seldom advisable. It can produce good results only in extreme cases, when society finds itself in the condition of a man desperately ill, and the only alternative is either a possible chance by a capital operation or sure death.

Since the object of the state is the good of the people that form the state, *the rights and duties of the government* must be determined by that object. Whatsoever action is necessary for the common good, the authority of the state must command, and whatsoever action is seriously detrimental to the common good, the government must forbid and prevent as much as possible. However, there are a few significant exceptions to this principle: 1. The state can never command or authorize an action contrary to the natural law, for the simple reason that the state, no more than the individual, is not autonomous but subject to God and to the will of God as clearly expressed in the natural order of the universe. 2. The state must never interfere with the essential rights of individuals or families except to safeguard and protect them from infringement, because these rights are anterior and superior to those of the state. The state exists for the family and for the individual, but the individual and the family do not exist for the state. 3. The state must not interfere with the rights of people except when necessary, and then not more than necessary. There is nothing more pernicious and subversive of the common good than a meddlesome government which seeks to regulate everything, even the things of most intimate privacy, from the books we read to our bill of fare. It is unfortunate that even democracies are not exempt from this dangerous tendency which, if persisted in, can terminate only either in angry revolution or, what is worse, in the enslavement of a whole nation.

From the foregoing explanation the rights and duties of the state can be reduced to a few heads:

1. In respect to its own life it is authorized to appropriate whatever goods are necessary for the attainment of its legitimate purposes, either by taxation or otherwise, provided there be no injustice in the appropriation and no extravagance in its expenditure.

2. In respect to the life of the people the state must provide a condition of public security and order and, generally speaking, such an atmosphere of social and civil freedom that every one can live his life, physically, intellectually, and morally, in his own way without undue interference.

3. In respect to matters economic the state must safeguard the property rights legitimately acquired as far as they are not contrary to the common good, must protect the economic liberty of all individuals and all classes according as they need pro-

tection, principally, the right of all to work when, where, and how they choose, and finally, it must create such an economic environment that none of its members lack the things necessary for their life and happiness.

4. As regards the education of the young, the state must be careful to respect the rights of parents, whose rights in this connection are prior and superior to those of the state. However, it may and, when necessary, must interfere to protect and safeguard the rights of the children as well as its own, by promoting the work of education and raising its standard in conformity with the cultural needs of the people, but never in contradiction with the rights and duties of the parents.

5. In matters religious and moral it is well to bear in mind the delicacy of their character because they are, more than any other, of private concern and belong to the jurisdiction of the individual conscience of each person.

　　Therefore, the state should be extremely cautious in exercising its authority in cognate matters. When intervention becomes imperative, it ought to be guided by these two simple viewpoints: Its positive influence should be devoted to the purposes of general promotion because religion and morality are the pillars upon which its own structure and security rest. Its negative or rather prohibitive and coercive power should never be used except to prevent or repair public scandal.

CHAPTER TWENTY

THE AIM AND END OF HUMAN LIFE

OBJECT AND SCOPE OF THIS CHAPTER

Our philosophical study of psychology is coming to its close. After first pointing out briefly the subject-matter and problems of psychology, we devoted our attention to the phenomena of life in its threefold order, using the analytical and inductive method of study in a desire to arrive at a knowledge of the nature and origin of plant, sense, and mind life. We called this analytical and causative psychology. Then we proceeded to consider the same subject-matter from another viewpoint, *i. e.,* with another purpose in mind. We were already in possession of the elements of human life, we knew their nature and causal relations, and on the basis of this knowledge we endeavored to find an explanation of the relations existing between the various actions of the same faculties and their natural object and aim, and also of the relations connecting the actions of the various faculties. This study we have termed synthetic and teleological psychology. In this work we are still engaged and we are about to carry it to its conclusion.

We have spoken a great deal so far about the object and aim of the various intellectual and volitional operations of human life and their interrelation, but have said nothing till now of the supreme object and aim to which all others are subordinate and subservient as means to an end. And yet this is the most important of all problems because, if there is, as we have found, a natural order of teleology in human actions, and if, as a consequence, there is a supreme object and aim in human life it is evident that the knowledge of this object and aim is of paramount significance, since whatsoever goodness and value there is in a subordinate object and aim is derived from its relation to its supreme object and aim. Hence the study of this chapter must give us the key for the interpretation of the value and signification of the whole human life, nay, even more than this—of the whole universe. We have had occasion repeatedly to draw attention to the objective order in the universe clearly expressing the fact that the lower beings, and the lower elements of a being, exist for the higher, and consequently, the inorganic world exists for the organic, the inanimate for the animate, the animal for man, and therefore, the supreme object and aim of man is also the supreme object and aim of the universe, in so far as this object and aim is in the universe itself.

When we speak of the supreme object and aim of human life, we may have in mind two distinct meanings. Life evidently must have a supreme object and aim to be realized in its present conditions, *i. e.,* in its mortal phase, in its terrestrial home. However, the human soul, being spiritual, does not die and consequently, will continue to exist and act in other conditions, and this is its ultra-terrestrial and immortal life. Our next task then must be to study the terrestrial supreme aim and end of human life. The knowledge thus acquired will aid us in the explanation of its ultra-terrestrial aim and end.

I. The Supreme Aim and End of Human Life on Earth

From the objective viewpoint, which is, of course, the one we are most concerned about, *the supreme aim and end of human life on earth is the full and proper realization of the moral order:* from the subjective viewpoint *it is perfect happiness, in so far as such a state is possible on earth.* The realization of the moral order and the state of perfect happiness are two aspects of the same reality. If a man realizes the moral order fully in his life, he is, as far as capable, perfectly happy, and there is no other way of attaining such happiness except by the proper and full realization of the moral order.

A. THE REALIZATION OF THE MORAL ORDER

When we speak of the realization of the moral order with reference to the individual man, we mean the actualization of the forces and faculties which are part of his nature in such a manner that their natural objects which opportunity brings within his reach are thereby attained. Evidently, such a realization will differ greatly in respect to people living in a different age or belonging to different races; more even, there never is or can be an identical realization of the moral order between two individuals, no matter how closely related their life and its circumstances may be, because each individual has his own distinct forces and faculties which, as regards the manner of their distribution and the degree of their capacity, are never duplicated, nor are the extrinsic opportunities, as regards their quantity and quality or in their manner of succession ever repeated in the life of two distinct individuals. Consequently, each individual has his own special objective aim in life which he is bound in conscience to realize as well as he may. Hence, the problems of life are individual problems, and therefore, the responsibility for the theoretical and practical solution of these problems is an individual responsibility. We may at best aid one another in the study of the problems, but in respect to their solution, above all their practical solution, the responsibility is absolutely personal.

I. THE OBJECTIVE STANDARD

From these self-evident principles we draw the natural conclusion that what is a full realization of the moral order for one, is not the same for another. For one it might be only a partial realization and for another it might pass by far his powers and opportunities. However, while the standard for the realization of human life is different for each person, and consequently, no general criterion can be used for its determination, yet there are general principles of the greatest practical value to the individual for the determination of his own personal standard, *i. e.,* such a full and proper realization of his life as would perfectly correspond with his intrinsic and extrinsic possibilities. These principles refer chiefly to the intrinsic possibilities of a person, *i. e.,* his forces and faculties, since over the extrinsic possibilities, the social environment and casual opportunities of life, a person has, generally speaking, little or no control.

The first principle in this connection is based upon the potentiality or capacity for development of the forces and faculties of our nature. When we are born, we are incomplete. We are, it is true, in possession of all the forces and faculties belonging to human nature, but we cannot use them to advantage because they are undeveloped. We are placed, normally, by the order of a kind providence into the atmosphere best adapted to their early development—that of the home. Apace with the development of the organism goes that of sense life, and very soon, indeed, as soon as the sensations become clarified, separated, and objectivated, and in this form remain and reappear when needed again on the surface of consciousness, the mind makes its first efforts at abstraction, and thereby the dawn of reason has set in to illumine the human horizon. From this period dates the beginning of man's own problems and his responsibility for their solution. This responsibility is minimal at first, but grows each day with the growing power of his intelligence and will, and as his responsibility grows, that of parents, teachers, and others in the child's environment diminishes, till, when fully developed, his responsibility is all his own. It is most important that during this period of formation the child should be aided to develop all his forces and faculties in adaptation to the changing years and his consequent changing dispositions and necessities. All these efforts should be inspired and controlled by the final result to be attained, *viz.,* the child's complete and harmonic development in virtue of which the body would be a perfect tool of the mind, and the mind a perfect instrument of the will.

Such is the standard of education for the individual. However, education is only a preparation for life, not the realization of life itself. To set up for ourselves the standard of individual life in its full and proper realization, other principles are necessary to regulate the use of our faculties after their powers are completely developed. The first principle in this respect tells us that *we must put our faculties to use and not let them rust.* They are talents that God has intrusted to our stewardship, and we must not bury them in a napkin.

The second principle refers to the manner of applying the faculties. *They must be used rightly, and rightly in two ways: as regards their object and as regards their proportion.* In regard to their object it is evident that they must never be applied to an object which is wrong. But even in regard to right objects, our faculties must not be applied indiscriminately, *i. e.,* we must not give much attention to insignificant objects, and little attention to important objects, but rather proportion our attention to the various objects according to their objective importance and to our subjective capacity and need. Furthermore, our faculties must be used, as we expressed it, in the right proportion. All our faculties are talents which, according to the Giver's intention, must be put to discreet profit. Thus, as it would be a disorder to devote too much care to the body and not enough to the soul, so it would also be a disorder to prefer the soul to the neglect of the body, and again, as it would be disastrous to cultivate the mental powers to the detriment of the moral, so it would be equally disastrous to apply the moral powers with no regard for the mental. The use of our faculties must be governed by the same law as their development: there must be harmony in both. And harmony is to be achieved in both cases by subordination of the lower to the higher powers, excluding or neglecting none.

To these principles must be added another. It is the most important of all, because it explains the supreme object and the manner of attaining it, and, as already pointed out, it is this object upon which depends the whole value and signification of the moral order that is to be realized. This object is God, because, being the Creator of the universe, He is the Author of the ontological order in the world, and consequently, also of the logical and moral order, since the logical order is but the intellectual reproduction, and the moral order but the deliberate application of the ontological order by man to his life and action. Hence, the intellectual basis for the full realization of the moral order is man's complete and clear knowledge, as far as his capacity permits, of the universe in its relation to God, *i. e.*, in so far as it manifests the power, wisdom, and goodness of God; and *the proper and formal act of realization consists in the definite and perfect approval and acceptance of the moral order as the best available means of presenting to God the homage of humble submission, profound reverence, and sincere gratitude which man, as a creature, owes Him.*

2. THE OBJECTIVE AND SUBJECTIVE RESULT

Such is the standard or objective criterion by which we may gauge and estimate human life in its general aspect and value. While, of course, this standard of human life refers to the individual, yet it may serve also as a basis for the evaluation of social life, since social life depends upon the individual as a means for an end. Consequently, that form of social life will be its standard which is best adapted to aid the individual members of the social body to attain the standard of individual life. It is evident that both the social and individual standards for the realization of the moral order are ideals which in the concrete conditions of life are never fully actualized. However, earnest, systematic, and persevering exertion on the part of man to approach the ideal, as far as his intrinsic powers and his extrinsic opportunities allow, will produce a definite result, which we may call *THE PERFECT MAN* from the objective viewpoint, and *THE HAPPY MAN* in its subjective aspect.

a. THE PERFECT MAN

The objective result of such a full and proper realization of the moral order is, with regard to the individual, a perfect man. Not absolutely perfect, but perfect in relation to his innate powers and capacity on the one side, and to the objective conditions of his environment for perfection on the other. He would be a man who had profited to the fullest extent by his gifts and opportunities, who had made the most of himself and his chances.

Such a man would appear to be an admirable specimen of manhood—his body trained and kept in condition to carry out the commands, wishes, and purposes of the soul. The soul itself with its various faculties and powers well developed into a state of calm poise and complete self-control: in his affections neither cold or indifferent, nor effervescent or sentimental; in his intellectual activity neither shallow or frivolous, nor abstruse or subtle; in his volitional life neither vacillating or fickle, nor stubborn or immovable: yet withal strong and warm emotionally, clear and thorough intellectually, firm and energetic volitionally, and what is more: all his actions would be performed under the guidance of a sound conscience, and would be normally ennobled by the purest intentions.

It is evident that such a man would be a complete personality, thinking his own thoughts and living his own life in conformity with his own convictions, a thorough character in whom the respect for authority would not be perverted into flattery to superiors, and the love for friends would not lead to injustice to enemies; and as the crown and seal of it all: the fundamental motive and the highest aspiration would be the realization of the moral order which represents and expresses the plan of God in the universe. There are four moral habits—the so-called cardinal virtues, which would account for the existence of such men in the world: prudence, temperance, justice, and fortitude. They would be the pillars upon which such a character can be built, the sources from which his actions would naturally flow. We will give a brief definition of each.

By *PRUDENCE* we apply, in an appropriate manner, the general principles of the moral order to the occurrences of daily life. It is the proficiency of the intellect devoted to practical decisions, based upon the relations of the end to be attained and the means available for its attainment. Wisdom, good sense, sound judgment, are names for similar qualities.

TEMPERANCE aids us to obtain and retain the control of our spiritual faculties over the powers and instincts of our animal life. Its object is the regulation of the relations between the spiritual and the animal part of human nature. Cognate virtues are, above all, chastity and sobriety.

In virtue of *JUSTICE* we respect the rights of others, those of God before all others, giving to all their due in the same way as we want others to respect our rights. The object of this virtue is a plain inference from its definition: to regulate the relations between ourselves and others. In its strict sense we speak of justice as *COMMUTATIVE,* which refers to the relations between equals, *i.e.,* where the mutual duties of justice are founded upon a common basis, *viz.,* the natural law. Inasmuch as justice regulates the mutual duties between superiors and inferiors, we call it *LEGAL* justice, inasmuch as it is based upon positive law. In a very special sense we call it *DISTRIBUTIVE* justice when we refer to the duty of authority to confer and distribute the honors and burdens of social life according to merit and capacity. Honesty, uprightness, integrity, fairness, equitableness, are virtues related to the same subject-matter.

Finally, we come to the fourth and strongest pillar of character: *FORTITUDE.* Its object is to strengthen us for the battle of moral life, to uphold our courage and the determination to persevere on the right path in spite of danger and all possible evils. Fortitude is, therefore, what we call the backbone of the moral man. Its correlated virtues are courage, patience, endurance, forbearance, perseverance, and others.

b. THE HAPPY MAN

So far we have examined the objective result of the full and proper realization of the moral order—the perfect man. We will consider briefly now its subjective aspect—the happy man. The perfect man is also the happy man; they are the distinct aspects only of one and the same thing.

Apparently, happiness is something altogether subjective, personal. What produces happiness in one, may produce unhappiness in another, and on the contrary, the things over which some feel extremely unhappy, may be the cause of intense happiness to others. There are people who are happy in the midst of sufferings, just as there are people who are unhappy in the midst of pleasures. Furthermore, there are people who seem to be more or less indifferent to happiness: they appear never very happy nor ever very unhappy, no matter what occurs. Such indifference might be the fruit of perfect self-control, but generally it is the result of dullness, or the lack of a natural disposition and capacity for happiness.

All these concrete facts indicate plainly the subjectiveness of happiness; and the reason for this subjectiveness is in the emotions. To feel happy means simply: I am satisfied with my present state of consciousness. Similarly, unhappiness expresses dissatisfaction with the actual contents of consciousness. Here we begin to perceive that happiness, while formally an emotional element of life and, therefore, the most subjective and volatile element of human nature, is based upon an objective foundation, which, while easily changeable, is to a certain extent under our control—the objective contents of consciousness. Consequently, if we were capable of constantly filling our consciousness with satisfactory objects, we would always be happy. And this is precisely what the perfect man does. His life is, in truth, a full life, and it is filled with the very objects which are by their nature disposed to give satisfaction. As far as he is capable of controlling his consciousness, there is nothing which ought not to be there, and there is everything that ought to be there. No wonder, then, that he is happy. Such a state evidently does not exclude the feelings of privation and sadness, even of pain and bitterness, but they do not produce unhappiness because they are admitted and welcomed as satisfactory objects of consciousness, since they are useful and even necessary as means for the acquisition of higher goods. The bitterest trials could only duplicate the sublime principle of Job: The Lord has given it, the Lord has taken it: His name be blessed!

These principles, which speak for themselves and have been justified by the experience of all good people in direct proportion to their state of perfection, and above all in the life of the Saints, are also in complete harmony with the psychology of the emotions. We have seen above that emotions are the natural concomitants of all conscious action. When the action appears in consciousness as satisfactory, *i. e.,* when its object is achieved by means of a natural, energetic, and successful conscious action, its emotional concomitant or result is joy or, at least, a general feeling of satisfaction. On the contrary, when the action appears in consciousness as in some way defective or excessive, and, consequently, as a failure, its emotional concomitant and result is sadness, or, at least, a general feeling of disappointment. The objective reason for this psychological process is obvious: actions when successful, appropriate, and proportioned to both faculty and object, complete and perfect human nature, whereas human nature, whose intrinsic tendency is towards perfection, remains unsatisfied because incomplete, when actions are for some reason or other unsuccessful, or when there is an incongruity or disproportion between the faculty and the object. Taking these psychological facts and their reasons for our premises, we come to the same conclusion, that the more perfect a man is, the more happy he must be, and that the happiest man can only be the most perfect man. From these principles we draw another important conclusion: the objective tendency in virtue of which all beings of the universe seek their natural completeness and perfection, is accompanied in man by the subjective tendency towards complete and perfect happiness, because, just as perfection and happiness are only the objective and subjective aspects of the same reality, so the tendency towards objective perfection and the tendency towards happiness or subjective perfection are really one and the same tendency from distinct viewpoints.

B. THE FAILURE TO REALIZE THE MORAL ORDER

It is a regrettable fact that the moral order is not always realized in the life of man. And since the moral order has for its objective basis and source the ontological order, the violation of the former has a disturbing influence upon the latter. Man is capable of violating the moral order, for he is free, and since man alone of all beings in the universe is free, he alone is capable of disturbing the order of the universe. This consideration sets before our mind vividly the awful responsibility attached to freedom, giving into man's weak and wavering hands the power to introduce an element of disorder into the world and thereby to upset, as far as he is concerned, the divine plan in the government of the universe. Bearing in mind this double character of man's responsibility —to govern himself freely and, thereby decide his own destiny, and to bear a part in the government of the universe,—it is clearly of the highest practical importance to discuss as briefly as we can, sin, its nature, and its natural and necessary consequences.

I. THE NATURE OF SIN

We call sin any violation of the moral order. Its objective element consists in a deviation from the moral law. Consequently, any action that deviates from the moral law, *i. e.,* is not in conformity with the principles of the moral order, is an objective, or, as we say, *material* sin. The *formal* character of sin is in the subjective element of the action, *viz.,* in the deliberate determination of the will to perform or omit the action, though to do so is contrary to the moral law. From the definition of sin a criterion for the judgment of its gravity is easily inferred. It depends on the one side evidently upon the objective importance, and on the other, upon the subjective perfection of the sinful action. Therefore, a sin is the greater, the more necessary an action is for the realization of the moral order and the more deliberate and free is the decision of the will. The freedom of decision being in direct relation to the clearness of judgment, whatever influences unfavorably the power of judging clearly, such as prejudice, ignorance, a state of mental distraction, as well as all kinds of emotional excitement, has a direct bearing upon the freedom of decision and thus, diminishes the gravity of sin. In the same manner the gravity of sin is lessened by factors which directly weaken the will, such as habits of sin which have gradually undermined its power of resisting temptations.

2. THE WICKEDNESS OF SIN

Sin, being a violation of the moral order established and sanctioned by God, is in its very nature a rebellion against the Divine Sovereignty. Inasmuch as we owe absolute allegiance to the Divine Majesty, every sin is, in the strictest possible sense, a crime of high treason and even implies idolatry because it is a service of the creature instead of the Creator.

In the second place, sin is a desecration of the Divine Dignity, an attempt to insult and debase the divine Majesty, because the moral order violated by sin is the created expression and reflection of the divine nature. This aspect of sin is analogous to an insult offered the flag or the ambassador of a nation, which is taken as an insult to the country which he represents.

Furthermore, sin is a violation and desecration of man's own dignity which, while infinitely small in the presence of the divine Majesty, yet is infinitely great when compared with the rest of the universe. Man was set by God upon a throne to be the lord and king of creation, upon an altar to exercise the priestly function of worship on behalf of those creatures which are not capable of divine worship; and in sinning, *i. e.,* abusing the royal and priestly prerogatives of reason and freedom, he descends from the throne and from the altar to become a slave and an apostate.

Finally, and this is perhaps the most awful attribute of sin, it is a most fruitful and practically inexhaustible source of evil and harm to the sinner, and, in many instances, to a number of others, not for life only, but often for eternity. Apart from the fact that usually one sins begets another and thus, each sin is likely to have an uncountable progeny, and that the effects of sin vary greatly according to the nature of the sin and the nature of the sinner, yet sin in every case tends to deteriorate the natural faculties and powers of man, weakening on the one side his native tendencies for good, and on the other, strengthening his inclinations for evil, in virtue of which influence it may happen, and unfortunately often does happen, that man, who was created a little less than the angels, through inveterate habits of sin becomes little less than a devil. No wonder that sin unfits man for the enjoyment of true happiness on earth and unfits him still more, indeed absolutely, for the attainment of perfect happiness in the life to come.

To this train of evil inherent in every sin must be added the manifold evil produced by many sins to others and in others, in so far as they are the victims of those sins, or take scandal and follow the attractions of sin themselves. In this regard, it is almost impossible to overestimate the multitude of new processions of evil thus originating from one sin. It is like the rock thrown into the midst of a calm lake: a circle of ripples forms and spreads in ever-widening circles till they are lost to the eye on the horizon. Such are the ever widening circles of evil formed by sin; they spread and scatter in every direction, lost in the end to the eye of man, but not lost to the eye of the Sovereign Judge.

3. THE IRREPARABLENESS OF SIN

If it were necessary to demonstrate the horror and awfulness of sin still more, we would call attention to its irreparableness. By this we mean the practical impossibility of undoing its depravity or repairing the evil and harm which it causes. Of course, we speak here from the philosophical viewpoint only and do not belittle in any sense the superabundant reparation for sin in the supernatural order by Christ's sacrifice of atonement.

It is possible for the sinner by true repentance and actions of a propitiatory character to repair the moral order which he has violated. However, it will always be a repaired and not an unviolated moral order, since the sinful act and its consequences can never be undone.

In a similar manner, there can be no doubt that God may and often does forgive the sinner's guilt if he sincerely repents and atones, as well as he is able, for the dishonor and shame he has brought upon the divine dignity. However, here again, there is an immense difference between the state of the forgiven sinner and that of the innocent person. The one is an innocent servant, the other but a pardoned criminal.

Not even the sinner's own personal dignity violated by his sin can ever be perfectly restored. Whatever he may do, he can never forget how he has debased himself, descending from the place of honor upon the throne and the altar upon which God had set him, no more than the prodigal son, back in his father's house and grace, could ever forget that he had left his place of dignity and honor to herd the swine of another.

This awful fact of the irreparableness of sin will come home to us still more forcefully when we think of the manifold evil and harm produced by sin in the sinner himself, and through scandal in others. We saw above how sin is as a rule the mother of many sins and how each sin starts a circle of evil which spreads and spreads till no human eye and no human measure can encompass it. It would be folly here to think of, or hope for, any sort of effective and comprehensive reparation. If this is true in general, it is especially true as regards the sinner's own nature and faculties. If sin has become a deeply rooted habit, the effect produced is a profound and permanent perversion for which there is hardly any remedy available in the natural order. In respect to the irreparableness of the consequences of sin in the future world, more will be said further on.

II. *The Ultimate Aim and End of Human Life*

The whole human race has ever believed and hoped in an ultra-terrestrial life, in which man's ultimate aim and end would find its perfect realization. There is a very strong presumption in favor of such a faith and hope in the fact that the moral order has never been and never will be, as far as history tells us and our own experience teaches, perfectly and completely realized either in the life of individuals or in the life of nations here on the globe. But, it would seem that either a perfect and complete realization of the moral order, or at least, a perfect and complete compensation for the failure of its realization would be necessarily demanded by the justice and holiness of Almighty God. Hence the faith and hope of mankind that the soul is immortal, and that the divine government of the world will find a perfect justification and the moral order a complete vindication, cannot appear extravagant and baseless to the philosopher, who, as a consequence, will devote his serious attention to the solution of this grave problem.

A. THE IMMORTAL LIFE

When we speak of immortality we speak of the soul exclusively, not of the body of man. While Christianity

plainly teaches that the body will ultimately participate in the immortal life of the soul, yet we consider this
doctrine a *mystery* in the strict sense of the word, *i. e.,* a
doctrine of Revelation which as such does not concern the
philosopher. The arguments for the immortality of the
soul are manifold, some direct and others indirect, some
conclusive, others only confirmative.

I. CONCLUSIVE ARGUMENTS FOR IMMORTALITY

To demonstrate the immortality of the soul conclusively, two things are required: 1. It must be shown
that the nature of the soul is such that, if left to itself, its
life never ceases, *i. e.,* it does not bear in its own being the
source of dissolution. 2. It must be shown that no external influence will bring about its destruction.

a. THE NATURAL IMMORTALITY OF THE SOUL

The demonstration of immortality as a natural and essential attribute of the soul is based exclusively upon
the proof already given in the first part of our study on
psychology, that the soul is spiritual. We showed there
that it is in the very nature of a spirit to exclude composition of integral parts, that it is essentially indivisible
and therefore, simple, in the same way as it is in the nature of a body to be composed of integral parts, to have
quantity, to be essentially divisible. For the same reason
that *a body may begin to be by evolution and cease to be
by dissolution because it is essentially composed of parts,
a spirit, because it excludes essentially all such component
parts, cannot begin to be by evolution nor can it cease to
be by dissolution,* since a being begins to be by evolution
when it acquires its last essential part, and ceases to be by
dissolution when it loses possession of one of its essential
parts. Being a simple substance, the soul can only begin
to be in its totality at once, *i. e.,* by creation, and for the
very same reason it can only cease to be in its totality at
once, *i. e.,* by annihilation. But neither creation nor an-

nihilation can be the act of the soul, nor of any other contingent agent; being an absolute and independent manner of acting, both can be attributed only to the one absolute agent, God. Hence, *the life of the soul, being spiritual, can never come to an end by an intrinsic principle of decay or disintegration, it is naturally immortal.* If it ceased to be at all, it could only be by violence from without, by an act of God.

b. THE NEVER-ENDING LIFE OF THE SOUL

The soul of man, being spiritual, is naturally immortal, and if left to itself will never come to an end. Even more than that, there is no power in heaven or on earth that can terminate its existence except of the omnipotent and absolute power of God. Hence the question that remains to be answered is this: can we prove conclusively that God will never annihilate the soul? There is no doubt that we can. We will show that *God does not annihilate anything* and therefore, does not annihilate the soul. We will even go farther and show that *God cannot annihilate anything,* because such a thing is contrary to His infinite perfection.

There is a law of nature which says that the mass of the universe never varies. It has been found by the most careful experiments that in all changes and transformations of bodies the mass remains ever the same, there is never any indication of matter disappearing from, or of new matter appearing in, existence. In other words, science never finds a creation or an annihilation of beings. The philosopher may accept the interpretation of the physicist in this connection without reserve. While *God is the Creator of the universe, He is not its annihilator.* He creates when it is His pleasure to do so, but He never annihilates anything simply because He is perfect. When He creates, He foreordains the purposes of His creatures and foresees their accomplishment. There can be no surprise that would or could produce a change in His plan and in His consequent will to which beings owe their existence. It is true, man is capable of destroying his own works because he is essentially imperfect and limited in both mind and will. His mind changes for better or for worse, either because it grows and develops, or because it yields to the influence of sense environment; and his will changes for better or for worse, either because it follows the better or worse light of the mind, or because it yields to natural fickleness or to the control of intrinsic inclinations and extrinsic influences. But such a charge is unthinkable in the infinitely perfect mind and will of God. Hence, we are justified in saying that *God never annihilates anything*. If this is true as regards material beings which, in conformity with their nature, are subject to never-ending changes, but not to annihilation, it is true, a fortiori, in respect to spiritual beings which, being essentially simple, are not subject to substantial transformation but continue to live on forever, preserving forever their substantial identity.

This argument, we believe, proves clearly and conclusively the never-ending life of the soul. However, we think that we can still more strengthen it by slightly modifying the assertory proposition which denies the fact of its annihilation by God, transforming it into an apodictic principle. Thus, we would add that not only does God not annihilate the human soul, but *it is intrinsically impossible for Him to annihilate anything, because annihilation would involve contradiction in the divine nature*. We will understand the power of this argument better after our discussion on the nature of God in metaphysics. For our present purpose it is sufficient to perceive the impossibility of succession or time in the life of God. Creatures are essentially subject to time because their nature is a mixture of actuality and potentiality: they possess at all times some elements of the being which they are capable of possessing, but never all the elements together and forever, since some elements are exclusive of one another. Thus all creatures are subject to time because they are subject to change, since they are constantly gaining or losing some of their elements. This process of gain or loss is necessarily successive, happening as it does by a series of phenomena, one of which follows another. Such is the condition of created existence because it is imperfect; but such cannot be the condition of the existence and life of God because He is infinitely perfect. There is no mixture of actuality and potentiality in God, He is pure and perfect actuality. He can neither gain nor lose anything, He is absolutely changeless, and, therefore, His existence and action exclude the idea of time or succession absolutely. Since an act of annihilation would introduce the idea of time into the divine life, therefore we deny its possibility. We reason as follows:

Things exist by a positive act of God—the act of creation. This act we call preservation when we look upon it from the creature's viewpoint, because, being subject to time, we distinguish clearly between the moment it came into being and every other moment in which it continues to be. With reference to God, evidently, preservation is identical with creation. However, it is not possible to apply the idea of annihilation to God in the same manner, because there is plainly a contradiction between creation and annihilation, which is totally absent between creation and preservation. Preservation is creation not suspended, but annihilation is creation suspended, it is its direct contradictory. But *two contradictory acts cannot co-exist in the same being simultaneously;* consequently, when attributed to the same agent they imply necessarily succession and, therefore, time in that agent.

Hence, *God does not annihilate the human soul because He does not annihilate anything; and He does not annihilate anything because He cannot annihilate anything; and He cannot annihilate anything because He can neither create and annihilate simultaneously,* since such a thing is absurd, *nor can He create and annihilate successively,* since the nature of God excludes succession of time in His acts.

2. CONFIRMATIVE ARGUMENTS FOR IMMORTALITY

There are a number of arguments on behalf of the immortality of the soul and its never-ending life which, though perhaps not strictly conclusive, are of great moral value in confirming the convincing force of the metaphysical arguments so far discussed. We will present briefly the most significant.

a. There is first the argument based upon the *unanimous voice of mankind*. It is true, this argument is not decisive in itself. Yet it is of great moral power. The intellectual authority of the whole race in a matter so vital is apt to create conviction in most thoughtful minds. However, its direct and immediate value is not conclusive, but presumptive. It produces the presumption that there must be convincing and clearly perceptible reasons for the immortality of the soul in order to account for the practical unanimity of such a conviction.

b. In the second place, man has a *natural horror of death*. He is enabled to conquer that horror only through faith in the immortal and never-ending life of the soul. Without this faith man is fundamentally incapable of happiness. With the horror of annihilation staring in his face he would live his days like the man condemned to the gallows, waiting for the hour of execution. His outlook would be enveloped in utter darkness with not the faintest ray of hope. Nevertheless, it is a fact that there is in the human soul an innate, ineradicable, and irresistible desire for, and tendency to, happiness. Such a natural desire and uncontrollable inclination cannot be explained unless God, the author of human nature, put it there. But what a strange anomaly it would be in the order of the universe if such a god-given desire and irresistible longing of human nature should be frustrated, should remain without its proper satisfaction! Hence, the wisdom and goodness of God appear to demand the immortality of the soul.

c. There is a third moral argument, probably the strongest of all: *the necessity of immortality for an adequate sanction of the moral law.* As we explained in the last chapter, there can be no doubt of the necessity of an adequate sanction for the law of nature. The infinite justice and holiness of God alike demand it: His holiness because the divine legislator cannot treat with indifference the voluntary fulfillment or the deliberate violation of His holy will, and His justice because there must be an adequate retribution in strict conformity with the degree of merit or demerit for the natural order that has been freely complied with, or departed from, by man. It is evident that such an adequate sanction does not find its accomplishment on earth. Prosperity and happiness are plainly not in exact proportion to virtue and merit, nor are the disadvantages and disappointments in life ever proportionate to sin and immorality. Often the very opposite is clearly apparent. Where, for instance, would be the adequate sanction for the law which demands the sacrifice of life, if death were the end of the soul's life also? Hence, there can be no explanation of an adequate sanction of this moral law without the immortality of the soul.

B. THE BLESSED LIFE

Following our whole course of discussions on human psychology consistently and persistently to its natural conclusion, we are led to consider the life of the soul after death as a life of blessedness. The objective realization of man's natural perfection is, as we have seen, accompanied by subjective happiness already on earth. Consequently, when beyond the grave the preparatory and provisional stage of human life has been transformed into a condition of definite attainment and permanent possession, the subjective aspect of perfection—happiness, will be naturally in exact proportion to the degree of objective perfection actualized and definitely attained. And since no further growth and actualization is possible on the objective side, so also on the subjective, the potentialities of the soul for the fruition of happiness have been fully actualized and permanently determined. Such is the general conception of what we mean by the expression: the blessed life of the soul.

I. THE SPIRITUALITY OF THE BLESSED LIFE

From reason unaided by faith, we are not able to know with certainty many things about the exact status of the blessed life. While we are quite sure from the knowledge we have of its spiritual nature that the soul is intrinsically capable of an independent existence and life, we can know nothing about the manner of its activity, when deprived of the concurrent action of the imagination without which the soul is incapable of action in its present condition.

From the fact of the consubstantial union of soul and body, and from the necessity of their concurrent action in the present life, some philosophers—amongst them Cardinal Mercier—draw the conclusion that the status of the blessed life demands the reunion of soul and body. In their opinion, the doctrine of the resurrection of the body is a natural truth of reason and not exclusively a mystery of faith. We do not think this conclusion justified. We can very well conceive the possibility of the consubstantial union of soul and body and the consequent necessity of their concurrent action, not only as a definite and absolute disposition in the divine plan, but as a temporary and provisional status of human existence for the purposes of the probationary character of human life on earth. There can be no doubt that the life of a spirit, which is independent of material conditions, considered in itself, is superior to that which is so dependent, and there is, apart from Revelation, no conclusive evidence to show that man, in reward for fidelity during the period of preparation and probation, might not be elevated to such a higher form of existence and life. If left to the exclusive guidance of our mind, we would probably find in the very condition of our present existence a reason that would rather incline us to expect such an elevation to a life of definite and permanent independence of matter. Surely, all will admit freely that, though the concurrence of sense is necessary and essential, the specific activity of the spiritual soul is, to say the least, as much restricted and hindered as it is aided and clarified by its consubstantial union with the organic body. But if this is the case, and consequently, if the soul in its state of separation could act more freely and more perfectly, we can conceive of no reason why it should naturally demand reunion with the body.

2. THE ESSENCE OF THE BLESSED LIFE

There are two courses of reasoning which lead naturally to a conception of what the blessed life of the soul consists in. The one we have followed in the first part of this chapter. There we dwelled upon the matter, showing how the full and perfect realization of the moral order was the destiny assigned to man on earth by His Maker, and how man's happiness was the natural correlated subjective concomitant of that destiny. Through death the boundary line between the state of preparation and promise and the state of definite acquisition and fulfillment is passed. The destiny as such remains the same, the only change being that from the struggle for its possession to the actual and absolute attainment of possession. Since this attainment is nothing else than the actual realization of the moral order which, again, concretely speaking, is nothing else than the perfectly satisfactory knowledge of the plan of God by the human mind and its complete and absolute approval and acceptance by the human will, it is quite evident that *the essence of the blessed life is the knowledge and the love of God.*

There is another way of reasoning which leads to the same conclusion. No one will seriously dispute the principle that a being's natural destiny is to be found in the adequate object of its highest faculties. The reason for this principle is obvious. Beings exist for action. But actions of lower faculties attain objects which are valuable only as means for higher actions. *Only the adequate object of the highest faculty has no longer the relative value of a means, it is an end.* Hence, the adequate object of the human mind and the human will must be the ultimate end of man's life and, consequently, the essence of the blessed life. Which is the adequate object of the mind and will of man? Surely, there can be no doubt about the answer. Every argument of this book tends to give it: God as the absolutely perfect cause of the universe is that object.

The knowledge and love of God as manifested in His works constitute the objective and essential element of the blessed life; the subjective element of such knowledge and love, which is their natural and necessary resultant and concomitant, *is* precisely what we have termed *blessedness or perfect happiness.* The perfection of blessedness is not absolute, but relative, it corresponds exactly to the relative perfection of the knowledge and love of God. We call this knowledge and love perfect in so far as it is as perfect as the individual dispositions allow: no soul could know and love God better than it does. For the very same reason we call its blessedness perfect because no soul could be more blessed than it is. Evidently, the relative perfection of both the knowledge and love of God on the one side and of the blessedness of the soul on the other, depend upon, and are in exact correlation with, the faculties developed, the habits and powers acquired, and the general character formed during the life of probation and preparation. Hence, there will be as many degrees of perfection in the knowledge and love of God, and consequently, also of perfection in the fruition of happiness, as there will be souls that have achieved their destiny.

It is hardly necessary to add that in the state of pure nature unaided by grace—and of this state alone have we been speaking, and we could not speak of any other in philosophy—such a knowledge of God, while incomparably more perfect than on earth, and all-sufficient to fill the capacity of the soul, would not be a Beatific Vision, *i. e.,* a direct intuition and contemplation of the divine nature; it could be but an indirect and inductive knowledge of the divine goodness and power, wisdom and beauty as manifested in God's creation.

3. THE LOSS OF THE BLESSED LIFE: HELL

Thus far we have studied the immortal life of the soul from the positive viewpoint. Unfortunately, there is also a negative aspect which we must not pass by. The blessed life is not the spontaneous and necessary fruit of human life, but depends absolutely upon the fact and the measure of the free and deliberate realization of the moral order by man on earth. We are well aware from history and observation that there are many who fail to realize the moral order, even in its most essential parts. This is not so strange when we consider the innate human weakness and imperfection on the one hand, and on the other, the environment in which the battle of life must be won. Hence, two questions arise: 1. What will be the state of such a soul after death? 2. Will its status be, like that of blessedness, permanent and irrevocable?

a. THE NATURE OF HELL

The answer to the question of the nature of hell is simple enough: it is the loss of blessedness, because the soul will be deprived of what constitutes its blessedness. Such a soul will be totally incapable of that knowledge and love of God which is the source and basis of blessedness of the future life. The reason for this privation is, again, of easy comprehension: the faculties of the soul have not been properly developed, its powers and habits acquired have not been properly directed, and its character has not been formed with a view of disposing and fitting it for its ultra-terrestrial activity.

That such a privation of its natural destiny must involve the loss of blessedness, cannot admit of any doubt. It must have a most terrifying and, at the same time, supremely saddening effect upon the soul. Such a soul is comparable to a fish cast upon dry land or to a child thrown into the water. However, in these two cases, the terror has a speedy end: both the fish and the child will soon be relieved by death. But what about the state of the soul that has lost the blessed life? In other words, is hell a transitory and provisional or a permanent and absolute condition? Is hell temporal or is it eternal? This is a tremendous question in itself and, besides, of the utmost practical importance from the moral and pedagogical viewpoint, since its solution is capable of exercising a decisive influence upon human life on earth.

b. THE ETERNITY OF HELL

No one believing in the immortality of the soul ever doubted of the eternal or everlasting state of blessedness. But many people do seriously question the eternity of hell. No wonder, when we look upon that awful prospect of never-ending privation and hopeless despair. However, its terrifying aspect must not prevent us from examining the problem fairly and squarely from every angle. Such a careful and comprehensive study will lead to this conclusion: *while there are various good reasons which point in the direction of an eternal hell, there is not one solid reason against it.*

An illustration will, perhaps, give us a better understanding of the problem than many explanations. For a man to utilize fully the internal gifts and the external opportunities of his life, he must be fitted for his task in his childhood and his youth: he must not neglect his education. If he does, the loss can never be made good, his life can never be what it otherwise would have been. In a similar manner, since the full and perfect realization of all human talents and opportunities does not come into effect till after death, our whole life on earth is like the childhood and youth in which we must be educated and properly fitted for the ultra-terrestrial life. If this education for eternity is neglected, *i. e., if death finds us unprepared and unfit for the blessed life, the loss can never be repaired,* we know of nothing capable to remove the soul's unfitness and to give it that fitness which only the patient educative labor of a life-time can give.

The sanction of the moral law seems to imply the same answer. There is no doubt the blessed life has the character of compensation: it is a reward for loyal service. *But if we assume that hell is not eternal, heaven is no longer a reward for loyal service,* as it would sooner or later be the possession of all without exception. Thus we would be compelled to conclude that there is no perfect divine sanction of the moral order, since in the end the just and the wicked would find themselves in the same condition of blessedness. Such a conclusion, however, is inacceptable because the goodness and wisdom as well as the holiness and justice of God demand the adequate sanction of the moral order.

The only reason to doubt the eternity of hell could arise from the possibility of a reincarnation of the soul and a consequent other life of probation. While it is true that we cannot positively prove that such a thing is impossible because it is not absurd in itself, yet there are nowhere, as far as history and personal experience are concerned, any positive signs or reasons in favor of a reincarnation. If we suppose that a second or third probationary life had ever been conceded by God for the purpose of amendment, evidently some people would be able to enlighten us about it, since the recollections of the experience of the former life and its result would be indispensable conditions of the later lives. However, there has never been any one able to furnish us with any reliable information on this subject. Hence, though perhaps we may not be authorized to assert that the eternity of hell is metaphysically certain, there can be no doubt of its practical certainty.

PART THREE

METAPHYSICS, THE PHILOSOPHY OF THE
TRANSCENDENTAL WORLD

CHAPTER TWENTY-ONE

METAPHYSICAL PROBLEMS AND THEORIES

GENERAL CONCEPT OF METAPHYSICS

In metaphysics the human mind reaches the extreme limit in its abstractive thought on the universe; and it is a limit towards which it tends irresistibly. It is in the very nature of the mind to desire, and labor for, a comprehensive, systematic, and profound knowledge of the universe so as to be able to render an adequate account of its existence and all its phenomena. Not everybody actually arrives at such a supreme philosophical synthesis or metaphysical conception of the world, but anyone who is at all intellectually interested in the study of his own nature and of his environment will not rest content until he comes into the possession of such a universal viewpoint of the world's nature, origin, and destiny. If, for one reason or another, he is not capable of basing his metaphysical knowledge on objective principles, he will create his own metaphysics, *i. e.,* he will explain the universe to his satisfaction on the basis of subjective assumptions. Thus we are in the presence of two kinds of metaphysics: *objective metaphysics, i. e.,* a supreme philosophical synthesis of the universe founded upon the objective data of cosmology and psychology, and *subjective metaphysics, i. e.,* a supreme philosophical synthesis of the universe built upon the subjective theories constructed by the mind itself, more or less independently of the objective facts and conditions of the world.

To understand the exact place and value of metaphysics in philosophy it is well to recall what we said of it in the chapter of the systematic structure of the logical order. There we spoke of metaphysics as a super-philosophy in a similar way as we called cosmology and psychology super-sciences. With this expression we mean to say that, in the same manner as the natural sciences of inorganic matter, such as physics, chemistry, geology, astronomy, etc., are preliminary studies to cosmology; and the natural sciences of life, such as biology, physiology, psycho-physiology, etc., are preliminary studies to psychology, so also cosmology and psychology are preliminary studies to metaphysics; in other words, just as cosmology and psychology are, in respect to the natural sciences, not co-ordinated but super-ordinated, so also is metaphysics, in respect to cosmology and psychology, not co-ordinated but super-ordinated. In cosmology and psychology we have studied the distinctive characteristics and their relationships of the two great divisions of beings that compose the universe, the living and the non-living separately. The very same subject-matter, *i. e.,* the beings of the universe, will form the object of our study in metaphysics. However, we study them here from quite another viewpoint, *i. e.,* the formal object of our study is different. It is no longer the differences, but the identity of the beings which we consider. In other words, we look upon the beings of the universe simply as beings, and not as beings of special types, and thus, we can group together all classes, orders, and divisions of beings in one homogeneous sum, since in being beings they are all identical. This, then, is the proper and specific object of metaphysics—the study of the universe in so far as it is a sum of homogeneous beings, which is equivalent to saying that it is the study of the universe from the most simple and therefore, also the most universal viewpoint.

I. Subjective Metaphysics

Though it is plainly impossible to arrive at a metaphysical conception and knowledge of the universe unless we have a clear and certain knowledge of the beings and their attributes which make up the universe, yet there have been in all periods of human history philosophers who formed their metaphysics, more or less, upon subjective grounds, being swayed to a large extent by non-intellectual motives, having their source, for instance, in their peculiar attitude on religion and morality, or in the flights of an exuberant imagination. Instead of trying sincerely and earnestly to solve purely intellectual problems upon intellectual grounds, they rather presented their metaphysics in the form of a plea for a certain cause, or in the guise of poems for the delight of their readers. To such synthetic views about the world we give the name subjective metaphysics, inasmuch as their basis is, if not entirely, at least in its characteristic bearings, not intellectual as it should be, but volitional and emotional as it should not be.

There are various kinds of subjective metaphysics in vogue today with an uncountable number of personal differentiations. For our purpose, however, we may reduce them to three heads: materialistic, pantheistic, and criticist metaphysics.

I. MATERIALISTIC METAPHYSICS

The theory of materialism as an attempt to account for the universality of things is as old as philosophy itself. But in virtue of the great progress in the knowledge of matter and material phenomena through the study of the physical and chemical sciences in the last few hundred years, which progress was unfortunately accompanied by a general decline in the study of the spirit and of spiritual phenomena, and particularly in consequence of the plausible and brilliant presentation of a materialistic interpretation of life in its various phases and multiform phenomena by Darwin in the last century, the philosophy of materialism seemed destined for a while to completely inspire and dominate modern thought. While during the last few decades a vigorous reaction has set in amongst thinkers everywhere against such a shallow, incomplete, and in every sense unsatisfactory interpretation of the universe, the name of its adherents amongst the masses of the half-educated and would-be cultured people is still legion.

a. MATERIALISM IN GENERAL

The metaphysical principles which in the mind of materialists are a perfect and all-sufficient explanation of the existence and the phenomena of the universe in its totality, are few in number. They are not entirely new to us, since we have already encountered and refuted most of them in cosmology and psychology.

First and fundamental is the arbitrary assertion that *there is nothing in the universe except matter*. In connection with the first is the second principle, not less sweeping nor less based upon fact: *All physical and chemical phenomena in the universe are reducible to mechanical modifications of matter*. The further assertions which speak of life in general as the function of the organism, and of the life of sense and of mind as the lower and higher functions of the nervous system, are not only superficial aspects of what they pretend to explain, but they explain absolutely nothing because they ignore the fundamental problems which refer to the qualitative aspects of those phenomena.

Such are the ultimate principles of materialism as regards the explanation of the nature of the universe. Those proposed to account for the origin of the universe are not more profound nor more solid: 1. *The universe is due to the evolution of eternal matter eternally in motion*. This is the fundamental principle of materialism in this connection. Apart from the arbitrariness of the assertion itself and from the obscurity and inconceivability of eternity as an attribute of both matter and motion, there is no objective metaphysical explanation whatever contained in the statement. Unless it can be shown positively and evidently that matter is not contingent, but necessary in its existence, its assumed eternity has absolutely no value or meaning in this

respect, because eternity refers to the time of its duration, not to the reason for its existence.

The second assumption, *viz., the assumption of spontaneous generation,* which is supposed to explain the existence of life in the universe, is not better founded on
fact, nor does it explain better what it is supposed to explain than the eternity of matter in eternal motion. We
have seen in psychology how biology rejects spontaneous
generation. But even if we were to assume, for argument's sake, that life were the spontaneous and fortuitous
issue of a most marvelous combination of physical and
chemical factors, its regular continuation and perpetuation
without any intrinsic or extrinsic principle of orientation
or direction of the manifold chemical and physical factors
necessary to life, would be the elevation of the miraculous
to the condition of the normal without any attempt at explanation. As a climax, we would have to look upon
sense and mind life as a vast accumulation of marvels,
together with the constant recurrence and perpetuation
of the same accumulated marvels, for which in eternal
matter in eternal motion there is not found the faintest
shadow of a reason.

b. VARIETIES OF MATERIALISTIC METAPHYSICS

Such is the metaphysics of materialism. It is, of
course, not metaphysics in the true and proper sense of
the term. No wonder that such metaphysical vagaries
have produced in many minds a mild contempt for the
deeper study of philosophy. However, even those who
pretend to despise metaphysics are often victims of this
false and hollow philosophy. We will mention a few of
such victims.

(1) In the *POSITIVISM* of Auguste Comte and his
School attention is chiefly paid to knowledge. There
is no specific human knowledge. Sense experience
alone is the full source and only test of all true and
positive knowledge. But sense experience never
comes into contact with substances, or causes, or

purposes, or other abstract relations. Consequently, only terms that express concrete realities and their concrete relations represent true and positive knowledge; all other knowledge is termed contemptuously metaphysics, *i. e.,* without positive meaning and value.

(2) Herbert Spencer, bringing to bear upon positivism the theories of the cosmic evolution proposed by Kant and popularized by Laplace, and of biological evolution proposed by Lamarck and popularized by Darwin, became the exponent of a philosophical *EVOLUTIONISM* which attempts to interpret and explain all phenomena of the universe, the intellectual, moral, social, and religious life of man included, by the simple and necessary processes of mechanical progressive evolution.

This metaphysical theory has exercised and still continues to exercise in shallow minds and philosophically inclined newspaper writers and their readers a vast influence, because for such people it has all the advantages of a philosophy with a certain appearance of a justification in a number of scientific facts, yet without involving any objective and serious burden from a religious or moral viewpoint.

(3) This very smal shallow interpretation of the universe is called *PHENOMENALISM* and *AGNOSTICISM;* phenomenalism when reference is made to the supposed exclusive object of all knowledge, *viz.,* sense phenomena; agnosticism, when reference is had to the underlying subjects in which these phenomena are realized, and to the relationships between those subjects, because phenomenalists proclaim complete ignorance in this respect, not only as a fact but as a necessity. The name agnosticism is applied also in a more restricted sense to positivism in so far as it assumes and asserts, with a special emphasis, the impossibility of any human knowledge about the existence and nature of the soul of man and about the existence and the nature of God.

2. PANTHEISTIC METAPHYSICS

While pantheism, as a rule, has also a materialistic aspect, yet it adds a new feature to materialism—it pretends to explain the universe, and consequently, its material as well as its spiritual phenomena, by the substantial identity of the world with God, for the fundamental principle of its metaphysics is the assertion that God and the world are one and the same substance. Elaborated as a metaphysical system by the Stoic and Neo-platonic Schools in ancient times, revived for a while in the Middle Ages by John Scotus Erigena, it acquired intellectual influence in modern times through Giordano Bruno and above all, through its perfect systematization by Baruch Spinoza.

In the pantheism of Spinoza the universe is the natural and necessary expansion of the divine substance, of which the material and spiritual worlds are but different modes in which the divine substance expands and expresses itself. There is no need of calling attention to the practical consequences of such a conception of the universe. It is theoretical and practical atheism, since in a pantheistic universe there is no room for a personal God. Furthermore, personal spirituality and the immortality of the soul, individual liberty and responsibility, and, therefore, morality in the ordinary sense of the word, are impossible. Finally, the pantheistic world is a fatalistic as well as the possibly best world, as evidently in such a world there can be neither sin nor error, since all phenomena are the necessary phases of the divine evolution. Apart from these awful consequences of pantheistic metaphysics, its intellectual basis is clearly untenable. It is hardly necessary to call attention to the manifold contradictions which result logically from the identification of the world and God, the finite and infinite, the contingent and necessary, the relative and absolute. It must seem strange that such a metaphysics should exercise any intellectual influence at all, and yet, as a matter of fact, outside the Catholic fold and the materialistic camp, there are not many philosophers who are not in some way or other influenced in their metaphysical ideas of the universe by pantheism, not to mention that the philosophy of the popular craze called Christian Science is, as far as there is any idea of philosophy in it, that of pantheism.

To understand this strange intellectual, moral, and social phenomenon we must bear in mind the antithetic and in part plainly contradictory attitude of modern intellectual, moral, and social life in the presence of the primary and fundamental necessities of human nature which we might call man's rational instincts. These rational instincts have clearly a religious basis and a moral aim which, when logically followed to their ultimate conclusions, imply manifold restrictions and painful acts of self-denial in individual and social life, because they demand absolute submission to the sovereign law of God.

On the other hand, however, the intellectual and social revolutions and upheavals of the last four centuries have had a tendency to produce in man a sense of personal autonomy and self-sovereignty, which has left generally, but especially upon the cultured classes of today, deep-rooted and powerful prejudices against the humble recognition of human dependence upon an ultramundane and personal God, and the consequent meek and submissive duty of obedience to His inflexible law with its irrevocable eternal sanctions.

In this dilemma pantheism presents itself as a redeemer. It offers a metaphysics which appears capable of bridging over that intellectually and morally irksome gulf between the sovereignty of God and the autonomy of man by assuming the substantial identity of both. No wonder that by minds which are not superficial enough to be content with the shallow philosophy of materialism, pantheism is welcomed as a deliverer from the hateful dilemma of having to accept either materialism, which is the philosophy of the brute, or theism, which in its practical religious and moral applications is to the average modern mind a philosophy of self-effacement. While this philosophy of pantheism is neither profound nor logical, it is obscure and subtle, and therefore, it lends itself very well to a semi-religious and mystical conception of human life as well as to a highly poetical personification and deification of the phenomena of nature which strongly appeal to cultured people who recoil from the brutal consequences of materialism.

3. CRITICIST METAPHYSICS

We call criticist the metaphysics of Kant and his School with its various ramifications. No other philosopher has exercised, and still continues to exercise, such a widespread and profound influence upon the modern mind as Kant. Of the men who at present occupy the chairs of philosophy at the great universities of the world, there are many thorough-going and avowed criticists, and there are very few whose metaphysical ideas are not colored by Kant's philosophy. Hence, a brief discussion of his metaphysical theory is of practical importance, as well as of speculative value.

a. KANT'S METAPHYSICS

Kant's philosophy has been termed *criticist* because, deeply convinced of the false metaphysical position of both rationalism and sensualism as repesented respectively by Descartes and Leibniz on the one side, and Locke, Hume, and Berkeley on the other, he proposed to put the whole subject and range of human knowledge to a thorough examination and *critical* test in order to verify the fundamental foundations and define the exact limits of human knowledge. According to his analysis, which undoubtedly was original and painstaking, man's great body of knowledge comprises three sections—science, metaphysics, and religion. Examining them critically we find that only scientific knowledge has been universally successful, whereas both metaphysical and religious knowledge has failed to a large extent, since everybody is in agreement about questions of science, while the whole world has ever been in disagreement about matters of metaphysics and religion. Of course, there must be a reason for the success of scientific knowledge and for the failure of metaphysical and religious knowledge. This reason, according to Kant, is a profound and well-defined difference between scientific knowledge on the one side, and metaphysical and religious knowledge on the other: Scientific facts can be examined and tested by all men in their own sense experience, whereas religion and metaphysics deal with concepts which cannot be so examined and tested; they are essentially beyond sense experience. From this the conclusion is drawn that only scientific knowledge has objective meaning and value, whereas religious and metaphysical knowledge is of a purely subjective character.

Now in Kant's own mind a strong counter-action arose against the total ruin of philosophy and religion which must follow such a theory. After all the philosopher of Königsberg was different from the shallow positivists—he was a thinker and he was not an irreligious man. He admitted that the human mind is so built that in the explanation of human life we cannot get along without the assumption of the spiritual soul as the absolute condition of human experience—especially necessary for the explanation of moral freedom; and that in the explanation of the phenomena of the universe we cannot succeed without the assumption of God as the absolute condition of all conditioned happenings. However, since these metaphysical concepts cannot be tested by sense experience, their basis is another type of knowledge, they are not the knowledge of speculative, but the *postulates of practical reason*.

Such is Kant's position in respect to metaphysics. Evidently, this is digging the grave for all true philosophy. Postulates or moral assumptions will be accepted by men of the simple and excellent moral character of Kant, but rejected by every one else. Where knowledge is based upon moral necessity, and not upon speculative conclusive arguments, it cannot stand, because morality itself depends absolutely upon the speculative mind to show it its goal and the way to the goal.

It is hardly necessary to call attention to the fallacies in Kant's reasoning: his premises are both false and, moreover, his deduction is faulty. Neither does science always succeed nor do religion and metaphysics always fail. Science does succeed more generally because many of its problems are of a superficial character and, therefore, their solution is easily perceptible. On the contrary, metaphysics and religion often fail because many of their problems are of a profound nature and therefore, their speculative solution demands a well-developed intelligence and a careful study, which are not found very frequently.

b. VARIETIES OF CRITICIST METAPHYSICS

Criticist metaphysics was meant by its founder to be *objectivist, realist,* and *dualist.* 1. It was meant to be objectivist because for Kant human knowledge—at least the various sciences—was representative of objects which were not considered identical with the knowledge itself. 2. It was realist because Kant accepted as evident the objective existence of the outside world apart from the existence of the mind. 3. It was dualist in a double sense because both the distinction between matter and spirit and that between world and God were quite evident in Kant's opinion.

Kant's disciples and intellectual heirs, such as Fichte, Schelling, Hegel, and a host of others less important, more consistent than their master, followed his principles resolutely and fearlessly to their ultimate conclusions, and thus transformed Kant's criticism into *SUBJECTIVISM, IDEALISM,* and *MONISM.* There is no reason to be surprised at such developments because they are perfectly logical. It can only be attributed to Kant's inconsistency with his own fundamental principles that he himself remained objectivist, realist, and dualist in his metaphysics. Such inconsistency can be accounted for in a mind so profoundly critical and subtle only because his practical common sense revolted against the ultimate disastrous philosophical, religious, and ethical consequences of his own speculative psychology.

(1) We have seen how in this psychological theory of knowledge the only link connecting the mind with the outside world is but a tiny thread—a factor impressing the passive senses. Of the objective nature and attributes of this factor nothing is knowable. But if the mind creates everything that characterizes it and belongs to it, why not also its existence? If everything else in the knowledge of a thing proceeds absolutely from the subject, why should we stop short at the first impulse unless it be for the necessity of the cause, *i. e.,* for the purpose of avoiding absolute subjectivism? *Thus we arrive at plain subjectivism and idealism.* From another viewpoint, the same principles will lead us to the conception of an idealism which is both pantheistic and monistic. If we examine seriously the assumed universality and absolute value of scientific knowledge with the view of discovering a real objective basis and source for these characteristics of knowledge, which are, according to the theory, the creation of the mind, we must evidently conclude that only the assumption of a universal mind can account for them. In this manner we come to the conclusion, not only justifiable, but necessary if we accept the premises, that not only world and mind are identical, but that also mind and God are consubstantial, and thus *we have arrived at the last logical consequence of criticist metaphysics—idealistic and pantheistic monism.*

(2) We saw above that Kant's metaphysical thought had a twofold aspect, proposed respectively in his two principal works: KRITIK DER REINEN VERNUNFT, and KRITIK DER PRAKTISCHEN VERNUNFT. While some of his disci-

ples developed the theoretical principles of the speculative reason, others, convinced of the absolute metaphysical sterility of those principles, devoted their attention to the development of the postulates of the practical reason and elaborated a system of metaphysical *MORALISM* and *PRAGMATISM* in which the very ideas of knowledge and truth, upon which all science and philosophy are built, are fundamentally changed. In this novel metaphysics the relation between knowledge and action and, consequently, between mind and will is completely reversed. No longer must the mind give guidance to the will, but light must come from the will to the mind because the object of knowledge is not the perception of truth so that human action may be based upon the firm rock of objective certitude, since such a thing is impossible, but action must determine knowledge because truth and falsehood are relative attributes of the action, depending respectively upon its success or failure. Consequently, any theory whatever, scientific, philosophical, or religious, is true in so far as it works well, and is false inasmuch as it does not work well. Evidently, such a metaphysics is *RELATIVISM* in its purest form.

II. *Objective Metaphysics*

It is a great joy to come out of the labyrinth of metaphysical subjectivism and relativism, which spell intellectual pessimism and philosophical despair, into the free and fresh atmosphere of the neo-scholastic metaphysics, the foundations of which were laid firmly in antiquity by Aristotle and reinforced with singular earnestness and success in the Middle Ages by such men as Albertus Magnus and Thomas Aquinas. While also in neo-scholastic metaphysics we meet with problems which are complex, profound, and of difficult solution, yet we are standing on the solid ground of the objective universe, to which, when our mind is bewildered on account of the number and complexity of the problems facing us, we can always go back to rest before making a new start.

I. SOURCE AND OBJECT OF METAPHYSICS

Though the subjective theories of metaphysics which we have briefly discussed, particularly positivism and criticism, have stirred up in the modern mind a strong hostility to the study of metaphysics, they have not been able to undermine its objective foundation. From the study of cosmology, and still more, from that of psychology, we have derived a clear and definite knowledge, based upon objective and conclusive evidence that the phnomena of the universe are realized in subjects which we called inorganic and organic bodies or substances, and that there are manifold and complex relationships between those substances. Our present aim—the object of metaphysics, —is to find out: 1. Which are the fundamental elements common to all substances indistinctively, no matter to what group or order they belong, and 2. which are the essential relations between those common fundamental elements; *i. e.,* we shall study the world no longer as the inorganic and organic world, but simply as the one undivided universe in its ultimate principles.

Such being the aim and object of metaphysics, our first problem is to define the primary elements that enter into the constitution of the universe as a unified whole, and not as a collection of groups. These primary elements are beings, for the universe is the sum of contingent beings. There are a thousand things in which beings differ from one another, and it is on account of these differences that they are divided into species and genera of different orders, but there is one thing that is common to all without exception: they are individual concrete beings, constituting, when summed, what we call the universe. This concept of a being as a being, and not as a being of such and such a type, or belonging to such and such a species, we call *absolute* and *transcendental:* absolute, because it

is considered exclusively in itself, without any of its relations to other beings; transcendental, because, considered in itself absolutely, it transcends the species and
genera of all categories of beings. Consequently, we
may idefine *metaphysics as the philosophy of the abso-*
lute and transcendental being. However, the absolute
and transcendental being is taken in a double sense: *viz.,*
being absolute and transcendental by abstraction and by
negation, and this is the proper sense of the term; and
being absolute and transcendental concretely and positively, and this is an analogical sense of the term. Therefore, the full study of metaphysics will comprehend two
sections, one dealing with ontology or general metaphysics; the other dealing with theodicy—the application
of metaphysics to God.

2. ONTOLOGY OR GENERAL METAPHYSICS

Ontology we call that part of metaphysics which studies
the absolute and transcendental being in its proper sense.
We refer here not to being in the abstract as it exists
in the mind, but to being in the concrete as it exists
in the objective world; not to the substance as such or to
its accidents as such, but to the whole individual being,
inclusive of everything which is found in a being as
a being. It is necessary to insist upon this because many
modern writers on philosophy speak of the object of
ontology in very vague and indefinite terms, as if it were
a reality which was neither substance nor accident, neither
actual nor possible being, neither real nor logical, but
inclusive of them all in a general and hazy way. This
is a great mistake. Aristotle is very definite. He calls
metaphysics the first philosophy, "philosophia prima," because it is the philosophy of the "substantia prima," which,
in Aristotle's mind, is the concrete being, *i. e.,* the being
that our eyes see and our hands touch, *i. e.,* the individual
being. Such being the proper object of ontology, the
objective character and value of metaphysics is clearly
apparent.

a. STATIC ONTOLOGY: THE INTERPRETATION OF BEING

The first philosophical efforts of the Greek mind were devoted to the question of the fundamental and intimate element of the universe, *i. e.,* the universe was looked upon as a sum of beings which, while infinitely differentiated in their appearances, were taken to be essentially stable and unchangeable, being considered as aggregations of that fundamental and intimate element. Hence, the first metaphysics of Greece was static ontology. This viewpoint is perfectly justifiable in philosophical studies, but it must not be exclusive as it was with those Greek philosophers. The universe is, indeed, a sum of beings, and at all times, no matter when we look upon it, it remains a sum of beings. Furthermore, there are certain characteristics and attributes found in all beings of the universe which are stable and unchangeable. It is this sum of beings and the universal and ever-present characteristics and attributes of those beings which we study in static ontology.

The reason which justifies the beginning of metaphysical studies with the static viewpoint is of easy comprehension: a being must first exist before it can act. Before we can engage in dynamic ontology, *i. e.,* before we can study the characteristics and attributes of the action of beings, we must evidently first know those of their existence. While in the analytical and inductive method of study the character of the action is first and the nature of the agent second, in the deductive and synthetic method which is the method applied in metaphysics, the nature of the agent is first and the character of the action second. From the study of cosmology and psychology we know the nature of the beings, and now, taking this knowledge as our basis, we endeavor to form an adequate synthetic interpretation of the universe.

b. DYNAMIC ONTOLOGY: THE EVOLUTION OF BEING

While the static viewpoint is the first, it is not the only metaphysical viewpoint. The universe changes because the beings which compose it act and by their action the ever varying phenomena of the world find their explanation. And not only the phenomena are subject to never-ending change, but the beings themselves are transformed by their action. Though the universe, as regards its total mass of matter and its total sum of energy is always the same, considered in its concrete totality it is never the same for two consecutive moments: it is its very nature to exist in successive phases of which, as we have seen before, the one that precedes must be taken to be the cause of the one that follows. So natural and obvious is this dynamic viewpoint in philosophy that in the second period of Greek philosophy the static viewpoint was entirely discarded and the study of the universe resolved itself into a metaphysical study of its changes. To them the world appeared exclusively as a flowing stream and the philosophical problems as the problems of its movement.

While the dynamic metaphysics of the universe is not exclusive, yet it is just as necessary and as essential as the static metaphysics, because the beings of the universe act as well as exist. By their action upon one another, they change, and change one another and, as we saw in both cosmology and psychology, those changes may be superficial (accidental) and profound (substantial). Thus, we learn to look upon beings not only as they are at any given moment, but as they are in their successive phases of accidental and substantial, progressive and regressive evolution. The various problems connected with the explanation of this interdependence of the beings of the universe constitute the subject-matter of dynamic ontology.

3. THEODICY: APPLIED METAPHYSICS

Theodicy is the philosophy of the absolute and transcendental being in its positive and concrete sense, *i. e.,* we apply the metaphysical ideas of absolute and transcendental to God, who is the primary source and adequate cause

of the universe. Our idea of the absoluteness and transcendence of the beings which compose the universe is
gained by abstraction and negation. We know that in their
concrete existence all beings of the universe are related
to, and dependent upon, one another in many ways, but
for the sake of a more complete and more profound
knowledge of their nature, we exclude from our consideration all their relations and connections with one
another. We know from cosmology and psychology
that there is a being—God, who by His very nature is
absolute and transcendent, and since our interpretation of
the universe, to be a full and adequate explanation of
its existence and nature, necessarily includes God, we
must, as philosphers, explain the nature of God as well
as we can.

a. THE EXISTENCE OF GOD

Before we focus our attention on the study of God's
nature, we must make absolutely sure of His existence.
Already in cosmology and psychology we were repeatedly compelled to assume the existence of an absolute and necessary Being for a full and adequate solution of our problems, but the importance of the matter,
both theoretically and practically, for the philosophy of
nature as well as for the philosophy of human life in all
its individual phases and social developments, is such
that a special chapter devoted to this problem is not
only justifiable but indispensable. This is so much more
necessary, because, as we saw above where we discussed
the subjective systems of metaphysics, it is chiefly owing
to anti-theistic prejudice that there is no objective basis
or common source of possible philosophical agreement
found in the various periods of the history of human
thought. We can readily understand this because in the
intellectual and moral world the acceptance of the existence of God is like the apparition of the sun on the
horizon of the physical world:—just as the presence
of the sun produces light and warmth and thus promotes
the growth and development of life on earth, so the

thought of God's existence gives intellectual light, emotional warmth, and moral life and power to the human world. We therefore consider it a sacred duty to devote to this paramount philosophical problem our closest attention.

b. THE NATURE OF GOD

Of the absoluteness and transcendence of the divine nature we are quite sure by reasoning because only an absolute and transcendent being can adequately explain the existence and the nature of the universe. However, having no intuition nor any direct and proper perception of the divine nature, our conception of absoluteness and transcendence is based upon what we know from the metaphysics of the universe, and consequently, when we apply these concepts to God, we apply them in another *viz.,* a higher sense than when we apply them to the world. The reason is simple enough: as we have seen, in their application to the universe they are abstract and negative, whereas in their application to God they must be positive and concrete. But this means that we do not use them in the same sense: referring them to the universe we use them in their proper sense as it is from the universe we have abstracted them, referring them to God we use them in an analogical sense, so far as things exist in the effect differently from the way they exist in the cause. This applies in a general way to all our concepts: they are proper when we speak of the beings that we know directly or indirectly by their action upon us, they are analogical whenever we apply them to God because we know God, not from His action upon us, but only in so far as He has expressed His likeness in the nature and attributes of creation.

However, we must not conclude from this that our knowledge of the nature of God has no value and therefore, is not worth acquiring. Though analogical only, it is not negative, but positive, *i. e.,* it teaches us many things which are positively attributable to God and to God alone. While we freely admit that such knowledge is neither perfect nor adequate on account of being based upon analogy and not representative of the nature and the essential attributes of God in their proper characteristics, yet in respect to God, by whose existence and nature alone an adequate explanation of the universe is possible, even the smallest amount and the most imperfect kind of knowledge, provided it be true, is of the highest possible value.

SECTION ONE

ONTOLOGY, THE PHILOSOPHY OF THE TRANSCENDENT ASPECT OF THE WORLD

CHAPTER TWENTY-TWO

STATIC ONTOLOGY

OBJECT AND SCOPE OF STATIC ONTOLOGY

Ontology is the philosophy of being as such. The object of static ontology is being in so far as it is a real objective fact at any given time. It excludes whatsoever change there is in a being and consequently, it does not consider what has gone before nor what is to follow. All questions referring to the changing of beings and their causality belong to dynamic ontology. Hence, static ontology is the philosophy of being inasmuch as it exists, and not inasmuch as it acts. However, it is inclusive of everything that is found in each and every being of the universe, because whatsoever is present in each and every being is a characteristic of being as such and is therefore, of an absolutely universal, or as we called it above, transcendental attribution.

From this determination of the object of static ontology it is clear that we refer here to being not in its abstract state as it exists in the mind, but to the real objective being having a concrete existence apart from our knowledge. Yet this metaphysical or transcendental being represents the fruit of the highest possible abstraction and, as a consequence, is the simplest concept of which the human mind is capable. It is on account of this extreme simplicity that it is of such universal application, *i. e.,* it is its supreme simplicity which makes it transcendental. However, it is well to bear in mind that this supreme simplicity of our conception of being does not mean that the being which this concept represents is in itself absolutely simple. In the analysis we have made time and again of the beings of the universe in both cosmology and psychology, we have discovered that each and every being is a complex structure of elements, and while these elements vary greatly in quantity and quality according to the different species and orders to which they belong, yet upon close examination we shall find that there are some fundamental elements and aspects present in each and every being, no matter to which class it belongs, and which therefore, form the subject-matter of this discussion. Hence, the problem of static ontology is threefold: 1. What constitutes the transcendental being as a concrete, individual being? 2. What constitutes the transcendental elements of its structure? 3. What constitutes the transcendental basis of its attributes?

I. *The Transcendental Individuality of Being*

The study of ontology has for its object the real objective being; but the real objective being is necessarily the concrete individual being. While we exclude from our consideration everything in which one being differs from every other being, yet it is still the individual being to which we refer. As a consequence, whatever we find present in one individual being will be equally applicable to every other real or even possible individual being since none of their real or possible differences is considered. The question now arises, what is this individuality which is a transcendental aspect of every being of the universe? Which are its constitutive elements?

1. DEFINITION OF ESSENCE AND EXISTENCE

In the concept of being there are two clearly distinct aspects. When we say that this tree is a being, or that dog is a being, or Peter is a being, we express two things at once; we say that they are *something,* and we say that they *are.* Inasmuch as we say *what* they are, we give their *essence;* inasmuch as we say *that* they are, we give their *existence.* In respect to their essence, or what they are, the three beings are very different, in respect to their existence, or in that they are, they are perfectly the same. Essence and existence are not elements of the same order because each of them includes the totality of the individual being in a different way.

To clarify these fundamental ideas, let us compare them with their opposites. The concept of existence has but one opposite—its contradictory: *non-existence, non-being*. The concept of essence is opposed to both that of *accident* and that of *contingent*. Essence is opposed to accident because it is a being having its own existence, not existing by nature in another; indeed, it is the source and basis from which and in which all accidents have their being. In this ontological sense essence is equivalent to *substance*. From a purely logical viewpoint we speak of the essential elements of a being as its distinctive characteristics.

The essence is opposed to contingent inasmuch as the elements that compose it are linked together by a bond of natural and intrinsic necessity and are, therefore, inseparable in their natural order of existence, whereas, what is contingent, is not expressive of necessary connection with the nature of a being.

Speaking of the concrete individual being—so when we say this tree, that dog, Peter—we include both essence and existence. In this respect we call the individual being an *actual being*. When we pay attention to the essence alone, not considering the existence, we speak of the *real being*. When we consider the essence without existence, *i. e.,* when we positively exclude the existence, we have the *possible being*. A being is intrinsically possible when the elements which constitute its essence are compatible, *i. e.,* not contradictory. It is extrinsically possible when there is a cause that can give it existence. Therefore, absolutely speaking, every being which is intrinsically possible is also extrinsically possible, inasmuch as it is in the power of God to produce it.

As explained, the actual being includes both essence and existence. The essence, considered as realized in the concrete being, was called by Aristotle the *first substance,* *"substantia prima,"* and considered in the abstract, *"substantia secunda."* Both the "substantia prima" and the "substantia secunda" are expressed also by the term *nature.* In the abstract, nature, essence, and substance are perfectly equivalent. In the concrete, when we use the term *nature,* we add to the "substantia prima" the *dynamic viewpoint*: *substance refers to existence, nature to action.*

The "substantia prima" is called an *hypostasis,* "suppositum," an individual being which expression implies self-sufficiency for existence and action. When an hypostasis is rational, we call it a *person,* because an hypostasis, being rational, is self-conscious and has the power of self-determination and, consequently, has a dignity and responsibility which no other hypostasis can possess. A person alone has rights and duties.

2. DISTINCTION BETWEEN ESSENCE AND EXISTENCE

The fundamental aspects of a concrete being are plainly its essence and its existence. However, are they aspects only of the same being, or are they distinct realities? If they were not distinct realities, they would be intrinsically identical. This is a rather delicate problem, and yet it is of no slight importance. With St. Thomas Aquinas we hold that they are really distinct.

A good reason for our position is given with their respective definition. The concept of essence is adequately distinct from the idea of existence; neither is inclusive of the other and yet both express the whole being. The one answers the question: *What is it?* The other replies to the question: *Is it?* Or does it exist? As already stated, concrete beings are very different from one another by *what* they are, they are exactly the same in *that* they are. Consequently, beings, being clearly different from one another in essence, and clearly identical in existence, essence and existence cannot be the same reality.

St. Thomas adds another reason for the real distinction of essence and existence which is convincing, but on account of its depth not of easy comprehension. He says that the beings of the universe are finite, and in finite beings essence and existence are really distinct, because a being whose essence and existence are identical must be infinite. Why? Because the limitation of a being does not come from its existence, but from its essence, since the essence of a being is its potential capacity for being which is actualized by existence. Existence as such, being an act, is not measurable but can be measured only by the capacity or potentiality which it actualizes, as a liquid is measured and limited by the capacity of its container. Consequently, where the essence of a being is its existence, there is no capacity, no potentiality which could limit or measure the existence, and therefore, it must be infinite. It is plain the perfection of a being is not measured by the fact that it *is*, but by *what* it is. How should we be able to conceive the limitations of being in a being whose very essence is *to be?*

There is yet another and more simple way of showing the real distinction between essence and existence. As we have seen time and again, and shall soon explain more fully, concrete beings are ontological structures, or systems of ontological elements. But these various elements constitute one being only, *i. e.,* they have one act of existence. If not, these elements would be as many beings, they would not be the one being which they are. But if the essence is manifold and complex and the existence one and simple, it is clear they must be really distinct from one another.

II. *The Transcendental Structure of Being*

After the study of the transcendental individuality of being, we proceed to discuss the transcendental elements of its structure. While it is true, that the concept of being is the most simple idea of the human mind, yet the concrete being to which we apply it is far from being really simple. We have just seen that it is composed of essence and existence; now, we will examine the elements which compose its essence, or constitute the being in what it is. The first division which imposes itself here is that of substance and accidents. This question has come before us in both cosmology and psychology. We must study it again from the metaphysical viewpoint.

A. THE SUBSTANTIALITY OF BEING

Substance is being considered as capable of having its own existence. It is the *"ens in se."* It needs no other being as a subject in which to exist. Its contradictory is the *"ens in alio,"* the being which is not capable of having its own existence, but needs another being as the subject in which it can exist. This being is called *accident*.

Though it seems incredible, there are many philosophers who deny the reality of the substance. Positivists and phenomenalists declare that we do not and cannot perceive any substance and consequently, must be, if we are consistent, *agnostics*. *Pantheists* proclaim that there is only one substance—the god-world.

The doctrine of pantheism is based upon a conceptual confusion. Instead of defining substance as the "ens *in* se," Spinoza, the father of modern pantheism, defines it as the "ens *a* se." Of course, this definition fits one being alone, God; it is not taken from experience, but is a mere assumption.

The proof that there are substances is easily established. While it is true that we cannot perceive the substance with our senses, because what acts upon them are the accidents of being, yet it is impossible to perceive any accident without implicitly perceiving also the substance in which it exists. Thus, the act of walking or speaking implies necessarily the walker or speaker, and the perception of a color or a size is impossible without the simultaneous perception of the body that is colored or has size. The reason is simple enough: *what we per-*

ceive is either itself a substance or it exists in a substance, since an accident has no existence of its own. Even the absurd supposition of an infinite series of accidents superposed upon, and existing in, one another, affords no adequate explanation of their real existence. Hence, substances do exist.

The absolute idealist alone has a certain right to deny the substantiality of beings because to him all beings are subjective mental creations. However, even he must accept his own subsistence.

B. THE ACCIDENTS OF BEING

Substances as such do not act because all beings have manifold and various activities, whereas the substances as such are unchangeable. Since any change in the substance would change the nature of a being, *i. e.,* cause it to cease to be what it is and become another being, we are compelled to assume other realities which explain the manifoldness and variety of the actions of a being, notwithstanding its substantial unity and permanency. These secondary realities we call *accidents.* They are the natural means and instrumentalities of a being for the attainment of its intrinsic tendency, and consequently, they are to us the expression of its nature. There are nine categories or supreme genera of accidents, which, with the main category—substance—comprise all reality which exists or can exist in the universe: *quantity, quality, relation,* the determinations of *time* and *space, action* and *passion, intransitive action* and *passive attitude* or *state.* Quantity, and time and space relations belong to cosmology, and enough has been said about them there. The last four, inasmuch as they are important in metaphysics, will have their place in the next chapter. Hence, relation and quality alone claim our attention now.

I. QUALITIES

After quantity, the most important of all accidents are qualities. *They are stable dispositions in virtue of which a being is such and such.* What the forma substantialis is to the being substantially, qualities are accidentally. In other words, just as the forma substantialis gives the being its substantial determination, which is one and unchangeable, so the qualities give it its accidental determinations, which are manifold and variable. We will limit our discussion to those kinds of qualities which are the most significant as ontological elements of being: powers of action, habits, and passions or powers of emotion.

a. POWERS OF ACTION

The *powers of action* are what in cosmology we called *forces,* and in psychology, *faculties. They are the immediate principles of action in a being,* the remote and fundamental principle being its nature. We have assumed several and various powers to explain the complexity and variety of the activity of a being, notwithstanding the unity and unchangeable permanency of its nature. The nature of a contingent being as such never acts, as such activity would destroy it, because every change in the nature of a being transforms the being. *Our specification of the powers of action depends upon the differentiation of the actions,* and *we determine the nature of the actions by the adequate distinction of their object.* Thus, we accept various species of mechanical, physical, and chemical forces, and, again, various species of both sense and rational faculties.

There is another very significant difference between forces and faculties—*the capacity for development;* it is present in faculties, absent in forces. *Forces* never change, they are *rigid,* whereas *faculties* are capable of improvement, they are *plastic.* In this respect, there is again a great difference between the faculties of sense and those of the spiritual soul, because *sense faculties,* on account of the great complexity of sense organs, *are* of *little plasticity,* whereas *the plasticity of rational faculties,* not intrinsically dependent upon organs, is *indefinite.*

These considerations explain the possibility of *habits*

and the profound difference there is between the *habits of animals and those of men*. Evidently, inorganic beings and plants are incapable of habits because their forces are rigid, admit of no improvement. There is a semblance of habits in animals, because senses are somewhat plastic, and therefore, susceptible of a certain development, but habits, in the proper and strict sense of the term, belong to man, because there is no set limit to the plasticity of his faculties. Hence, *the animal,* being plastic to a certain extent, *can be trained, man,* being perfectly plastic, *can be educated.*

b. HABITS

There can be no doubt about the speculative as well as practical importance of these new qualities of a being which we call *habits.* We refuse to ascribe them in the strict sense of the term to animals, because the developments and improvements brought about by the exercise of sense faculties are, on account of the great complexity of the nervous system upon which they absolutely depend, not sufficiently stable to deserve the name of qualities. It is different with man, whose distinctive powers are spiritual, and as we have seen, spiritual faculties as such are absolutely plastic and therefore, indefinitely perfectible. Nevertheless, the plasticity and perfectibility of the mind and will of man are not absolute and unlimited, because they participate, to a certain extent at least, in the limitations and imperfections of the sense faculties upon which their action is necessarily dependent as their consubstantial organic instrument.

Habits may be defined as qualities produced by repeated action. *They are stable dispositions superadded to a faculty in consequence of which the action of that faculty becomes more easy, its direction more stabilized, and its result more perfect.* This stable perfective disposition is exclusively due to exercise and depends proportionately on the nature of the action—its intensity and success, and on the number of judicious repetitions. While each action tends to perfect the faculty in the form of a habit, as a rule a deep-rooted habit is not established except by many repetitions of the same act. If carefully and sufficiently reproduced, the habit becomes as stable almost as the faculty itself! "Consuetudo est altera natura," Habit is a second nature. When actions are very intense, a few repetitions may suffice to produce a habit, particularly in matters intellectual. The same is true as regards moral habits, the object of which is the gratification of natural inclinations.

c. PASSIONS

There is another species of qualities which claims our attention: *passions or powers of emotion.* They are qualities or stable dispositions since they are plainly the cause of permanent individual differences. However, they are *passive dispositions;* while they are actualized only by and with conscious action, yet they are not faculties or powers which explain that action.

From the study of psychology we remember that every conscious action produces in the agent a certain passive state in virtue of which he is affected in an emotional manner, which state in its lowest degree simply is characterized as satisfactory and pleasurable, or unsatisfactory and displeasing. However, in conformity with the variety and intensity of the conscious actions, the emotions are greatly differentiated in quality and quantity from an ecstasy of love, joy, and enthusiasm to a frenzy of hatred, anger, and jealousy, from the exaltation of unbounded admiration, desire, and hope to the depth of repugnance, fear and despair.

Passions, being natural concomitants and consequences of conscious actions, are integral elements in both animal and human nature. *Biologically,* they have for their object the protection of the life of both the individual and the species. *Psychologically,* their relation to the will and, consequently, to the activity of man corresponds to the relation of the imagination to mind and knowledge. While not spiritual in their specific nature they share in the spirituality of the will, whose instrumental causes they are. From the *moral viewpoint,* passions, like the faculties, are in themselves neither good nor bad, but may become either by their direction. Their presence is of the highest importance to man, as without them he would be deprived of the greatest attraction of his human personality, since they impart a peculiar charm of color, tone, and warmth to human character and life. Moreover, to the will they serve in the capacity of driving forces of the first order for which there is no substitute possible. Hence, they should be carefully cultivated and trained, and not suppressed. If not trained and kept under the control of the will, they are as dangerous as the waters of a mighty river when they break their levees.

2. RELATION

Relation is of all accidents the least real because it is the only one that is not absolute in any sense, *i. e.,* it implies necessarily the existence of two beings which are bound together in a certain manner. It is nothing in itself: all its reality depends upon the beings related to one another.

There are multiple relations between beings, because they can be compared with one another from various viewpoints, and each comparison presupposes a relation between them. A created world without relations is impossible to conceive. The absolute being alone does not imply any necessary relation.

In every instance, relation expresses *order,* and order involves at least two elements. Order is of two kinds: of *co-ordination,* when the elements related possess the same relative dignity, such as parts of a whole or members of a system. We call this the *static order,* and inasmuch as it is the ontological basis of beauty, it is also termed the *esthetic order.* The second kind of order is that of *subordination,* in which the elements related are of unequal dignity, because their relation expresses dependence such as we find between cause and effect, end and means. This order we call *dynamic,* as it is based upon the action of beings, and *teleological,* as expressive of the correlation of their activity.

III. *Transcendental Attributes*

We come now to the third part of our study—the transcendental attributes of being. By transcendental attributes we mean such as are attributed to, or predicable of, every being because it is a being. Hence, not every transcendental term is "eo ipso" a transcendental attribute. Thus, the scholastics enumerate six transcendental terms: "Ens, res, aliquid, unum, verum, bonum." Of these six terms, the first three are not expressive of attributes of a being, but of the being itself. By *"ens"* is meant the concrete being; it refers to its individuality. By *"res,"* the essence of the being is expressed; it alludes to its substantiality. By *"aliquid"* (aliud quid), we refer to the same being inasmuch as it is distinct from non-being or from another being.

None of these terms adds anything to the transcendental being but simply expresses it from a distinct viewpoint. It is different with the other three—*"unum, verum, bonum."* They add something positive which is not included in the term being, though the being as such is the natural basis for the threefold transcendental attribution.

1. THE TRANSCENDENTAL ATTRIBUTE "UNUM": UNITY

"Omne ens est unum": *Every being is one.* While each being is distinct from non-being and from every other being, it is in itself indistinct, undivided. This *indivision or unity* of a being is not equivalent to indivisibility or simplicity. All beings of the universe are indeed compounds and therefore, divisible, but they are not actually divided. They are constituted by parts, but the parts have no existence of their own, they exist as parts of the whole being, which alone is self-sufficient for existence.

a. COMPOSITION AND DISTINCTION

Compositions in beings we know from cosmology and psychology. Let us recall some: 1. Composition of materia prima and forma substantialis. 2. Composition of substance and accidents. 3. Composition of integral homogeneous parts—quantitative composition. To these we added above, 4. Composition of essence and existence. These are four kinds of real composition in which each part is distinct from every other part by a real distinction.

Besides the real we have *logical distinctions* which express divisions introduced by the mind. They are *purely logical* when there is no objective foundation for such a division as when we make a distinction between the definition and the defined. When there is an objective foundation, our distinctions are called *virtual or metaphysical,* as they are based upon what is called a metaphysical composition. For instance, while man in the concrete is constituted of real parts in a fourfold manner as just described, yet our concept of man, or what is the same, man in the abstract, is simple. However, to clarify our concept we divide it in defining man as a rational animal. This distinction is virtual because, though man is essentially one, there is in the complex activity of human nature an objective foundation for such a distinction.

In a real distinction we have numerically distinct parts —one part is not the other part. However the real distinction in a being does not necessarily imply the separability of its parts. Thus, of the four kinds of real distinctions given above only one is a separable distinction— the parts in quantitative composition. The reason is obvious. The other three compositions refer to compounds of heterogeneous parts which by their very union constitute the being: no part being able to exist by itself, no part is separable from the others.

In purely logical distinction there is no real basis for it, it is merely the work of the mind. Such is the distinction between the term man and the complex term rational animal. They are perfectly equivalent, though one expresses the object with greater clarity. In virtual or metaphysical distinction, while also formally the work of the mind, there is a real basis in the object. On account of the complexity of the object our mind directs its attention first to one side and then to another. Here evidently, the mental is not perfectly equivalent to the real object, as it represents but one side of it. Such is the distinction between animal and rational when we speak of man. While the concept of man is essentially one, our ideas of animal and rational are clearly distinct aspects of its object, each expressing something different of the same.

b. NUMBER AND MULTITUDE

The concept of unity leads to that of number and multitude. When we first pay attention to a being as one in itself and distinct from others, and then, while keeping that one in mind, turn our attention to another being, we have the idea of number. When the number of beings we thus include in our idea is not known, we speak of a multitude. It is evident that a number is finite because its last unit is known, but it is by no means clear whether a multitude cannot be infinite. There is another origin of number. When we divide a quantity into its homogeneous parts, we obtain an indefinite multitude of parts because quantity is indefinitely divisible. There are three kinds of quantities: time, space, and mass. We measure them by taking one conventional part as a unit. Thus, we have a second, a centimeter, and a gram as the fundamental units of time, space, and mass. Unity or unit in this connection is predicamental and must not be confounded with transcendental unity. It belongs to one category or predicament alone—quantity.

2. THE TRANSCENDENTAL ATTRIBUTE "VERUM": TRUTH

"Omne ens est verum": Every being is true. Truth is the second transcendental attribute of being. In the

same way as unity is a transcendental attribute of being because it is a necessary condition for its existence, truth is a transcendental attribute of being because every being which exists, if brought into relation with an intelligence, is knowable. The formal characteristic of truth is not in the being known, but in the mind that knows it. However, the material or objective element of truth is the being known. *Since every being, in so far as it is a being, is knowable, every being is objectively true.* It is evident that in this transcendental sense, we could never speak of a being as false, because in favorable conditions there is no being which is not knowable such as it is, since being is the proper object of intelligence. *When a being is known such as it is, we speak of it as formally true.*

It is well to recall here what we learned about the fundamental characteristics of knowledge in psychology. To know the truth about a thing is to know it as it is. This knowledge is not achieved in its perfection by an act of simple apprehension, but by an act of judgment. Consequently, truth is formally a relation, since judgment is essentially the enunciation of a relation between two concepts. Truth has been defined traditionally as *conformity between the intellect and the reality* which is its object. If we understand by the intellect the object habitually known, *i. e.,* the abstract concept which serves as predicate in the proposition in which the relation is expressed, and by the reality, the object that is actually placed before the mind and serves as the subject of the proposition, this definition of truth is acceptable. Truth in this sense is the ontological truth—it is the *correspondence between the being habitually known and the being coming presently before the mind.*

There is a great difference between ontological and logical truth: Ontological truth is in the things known, logical truth is in the mind that knows. When we judge, *i. e.,* when we affirm or deny one concept of another in conformity with the relation which exists between their objects, we have logical truth. Hence, logical truth is based upon the ontological: the one refers to the relation between the things known, the other to the judgment about such a relation. From this explanation it is clear that error or falsehood is an attribute of the mind that judges, and not of the being which is its object. All beings are true because all are knowable such as they are.

3. THE TRANSCENDENTAL ATTRIBUTE "BONUM": GOODNESS

While we do not take goodness here in the sense of kindness, it is well to mention its distinctive characteristic. In this sense goodness is a tendency to communicate to others of our own perfection and advantages: "Bonitas est diffusiva sui," goodness is characterized by a diffusion or expansion of self. It is the very opposite to what we call selfishness. Evidently, goodness in this acceptation is not a transcendental attribute, but a perfection of the free will and, therefore, belongs to rational beings alone.

In the sense of our present discussion, *i. e.*, in its ontological sense, *every being is good:* "Omne ens est bonum." In the same manner that truth is a transcendental attribute of being, goodness is also, *i. e.*, in its objective and material sense. To be formally good, a being must be brought into relation with a will, the same as to explain truth in its formal character an intelligent agent is necessary. From the transcendental viewpoint, as true is equivalent to knowable, good is equivalent to *desirable*. Whatsoever makes a being desirable, makes it good. The question which would naturally arise in this connection is this: Is every being good or desirable simply because it is a being, just as every being is knowable and true because it is a being?

We call good anything and everything which tends to complete and perfect a being, because it is evidently desirable from the viewpoint of the being itself that it should be complete and perfect. While every contingent being is imperfect by nature, it is a fact that it has first a natural tendency to its perfection and, secondly, an activity by means of which it approaches that perfection. It is evident, therefore, that every being is good in various ways and for various reasons: 1. Because it exists, and existence is good inasmuch as it perfects its essence, actualizing it; 2. Because it has a natural capacity for greater perfection; and 3. It acts in many ways, and every act completes and perfects its being.

What completes and perfects being in a conscious individual produces *pleasure*. This pleasure itself is a good inasmuch as it tends to increase the natural activity and thereby the perfection of the being. This is the *"bonum delectabile."* Being a means for an end, it is subordinate to the higher good—the perfection of its nature which, in rational beings, constitutes the *"bonum honestum," the moral good*. The means is a *relative* good, it is the *"bonum utile,"* whereas the end is the *absolute* good. The end may be the means of a still higher good, and thus only the really supreme end is the absolute good, in whose goodness all subordinate ends participate.

Evil is the contradictory of good. However, it is not a mere negation, since there are no concrete negative beings. It is the *privation of a good, i. e.,* a good is absent that ought to be present, such as blindness in man. When an evil is known and formally approved by a rational being, it becomes a *moral evil*. It must not be forgotten that a physical evil may be the useful and necessary means for the attainment of a higher good or of a good of a higher order. In such circumstances it ceases to be an evil since it participates in the nature of the higher good.

4. THE QUASI-TRANSCENDENTAL ATTRIBUTE "PULCHRUM": BEAUTY

There is a fourth attribute which, while not transcendental in the strict sense, is closely akin to it and, therefore, may be called a quasi-transcendental attribute—the beautiful. It shares in the distinctive nature of the other three, but has a characteristic of its own not found in the others; in other words, there can be no beauty where there is no unity, truth, or goodness, and yet a being is not beautiful simply because it is one, true, and good. There are two plainly distinct aspects to beauty—the subjective and objective, to which we must briefly call attention.

The subjective aspect is presented by St. Thomas Aquinas when he determines as beautiful things which, when seen, please: "Pulchra sunt quae visa placent." Evidently, the prince of the scholastics does not limit the perception of beauty to the eyes. "Visa"—seen, means here as much as perceived, known. Consequently, *beauty is that attribute of a being the perception of which causes joy*. Its direct relation is not to the faculty of appetition—the will, but to the faculty of knowledge in man—the mind. In this connection, beauty resembles truth rather than goodness. But it adds something to truth. Not every truth causes joy. Nevertheless, it is the joy of the intellect rather than that of the will; it is quite foreign to the pleasure of possessing a thing which is perceived as good, or the anticipated pleasure of desire and hope for the desirable good. The things which thrill us by their beauty inspire no desire for possession, no interested effort for their acquisition. It is the joy of knowledge simply—beauty begins in contemplation and ends in admiration.

The objective aspect of beauty was aptly determined by St. Augustine when he called it "splendor ordinis," the brilliancy of order. And in this respect we find an intimate relationship of beauty with both unity and goodness. Order is the harmonious result of a combination of realities, and as realities are good inasmuch as they are realities, order is the harmonious result of a combination of good elements. The result of such a combination approaches the ideal of order in proportion as the unification of the elements is more perfect. It is this perfection in the unification of the various elements which characterizes the ideal order, which St. Augustine calls its lustre, its splendor. Thus we might explain the *objective element of beauty as the shining, or clearly apparent unity in a great variety of realities*. Such a definition of the objectively beautiful would account in a rational manner for the esthetic enjoyment of the beautiful, because it cannot appear strange that the action of the intellect should produce an emotion of joy, when the knowledge of a great variety of elements adds considerably to the wealth of consciousness if such an addition is realized quickly and easily on account of the striking unity and harmony of the various elements.

From the nature of the case it is clear that esthetic enjoyment, *i. e.*, the fruition of beauty, is proper to man and not found in animals; only the intellect can perceive unity in multiplicity. Even in man a certain development of the esthetic taste is required to enjoy to the full the treasures of beauty present in nature and in the manifold works of art produced by man. Though the emotions which accompany and follow knowledge as such are, generally speaking, feeble in comparison with the passions roused by appetition, yet their influence upon human life and character is by no means contemptible, and in the life and character of people who are by nature more susceptible or by education better adapted for the enjoyment of the beautiful, very often the esthetic emotions have a strong influence.

One other remark will show the quasi-transcendency of beauty. As a matter of fact, each and every being of the universe is an admirable combination of a multitude of elements of great variety. This is clearly apparent from all the various discussions of this chapter. If we add to this absolutely evident combination of metaphysical elements the vista of the infinitesimal chemical elements and imponderable electrons and ions which have been suggested by the discovery of radio-activity and similar phenomena, and in view of the striking unity and harmony of all these many and various elements as characterized by the substantiality and the individuality of the being, who can doubt that to a highly developed intellect the knowledge of a being as such may be productive of estheic pleasure and, consequently, fully merit the attribute of beautiful?

CHAPTER TWENTY-THREE

DYNAMIC ONTOLOGY

OBJECT OF DYNAMIC ONTOLOGY

We have studied being in its double transcendental aspect—as being and as being something, *i. e.,* the existence and the essence of a being. We called this static ontology. Though static ontology is the necessary source and foundation for the comprehension of the universe, it is by no means a complete presentation of its object. It presents the universe at rest, as it were, in a state of equilibrium, in full possession of its elements. In reality, the universe is very different—it is never at rest, never in a state of stable equilibrium, never in full possession of all its elements. The reason is plain enough: the universe is the sum of contingent beings; but contingent beings, in which essence and existence are really distinct, depend for their existence upon the action of other beings, and since the action of contingent causes is again contingent and dependent, and not necessary and absolute, and since such action is, therefore, neither instantaneous nor permanent, the universe is never the same in two consecutive moments—it is naturally and intrinsically subject to change. It is evident that, unless we arrive at a rational interpretation of this continuous series of transformations through which the universe passes incessantly, and of the influences that produce, and bear upon, these transformations, our metaphysical study of the world will remain incomplete and unsatisfactory. It is this viewpoint in metaphysics which we call dynamic ontology.

Let us bear in mind that the universe is the sum of contingent beings. However, all contingent beings change. Not having the reason for their existence in themselves, *they depend upon the action of others for their being;* even more than that—to acquire it in its natural fullness, *their own action is indispensable.* Consequently, contingent beings acquire their being gradually, step by step as it were, and in this gradual acquisition of being,—let us call it *ontological evolution*—various intrinsic, and extrinsic elements are necessary. Our task then is naturally twofold: to study ontological evolution in itself, and in its causes.

I. Ontological Evolution

Ontological evolution is not the same as cosmic or biological evolution. Cosmic evolution refers to the inorganic universe. We studied its phases and examined the reasons upon which it is based in cosmology, and we accepted it as a scientific theory of great value and the highest probability. In a similar manner we studied and examined biological evolution and accepted it, at least within certain limits, as a very convenient and probable scientific interpretation of the manifold facts of organic life. In ontological evolution we do not consider the living or non-living beings in their distinct characteristics, but, as in static ontology, being as such will be our object, and, consequently both the living and the non-living must be included in our study in exactly the same manner.

Furthermore, there is a great difference in the degree of certainty. Though cosmic evolution is highly probable, indeed, appears to us as practically certain, yet its certainty is by no means absolute, because its grounds are not clearly evident. Still more does this possibility of error apply to biological evolution. Though many cumulative reasons give it also a high degree of probability, none of those reasons are conclusive. Things might have happened differently from the way evolution supposes. The certainty of ontological evolution is of a different type—there is no room for doubt left. Its evidence is not open to question because it is based upon the analysis of the most simple processes which we find everywhere and always. We proceed to study ontological evolution first in itself and then in its various applications.

I. ANALYSIS OF ONTOLOGICAL EVOLUTION

As already explained, every contingent production or acquisition of being is gradual and not instantaneous. A being is first less perfect and then more perfect, *i. e.*, it first possesses less reality and then more reality. This process by which it acquires more reality and thereby becomes more perfect, we call an *ontological movement or evolution*, the "kinesis" of Aristotle, the "motus" of the scholastics. The terms are appropriate. We may indeed call "terminus a quo," the point of departure, the being considered before the process sets in, and "terminus ad quem," the point of arrival, the being considered when the process stops, and thus, the process itself—the passage from the "terminus a quo" to the "terminus ad quem"—appears truly as a "kinesis," a "motus," an ontological movement. In Aristotelian philosophy, anterior to its process of ontological evolution, the being is called the *potential being*—the "ens in potentia," and after the process, the *actual being*—the "ens actu." Equivalent to potential being is the being in a state of determinability and perfectibility; it refers to its capacity for receiving new degrees of being or reality. Equivalent to actual being is the being in its state of determination and perfection, *i. e.*, in the possession of the new degrees of being. Since this process, changing the being, carries it forward from the state of potentiality to the state of actuality, we may also call it appropriately the *actualization of the being*.

It is clear that the terms potential and actual are correlative; they refer to the same concrete being in its natural course of evolution, *i. e.*, to different stages in the acquisition of its full being. What is actual in regard to a past state of the being is potential in regard to its future state. Again, not only to the progressive development of a being are the terms applied, but also to regressive evolution. Hence, speaking of concrete beings, the concepts of potentiality and actuality give us the key for the interpretation of all the changes that take place in the universe, the substantial as well as the accidental. Thus, cold iron is potential when compared with hot iron, and again, the oak is the actualized acorn. In the same way the elements of oxygen and hydrogen are potential water, and again, the child is the potential man or woman.

2. TRANSCENDENTAL APPLICATION OF ONTOLOGICAL EVOLUTION

The transcendental character of ontological evolution is quite obvious—changes are universal, and consequently, their metaphysical interpretation is also of universal application. However, it will be illuminating to mention a few of the most important concrete cases to which it applies.

The fundamental application refers to the substantial constitution of the being. The substantial ontological elements of a being are the materia prima and the forma substantialis. There can be no doubt—the materia prima is the potential being. When determined by the forma substantialis we have the actual being. The *specific determination of the materia by the forma is the actualization of the materia*, it is the first ontological evolution of the being of which the constitution of the substance is the result.

In the natural order a substance is never isolated, but is endowed with its specific group of accidents. Also here the correlation of potential and actual being finds its application—*the accidents actualize the substance*.

Even the accidents themselves are correlated to one another in the same manner. Every bodily substance is ontologically determined by quantity, and quantity, again, by extension, and extension, again, by the exact form or figure of the natural body. Hence, it is *quantity* which *directly actualizes the substance,* and *extension actualizes quantity,* and the *external form actualizes the extension of the body.*

From another viewpoint the *extended substance is potential with reference to its actualization by the mechanical, physical, and chemical forces.* So also the *inorganic body is actualized by life.* And again, *the organic body is potential in respect to the psychical powers* which determine its distinctive character and convert it into an animal. Even *the spiritual substance,* such as the human soul, is *actualized by its intellectual and volitional faculties.* In such a way from the dynamic viewpoint the concrete essence of a being is constituted.

We have not yet the concrete being in its fullness. The *concrete being is but potential in regard to its action,* which is in a sense the most characteristic actualization of a being. Again, to some extent in sense powers, but especially and properly in rational faculties, through repeated action, a new ontological element is produced—the *habit,* which is another *important actualization of the faculties* and, of course, indirectly of the agent.

Have we exhausted the applications of the correlated concepts of potential and actual in the universe? The most significant of all remains to be mentioned—essence and existence. As we saw in our last chapter, in the contingent being the complete and perfect constitution of a being, *i. e.,* all its elements, the substantial and accidental combined in one being, does not necessarily imply its existence, and it is the act of existence which is the crowning actuality of a concrete being—*to be is its supreme actualization,* as the scholastics said: "Esse est ultimus actus."

These few considerations show clearly the transcendental application of ontological evolution. And even to the logical order we apply the same metaphysical interpretation in a sense of analogy. Thus, we speak of the transcendental concepts as being the most potential, which are actualized by the categories or supreme genera, and these are potential concepts when compared with the intermediate and the lowest genera, and again, the lowest genera are potential in respect to the species, and finally the specific concepts are actualized by the concept of the individual.

Another remark is here apposite. As the materia prima and the forma substantialis represent the primary and fundamental application of these correlated concepts, they have become identified with them in meaning. Consequently, we speak of *material in exactly the same sense as we speak of potential, and of formal in the same way as we speak of actual.* Thus, we apply correctly the term material even to purely spiritual elements, as when we say that the acts of the mind are the material object and their correlation the formal object of logic.

II. The Causes of Ontological Evolution

To explain the presence of both potential and actual beings in the universe and the manner in which they pass from the state of potentiality to the state of actuality, action is necessary. In the first instance, we cannot explain adequately the presence of any being in the universe, whether actual or potential, except upon the assumption of an absolute cause—God, who called them into existence from nothing by His divine fiat. This fact has been abundantly demonstrated both in cosmology and psychology. However, at present we are not concerned with creation; but we are concerned with the explanation of the manner in which the actual beings of this world, which already exist and constantly change their existence under our eyes, pass from one state and form of existence to another. We believe that to explain these changes in the universe we need not appeal directly to the primary and fundamental cause of the universe—creation, but that the action of the contingent beings is sufficient. Taking for our basis the analysis of ontological evolution which we gave in the first part of this chapter, it will not be difficult to determine the nature and the number of contingent causes necessary to account for the dynamic aspect of the universe.

I. DEFINITION OF CAUSE

Before we enter upon our discussion of causes, let us clearly determine the meaning of the term. We call cause any being and any action which directly or indirectly contribute to the production of a being or a phenomenon. This concept will be clarified by a comparison with synonymous expressions. *Cause* is partly equivalent to *principle,* to *element,* to *reason,* but only partly so. *Cause applies to the ontological order only, principle to both the ontological and the logical order.* Thus, the sun is the cause or the principle of heat and light on earth, but the premises are the principles, not the causes, of a conclusion.

Similar is the relation of cause to element. *Elements are the result of an analysis,* but since there are both real and logical analyses, elements, like principles, *apply to both the ontological and logical order.* Thus, hydrogen and oxygen are the causes or elements of water, but concepts are the elements, not the causes, of a judgment. Moreover, not even every cause is an element, because an element is always a part of the being to which it belongs, whereas there are causes which are extrinsic. Thus, while elements are more extensive than causes in one respect, they are less in another.

Reason refers to the mind. Anything whatsoever, whether it be a cause, principle, or element, which helps us to explain a thing in our own mind, is a reason. Consequently, reason is of all synonyms the most general. *Occasion* is a circumstance favoring the action of the cause, *condition* is a necessary circumstance. Also occasions and conditions are reasons. Neither occasions nor conditions are causes.

2. CONSTITUTIVE OR INTRINSIC CAUSES

The first potential being in an ontological evolution—the "ens mobile" as the scholastics would say,—is the materia prima. It must not be conceived as a mere negation nor as a pure possibility of being, but as a real positive element of perfectibility, or as a positive capacity for further development of being. This is the "terminus a quo" of the evolution. The "terminus ad quem" is the actual being in its concrete reality. It is the same potential being after it is actualized, *i. e.,* after its natural perfectibility has been transformed into substantial perfection, its determinability into specific determination. Thereby a totally new element has been acquired. This is the forma substantialis. The potential being is the *material element,* the new element which perfected and determined substantially and specifically the potential being—the forma substantialis—is the *formal element.* Since both elements constitute the actual being, they are the *constitutive elements,* and as they enter into the being's very nature, they are the essential elements of the being. Furthermore, because these elements are causes of the being, since they positively constitute it by their union, their proper name is *constitutive* or *intrinsic causes.*

"Mutatis mutandis," this interpretation applies also to accidental transformations and, consequently, to every ontological evolution. The subject in which a change is realized is always the material element, the "ens mobile," the potential being; the element acquired by the change is always the formal element, with this difference that in accidental changes, the potential being is a "materia secunda" and the new reality is a "forma accidentalis." But also the "materia secunda" and the "forma accidentalis" are constitutive or intrinsic causes of the being, with the difference that their causality is not substantial but accidental. Thus, in hot iron, iron is the material, heat the formal cause.

3. THE EFFICIENT CAUSES

How must we interpret the ontological evolution itself, *i. e.,* the passage of the potential being, the "ens mobile," from its "terminus a quo" to its "terminus ad quem"? In other words, what explains the actualization of a potential being?

If we take the "ens mobile" for a vehicle, an illustration which the expression itself spontaneously suggests, the question would be: What is the power that moves the vehicle from its "terminus a quo," its starting point, to its "terminus ad quem," its destination? It may be a horse, it may be a mechanical motor of some kind driven by steam, electricity, or gasoline. In every case it is moved by an external action, by the force of another agent. The vehicle is not and cannot be, strictly speaking, automotive.

While this illustration suggests the solution of the question, we must not be tempted thereby to remain on the surface of things. Evidently, the true problem consists in explaining the coming into actual existence of the new ontological element, the new positive reality or perfection, either substantial or accidental, which we called the forma substantialis and accidentalis respectively. This new element cannot come solely from the material subject or potential being, as this is by supposition in a state of potentiality regarding it. Therefore, an outside influence is necessary to explain its appearance. The being from which this influence proceeds we call *"causa efficiens."* It is the "ens movens," or the motor of the movement, the *efficient cause of the ontological evolution.* It is not like the material and the formal element of a being an intrinsic cause, but exercises its causative influence from without by means of an action the object of which is precisely the realization of the evolution which we are explaining.

It is evident that every contingent being is an efficient cause, because every being is an agent; and being a material agent, whenever it acts, it acts upon others. It is well to remember in this connection that even the actions of organic beings are not, strictly speaking, immanent, because it is always the case of one part or organ acting upon another part or organ of the organism. Only purely spiritual agents can be strictly immanent efficient causes, in the activity of which the efficient causality is not necessarily exercised upon another being. Since all agents in the universe are material agents, their action always involves an efficient causality of the type explained.

The efficient causality of a being may be direct and simple, or indirect and complex. When it produces the effect directly, *i. e.,* when the power of action, such as physical forces, is applied directly to the being which is thereby changed, we have a simple efficient cause. In higher organisms, especially in man, efficient causality is often complex; indeed, every specifically human action has a complex causality. The rational agent, the human individual, is the *principal cause*—the being from which the action originates and to whom the action is ascribed, because he is the agent. The external beings, and even the human body itself, by means of which the action produces its effect in other beings are the *instrumental causes.* Such are the hand and the pen, for instance, with which we write down our thoughts. The beings which serve as instrumental causes have their own specific action, but inasmuch as they are instrumental causes, they share in the power and dignity of the principal cause. This applies to all instrumental causes, but particularly to the human body as the organic and consubstantial instrumental cause in human activity.

We have touched in psychology upon the problem of how principal and instrumental causes concur in producing one and the same action. It is one of the greatest difficulties in philosophy. But while it is plainly difficult to conceive and explain the concurrence in detail, it is absolutely impossible to conceive and explain human activity without such concurrence.

Another remark on this subject will not be useless. Its object is the relation between the action of the necessary and absolute Cause—God, and the action of contingent causes. The action of God is the first and primary efficient causality of the universe, the contingent agents are but second efficient causes, or causes of a secondary order for the explanation of the universe. While it is a simple and self-evident principle in philosophy and science never to appeal to a direct divine intervention whenever the action of contingent causes can account for an effect, yet we must not forget that any explanation by the causality of a contingent agent is never adequate and final, but necessarily partial, provisional, and conditional, since the action of a contingent agent is itself contingent. An adequate and definite explanation must ultimately rest upon a causality which is not contingent, but absolute, *i. e.,* the causality of the First Cause.

4. THE FINAL CAUSES

In our attempt to find an explanation for the acquisition of being, which we characterized as an ontological evolution, we have discovered and analyzed a twofold source and cause: the intrinsic, passive principle, *i. e.,* the subject in which the new element is received, and the extrinsic, active principle, the efficient cause or the agent, by whose influence the natural capacity of the first is brought to actual realization, and thereby the new intrinsic element, the active consubstantial principle—the forma—is brought into existence.

a. REALITY OF THE FINAL CAUSES

While the constitutive and efficient causes are undoubtedly necessary to explain the production of an actual being, they are not sufficient for a full and perfect explanation, because such productions do not proceed at random, and the products themselves are not irregular or chaotic. On the contrary, the natural processes of ontological evolution, as we know them from cosmology and psychology, are expressive of absolute regularity; and, apart from the marvelous order which regulates the complicated processes themselves, there is a most wonderful order in the result, so that in spite of the ceaseless and infinitely complex transformations and modifications of the uncounted billions of beings of the universe, the universe itself, in all the stages of its cosmic and biological evolution, manifests a striking unity and an imposing harmony. But order of any kind is unthinkable without a principle of direction. In both cosmology and psychology we saw that this principle of direction is intrinsic, *viz.*, an immanent tendency in the being by which its activity is controlled in a definite sense. It adds neither active energy nor passive capacity to a being, but it is a principle of orientation, drawing its evolution in a given direction. Furthermore, since each being has its own well-regulated and perfectly determined course of evolution, this directive factor is plainly a specific principle, intimately associated with the forma substantialis of which it is the natural sign and expression. This principle of orientation acts in the manner of a *physical cause* in all beings which, having no reason, are not capable of any other influence; in rational agents it is a *moral cause,* inasmuch as it exercises its action by means of an aim in the mind.

These few considerations are sufficient to prove that this principle of direction has a positive and most important influence upon the final outcome of ontological evolution and has therefore been termed justly the *final cause*.

It seems strange that anybody with eyes open could deny the presence in the evolution of the universe of this causality, without which there is no way of accounting for even such simple phenomena as the various laws which regulate so perfectly the mechanical, physical, and chemical actions of beings, not to mention the wonderful regularity in the manifold and complex functions of the living beings from the lowest to the highest species. We may well repeat here what we said above in another connection: if it is difficult to conceive in detail how this causality is accomplished, it is infinitely more difficult, indeed, absolutely impossible to explain the manifest teleology in the universe without final causality. Since there is no question and cannot be a shadow of doubt about the facts, this, the only possible explanation, apart from a direct divine intervention, speaks for itself.

b. INTERPRETATION OF FINAL CAUSALITY

There is hardly any need to call attention to the fundamental source and basis for a rational interpretation of final causes. Evidently, we cannot account adequately for the influence of such causes except on the assumption of an omnipotent and all-wise Creator of the universe. Being conceived as the action of the principle of direction and orientation, from which the grand order of the cosmos originates and which alone offers a key for the rational interpretation of the marvelous processes of the evolution of life in the individual and in the species, final causality can be explained only as the expression of the mind and will of God, who, being the designer as well as the creator, assigned to each species and genus of being its own distinctive nature, and to each individual its own specific immanent tendency to direct and control its course of activity in conformity with the divine design and plan.

The manner in which the action of the final causes is accomplished is twofold: it is realized both in the subject or material cause, the potential being, and in the efficient cause or the agent, to whose action the evolution is due.

The final cause is active chiefly in the material cause—the subject which is to evolve. The potential capacity for actualizations in a given subject is not indefinite but clearly determined by its very nature: a certain number of definite courses are open to it. Whenever an outside influence comes to bear upon it, it takes one of these courses in its evolution, and never any others. Here we have, then, one principle of direction: the immanent tendency in the material cause.

For instance, in the case of a chemical reaction between carbon and oxygen, there may be a combination of one atom of carbon and one atom of oxygen, or it may be a combination of one atom of carbon and two of oxygen. Again, who does not know that the same amount of heat applied to various kinds of beings produces a distinct result in each distinct kind?

There must be another principle of direction in an evolution, because, if there is a number of well-defined courses which the potential being may take in its progress, why does it not take any one of the several courses open to it? Because also in the efficient cause—the agent who acts upon it,—there is the same kind of immanent principle of direction which controls the influence of the efficient cause upon the material cause, and thus, directed by the harmonious action of this combined final causality, regularity and order in the processes of the universe are achieved.

Let us take again the same chemical reaction as an illustration. In a given concrete situation the combination will be either one atom of carbon and two of oxygen, or one of each species. Which of the two combinations is realized depends upon the external causes. In the same way, if we apply heat to water, the effect will be directly in proportion to the amount of heat we apply.

SECTION TWO

THEODICY, THE PHILOSOPHY OF THE TRAN-
SCENDENT AUTHOR OF THE WORLD

CHAPTER TWENTY-FOUR

THE EXISTENCE OF GOD

Our Capacity for the Knowledge of God

Before we engage in studying the problems of theodicy or the philosophy of God, let us determine the preliminary question of our capacity for the knowledge of God, since without it, our study would be fruitless and useless. We have already dwelled upon the fact of the undoubted difference between our knowledge of the universe and our ideas which represent and express the nature of God—the former is proper, the latter analogical. We have come to the conclusion that even the analogical knowledge of God is of supreme value and significance to us, speculatively as well as practically. But what is still more important to know and what concerns us most directly in this chapter, is to investigate the fundamental capacity of our mind to arrive at a certain knowledge that there is a God, since every other problem of theodicy is dependent upon the solution of this preliminary question.

Positivists, agnostics, skeptics, and materialists generally, assert that there is no God, or at least, that the knowledge of God, if there be such a being, is absolutely beyond the power and scope of the human mind. The pantheists identify God with the world, and consequently, their god cannot be the same as the personal and extramundane and supermundane God of theism and Christianity. Thus, from our viewpoint, pantheists are equivalent to atheists. Even Kant thought he had shown that, while the existence of God was practically certain on moral grounds, there is no possibility of a certain speculative knowledge of it, *i. e.,* that we cannot logically demonstrate it.

Against them all we shall prove in a speculative manner that God exists, because our knowledge of God's existence is of the same order and based upon the same laws of logic as apply to the knowledge of the objective existence of the world in which we live. It is only of ourselves, *i. e.,* of our own existence, that we have an intuition or a direct knowledge—we perceive ourselves in every conscious act. The existence of every other being, as we have seen in criteriology, is known to us only indirectly, *i. e.,* such knowledge is founded upon the principle of causality: we perceive a being only inasmuch as it acts upon us directly or indirectly—we perceive the cause in its effect. But this principle of causality is a proposition of absolute value and, consequently, of universal application; and no matter what positivists, agnostics, and criticists say to the contrary, this principle is evident, it is even of immediate evidence because its negation implies direct contradiction. A few words will show this clearly.

The Logical Basis for Our Knowledge of God

From the dynamic viewpoint, Aristotle's presentation of the principle of causality is the most characteristic: "Quidquid movetur, ab alio movetur," *whatsoever is moved, is moved by another.* Aristotle speaks here of movement in the metaphysical sense as explained in our last chapter. Hence, the proposition means that every acquisition of being needs another factor besides the "ens mobile," the potential being itself, to explain it. This is evident because, as it cannot come from the "ens mobile" itself, which is, by supposition, in a state of potentiality, it must come from without.

From the static viewpoint we may give an even more simple presentation of the same principle: *The existence of a contingent being is due to the action of another.* The proposition in this form is, again, quite evident. Every existing being is either an "ens a se," *i. e.,* it exists because it is its nature to exist, or it is an "ens ab alio," *i. e.,* its existence is due to the action of another. Consequently, the contingent being, not being an "ens a se," *i. e.,* not having it in its nature to exist, is manifestly an "ens ab alio," *i. e.,* its existence is necessarily due to the action of another being.

I. The Demonstration of the Divine Existence

Both in cosmology and in psychology we have had occasion to show that the only possible adequate interpretation of the universe is based upon the concept of its creation by an absolute uncaused cause—the necessary being whom we call God. While the arguments then proposed are perfectly conclusive, yet the paramount speculative and practical importance of the problem of the existence of God for the human race induces us to devote a special chapter to this subject, studying it more profoundly and more completely. Bearing in mind the far-reaching consequences of this problem, it is but natural that the greatest minds of the race have consecrated their deepest thought to this matter. The great Plato and his still greater disciple, Aristotle, presented demonstrations which have illumined the way of the philosophers of all ages; some of their arguments are still classic and have never been improved upon. Especially is this true of Aristotle's. He is indeed the father of theodicy, just as he is the father of cosmology, psychology, and ontology.

However, the arguments used by the philosophers of the past to demonstrate the divine existence, have not all been of equal value, indeed, some have had no demonstrative value whatsoever. To proceed methodically in our work we will consider first the most renowned arguments for the existence of God which are not conclusive. In the second place, we will present those which are conclusive.

A. INCONCLUSIVE ARGUMENTS FOR THE DIVINE EXISTENCE

The arguments for the existence of God which, while not absolutely without value, are not conclusive, are of two kinds, *ideological* and *moral*. Both kinds are associated with some of the greatest names in the history of philosophy.

The source of the ideological arguments are platonic ideas, especially the platonic conception that the material beings of the universe are but the shadows of intelligible beings—the separate ideas, *i. e.*, ideas which in Plato's mind have an existence of their own in a spiritual world apart from the human intellect, and which are therefore the standard and criterion of our knowledge. Such a conception, modified by the teachings of Christianity, exercised great influence upon the arguments used on behalf of the existence of God by St. Augustine, St. Anselm, St. Bonaventure, and many others, even in our own days.

The moral arguments are based, as their name implies, upon moral grounds, *i. e.*, they take certain evident facts in the moral and social life of man and build upon them the assumption of God, claiming that only the existence of God can explain them adequately. There is hardly any philosopher of note dealing with this subject, who has not used this kind of arguments, and being at the same time of a more facile presentation and having a stronger appeal to the imagination than the others, the moral arguments enjoy the favor of popular speakers and writers.

I. THE IDEOLOGICAL ARGUMENTS

The ideological arguments have a common basis: in an open or veiled manner they deduce the existence of God from the idea of God in particular, or from the idea of the absolute, the infinite, the perfect in general. They have no logical value, *i. e.*, they do not prove the objective existence of God, because they all involve explicitly or implicitly a transition from the ideal to the real order, which, in logic, is not legitimate, according to the Schoolmen's sentence: "De posse ad esse non valet illatio."

a. The ideological argument in all its purity is *St. Anselm's*. It is generally called the ontological argument, but in our opinion wrongly so, because it has its source not in the concrete being which alone is the proper object of ontology, but in being as it exists in the mind which is the object of logic. Here it is: God is the most perfect being that can be thought of. But such a being must exist, because, unless it existed, it would not be the most perfect being we can think of, since we can in our thought include existence as one of its perfections.

Though this argument was proposed by a great doctor of the Church, adopted by Descartes, conceded by Hegel, and, with slight modifications, used also by such eminent minds as St. Bonaventure, Duns Scotus and Leibniz, yet it is plainly without demonstrative value. The only legitimate conclusion which can be drawn from it is this: the concept of the most perfect being conceivable includes existence as a part of it, *i. e.*, of the concept. About the concrete objective existence of such a being it says nothing.

b. *Descartes* proposed another ideological argument which was accepted by Fénelon and others: We have the idea of the infinite; but, then, the infinite must exist because we cannot explain the idea of it unless God put it in our mind. The fallacy of this argument is quite obvious. Our idea of the infinite is not positive, but negative; it is the idea of being in general, to which is added the negation of any limit. Mental abstraction explains such an idea perfectly without any appeal to the existence and action of God.

c. The most famous as well as the most plausible ideological argument is the one cherished by *St. Augustine* and used by many medieval and modern Christian philosophers. It is based upon the eternity, necessity, universality, and immutability of our ideas in general, and upon the eternity, necessity, universality, and immutability of the logical and moral orders in particular. The argument assumes that there can be no adequate explanation of the absoluteness of the ideal and moral orders unless we accept the ideas in the Divine Mind as its foundation.

Evidently, we have here an adaptation of Plato's ideas to Christian teaching. There can be no doubt about the appropriateness and beauty of such a conception, which looks upon the universe as the created realization and expression of the ideas of the divine mind; in the chapters on logic and ethics we have repeatedly called attention to it. However, for the conclusive demonstration of the objective divine existence the argument has no value whatsoever. Abstraction and negation are adequate to explain the eternity, immutability, universality, and necessity of the ideal and moral orders.

2. THE MORAL ARGUMENTS

We come now to the so-called moral arguments for the existence of God. There is a number of them and they are presented in various ways. For our purpose it will be sufficient to deal with the three most important. They are: *The consensus of mankind, man's natural desire for perfect happiness,* and *the obligation and sanction of the moral law.* As we shall see, they all have their value. However, their importance in the history of philosophy and in practical human life is greatly exaggerated. Their value is either presumptive or confirmative, never demonstrative or conclusive.

a. In the first instance we have the *consensus of mankind:* the human race has ever been practically unanimous in its belief that there is a God, or some Supreme Power controlling the universe. But such a universal consensus cannot be explained except on the assumption that there is such a being. Consequently, God exists.

While we may concede the minor premise, the fact of universal consensus, the major, is inacceptable because it implies an "ignoratio elenchi"—it proves too much. Mankind has been unanimous on various questions on which, as the progress of science showed, the consensus was based on error. All that, in this instance as in any other, human consensus proves is that there must be good and obvious reasons for the belief in God. An absolute rational assent is not possible till the mind examines those reasons and finds them logically conclusive. Hence, the argument has presumptive value only.

b. The second moral argument is based upon the *innate desire in man for happiness*. It is claimed: 1. There is in human nature an irresistible inclination to the enjoyment of perfect happiness; and 2. God alone, the infinitely perfect being, can be the adequate object of this natural desire, because we know from both history and our own observation and experience that there is no contingent being nor any sum of contingent beings which can perfectly satisfy it. Hence, it is concluded, God must exist.

In this argumentation the premises are true, but the conclusion is not contained therein and, consequently, is not legitimate. The logical conclusion of the premises would be: If there is an adequate object to that human desire, God alone is it. In other words, to convert the argument into a logical syllogism, we must make the first proposition a truly major premise by adding: and there must be an adequate object to such a desire. But analytically, this addition is a mere assumption which cannot be proven by itself. Synthetically, however, *i. e.*, basing it upon the knowledge of the divine existence, this argument is of great confirmative value, as it gives a very satisfactory interpretation of man's undying desire for perfect happiness.

c. The argument for the existence of God derived from the *moral order* is of a similar nature and power. It is often proposed in this manner: The obligation of the moral order is absolute and its sanction is perfect. But there can be no absolute obligation nor perfect sanction, unless they come from God. Consequently, God exists.

Undoubtedly, the conclusion would be perfectly acceptable if the minor were analytically demonstrable, but it is not. The absoluteness of moral obligation and the perfection of moral sanction are assumptions which cannot be proven a posteriori. Just as in the preceding argument, so here: if we concede the divine existence as a fact, the characteristics of absoluteness in moral obligation and of perfection in moral sanction are easily deduced, and thus, from a synthetical viewpoint this argument possesses a striking confirmative power. In the same way as it is desirable that man's thirst for perfect happiness should find an adequate satisfaction, it is desirable that there should be an absolute obligation and a perfect sanction of the moral order. Nevertheless, this desirability alone does not prove their existence.

d. A word or two must be said here on another so-called moral argument famous in the history of philosophy, to which reference has already been made. After Kant had undermined in his criticist philosophy the foundation for a speculative demonstration of God, he assumed His existence as *a moral postulate*. Though it is impossible to prove God theoretically, he argues, human life, individual and social, is such that the idea of God is indispensable as an absolute condition of a workable interpretation of the world. Therefore, we postulate it.

What is the meaning and value of such a moral postulate? While its presentation is faulty, yet in reality this argument is not a simple postulate or merely a moral argument, but a genuine speculative and metaphysical argument equivalent to those which we will discuss immediately. If it can be clearly proven that without God there can be no adequate explanation of human life, it is evident that God must exist, because if the effect exists, its necessary cause must also exist.

B. CONCLUSIVE ARGUMENTS FOR THE EXISTENCE OF GOD

Having studied the ideological and moral arguments, which are not conclusive, we will now consider those that are and therefore demonstrate the existence of God. We call them metaphysical because they are based upon the nature of beings as we study them in metaphysics. Here again, we have no intention of examining or even presenting all the arguments which have been or may be suggested for the demonstration of the divine existence, but we will limit ourselves to the most important, which are the basis upon which every other possible argument must rest. They are the famous "tres viae" of the Summa of St. Thomas Aquinas. Finding them, at least in substance and implicitly, already in Aristotle, they have been used and their peremptory logical value acknowledged by practically every theistic and Christian philosopher. *They are founded respectively upon the contingent nature of the universe, on an analysis of ontological evolution,* and *on the existence of order in the world.* The first argument is often called *cosmological,* but we prefer to call it *ontological,* because it has its source not in the existence of organic or inorganic beings as such, but in the existence of contingent beings as such, which are studied, not in cosmology or psychology, but in ontology. The second is called *kinetic,* from *"kinesis,"* i. e., motion, and the third, *teleological.*

I. THE ONTOLOGICAL ARGUMENT

The ontological argument is not new to us. We used it in both cosmology and psychology to give an adequate explanation of the existence of the inorganic and organic beings that compose the universe. The universe, as we showed, is contingent, but no contingent being nor any sum or series of contingent beings find the adequate reason for their existence in themselves and must, therefore, find it ultimately in the action of a necessary being. This argument leads to God as the *"ens necessarium"* or the *"ens a se," i. e.,* the being that has the reason for its existence in itself and is therefore absolute. For greater clarity, let us present the argument in syllogistic form.

MAJOR: No contingent being, nor any sum or series of contingent beings, can find an adequate explanation for their existence either in themselves, or in any other contingent being, or in any sum or series of contingent beings.

MINOR: The universe is a sum of contingent beings.

CONCLUSION: The universe can find its adequate explanation neither in itself, nor in any other contingent being, nor in any sum or series of contingent beings.

The inference from this conclusion is inevitable: The action of the necessary being, the absolute Cause, alone can adequately explain the existence of the universe. This inference is inevitable because the two terms are plainly contradictory, and consequently, if existence cannot be due to a contingent cause, it must be due to a non-contingent or necessary cause.

Neither the major nor the minor premise needs any real demonstration. The minor is plainly evident from almost every page of this book. There can be nothing more certain in our mental life than the fact of the changeable nature of the universe. But only contingent beings can be subject to change.

The major is not less evident. Every contingent cause is only a provisional and hypothetic explanation of a being: it is an explanation only inasmuch as it is itself explained. But no contingent cause explains itself, and therefore, each needs another explanation. Hence, no contingent cause can give a definite, absolute, and adequate explanation of any contingent being.

It will be well to recall here the various applications of which this argument admits and upon which we enlarged in chapters seven, nine, eleven, and fourteen. The ontological argument for the divine existence finds a solid and unshakable basis for its compelling logical power in every one of these four evident facts: 1. The existence of the inorganic world. 2. The existence of plant life in the world. 3. the existence of sense life in the world. 4. The existence of each human soul.

2. THE KINETIC ARGUMENT

The kinetic argument is based upon Aristotle's well-known principle: "Quidquid movetur, ab alio movetur," whatsoever is moved, is moved by another. It refers to ontological evolution. Its basic foundation is the same as in the previous argument, indeed, there can be no other; but it is derived from a dynamic interpretation of the existence of the universe.

There are two distinct applications of this argument, both equally compelling in their logic. *The evident fact upon which both are based is the ontological evolution of the universe*. We have learned from the metaphysical analysis of evolution that, to explain the course of progressive and regressive evolutions which constitutes the history of the universe, we must assume two series of causes, the intrinsic passive causes—the "entia mobilia" or potential beings which evolve, and the extrinsic active causes—the "entia moventia," *i. e.*, the efficient causes or motors which cause the evolution. Let us direct our attention first to the "entia mobilia," the beings which are the subject of evolution.

a. If we consider one evolution by itself, it is evident that the being evolving is first potential and then actual, because its evolution is nothing else than the actualization of its potentiality. But if we consider the whole series of evolutions the sum of which constitutes the universe, we must assume that the very first being—the "ens primum" from which the whole series originates, could not be a potential being, because being potential, it could not actualize itself, and being the "ens primum," there could be no prior being to cause its actualization. Hence, the "ens primum," the being that started the series of evolutions in the world, could only have been an actual, not a potential being.

Furthermore, the "ens primum" must be conceived not simply as an actual being but as purely actual, *i. e.,* it must exclude from its nature all mixture of potentiality because, being the first being, there is no other to explain by its action the passage from the state of potentiality to the state of actuality, and therefore, an explanation of its evolution would demand an actualization "ex nihilo," which is absurd.

Finally, the "ens primum," besides being necessarily and purely actual, must have possessed supreme, absolute, and infinite actuality, as it must have contained, at least implicitly, or rather supereminently, the actuality capable of accounting adequately for all the power expended in the actualization of the whole series of ontological evolutions, inclusive of man, and all human activity and products.

Hence, the "ens primum" from which the universe draws its origin, is, as Aristotle clearly perceived, a supreme extramundane and supermundane *ACTUS PURISSIMUS, pure and absolute actuality.*

b. This same kinetic argument admits of another presentation. Instead of considering the series of "entia mobila," the passive causes, let us pay attention to the "entia moventia," the active motors. In truth, they are but one and the same series of beings from two distinct viewpoints, because each concrete being is both "mobile" and "movens," since it is both passive and active, and, again, for the very same reason, each being is both potential and actual. Inasmuch as the series of beings the sum of which constitutes the universe, are "entia moventia" or motors, they are without exception intermediate motors, because, being moved themselves, they are moved by another, and therefore, depend upon another for their power to move. But where there is a series of intermediate motors there must necessarily be a first motor, a "primum movens," from which the intermediate motors draw their power to move, because intermediate motors move only inasmuch as they are moved by another motor. To assume an infinite series of intermediate motors would not solve the problem, it would only multiply and obscure it.

This "primum movens" cannot be an "ens mobile," *i. e.*, it must itself be immovable, because, if it were itself moved, it could not be the "primum movens," as it would be necessarily moved by another.

Thus, we are led by the kinetic argument to conceive God as the *immovable Prime Mover of the universe* or, as the scholastics would say, the *"MOTOR MUNDI IMMOTUS."*

3. THE TELEOLOGICAL ARGUMENT

Of all the arguments for the existence of God, the most obvious as well as the most forceful is the *teleological.* Its appeal is direct and universal. *Its solid foundation is the manifest order in the universe perceptible even to the untrained eye and undeveloped mind of the savage.* It is an absolute order constituted by the unity found in the complex parts and various actions and forces of the same being, particularly the living being, and a relative order constituted by the manifold interrelations which exist between the different species and genera of beings, based upon a most wonderful, regular, and indispensable interaction and interdependence. The fact of the order being undisputed, the teleological argument is of compelling logical force. It may be presented in this simple manner:

Wherever there is order, *i. e.,* where several elements produce unity or where various actions subserve a common end, not once, but regularly, in conformity with definite laws, there must be direction; wherever there is direction, there must be a design, a plan; wherever there is a design and a plan, there must be an intelligence. But only the infinite intelligence of the Divine Mind can adequately explain the plan that directs, controls, and harmonizes the whole universe.

That the infinite intelligence of the Divine Mind is required to explain adequately the conception and execution of the plan of the universe is of facile comprehension, if we bear in mind what it involves: 1. It must account for the marvelous cosmic order so manifest in all the stages of cosmogonic and geogonic evolution with its immensity of time and space. 2. It must account for the still more marvelous order so clearly apparent in the production, continuation, and perpetuation of life on the globe, with its uncountable billions of individual representatives, and its wonderful variety and complex interdependence of the uncounted species and genera, families and orders of both plants and animals. 3. Last, not least, it must account for the lord and king of all, man, the most marvelous order in the cosmos, indeed, a true *microcosmos* reproducing in himself the whole *macrocosmos,* reflecting and representing all its marvels, and partly imitating and reproducing them, through the supreme created power and prerogative of reason and free will.

In this argument God is not revealed to our mind as the "ens necessarium," or the "motor immotus," or the "causa non causata," *i. e.,* not as the absolute *"causa efficiens"* or principle of action, but as the supreme *"causa finalis"* or principle of direction and orientation, and consequently, as the *"SUMMUS MUNDI FINIS,"* the supreme end of the universe.

It is in this argument and its conclusion that we have the logical basis for our conception of the universe as the created imitation and expression of the divine nature. God being the supreme "finis mundi," therefore, the object and end, from which everything in the universe must derive its meaning and value since everything in the universe is but a means or subordinate end in respect to the supreme end, we cannot conceive the object of the universe being any other but that of manifesting in a created and imitative manner, as far as such a thing is possible, the mind and the will of the Creator.

A few remarks on the so-called *scientific arguments* for the existence of God may not be needless, because some authors on the subject make much of them. There are no scientific arguments in the strict sense of the term. The divine existence cannot be proven experimentally or mathematically, but only philosophically, as we have done. However, it is well to remember that philosophical argumentations are properly and strictly scientific when they are founded upon compelling logical deductions from evident principles.

Science however has not been entirely without effect upon the philosophical arguments for the existence of God. The great progress in the scientific knowledge of the world has revealed and established a vast multitude of facts which, while not changing fundamentally our conceptions of the universe, have aided us in perceiving the wonderful order in the universe more clearly, and thus, the old arguments may be presented under new and more striking forms, and particularly the minor premise of the teleological argument has thereby been powerfully enriched and fortified.

II. The Problem of Atheism

Notwithstanding the clear and evident proofs for the existence of God, there is today, and always has been, the problem of atheism in the world. It is a matter of fact, visible to everybody, that the world at present is full of *practical atheists, i. e.,* people whose life is not influenced by the idea of God and the divine government of the world and of human life. At all times of human history there have been many such, but perhaps never more than today. Evidently, this is a serious social condition. But still more serious is the presence of many *theoretical atheists* in the world, especially, if they are of an aggressive atheism, secretly and openly preaching their doctrine, from the soap-box on the street corners, on the stage, in the press, in schools and colleges, and wherever they find a willing ear to listen to them. No doubt, they attract many to their banner, and their soldiers rarely desert, because the doctrine of the absolute freedom and unconditional sovereignty of man has the charm of a siren's voice and the sweetness of a well-concocted poison. This charm and sweetness of atheism appeal to all kinds of people alike, to the highbrows of science and art, to the princes of finance and industry as well as to the masses that live in poverty or abject economic dependence; but above all they appeal to the undeveloped mind and untutored will of passionate youth who abominate every restraint, like an unbroken horse its bit. Therefore, woe to the nation in whose educational institutions the theory and practice of religion are eliminated or even undervalued.

The reason for atheism's attractive power is not far to seek. We all possess in our conscience a stern teacher and uncomfortable warner. What a feeling of relief it would be in many instances, if we could simply silence its voice by declaring: I am free to do as I please, I am responsible to no one, because there is no God. No wonder that many fall a prey to the temptation and become atheists, not only in practice, but in theory as well. Little do they seem to reflect that, if the conviction of atheism were to become universal, a social Armageddon would follow, which would be such that the Great War would appear as a child's play. Hence, atheism is a profound and tremendously practical problem of the world at present, and consequently, we must examine the alleged foundations of its philosophy in all earnestness.

I. MATERIALISTIC ATHEISM

Positivists, evolutionists and materialists generally, assert that there is no God because we need no God to explain the universe, since the universe explains itself. They add that, even if there were a God, we do not and cannot know anything about Him. We have shown above with all the clearness of logical evidence that both assertions are not only arbitrary and without any shadow of proof, but directly and unequivocally false. From every one of the three metaphysical arguments for the existence of God, it appears evident that the world does not explain its own existence and that it can be explained adequately in no other way but by the assumption of the action of the Infinite God. But as soon as it has been clearly shown that only the action of God can explain the universe, the inference is inevitable that we are capable of knowing Him because we are able to study the agent in his actions, the author in his works.

a. A specific objection to the existence of God by materialistic philosophers and scientists is the difficulty of conceiving the act of creation. This difficulty is the fruit of a misconception. We have pointed out before that the act of creation is by no means *inconceivable,* but only *unimaginable.* We cannot imagine it because we have no sense experience of it, but we can well conceive it, at least, we can conceive the act of creation much more easily than we can conceive a contingent world without creation.

To conceive creation, all that is necessary is to abstract from contingent action, which we know perfectly, the conditions and attributes which make it contingent. Thus, we acquire the idea of an absolute action. The act of creation is such an absolute action, for it is the absolute production of a new being. We know from experience that contingent causes produce new beings, but their action is not absolute; it is contingent upon many conditions such as a pre-existing subject and instrumentalities of various kinds. However, it is not only not preposterous that the absolute cause should not be so restricted and conditioned in its action, but, on the contrary, it is rather in perfect harmony with our conception of its absolute nature that also its action should be absolute and free from extrinsic limitations and conditions, because "operari sequitur esse," which means that the nature and manner of a being's action is in perfect correlation with the nature and manner of its existence.

b. Another very ancient and ever new source of objections is the existence of evil in the world. It is claimed that the idea of an infinitely perfect being is incompatible with evil. This claim of course, is a mere assumption. Our idea of infinite perfection is analogical and negative because taken from the finite universe; but surely it is the height of folly to build upon a negative and analogical idea the peremptory interpretation of the facts which we find in the universe. It is to the facts we must go to obtain our ideas, and not vice versa.

Basing our concept of infinite perfection upon the knowledge of the facts, it would rather appear to us as quite evident that evil, moral and physical, is unavoidable in a universe in which the inorganic world subserves the purposes of the organic, in which plant and animal life subserves the purposes of rational life, and in which rational life, by free self-determination, should subserve the sovereign plan of God. It is true that there would be an insurmountable difficulty to our mind in the existence of evil in the world, if evil were the normal or main feature in the phenomena of the universe, or if evil were to come out victorious in the end. However, the order in cosmic and biological evolution in the universe is quite manifest, nor does the history of the inorganic and organic world, or the history of mankind, justify the assumption of the ultimate triumph of evil in the world. On the contrary, the facts of the past and of the present all point in the other direction, since order is in its very nature a victory of good over evil.

2. PANTHEISTIC ATHEISM

It is an axiom that too much of a good thing is an evil thing. So it happens with pantheism. Its claim is that all is god, but since all cannot be God, in reality pantheism is equivalent to atheism, because the god of pantheism is not a personal extra- and super-mundane God, but the world-substance itself. Such a god is neither the absolute Creator of the world nor the sovereign Lord and Master of human destiny—it is simply the universe personified and deified.

a. The *peculiar attraction in pantheism* is the very nebulosity and obscurity of its fundamental principle. It is in virtue of this nebulosity and obscurity inseparable from the concept of consubstantiality of God, who is infinite, absolute, incomprehensible, and ineffable, with the universe, which is obviously made up of finite and contingent beings, that pantheism has in its appeal to the human mind and heart all the advantages of materialistic atheism, and none of its disadvantages. It has its advantages because in denying the existence of a personal and ultramundane God, it has the same force as materialism itself in stilling the unpleasant voice of conscience and in escaping the burdensome and awful religious and ethical consequences of the belief in God, and yet it has none of its disadvantages because it does not deny the profound religious instincts in human nature, but, on the contrary, it appears to satisfy them in a magnificent manner through the idea of the consubstantial union of the soul with God. Even in the highest possible aims of the mystical theology of Christianity there is nothing comparable with the apparent depth and intimacy of the soul's union with the divinity as we find it in the very conception of pantheism. Pantheism is indeed a mystical apotheosis of self, and such an incomprehensible and ineffable deification is achieved without the necessity of any disagreeable sacrifice, or any bitter act of self-denial. No wonder that such a religion as pantheism offers, which apparently combines a most sublime mysticism with no demand whatsoever upon personal comfort and no outlook of awe and terror such as an eternal hell, has found and is still finding in the form of Christian Science many thousands and hundreds of thousands worshippers, because, in truth, they do not worship God but themselves.

b. As regards *the rational basis for pantheism* in general and its curious religious coloring and tone, we must be brief, as we do not want to repeat what we said in our introductory chapter on this subject. To the sober mind that looks for objective rational foundations and logical connections, the success of pantheism in ancient and modern times must appear a mystery. Apart from the purely subjective and arbitrary character of its main principles we may recapitulate the reasons for its rejection as follows: 1. Pantheism is built upon a foundation the elements of which are antithetic and exclusive of one another. 2. It presents a vast subject-matter, opens up a world of problems, and suggests a thousand questions, but leaves the subject-matter undefined, the problems unexplained, and the questions unsolved. 3. It is a bizarre identification of poetry, religion, and metaphysics, but in every aspect its appearance is monstrous: As poetry it has neither soul nor body, *i. e.,* neither any definite meaning nor intelligible expression; as religion it has its altar erected in the clouds with a headless, heartless, and shapeless idol upon it; as metaphysics it is lost in a tractless and trailless forest of contradictions.

3. KANT'S SPECULATIVE ATHEISM. CORRELATION BETWEEN REASON AND FAITH

From the practical viewpoint Kant was all through life a religious man of excellent moral character and conduct. However, from the viewpoint of speculative knowledge he proposed and defended with rare consistency and persistence principles which, if followed to their ultimate logical conclusions, must lead to atheism. This contradiction in Kant's thought and life is due to his rigorous distinction between speculative and practical knowledge. In respect to practical knowledge he was a religious believer, in respect to speculative knowledge he was a religious agnostic, because in his theory faith in God and in the immortality of the soul is based upon moral and not upon rational grounds, and thus, he was in practical life a religous man although he firmly maintained that we have no logically conclusive evidence for the existence of God and the immortality of the soul.

Evidently, this position is quite contradictory, as it establishes a division in human nature and life which is contrary to every law of logic and metaphysics. In doing this, Kant unwittingly revived in a new form the age-long claim of an antithesis between reason and faith expressed in the notorious adage: "Credo quia absurdum," which, freely translated, means, we accept on faith the things which are unintelligible to reason.

The grounds upon which Kant based the indemonstrability of the existence of God and of the immortality of the soul, are his psychological principles, according to which only those judgments are objective knowledge, *i. e.,* knowledge of absolute value and universal application which can be put to a critical test by sense experience. It is clear that the judgments that there is a God and that the soul is immortal, do not belong to this class. Indeed, in Kant's mind, these judgments must be purely subjective, since the ideas of God and soul have only subjective value and meaning, being metaphysical and transcendent, *i. e.*, ideas beyond sense experience.

We have seen above how Kant's immediate successors discarded his practical philosophy and quite logically developed his speculative criticism into pantheistic idealism, which, of course, is equivalent to atheism. Some philosophers of the past and present generation, convinced of the theoretical sterility and concerned about the dangerous practical consequences of Kant's speculative atheism, have turned their back on all metaphysical studies and plead for a return to Kant's moral postulates as the only possible way to save the intellectual world from ruin. This pragmatist and modernist revival of Kant's moral philosophy will not succeed. A religious faith based upon the will which is blind and fickle, or upon the emotions which are even more blind and more fickle, is building a temple upon sand. Such a religion, if inspired and accompanied by zeal, would naturally degenerate into fanaticism.

Like the wren in the fable which flew higher than the eagle but not without the eagle, so faith goes beyond reason but not without reason. Faith depends upon reason even more than the wren upon the eagle, because the wren left the eagle behind, but faith can never leave reason behind. The reason is obvious: Faith is formally an act of the will, but as the will is in itself blind, reason must guide its every step. The necessity of reason is ·strikingly apparent when we look upon the objects and tenets of faith as a system. Its whole structure is built upon the logically conclusive evidence that there is a God, and that God has spoken to man. But it is plain that speculative reason alone is capable of laying this foundation. Thus, the conclusion imposes itself ·that *to divorce faith from reason is even more disastrous than to divorce reason from faith.*

About the untenableness of Kant's speculative religious position little need be said. Also in this connection, his arguments stand or fall with his general psychology. We have seen repeatedly, how arbitrary are his main assumptions, how contrary to plain facts, how inadequate to explain the objectivity and absoluteness of knowledge of any kind.

Kant's objection to the use of the principle of causality in the demonstration of God is not better founded or reasoned. It is supposed to vitiate every argument for the existence of God because it has no objective value except when applied to sense phenomena. In the introduction to this chapter we have shown clearly, we believe, that the principle of causality is an objective and metaphysical principle of immediate evidence and consequently, of absolute value and universal application.

CHAPTER TWENTY-FIVE

THE NATURE OF GOD

THE VALUE OF OUR KNOWLEDGE OF THE DIVINE NATURE

We have examined the fundamental problem of theodicy—the existence of God—and have found that the affirmative solution is based upon a solid foundation: Our knowledge of the existence of God is not only a practical assent due to our individual attitude on the moral issues of human life, but the logical conclusion from evident principles. The second great problem in theodicy refers to the nature and attributes of God. Here again, we have first to solve a preliminary question: What kind of knowledge can we obtain of the divine nature, and what is the precise meaning and value of such knowledge?

It is quite evident, and we have alluded to this matter before, that our ideas, when applied to God, cannot have exactly the same meaning as when applied to the material world from which we have abstracted them, because if this material world is the proper object of the human mind, purely spiritual substances are not, and much less the absolute divine substance. When we use our ideas in connection with the things of this world, we call it proper knowledge, whereas, when we refer them to purely spiritual, and especially, to divine things, we call it analogical.

Even when we apply our ideas to the different beings of the world, we do not apply them always in exactly the same sense. Thus, the idea of life, used in connection with animals, has an object very different from the idea of life when we speak of plants, to say nothing of the still greater difference when the same idea is applied to the human mind or will. There are philosophers who speak of life as a proper term only in its application to vegetable life, from which the fundamental characteristics of all life—continuity and immanence, are abstracted; whenever they use the term with reference to a higher type of living beings they consider it analogical. However, we believe that it is preferable to use other terms to show the partial difference of meaning which results from their application to different species of the same genus. It is surely logical to call the ideas we abstract positively, either directly or indirectly, from the world in which we live, which is the proper object of the mind, *proper* ideas. To distinguish their meaning when differently applied, we prefer to call them *univocal* when used in exactly the same sense, as when we speak of the life of an insect and the life of a bird, and *equivocal* when we speak of the life of wheat and the life of a dog, or of the life of a dog and the life of a man. The specific sense of the terms is either the very same or is very different, but it is always *proper* as based upon positive abstraction by our mind.

No matter how great the difference in meaning of our terms according to the difference in their application, there is always an identical and common basis when we apply them to the universe—the transcendental sense of the term being. The transcendental term being applies univocally to all beings in the universe because they all exist in the very same manner; they all are contingent, depending for their being and action upon one another. Consequently, even when we know the beings in the universe only indirectly, *i. e.,* by their effects, we know that no matter what specific characteristics they may have which are not expressed in the effects, their fundamental and transcendental characteristic of being is ever the same:—they have their being from another, they are relative, not absolute beings. This applies to all beings except God. Speaking of God, even this fundamental and transcendental idea of being must be used in quite another sense, and since this is the basic content of all our ideas, all our knowledge without exception, when applied to God, is not proper but analogical, *i. e.,* based upon a certain likeness of God impressed upon the universe.

THE PROCESS OF OUR KNOWLEDGE OF GOD

The source of our knowledge of God is found in the universe inasmuch as a divine likeness is impressed upon it. Imperfect and incomplete as such knowledge must be, it is true and exact as far as it goes and the object of it being the Creator of the universe, it is of peerless value, even though only analogical. To realize the truth of this statement let us use some illustrations. It surely is impossible to know fully and perfectly a man whom we know exclusively from his works. But are we not able to form any valuable judgment at all about Michael Angelo, Shakespeare, or Richard Wagner? We have never seen them or come into personal contact with them, but if we have studied their works intelligently, we have found therein their likeness much more perfectly expressed than any portrait or even biography could give it. Thus, we have learned to know and admire them.

Such is the source and nature of our knowledge of God and the divine perfections. We attribute to Michael Angelo, Shakespeare, and Richard Wagner whatever excellence and beauty we discover in their works with the implied admission that such excellence and beauty existed in the artists in a higher form and manner than they could possibly exist in their products, because in them they were living spiritual realities, whereas in their works they are but a material expression of those realities. In the same manner, whatsoever perfection and excellence we find in the universe, we attribute to its divine Author, with the same reservation that they exist in God in a superior and nobler form and manner than they could exist in the universe, and with this other reservation added that whatever imperfection and limitation is necessarily attached even to the highest perfections in creation, must not be attributed to the Creator.

Thus, the process by which we arrive at a conception of what God is, is threefold. The first is a process of *attribution*. We attribute to God all the perfections we find in the universe. It is evident that in some form or other all actual and positive realities in the universe must be present in the fundamental cause from which they originate.

Our second process is one of *negation* or *elimination*. In the universe there are many perfections which, while good and necessary for the beings that possess them, imply in their very concept limitations. We call them *mixed* or *relative perfections*. We do not attribute them to God because there can be no doubt that the infinitely perfect being cannot possess any except unmixed or simple and absolute perfections.

The final process is one of *ontological sublimation*. We ascribe the simple and absolute perfections in the universe to God not in the sense in which creatures possess them. His manner of possessing them is *super-eminent and sublime* because His is an absolute and necessary, not a dependent and contingent possession. In consequence of this threefold process the contents or constitutive elements of our idea of God, though only analogical, are positive and instructive.

They are attributable to God and to God alone. Hence, they define God, and while this definition of God is not and, of course, cannot be adequate by any means, yet it is a true definition: it fits the being defined and no other; and besides, being an interpretation of the nature of God, it is of supreme value and paramount importance.

I. The Divine Nature

In discussing this great and vast subject we must necessarily limit ourselves to a mere indication and brief analysis of the rich and complex contents of the idea of God. We will call attention first to what is termed the nature of God. Trying to define the nature of God, we do not mean to be presumptuous. We have no intention to deny that, strictly and properly speaking, the divine nature is incomprehensible, ineffable, and, consequently, undefinable. All we intend to do is to point out amongst the perfections which we attribute analogically to God that perfection which is fundamental ontologically and logically, *i. e.,* the perfection from which every other perfection flows as from its natural source, and to which every other perfection may be logically reduced as to its primary principle.

I. DEFINITION OF THE DIVINE NATURE

We have already defined and expressed the divine nature as clearly as it is possible for us to do when, in our demonstration of God, we came to the conclusion that God is the *"ens necessarium,"* the *"causa non causata,"* the *"motor immotus,"* the *"actus purus,"* the *"finis ultimus."* Every one of these expressions defines God: they refer to Him and to no one else. Analyzing these phrases, we find that there is no real difference between them: from a different viewpoint they express the same concept.

Calling God the "ens necessarium" we determine Him as the being that exists necessarily, *i. e.,* the being whose nature it is to exist, or the being that has the reason for its existence in its own nature.

The "causa non causata" and the "motor immotus," the Uncaused Cause and the Immovable Mover, express the same idea from an external viewpoint. God is the efficient cause of all things, but He is independent and absolute Himself. He is exclusively cause and not effect in any sense. He is capable of action, but not susceptible of reaction, He is an agent, but never a patient.

This is the reason why the Church has rejected the definition of God by the great Origen, who defined God as *"CAUSA SUI,"* cause of Himself, because such a definition implies evolution in God. Instead of *"causa sui"* we might say correctly *"RATIO SUI"*— He is the reason of His existence, *i. e.,* His nature explains His existence.

Calling God the "finis ultimus" the idea is fundamentally the same, but it expresses the teleological, not the causative viewpoint.

Finally, using the expression "actus purus" we call attention to the pure and absolute perfection of God's being, to which no kind of limitation and not a shadow of imperfection are attached. Whatsoever He is, He is necessarily and absolutely, He never acquires or loses anything, He never grows or decreases in any respect.

Such being their premises, philosophers have defined God as the *"ESSE SUBSISTENS,"* *i. e.,* the subsisting act of existence. In other words, *to be, to exist* is the divine nature. Evidently, this definition implies the identity of essence and existence which is equivalent to the identity of nature and act. In defining other beings, we say *WHAT they are,* in defining God we say *THAT He IS,* because *He IS being,* while all others *HAVE being.* Therefore, to say *THAT* He is, is saying *WHAT* He is, because *TO BE* is His nature.

As a general conclusion from this analysis we may accept as well founded the determination of the divine nature given by many philosophers: He is the *"ens necessarium"* or the *"ens a se."* All other beings being contingent and therefore, "entia ab alio," *i. e.,* beings whose existence is due to another, this determination points out that attribute in God which is fundamental. We shall see further on how easily every other divine perfection is deducible from it and reducible to it. The scholastics coined the latin term *"ASEITAS"* to express it. We may translate it by *ONTOLOGICAL ABSOLUTE-NESS.*

It is interesting to note that this fundamental divine characteristic of ontological absoluteness is in perfect harmony with the name and definition God gave of Himself to Moses in the desert when He spoke to him from the burning thorn-bush—*YAHWE, He who is.*

2. INTERPRETATION OF THE DIVINE NATURE

We know now that the nature of God is *TO BE,* "*Deus est ipsum esse.*" In Him existence is due to Himself, to His own nature, He is the "*ens a se.*" However, though the one term *being* in its supereminent and absolutely perfect sense, *i. e.,* when it expresses at once the essence and the existence of a being, defines the divine nature, yet it tells us very little about God. After all the transcendental term being, though the highest in quality, is the lowest in quantity, because it contains one element only: it expresses as little as any term can possibly express; indeed, it is on account of its extreme simplicity that it is a transcendental term. Yet we are naturally anxious to learn more about God, if such a thing is at all possible. Fortunately, it is possible and, in truth, not only possible, but necessary, as knowledge to be a faithful intellectual mirror of the reality must give as many elements of it as possible.

In the first instance, the divine nature is not only *being* but also *life;* the divine existence is a *living existence.* There can be no question about the fact itself. Life is one of God's products, consequently, it must be in Him. However, it is not in God as it is in the universe. In the universe life is characterized in a double sense: it is immanent action and it is continuous. For an action to be immanent is a pure and simple perfection, to be continuous is a relative perfection, as without continuity immanent action would be inconceivable in a material agent. Hence, since in the divine nature, being an "actus purus," no real composition of any kind is possible, *God's act of existence is an act of life, inasmuch as life is an immanent action.*

God is life as well as being. So much is established. But His nature comprises more than that. His life is *spiritual life* because it is purely and perfectly immanent action. In material agents, apart from the mixed perfection of the characteristic of continuity, the immanence of action is never perfect and absolute. It is immanent in respect to the whole organism; but taken by itself each vital action involves a transition from one part to another of the organism, it is not strictly immanent, but transitive, it is not an action without a passion, not a cause without an effect. Such an immanence is foreign to the divine nature. But if so, the divine life is evidently spiritual life, spiritual action.

We have been amplifying our idea of God gradually, but we are still far from its completion. God exists, lives, and acts as a spiritual being. It is plain that the most characteristic spiritual action is *knowledge*. Inasmuch as knowledge is perfect and absolute, it surely must be attributed to God, since we find it in His creatures. Of course, sense knowledge is not attributed to God, not only because it is organic knowledge and the divine nature is spiritual, but also because sense knowledge is itself a necessarily mixed perfection, implying in its very concept manifold limitations. *God's knowledge, then, is intellectual*.

Furthermore, God's knowledge being not only intellectual but also perfect and absolute, the object of His knowledge must not only be directly intelligible, but also perfect and absolute. Therefore the knowledge of God is the *knowledge of Himself*. In His knowledge subject and object are one and the same. He is the one that knows and the one that is known.

Clearly, this is a perfection of knowledge by which God plainly transcends the knowledge of human intelligence. In the human mind the knowledge of a being is the representation of the object and, therefore, depends absolutely upon the being known: the being in virtue of its assimilation by the intellect comes into the mind. Consequently, human knowledge, though an act of the intellect, is passive and receptive, since it is the reception of the object into the mind. There can be no doubt that such is not the perfect and absolute manner of the divine knowledge. It is not only independent of its object, since its object is the divine knowledge itself, but there is nothing passive and receptive about it, it is pure action; in other words: *to know and to be known* are one and the same act in the divine knowledge.

This act of divine knowledge is evidently a knowledge of inexhaustible depth, width, and sublimity, because it is infinite in every aspect, and being at the same time instantaneous and simultaneous, without effort or labor, and withal absolutely transparent in its clearness and perfectly simple in its comprehensiveness, its necessary fruit and natural concomitant must be an incomprehensible and ineffable *esthetic joy* for which there can be no adequate analogy in the knowledge of the creature.

There is one other aspect of the divine nature which must be essential in a spiritual agent whose life is the knowledge of such incomparable perfection and peerless beauty—*absolute approval of such perfection and beauty,* and *perfect complacency in their possession.* Hence, parallel to, and yet identical with, the divine knowledge and the consequent esthetical joy is the *divine love with its consequent fruition,* the height, depth, intensity, and sweetness of which are necessarily such that any comparison, even with the highest possible exaltation of human love and the greatest possible joy of its possession, would be blasphemous.

Consequently, our concept of the divine nature has been wonderfully enriched by the very simple process of logical deduction. God is *being,* perfect, absolute, infinite being, because He is the *"ens a se."* But such a being is *life,* life in its supereminent perfection and energy. Again, life which is perfect and absolute is *spiritual* life, is *knowledge,* and this knowledge is, on account of its infinite perfection, accompanied by an infinitely intense and inexpressible *esthetic joy.* Finally, to the infinitely perfect knowledge and its special joy corresponds the infinitely perfect *fruition of love* with its incomprehensible and ineffable *bliss.* And being, life, knowledge, love, and joy are one and the same act, an act that had no beginning and will have no end, cannot grow in width and cannot decrease in intensity because it is absolute and perfect in every respect.

II. The Divine Attributes

The simple analysis of the term being in the exclusive, supereminent and sublime sense in which we apply it to God, led us to define the divine nature as an absolute and perfect act of spiritual life, and therefore as absolute and perfect knowledge, as absolute and perfect love and as absolute and perfect joy. Thus, we have acquired a rich and beautiful concept of the Deity. However, it does not portray completely, not only all the wealth of perfection that is contained in the divine nature, but not even all the wealth of ontological reality which we are able to grasp and understand. The reason is simple enough: Our intelligence is so imperfect and limited that it can mirror the divine perfection only in a number of various concepts of which each represents not the whole divine essence but only a certain limited aspect of it. If we were to attribute to God Himself such divisions in His natural perfection, our knowledge of God would not be true; but we are quite aware that such a variety of concepts necessary to portray the nature of God completely, is not due to the object, the divine nature, which is absolutely simple, but to the natural condition of our limited mind. Thus, while our knowledge of God is clearly imperfect because it does not represent the divine nature such as it is, it is nevertheless true and of precious value because there is in the divine nature the objective foundation for each one of the many concepts which are indispensable to picture, as well as we can, the immeasurable wealth of the divine being.

The foregoing explanation establishes the basis for our discussion on the attributes of the divine nature. They are in God perfectly identified with one another, and each one with the divine nature, but to our human consideration they are plainly distinct, nay, some are apparently exclusive of each other. We will first consider and analyze those attributes which must be predicated of God apart from the existence of the universe, and then study those which depend upon His relation to His creatures.

The principal divine attributes in this connection are God's *unicity* and *simplicity,* His *infinitude* and *immutability,* His *eternity* and *immensity.* They are divine attributes because, whatever they express has its objective basis in the infinitely perfect and absolute divine nature. Their study, inasmuch as it aids us in the knowledge of God, is evidently of inestimable service.

I. THE UNICITY AND SIMPLICITY OF GOD

a. The unicity and simplicity are both expressive of unity: unicity is absolute unity in kind and number, simplicity is absolute unity in nature and constitution. *The unicity of God* is the most important attribute of the divine nature. It has never been seriously disputed. Apart from some oriental philosophies which assumed two absolute principles, one to explain the perfections in the universe, the other to account for the existence of evil, polytheism has never been taught by any philosopher of note. This fact is naturally explained by the very definition of the divine being.

There is only one God because the nature of the being whose essence and existence are identical, excludes plurality. As is obvious, beings are distinct from one another not in their existence or in that they are, but in their nature or in what they are. Consequently, if we suppose two or three gods whose nature is to be, they would be totally the same or indistinct from one another, since their nature, as well as their existence, would be identical, and yet we would be compelled to say that they are not the same but totally distinct from one another since they are supposed to be two or three and not one. Hence, *plurality in the divine nature is contradictory.*

The concept of the *ontological absoluteness* which we determined as the fundamental characteristic of the divine nature, *is another evidence for the unicity of God.* To be absolute in its being clearly excludes any necessary relation with any other being: indeed, absoluteness is the same as unrelatedness. But if there were more than one God, not one of them would be absolute, as ontological equality would logically result in a number of necessary relations.

There is *an obvious indication of the unicity of God in the order of the universe,* which, comprising all parts and elements of the universe, implies one cause only. To assume the co-operation of several divine agents would involve imperfection, because the joint co-operation would be considered either necessary or free; if necessary they would be imperfect, and if free, also, because we would have to assume the possibility of frustration of the created order by any one of them.

b. *Simplicity* is the highest possible perfection of unity, and unity itself represents a decisive ontological victory over division. The unity of God's nature is supreme, because it excludes not only all actual, but also all potential division. It is not only indivision, but indivisibility. There is in God neither quantitative composition nor a composition between substance and accident, neither a composition between essence and existence nor betwen nature and act. The direct evidence for the absolute and perfect simplicity of God is *the idea of "actus purissimus,"* to which the demonstration of God's existence led us, and which excludes *all divisibility when it excludes all potentiality.*

We have repeatedly pointed out that in God being, life, knowledge, love, joy, and even the various attributes which we are discussing now, are not as many really distinct elements composing the divine nature, though our concepts are plainly distinct, each representing distinct objects or objectively distinct aspects of the divine nature. The reason for essentially identifying these various distinct objects of our concepts about God is precisely the divine simplicity which excludes all real composition. The distinction we introduce into the nature of God by representing Him by means of various objectively distinct concepts is based upon *metaphysical composition.*

2. THE INFINITUDE AND IMMUTABILITY OF GOD

a. By *infinitude* we mean God's infinite perfection. This concept implies two things: 1. God possesses all the simple and absolute perfections that exist in creation; and 2. He possesses them in the absolute plenitude of their being. That He possesses them all is plain, because there can be nothing in an effect that does not in some way exist in its cause, and that He possesses them in absolute plenitude is also plain, because in a being whose very nature is to be, there can be no principle of limitation or nonbeing.

Hence, God possesses all perfections which do not necessarily involve imperfection. But He does not possess them in the manner in which contingent beings are able to possess them. These possess them to a certain extent, *i. e.,* in a limited degree, because they possess them in so far as they have received them, and as a consequence, their being, since it is essentially due to communication from without, is a participation in being only, not a full and proper possession of it. Therefore, while they *have* being, they *are not* being. God on the contrary, possesses all possible simple perfections not only in all their fullness, but He possesses them in Himself, not as received from another source, but due to His own nature. Therefore we say that He possesses them absolutely. Thus, God not only *possesses* being, but He *is* being.

b. The *immutability* of God is intimately related to His infinitude, indeed, *He is essentially and absolutely unchangeable because He is essentially and infinitely perfect.* Being by nature and necessarily in the fullest possible possession of all possible perfections, He can neither gain any new kind or degree of perfection, nor can He ever lose any. But since change necessarily implies either an increase or a decrease in perfection, there can be no possible change in God.

The very same conclusion is drawn from the simplicity of God. *A being which is absolutely simple cannot change,* because there can be no real change in a being without either the loss or the gain of some real element. God, being absolutely simple, cannot change because, gaining an element, He would cease to be simple, and losing an element, He would cease to exist altogether; but evidently, God can neither cease to be simple nor cease to exist.

3. THE ETERNITY AND IMMENSITY OF GOD

These two attributes are, from the human viewpoint, negative rather than positive: they eliminate from the concept of the divine existence the conditions of time and space to which the whole universe is subject. However, in relation to the divine nature, the exemption of existence from the conditions of time and space implies undoubtedly a great and positive perfection.

a. *When we speak of God as being eternal, we exclude time as the condition of divine existence.* All contingent beings exist in time because they change. They evolve, and as their evolution, like all movements, is gradual, it is measurable, because it is a continuous quantity of which one part follows another, one act another. Consequently, there is necessarily a before and an after, or as we say, they are subject to time.

It is evident that it cannot be so in the absolutely perfect, simple, and unchangeable God. There is no evolution possible, neither progressive nor regressive, there is no succession of parts or of acts, there is no before and no after, no past and no future, only an undivided, indivisible, unfailing and ever permanent present. This we call the eternity of God. In a larger sense, *i. e.*, when we compare God's manner of enduring with that of the universe, we speak of eternity also as an equivalent to time without a beginning and without an end.

b. Just as we exclude time as a condition of the divine existence by eternity, so *by the immensity of God we exclude space as a condition of divine existence.* God is not a body and therefore does not occupy a position in space. We cannot speak of Him in the proper sense as being here or there or somewhere. Having no local position He is in truth nowhere, by which we simply mean that He is in no way restricted by spatial relations.

About the fact of divine immensity there can be no doubt. God is neither subject to space in the sense in which a body is subject to space, which is evident, nor can He be subject to space in the sense in which a contingent spirit is subject to space. The manner in which a spirit can be subject to space is known to us from our personal experience. Our soul is limited by space because it lives and acts in and through the body and therefore shares in the spatial relations and limitations of the body itself for the general reason that the principal cause of an action is affected intimately by the nature of its instrumental cause. Such a manner of subjection to space cannot be attributed to the perfect spirit of God, whose action is absolute and in no sense dependent upon material subjects or bodily instrumentalities.

In the same way as we bring the eternity of God into relation with the duration of contingent beings, and thus, speak of eternity as an equivalent to time without beginning and without end, we also compare the immensity of God with the extension of the universe, and thus consider immensity as equivalent to space without limit. In this respect, eternity is infinity of duration and immensity is infinity of extension. In consequence of this broad acceptation of the two terms we speak of God as acting in the past or in the future, and existing here and there and everywhere. The reason for such an analogical application of the eternity and immensity of God is, again, the natural limitation of our intellect. As we are subject to time and space in every act of our experience, we find it hard to conceive the existence and action of a being that does not exist and act at a definite time and in a specified space.

B. THE RELATIVE DIVINE ATTRIBUTES

What we have said so far concerning the divine nature and attributes applies to God independently of His creation. However, there are aspects in the Deity of another type which have their source and basis in the free divine act by which the universe was called into being. We speak of them as the relative attributes of God. Their study, while not so directly and intimately expressive of the divine nature, ought to be, nevertheless, of the greatest interest to us because much of it concerns us immediately and personally.

It may be instructive to mention another difference between the two sets of divine attributes. This difference is based upon the logical viewpoint. Our discussion of the absolute divine attributes was deductive and synthetical. From the knowledge we had gained analytically of the divine existence, we formed our judgment on the divine nature, and from the knowledge of the divine nature we drew by logical deduction our conclusions about the divine attributes. We proceed quite differently in the study of the relative attributes. The direct source of their knowledge must be the universe inasmuch as it is the work of God. Consequently, we study here the universe to discover and determine its relation to God, *i. e.,* if, and how far, the divine nature is communicated to, and expressed in it.

I. THE DIVINE WISDOM AND OMNIPOTENCE

a. If, in discussing the divine attributes of wisdom and omnipotence, we wish to proceed logically, we must discuss first wisdom and then omnipotence. The *divine wisdom* shines forth in the plan of the universe and omnipotence in the execution of the plan, but evidently, the plan must be made before it can be carried out.

It would be preposterous for any man, no matter how gifted and thoroughly instructed, to claim that he knows the whole and full plan of Almighty God in respect to His creation. The universe is too vast in the immensity of its masses as well as in the staggering figures of their distances and of the periods of their evolution! Such are the facts plainly demonstrated by modern astronomy and cosmogony. Furthermore, on our globe, one of the smaller groups of these unnumbered masses, and, therefore, probably on many of them, there are uncountable billions of individuals which are differentiated in structure and function in a million ways, constituting as many kinds of minerals and as many varieties, races, species, genera, families and orders of plants and animate beings. Again, these masses thus differentiated in such marvelous ways retain their differentiations in an ever-recurring regularity by means of extremely manifold and complex interactions and interrelations, the mysterious passive, active, and directive sources of which are hidden in the inner nature of the beings themselves. Finally, there is man, the marvel of marvels, who represents, in miniature as it were, the whole visible universe, and who by the spirituality of his soul and the liberty of his action is elevated to kinship with the divine nature of the Creator.

Such is in bare outline the divine plan as it is revealed in the universe even to the most superficial observer. The deeper, fuller, and exacter our knowledge of the wonderful order of the universe grows, the more profound and the more comprehensive becomes our conviction of the infinite wisdom of the divine designer. While in the vast immensity of creation there are obscurities and mysteries aplenty which, by our short intelligence in our brief experience and from our narrowly limited standpoint, we cannot fathom, the reality itself of an infinitely wise plan, which diffuses its light into every nook and corner of the universe, is not open to discussion.

What is the object of the divine plan? There can hardly be any doubt about it since the very existence of the universe in its imposing magnificence and grandeur, and in its splendid manifestation of order and harmony, reveals it with unmistakable evidence: The universe is a mighty expression of the infinitude and majesty of the divine nature and, consequently, a hymn of praise and glory to its Creator.

b. The universe is the product of *omnipotence*. While the divine wisdom is known from the order in the world, the omnipotence of God is shown forth in its very presence. We have seen, time and again, that there is no other possible way to explain adequately the existence of a contingent being except by creation. But creation is the act of omnipotence exclusively. The very concept of creation proves this clearly. To create is to produce a being from nothing, *i. e.*, it is acting without any pre-existing material, without any available instrumentalities. Therefore, it is acting absolutely, not dependently on certain conditions. But to act in an absolute manner, to act without any other dependency but the will to produce, is surely exclusively proper to an absolute agent. Hence, God alone is Creator.

Is creation alone sufficient evidence for omnipotence? Undoubtedly. If creation is the absolute independent act of the free will, evidently it is in the discretion of the free will to produce anything whatsoever it pleases; and such is our idea of omnipotence. There can be no limitation to the power of God except by His free will. Hence, God can do all things that are intrinsically possible. The fundamental source of intrinsic possibility is inexhaustible, for it is the infinite imitability and expressibility of the divine nature.

Authors generally speak of three divine acts with reference to the existence and action of the universe: creation, preservation, and the so-called "concursus" or co-operation in the action of contingent agents. We believe that creation is the only divine act necessary and sufficient for the explanation of the universe. Preservation is simply the act of creation not suspended, but continued. We do not think either that for the action of contingent beings any special divine concursus is necessary, because beings exist for action. Consequently, the divine act, which explains the existence of contingent agents with all their natural ontological elements, explains also their action, as the action follows necessarily upon the presence of the essential conditions.

2. THE OMNIPRESENCE AND OMNISCIENCE OF GOD

a. *Omnipresence* is the application of the immensity of God to the universe. God is everywhere because He is not subject to space in any sense, *i. e.*, because He is immense. The specific reason for the presence of God everywhere in the universe is the act of creation and preservation. We cannot conceive an act without the presence of the agent, and thus, we conceive the omnipresence of God as the necessary condition for any being whatever to come into existence and to continue in existence.

The best analogy we have for the omnipresence of God in the world is the omnipresence of the soul in the body. As the soul is present everywhere in the body and in every part and organ of it, whole and undivided, because it informs, vivifies, and animates the whole body and every part of it, so God is present everywhere in the universe and in every individual being of it, because by His power He brought it and keeps it in existence. However, there is this important discrepancy between the omnipresence of God in the universe and the omnipresence of the soul in the body: the soul's presence is limited by and to the body, whereas the presence of God is not limited in any sense neither by, nor to, the universe.

b. By means of the omnipresence which we have just discussed, we are present in the divine will that keeps us in existence; but it is evident that we could not be present in the divine will, if we were not already present in the divine mind. This presence of the universe in the divine mind we call the *omniscience* of God. The universe is also present in the divine mind through His wisdom, but not in the same manner. By His wisdom He planned the universe individually and collectively; and thereby established both the order that regulates the manifold interdependence and complex interaction of the various elements and forces which constitute the individual beings, and the order which regulates the still more manifold interdependence and vastly more complex interaction of all the beings and all the masses which compose the universe. Consequently, wisdom expresses the divine knowledge of the teleology of the universe, *i. e.,* of the relations between beings as means and end. On the contrary, omniscience refers to the causal relations of the universe, *i. e.,* it is the divine knowledge of the nature of beings, of the ontological elements which constitute them, and of the origin which explains their actual existence. Though divine wisdom, because it accounts for the wonderful order in the universe, appears to us of superior excellence and value, yet it would be impossible without divine omniscience. To propose an aim to which the whole universe must be subordinate and subservient, it is indispensable that the beings composing it must be perfectly known in all their elements, powers, and possible relations. Consequently, as the divine wisdom is clearly evident from the order of the universe, so also the omniscience of God is evident, inasmuch as it is its absolutely necessary condition.

We may define *omniscience as the divine knowledge of all things that are knowable.* However, in order to be knowable things must exist in some way. Negations as such are not knowable. It is quite evident that to the infinitely perfect mind of God there can be nothing hidden. The things past and also the things future are present before Him. We can understand that because they have had or will have their being, and in God there is no succession, no time. But what about the things that might have been, but never were because certain conditions did not materialize? Or about conditional events of the future that will not happen? They have not had or will not have any being. Yet we cannot well say that God does not know them, as in case of their occurrence they would enter or would have entered as elements into the divine plan of the universe. To say that God knows them because He perceives all things possible in the infinite imitability and expressibility of His divine nature, is perfectly true, but does not explain this mysterious problem, because such knowledge is purely ideal, whereas the problem refers to the real and concrete order.

There is another problem just as profound and mysterious concerning divine omniscience. It refers to the compatibility of the divine fore-knowledge with human freedom. If God has an infallible fore-knowledge of our acts, how can we determine them freely? They have no being till our decision gives it to them. How does God know these free decisions before they are made? Yet He must know them, as they and their consequences enter into the general plan of the universe. To say that our free acts do not happen because God has fore-knowledge of them, but that God has fore-knowledge of them because they happen, is not a solution of the problem. We may suggest that, there being no time or succession in God, the free acts of man are present permanently before Him as free "ab aeterno." But, even so, the question remains obscure.

3. THE DIVINE GOODNESS, HOLINESS, AND JUSTICE

So far we have discussed four of the relative attributes of God: His wisdom, His omnipotence, His omnipresence, and His omniscience. Each of them has helped us positively to understand the nature of the relationship which exists between God and the universe created by Him. However, while necessary, they are not sufficient for a full and adequate explanation, not any one of them separately, nor any combination of them, nor even the sum of them. They are not sufficient because they do not give the fundamental reason and motive for the act of creation. The main question: why did God create the universe, remains unanswered. We will now try to answer that question.

a. Whenever a rational agent acts, he must have an aim in view. That aim we call the object of his act. What was the object which God intended to attain by the act of creation? Evidently, such an object must have been something desirable, a good. The good which God intended to accomplish by creation, must be considered either as a means or as an end, *i. e.*, either as a good in itself, an absolute good, or as an object desired for the sake of another, a relative good. It is clear that the universe in itself could never be willed by God for its own sake; being essentially contingent and dependent, it can only be a relative good, a means and not an end. God alone, being absolute in His nature, can be an absolute good, a final end. Hence, the universe must be conceived in God's creation as a means to an end. But the universe, in respect to God, could be a means only in two ways: Either because it would be able to give God something which God does not possess, *i. e.*, it would complete and perfect the nature of God, it would make Him good; or because it would be able to show forth and express the goodness which is in Him. Evidently, the universe can give nothing to God which He does not already possess supereminently. Consequently, *the only possible object of creation was the manifestation and expression of the divine goodness.*

We shall understand this divine goodness better if we bear in mind what we said above about the nature of goodness: "Bonitas est diffusiva sui," goodness has the tendency to diffuse itself, *i. e.,* to communicate itself to others. Such is the act of creation in God: an evidence of the divine will to communicate Himself, to have others participate in His own nature. However, God, whose nature is His existence, can not possibly communicate His own nature as such to others, as thereby He would cease to be, but He can give an imitative participation in His being, and this is precisely the nature of created being. Consequently, the universe, being by its very nature a participation in being such as is possible for a contingent being to possess, its goodness consists in manifesting and expressing the divine goodness.

b. From the concept of the divine goodness as manifested in creation, we deduce directly the concept of the divine *holiness*. In truth, the source of the holiness of God is the divine appreciation of His own perfection and goodness. No doubt, God loves His own perfection with an infinite love because it is infinitely lovable, and for the very same reason He loves the created reproduction of the divine perfection in so far as it imitates and expresses it. But since we know plainly from former discussions that the clearest and most forceful expression of the divine goodness and perfection is found in the moral order, which regulates the life of man, there is no doubt that the moral order is the special object of divine love. The moral order, being intrinsically good and lovable inasmuch as it imitates and expresses the divine goodness, God loves what is morally good necessarily in exact proportion to its goodness and, for the very same reason, He hates what is morally bad necessarily in exact proportion to its opposition to the moral order, *i. e.,* to its wickedness. It is this divine love for what is good and this hatred for what is evil which we call the divine holiness.

c. In the same manner as divine holiness follows

from divine goodness, divine *justice* follows from divine holiness. In other words, *God is holy because He is good* and *God is just because He is holy*. In our discussion of the moral order we saw that, because God is holy, there is a divine sanction of the moral order in virtue of which those that realize it, attain happiness on earth and blessedness after death, and those who violate it, are unhappy on earth and lose the ultra-terrestrial blessedness. However, the respective state of happiness or unhappiness, terrestrial and ultra-terrestrial, which follows naturally and necessarily upon the realization or frustration of the moral order, is not absolute but relative, and the relation is one of exact proportion to the relative perfection of that realization and to the relative gravity of its frustration. It is this disposition of the holy will of God, in consequence of which reward and punishment for the fulfillment or violation of the moral order are apportioned in the exact measure of merit or demerit, which we call divine justice. Thus, just as the sanction of the moral order finds its source in divine holiness, the vindication of it has its basis in divine justice. Divine justice is the manifestation and expression of divine holiness in the same manner as divine holiness is the manifestation and expression of divine goodness.

From the comparative study of the relative divine attributes, two important conclusions are easily drawn: 1. The moral attributes, goodness, holiness, and justice, surpass all others in dignity and excellence, and 2. The queen of the moral attributes is undoubtedly divine goodness. We have seen how goodness constitutes the primary reason and the supreme motive for the creation of the universe, and since the reason and motive for an act are the aim in the agent's mind and the intention directing his will, it is evident that in divine goodness we have the most profound and most adequate explanation possible of the nature and signification of the universe as well as the key for the most perfect possible interpretation of the divine nature. On the one side, divine goodness presents the universe to our contemplation and admiration as the magnificent and glorious though contingent representation of the infinite and absolute perfection, beauty, and glory of the Creator, and on the other, divine goodness leads us to a deeper and fuller comprehension of the most sublime definition of the divine nature which the human mind has conceived and human lips have uttered, namely, *"Deus est caritas,"* God is love.

BIBLIOGRAPHICAL NOTES

I. SOURCES

The basic principles of the philosophical interpretation of the universe, as developed in the present volume, are Aristotelian and Thomistic. The best edition of Aristotle's works in the original Greek has appeared in Berlin, prepared by J. Bekker. Of St. Thomas Aquinas' works we have an excellent edition published in Rome on the initiative of Pope Leo XIII.

There are English translations of both Aristotle and St. Thomas. We have the works of Aristotle in six volumes, published in 1876, by George Bell & Sons, London. The translation was made by various Oxford professors. Though perhaps valuable from the philological viewpoint, they are almost worthless for the study of philosophy. An excellent German version has appeared recently in a very handy edition at Felix Meiner's, Leipzig.

The most important and characteristic of the works of St. Thomas, the two great Summas, have been made accessible of late to English speaking students: the "Summa Contra Gentiles" under the title of "God and His Creatures" by Father Joseph Rickaby, S. J. (Burns & Oates), and the "Summa Theologica" in a literal translation by the English Dominicans (R. & F. Washbourne).

II. BOOKS OF REFERENCE

A great number of works have been published on scholastic philosophy in various countries, especially in Italy, Spain, Germany, France, and Belgium, since Leo XIII wrote his famous encyclical letter *"Aeterni*

Patris" on the study of philosophy, in 1879. We recommend the following:

A. COMPLETE AND SYSTEMATIC EXPOSITIONS

"Manual of Modern Scholastic Philosophy," translated from the French of Cardinal Mercier and other professors of Louvain University. This is a brief but comprehensive compendium for school purposes, published by Kegan Paul, London, and Herder, St. Louis, Mo.

For a more complete and more profound study the reader is referred to the works of the same authors from which the "Manual" is a condensation and adaptation, viz.:

D. Nys, "Cosmologie."

Cardinal Mercier, "Psychologie"; "Métaphysique Générale"; "Logique"; "Critériologie Générale."

M. De Wulf, "Histoire de la Philosophie Médiévale."

All these works have appeared at the "Institut Supérieur de Philosophie," Louvain. They represent the ripest fruit of the famous school of Neo-scholasticism founded by Cardinal Mercier.

To the scholar who wishes to make a profound study of scholastic philosophy, we recommend the "Philosophia Lacensis," published by B. Herder, Freiburg and St. Louis, Mo.

B. MONOGRAPHS AND PARTIAL EXPOSITIONS

There is a great variety of treatises of this kind. The following, most of them of easy access, we wish to mention particularly:

William Turner, "Lessons in Logic"; Catholic Education Press, Washington, D. C.

George Hayward Joyce, S. J., "Principles of Logic"; Longmans, Green & Co., London and New York.

Hubert Gruender, S. J., "Experimental Psychology"; Loyola University Press, Chicago.

Michael Maher, S. J., "Psychology, Empirical and Rational"; Longmans, Green & Co., London and New York.

Peter Coffey, "Ontology or Theory of Being"; Longmans, Green & Co., London and New York.

John Rickaby, S. J., "General Metaphysics"; Longmans, Green & Co., London and New York.

Jos. Rickaby, S. J., "Moral Philosophy"; Longmans, Green & Co., London and New York.

Two works, one on Cosmology, the other on Psychology, which have appeared recently in German, deserve special mention as they are both up to date and thorough:

Joseph Schwertschlager, "Philosophie der Natur"; Heinrich Schoeningh, Münster:

Dr. J. Geyser, "Lehrbuch der Allgemeinen Psychologie"; Joseph Koesel, München.

Regarding the vital issues of evolution, cosmic and biological, two works, one published by Herder, Freiburg and St. Louis, Mo., and the other by Aschendorff, Münster, I. W., will prove useful to the student, namely: E. Wasmann, S. J., "Biology and Evolution"; and C. Braun, S. J., "Kosmogonie."

INDEX